At Home and Abroad

At Home and Abroad:
Historicizing Twentieth-Century Whiteness
in Literature and Performance

Edited by La Vinia Delois Jennings

TENNESSEE STUDIES IN LITERATURE
Volume 44

The University of Tennessee Press • Knoxville

Copyright © 2009 by The University of Tennessee Press / Knoxville.
All Rights Reserved. Manufactured in the United States of America. First Edition.

"Without Me" by Malcolm McLaren / Trevor Horn / Kevin Bell / Marshall Mathers /
Jeff Bass / Anne Dudley © 2002 by *Malcolm McLaren*. McLaren's share is administered by
Peermusic (UK) Ltd. All Rights Reserved. Used by Permission.
Library of Congress Cataloging-in-Publication Data

At home and abroad: historicizing twentieth-century whiteness in literature
and performance / edited by La Vinia Delois Jennings.
p. cm. — (Tennessee studies in literature: v. 44)
Includes bibliographical references and index.
ISBN-13: 978-1-57233-656-8 (acid-free paper)
ISBN-10: 1-57233-656-0

1. Whites in literature.
2. Literature, Modern—20th century—History and criticism.
3. Race awareness in literature.
I. Jennings, La Vinia Delois.

PN56.3.W45A8 2009
809'.93355—dc22   2009006149

To
the residents of the batey community of Palmarejo
in
Santo Domingo, the Dominican Republic
and
the Haitians of the African diaspora

Contents

Acknowledgments   ix

Introduction: The Race for Whiteness in the Twentieth
Century   xi
La Vinia Delois Jennings

PART I

Literature

Argentina White   1
Amy Kaminsky

A Dream of a White Vienna after World War I: Hugo
Bettauer's *The City without Jews* and *The Blue Stain*   29
Peter Höyng

From "Yélida" to Movimiento de Mujeres Dominico-Haitianas:
Gendering Resistance to Whiteness in the Dominican
Republic   61
Dawn Duke

Romancing Whiteness: Popular Appalachian Fiction and
the Imperialist Imagination at the Turns of Two
Centuries   93
Emily Satterwhite

The Threat to Whiteness: White Women's Marital Betrayals
in Colonial Settings   119
Suzanne Leonard

PART II
Performance

The Suspect Whiteness of Spain   147
Baltasar Fra-Molinero

The Myth of Whiteness and a Changing Italy: Historic
   Memory and Colonialist Attitudes in *Lamerica*   171
Renée D'Elia-Zunino

"Claiming": White Ambition, Multiracial Identity, and the
   New American Racial Passing   197
Meredith McCarroll

Beyond the White Negro: Eminem, Danny Hoch, and Race
   Treason in Contemporary America   221
Kimberly Chabot Davis

Stalling Zion: Hegemony, Whiteness, and Racial Discourse
   in the *Matrix* Phenomenon   255
Douglas A. Cunningham

Contributors   285

Index   289

Acknowledgments

My teaching and travel, both professional and personal, gave rise to *At Home and Abroad*, and I wish to thank those near and far who assisted in its production.

First and foremost I must acknowledge the fine work and extensive patience of the contributors whose essays appear between these covers and those whose do not. I especially wish to single out Kimberly Chabot Davis, who waited longest and best.

I thank my graduate assistant Meredith McCarroll and the Nathalia Wright Research Assistantship that compensated her for the time and energy that she devoted to reading submissions and corresponding with contributors.

I wish to thank the internal and external readers whose thorough reports stand as testaments to the intensive work that members of our profession perform anonymously and all too often without proper acknowledgment and remuneration.

In the Dominican Republic, I thank poet and television host Blas R. Jiménez; his sister, Eulalia Jiménez; the curator Juan M. Rodríguez of Museo del Hombre Dominicano; MUDHA director Sonia Pierre; the former ambassador to Haiti, Alberto Despradel; and Farah Halal, her husband Hector, and their daughter Itzel (Mariposa). In Haiti, I am eternally grateful to Nicole Grégoire in the Ministry of Foreign Affairs.

I thank Richard Dyer for his kind response to my letter. I thank you, John Edgar Wideman. And I thank Jenn Fishman and the John C. Hodges Better English Fund.

And last, I am indebted to the anonymous patron of the Jefferson Prize. Since receiving your generous gift, I have completed *Toni Morrison and the Idea of Africa* (Cambridge University Press, 2008) and this edited collection of scholarly essays. Another on Zora Neale Hurston is being readied.

La Vinia Delois Jennings
Knoxville
March 2008

Introduction

The Race for Whiteness in the Twentieth Century

I want every one of you to think about this the next time you get mad at one of your colleagues on the other side of the aisle. This fall, at the White House, Hillary had one of her millennium dinners, and we had this very distinguished scientist there, who is an expert in this whole work in the human genome. And he said that we are all, regardless of race, genetically 99.9 percent the same.

Now, you may find that uncomfortable when you look around here. [*Laughter*] But it is worth remembering. We can laugh about this, but you think about it. Modern science has confirmed what ancient faiths always taught: the most important fact of life is our common humanity. Therefore, we should do more than just tolerate our diversity; we should honor it and celebrate it.

—President William Jefferson
Clinton, state of the union
address, January 27, 2000

The concluding remarks of President William Jefferson Clinton at his last state of the union address before a joint session of the U.S. Congress concerning all peoples' genetic sameness and common humanity capped a millennium and a century that had begun with escalating anxieties about perceptions of human physical differences. From the Norman Conquest of 1066 to the mid-twentieth-century rise of Aryanism, Adolf Hitler, and World War II, peoples of Northern European descents increasingly perceived themselves as innately superior to peoples of other geographical and genealogical origins. Northern Europeans' belief that intrinsic differences defined specific groups of people had already been shaped before their incursions into non-European territories where they encountered populations markedly different from them in culture and appearance. But as film studies critic Richard Dyer points out, European encounter with others unlike themselves led to "the conflation of body and temperament" and the evolution of "a full concept of race" (18–19). Well before the second millennium ended, peoples of Northern European descents had positioned themselves globally as the exclusive progenitors of intellect, power, beauty, and civilization. Routing notions of Northern European racial superiority long entrenched in the American and global psyche, Clinton's televised statement in 2000 from the helm of a world superpower proclaiming the incontrovertible genome research of Eric Lander[1] and a cadre of geneticists worldwide was politically bold and historically unprecedented. It was also historically ironical since the "problem" of the twentieth century, as the distinguished educator and civil rights activist W. E. B. Du Bois had rightly predicted in 1903, had been "the problem of the color-line" (1).

Du Bois's prophetic assertion focused exclusively on America's problematic white over black color-line—conflicts between individuals who claim exclusive European descents and those of African and part-African ancestries. It did not anticipate the twentieth-century phenomenon of persons of African descent in Africa and its diaspora inaugurating a new color-line category by denying their genealogical ties to Africa even when the continent's phenotypic traits marked their bodies as definitively African. Nor did it critique ideologies and hierarchies of biological and genealogical whiteness already in popular circulation on both sides of the Atlantic Ocean. Less than two decades after Du Bois's color-line assertion, American eugenicists Lothrop Stoddard and Madison Grant published books asserting that a rising tide of color—whites labeled as Alpines and Mediterraneans who failed to measure up to the Nordic ideal in addition to nonwhites—threatened "white world-supremacy."[2] The racialized fears their works chronicled were not new. Three-quarters of a century earlier, the French diplomat and scholar Arthur de Gobineau in *The Inequality of the Human Races* (1853) also had alleged that the greatness of Aryan aristocracy was under assault by the inferior races. His racially biased treatise, too, was not groundbreakingly novel since it simply recapitulated ideologies of whiteness that had gained currency in the half century before his work appeared. *The Inequality* did, however, contextualize radical concepts of race privileging whiteness that had been sown in the seventeenth and eighteenth centuries,[3] that took firm root in the nineteenth century, and that would undergo countless propagations globally in the twentieth century.

While "reading" the human body has always presented a slippery slope in accurately validating a person's "race," "[a]ll concepts of race," as Dyer succinctly notes, "are always concepts of the body and also of heterosexuality. Race is a means of categorizing different types of human body [*sic*] which reproduce themselves. It seeks to systematise differences and to relate them to differences of character and worth" (20). Skin color proved to be the first and easiest reproduced demarcation of difference. Yet the visual absence or presence of color in one's skin has never been the sole arbiter of the conference of whiteness or nonwhiteness. In fact, molecular biologists have documented that most of us, "regardless of skin color, have quite enough tyrosnase [the master enzyme that assists in pigment or melanin production in our melanocytes] . . . to make us very black" (Wills 13). The visual presence of melanin in the skin, as scientists have theorized based on laboratory research, follows the trajectory of evolutionary adaptations affected by environmental conditions. To survive the ravages of ultraviolet light and excessive vitamin D production leading to harmful levels of calcium deposits in human tissue, the bodies of homo sapiens native to equatorial regions screen the ultraviolet rays of the sun with melanin-darkened skin. Inversely, to militate against deficient absorption of vitamin D essential for proper calcium production and bone development, the bodies of peoples indigenous to high altitudes and frigid, geographical climates far removed from the equator produce a tyrosinase inhibitor that radically reduces the formation of ultraviolet-blocking melanin in their skin (14). Therefore, the varying displays of melanin in the skin, the largest organ of the body, encodes much about the human body's adaptability in the past for survival and under what environmental conditions that survival occurred, not who is intellectually or culturally superior or inferior.

Christopher Wills states that "because [melanin's] effects are so visible in our skin, it has for centuries been made to bear an utterly undeserved burden of sociological and political significance. There are far more genetic differences among the people who make up these arbitrary constructs we call races than there are difference between races" (14–15). In 1998, the American Anthropological Association released the following statement on race that supports Wills's assertion:

> Evidence from the analysis of genetics (e.g., DNA) indicates that most physical variation, about 94 percent, lives *within* so-called racial groups. Conventional geographic "racial" groupings differ from one another only in about 6 percent of the genes. This means that there is greater variation within "racial" groups than between them.

Therefore, significant genetic differences between people who evolved in disparate geographic spheres of the world have negligible scientific backing; and race, as scholars have now come to understand it, is definitively a sociopolitical construct. That social construction, however, is still the principal determiner of the economic, psychological, and emotional realities of countless peoples in their native and naturalized homelands across the globe.

While the twentieth century will be remembered for its championing of multiculturism, its calls to tolerate and celebrate human diversity, and its seemingly infinite explorations of the interlocking effects of race, class, gender, and sexuality, the socially constructed racial playing field has yet to be leveled. White people and their sociopolitical agendas remain central and ascendant. The paradigm of the medieval, classical Great Chain of Being, which later acquired a Eurocentric bias, best exemplifies the ascent of whiteness, the descent of blackness, and the (un)conscious disparity cementing the character and worth distinguishing the two. The chain's tiers locate the bearers of whiteness closer to God and next to the angels. Conversely, blackness positions its bearers one rung above animals as the missing link between man and ape. Whiteness reifies its holders' humanness as approaching godliness and secures the power of those qualified as such. Blackness confers to its holders subhumanness akin to the simian and Satan, relegating them to savagery and powerlessness. That disempowering connection to subhumanness has motivated some on its lower rung to disavow their nonwhite roots in order to ascend the whiteness hierarchy.

In the twentieth century and now, almost a decade into the twenty-first century, various peoples' denial of their African ancestries constructs a neonarrative of modern and postmodern "racial" passing that reveals a deep-seated desire not only to be "raced" as white but also to be racially "othered" as anything but Black, that is, having African ancestry. While narratives of fictional and real-life light-complected individuals passing for white are numerous in the United States, a seemingly intractable preoccupation with whiteness and the quest to ascend its hierarchy among postcolonized and postenslaved peoples have emerged in divergent parts of the world. Some who aspire to whiteness wish to circumvent a racial legacy of economic and social oppression. Some are ashamed of their subordinate, subjugated pasts and strive to disassociate themselves from the stigmatizing heritage of slavery and involuntary servitude. And some, believing in the innate superiority of whiteness, seek to rise on what might be thought of as the present-day Great Chain of Being by claiming whiteness.

Along the Swahili coast of East Africa, various peoples in Kenya, Tanzania, Lamu, and Zanzibar claim exclusive Arabic and Persian descents rather than acknowledge mixed ancestries that include African forebears. And it is those African forebears that explain their broad noses, kinky hair, and melanin-rich skin.[4] When Henry Louis Gates Jr., during his African odyssey along the Swahili coast, questioned Sheik Badawi, a venerable scholar and native of the island of Lamu, about the Lamu people's possession of African antecedents, Badawi responded that Lamu was an Arab civilization for more than one thousand years and affirmed his direct descent from Muhammad. Even though the phenotypic signs of Africa are writ large on their bodies, his disclaimer, "We don't have African ancestry, but we try not to think badly of those who do," speaks not only to African genealogical denial but also to the historical assignment of an inferior worth to Africanness ("Swahili Coast"). Badawi's response to Gates's query exemplifies that with respect to nullifying one's visible blackness, "what can't be won on grounds of biology can be assaulted on genealogy" (Dyer 23).

Across the Atlantic in the Dominican Republic, the multiracial nation that shares with Haiti to its west the island once known as Hispaniola, many African Dominicans choose to claim genealogical linkage with the nation's Spanish Conquistadors and the long-decimated

Taíno Indians, who populated the island prior to Spanish conquest. They do so to erase Africa from their genealogy if not from their bodies. Because the Dominican Republic's color-line is less fixed with respect to the visual, one does not have to bear a light complexion to declare oneself white. In fact, many "white" Dominicans have quite a bit of melanin visually present in their skin. In order to be "white," one only needs to possess a physical body that approaches the claimed genealogy and that locates his or her Dominican body in stark relief to the Haitian (read African) body. Although Lamu and the Dominican Republic are referenced here as geographical sites where biological characteristics and genealogical realities collide, throughout the world, the privileged "lens" to read race has been and still is sight. The visual reading of race on the body, however, has never been 100 percent reliable or historically stable.

Perhaps the greatest historical irony of all with respect to the denial of African precursors is the erasure of nonwhiteness from and by whiteness itself. Compiling groundbreaking, archaeological, documentary, and linguistic evidence that white Europe purged its near Asian and East African antecedents, Martin Bernal, in the first three volumes of a projected four-part study, *Black Athena: The Afroasiatic Roots of Classical Civilization* (1987, 1991, 2006), asserts that nineteenth-century white scholars discarded Egypt and inserted an Aryan model, Indo-Europeans from the north and an older indigenous population of non-Indo-Europeans, as the cultural founders of Greek civilization. But Bernal offers up compelling proof that Classical Greeks knew nothing of the Aryans from which nineteenth-century historians claim they sprung. In fact, Greece's own "ancient model" attributes its political, scientific, philosophical, and religious institutions as originating generally from the East and specifically from Egypt. In the past two centuries, white scholars have systematically erased these Afro-Asiatic roots because "in an age of imperialism, such an idea was intolerable. Greece was seen as the cradle of Europe, but something had given birth to Greece, and that had to be compatible with the European sense of self and could not therefore be located in Africa" (Dyer 21). Bernal's scholarship calls for acknowledging the role Egypt and Phoenicia played in founding ancient Greece.

Within whiteness, internal hierarchies and unfixed borders have historicized whiteness as an unstable category. The ranking of the subspecies of the white race "in genetic worth well above the various colored races" but placing the Nordic race "far and away, the most valuable type . . . standing at the head of the whole human genus" (Stoddard 162) resulted in some white groups, despite possession of white skin, being less securely white than others. Nordics—Anglos, Scandinavians, and Teutons—elevated themselves to the top of the racial totem pole and secured their white status under British imperialism, U.S. development and expansionism, and Germanic Nazism. Ethnics—Southern or Eastern Europeans such as Latins, the Irish, Asians, and Jews—were granted unsecured whiteness. Their worth as white subspecies has risen and fallen in direct correlation to economic imperatives and historical mandates. These ethnics have sometimes been included in the category of white and at other times treated as buffers between Nordics and black or indigenous red peoples. Because top-tier whiteness grants practically unlimited access to societal rewards and privileges that are otherwise limited or closed to nonwhites and ethnic whites, it is not surprising that crossing over into whiteness or ascending its internal hierarchy is well worth the pursuit, with much to be gained if one is successful in its ascension. Thus the historically shifting border of whiteness proves a boon to twentieth-century nonwhite and ethnic whites who can meet its biological and genealogical requisites to access its social and economic perquisites.

It is scientific fact. With small variation between different "racial" groupings, we are all genetically the same. And given the capacity of normal humans to achieve and function within any cultural institutions, "present-day inequalities between so called 'racial' groups are not consequences of their biological inheritance but products of historical and contemporary social, economic, educational and political circumstances" (American Anthropological Association). To justify extermination and enslavement of other human beings and their own licentiousness, upper-rung whites created psychological "distance" between themselves and the human beings they stripped of humanity. Similarly, ethnic whites elected to class and caste themselves off from lower-rung ethnics and nonwhites to ensure a distinguishable distinction between themselves and the next rung down. Especially when their own visible melanin, broad features, and not-so-straight hair threatened their economic well-being and others' positive assessment of their social and human worth, ethnics dog-gedly policed separatist borders and racist practices. Nonwhites who wished to pass for white and possessed the visible requisites to do so did so, while other nonwhites of light and ambiguous skin coloring now ascend into neo- or pseudo-whiteness by claiming otherness but not (exactly) Africanness. While it is easier to gauge the psychologi-cal impact that socially conceding to or laboring under whiteness has had on those at its lowest rungs, it has certainly fostered fictional identities and fractured psyches for those at its apex as well. For both whites and nonwhites, the pursuit of whiteness has been ignoble and required high psychological maintenance. But when the acquisition of its societal rewards and privileges are weighed against economic denial and sociopolitical disenfranchisement, it is no wonder that in many sectors of the world the race for whiteness persists.

Comprised of ten critical essays written by scholars with ties to Europe, North America, South America, and Africa, *At Home and Abroad: Historicizing Twentieth-Century Whiteness in Literature and Performance* collectively treats global spaces whose nation building and identity formation turned on biological and genealogical exigencies to whiten themselves. Within these pages, in addition to its physical manifesta-tion, whiteness as identity, symbol, racism, culture, social formation, political imposition, legal imposition, innocence, purity, or pathology is outed into the visible, even in national spaces where the term "white-ness" has yet to be translated and adopted into the official lexicon. Drawing upon racialized, national practices implemented in selected geographical spaces prior to and during the global propagation of whiteness in the twentieth century, these essays enlist representations from literature and the performing arts that reflect the sociopolitical imperatives that secured whiteness in the respective locations that they treat. Although the study of representation is more limited than the study of reality, the examination of imaginative representations is a credible means of exposing the ways whiteness (re)produces and (re)secures itself since the study of representation is a useful method of accessing knowledge of reality (Dyer xiii). Representations of people and their actions in literature and performance are by design mimetic and have the power to chronicle histories that reflect the behaviors and lived realities of our selves.

In discussing seduction theory and the possessive geographies of whiteness where the racing of others may occur below the conscious, Shannon Sullivan writes that the "unconscious racing of bodies and space is unique neither to the United States nor to contemporary times. Especially in its binary division of a civilized 'us' from a wild 'them,' the phenomenon has a long history that stretches across Europe and, through European imperialism and colonialism, across the globe" (150). She further asserts that "[e]nigmatic messages about white privilege can be unconsciously communicated between portions of the world geographically quite distant from each other, which means that the national and geographical habits of various countries and areas of the world help form the unconscious raced habits of other peoples and nations" (95). One way that unconscious, global communication about whiteness took place in the twentieth century is through its sharing of literature, cinema, and music. Movies, magazines, songs, poetry, and even comic books "are seen as frivolous and pleasurable, as mere entertainment, but their frivolity is what makes them so insidious. The values they convey slips into one's thinking smoothly, without much (if any) conscious attention or psychical disruption" (98). The ten essays in this volume provide historical, literary, and performance examples of the ways that ethnic whites and nonwhites, as well as whites at the apex of the whiteness hierarchy, have (re)secured white ascendance. They feature the use and power of national epics, best-selling novels, films, popular songs, and other forms of the literary and performance arts to mirror, (re)secure, and indict the fabrication and privileging of whiteness within and between national spaces.

Part I of this collection, "Literature," contains five essays that investigate representations of whiteness in poetry and the novel and the ways those literary representations intersect with and expose the (re)securing of biological and/or genealogical whiteness in Argentina, Austria, the Dominican Republic, Appalachia in the southeastern mountains of the United States, and British colonial Rhodesia, Jamaica, and India. The authors of these chapters discuss popular national epics and best-selling novels to historicize the descent of otherness and ascent of whiteness in these spaces.

In "Argentina White," Amy Kaminsky contends that Argentina's self-identification as a totally white nation is a myth of racial superiority produced largely through a range of texts and historical practices. For more than a century, elites in Argentina, to solidify the South American country as the "most European" on the continent, forwarded a discourse of whiteness aimed at increasing the number of whites and reducing the number of blacks and indigenous peoples through dilution and genocide. Their ultimate goal was to claim Argentina a place in the politically and economically dominant family of European nations. Kaminsky places Argentinean ideas about race in the context of racial constructions in Spanish America, which are different from those in the United States, particularly around the stability of whiteness. She draws upon the theme of black extirpation in Argentina's national epic, José Hernández's *El gaucho Martín Fierro* (*The Gaucho Martín Fierro*, 1872), and the erasure of blackness—for example, subverting the fact that both Argentina's first president and national dance, the tango, have African roots—from dominant accounts of Argentine history to elevate its whiteness. Argentina's projection of itself to Europe at the 1900 International Exhibition in Paris, a particularly blatant attempt at self-whitening, contrived to expunge its black and indigenous past. Kaminsky concludes her thesis by offering up examples of European authors' complicity in the construction of Argentina as a white nation.

Peter Höyng's "A Dream of a White Vienna after World War I: Hugo Bettauer's *The City without Jews* and *The Blue Stain*" enlists the prolific Austrian writer's 1922 novels, the bestseller *Die Stadt ohne Juden* (*The City without Jews*) and *Das blaue Mal* (*The Blue Stain*), to expose Bettauer's whitening of the racial other to gain white approbation and inclusion. According to Höyng, the significance of *The City without Jews* rests in its address of overt anti-Semitism in Vienna prior to Nazi occupation in 1938 and Bettauer's almost clairvoyant anticipation of the Nazis' brutal racist politics. The plot of the satirical novel argues anti-Semitism in Vienna is not viable because the European metropolis presumably cannot lay claim to cultural preeminence without taking into account the contributions of its Jewish citizens. Höyng maintains, however, that scholars have overlooked the novel's and thus Bettauer's implicit racism since the novelist whitewashes Vienna by excluding Orthodox Jews—by far the largest number of Jews in Vienna after World War I—from the Viennese setting. The otherness of Orthodox Jews has to disappear in order to make the case that non-Jewish Viennese are foolish to eject Jews who are indistinguishable from the white Austrian-German majority. Bettauer's own white myopia becomes even more transparent when the reader compares the plot of *The City without Jews* with *The Blue Stain*, a Bildungsroman that to date has attracted little scholarly attention. Its plot absents racism from Vienna and "exports" it to the United States, where the protagonist, the son of a Viennese professor and a Georgia slave girl, discovers he is not white as he has been reared to believe. Through the course of hardships and unusual circumstances, his "true" identity, in this case his "blackness," is revealed. Yet as in *The City without Jews*, Höyng asserts, Bettauer expresses a desire to reify whiteness since its protagonist's blackness is only acceptable assimilated into whiteness.

Dawn Duke draws a symbolic connection between Tomás Hernández Franco's celebrated poem, "Yélida" (1942), and the Dominican grassroots Movement for Dominican-Haitian Women, the only organization of its type operating today that is invested in the uplift of the Dominican Haitian in the Dominican Republic. Duke's yoking of Hernández Franco's poem and the Dominican-Haitian female experience in "From 'Yélida' to Movimiento de Mujeres Dominico-Haitianas: Gendering Resistance to Whiteness in the Dominican Republic," becomes relevant in so far as it provides insight into the broader national preoccupation with nation whitening. A struture of neo-whiteness exists in the Dominican Republic connected to the national identity constructed around Dominicanness claiming whiteness through Spanish and Taíno antecedents and fiercely rejecting African ancestry and otherness, coded as Haitianness. While Duke's study contemplates the intricate maneuvers needed to ascend and secure whiteness through genealogy if not through biology, it filters the discussion specifically through the Haitian female figure, a perspective that uncovers deep-rooted forms of gendering white inclusion and nonwhite exclusion.

To investigate the ways in which popular representations of the Appalachian region served as a celebration of nationalism grounded in readers' embrace of an essentially white and rural America, Emily Satterwhite's "Romancing Whiteness: Popular Appalachian Fiction and the Imperialist Imagination at the Turns of Two Centuries" examines fiction set in the southeastern region between the turns of the twentieth and twenty-first centuries. The late-twentieth-century resurgence in the national popularity of regional fiction must be understood as arising, in part, states Satterwhite, from some of the same symptoms that fed the late-nineteenth-century local-color writing fad. These symptoms include well-to-do white American readers' anxieties about immigration, race, and group difference; their commitments to American nationalism and imperialism; and their sense of alienation from sustained relationships to other people and places. By configuring Appalachia as wholly rural and largely homogenous, late-twentieth-century best-sellers implicitly promised their readers the possibility of retreat from the diversity of races, creeds, and nationalities often associated with urban places. Furthermore, readers' designation of white, mountain folk life as the root of "real America" constructed Appalachia as "home" in contrast not only to heterogeneous domestic cities but also to "sinister" foreign places that seemed to threaten "home." Even as authors asserted the whiteness of their Appalachian characters, however, they undermined or romanticized that whiteness by suggesting Celtic, Indian, or other "not-quite-white" influences. In the early twentieth century, stories with such characters permitted readers imaginatively to rule Appalachia as an internal other—an impulse consistent with contemporaneous U.S. imperialist ambitions toward people of color abroad.

Suzanne Leonard's "The Threat to Whiteness: White Women's Marital Betrayals in Colonial Settings" focuses on three novels set in British colonial contexts, Doris Lessing's *The Grass is Singing* (1950, Rhodesia), Jean Rhys's *Wide Sargasso Sea* (1966, Jamaica), and Ruth Prawer Jhabvala's *Heat and Dust* (1975, India), to argue that all perform a discursive "blackening" of the white wife who fails to protect a designated racial/sexual hierarchy. Offering symbolic confirmation that the security of the colonial project rested in part with the white wife's sexual and emotional fidelity to her race, each novel narrates the story of a white wife whose whiteness is figuratively destabilized by an imagined or real sexual/reproductive breach. Leonard makes it clear that the white wife's symbolic punishment is thus frequently exacted not in response to a committed sexual transgression but as a response to a possible sexual breach. The intent of the punishment is to ward off the devastating consequences that result from miscegenation, the biological disruption of white reproduction leading to the dissolution of white race hegemony. Highlighting the fact that patriarchal constituencies police white women's racial and sexual identities to safeguard colonial dominance, Leonard implicates the marital institution in the larger ideological project of reifying whiteness.

The five essays appearing in Part II, "Performance," draw upon Spanish and Italian cinema and American cinema and theater to exemplify the power film and stage representations have in reflecting and shaping the national and individual consciousness concerning whiteness. Like their literary counterparts, the essays expose the (re)securing of national whiteness and the instability of the whiteness hierarchy.

Spaniards, states Baltasar Fra-Molinero, have seen themselves as white since early modernity, and other Europeans, who tied the Spanish imperial adventure to an illegitimate political enterprise due to Spain's Muslim and Jewish past, early on contested Spain's whiteness. In "The Suspect Whiteness of Spain," Fra-Molinero contends that as whiteness replaced the concept of Christendom, Spain became the object of other Europeans' orientalizing gaze during the nineteenth century. Their objectification created a feeling of fear and suspicion of Spanish whiteness among intellectuals and in the popular opinion, which led to Spain internalizing others' view of itself. The Franco regime, which lasted from 1939 to 1975, created a contradictory discourse of a nation wanting to be modern and European and thus white while simultaneously selling its Gypsy image as a prop for the tourism industry of the 1960s. Ironically, Spain's dark-skinned Gypsies were and still are the most racially marginalized and rejected ethnic group in Spanish society. Spanish filmmakers have addressed and continue to address the shifting national racial identity that has come about since Franco's death in 1975, since Spain's instauration of a parliamentary democracy, and since the nation's incorporation into the European Union in 1986. Following Richard Dyer's theoretical framing of whiteness, Fra-Molinero targets three areas of representation and symbolic social practice in Spain: the cinematic reproduction of Gypsy identity in the post-Franco years; the presentation of the African immigrant in Spanish films, notably in those of Montxo Armendáriz, Imanol Uribe, Inciar Bollaín, and Pedro Almodóvar during the 1980s and 1990s; and the shifting redefinition of Spanish whiteness through the new sexual politics of the Spanish state under democracy, culminating in the legalization of gay marriage in 2005.

Renée D'Elia-Zunino's "The Myth of Whiteness and a Changing Italy: Historic Memory and Colonialist Attitudes in *Lamerica*" explores the unprecedented cultural transformations that Italy has undergone in the last quarter of a century. For a long time a bridge between the African continent and the rest of Europe and a vacation retreat for Eastern countries, Italy today has become the home of thousands of immigrants seemingly overnight. Although some Italians prefer to call themselves xenophobic toward newcomers from surrounding countries, evidence shows that a racist mentality and attitude has established itself among many. D'Elia-Zunino points to Gianni Amelio's film *Lamerica* (1998) as a recent cinematic indictment of native Italians' racing of others, in this case neighboring Albanians, as the nonwhite, while they themselves, ironically, have forgotten their own emigrant history of being relegated to a lower rung of whiteness. Amelio's film, D'Elia-Zunino admits, also perpetrates a colonialist attitude by performing whiteness mythically, as perfection and normalcy. In the film, as in everyday life, pervasive white power remains invisible and unexposed for the sake of economic expedients, a reality that allows racial misconceptions and national prejudice to thrive unchecked.

Racial passing of the early twentieth century allowed individuals who had been socially, biologically, and genealogically relegated to blackness to cross the color-line and live as white. Because these passers met the physical biological and behavioral requisites for whiteness, their bodies were read as white and they were granted unearned social privilege and access. Meredith McCarrroll posits in "'Claiming': White Ambition, Multiracial Identity, and the New Racial Passing" that in the wake of the 2000 U.S. census, which allowed citizens for the first time to select multiple racial categories, claiming multiracial identity formally rose and continues to be on the rise as the new form of racial passing in the twenty-first century. McCarroll's essay begins by historicizing racial passing and drawing the conclusion from history that although some passers imagined radical subversive/deconstructive race potential in the act of passing, whiteness maintains its superior, ascendant position in the conventional racial hierarchy.

Recent claims to multiracial identity offer a similar promise to deconstruct race. McCarroll's evaluation of claiming multiracial identity, however, exposes its subversive potential fails to dismantle whiteness and instead recenters it by decentering blackness in favor of embracing, ostensibly equally, competing ethnicities that historically have higher ranking on the whiteness hierarchy. Golfer Tiger Woods and actor Vin Diesel, who both claim multiracial identities, exemplify that rather than deconstructing the conventional whiteness hierarchy, "claiming" only supports white ambition in much the same way as "passing" of the earlier era.

"Beyond the White Negro: Eminem, Danny Hoch, and Race Treason in Contemporary America," Kimberly Chabot Davis's essay, critiques the ahistoricizing tendency to view all white hip-hop artists as reincarnations of Norman Mailer's "white Negro," a hipster who appropriates a romanticized image of black potency and ventriloquizes black culture. She argues that the white Negro paradigm of imperialist co-optation is inadequate to explain the diversity of white affiliations with African-American popular culture in contemporary America. Some of these instances of crossover, she contends, have the potential to function as radical acts of race treason against white privilege. The essay draws political distinctions between two white performers working in the hip-hop and film media—Eminem, a.k.a. Marshall Mathers (*8 Mile*, 2002), and Danny Hoch (*Whiteboyz*, 1999), a Jewish writer and performance artist who founded the New York HipHop Theater Festival. Eminem is neither a white Negro (in Mailer's terms) nor the race traitor that he imagines himself to be. In comparison, Danny Hoch's cultural work lives up to the original hip-hop imperative of racial protest, by offering a powerful deconstruction of institutional whiteness and a model for the development of antiracist forms of white identity. Hoch views race and ethnicity as a function of culture and environment, a state of mind—in short, an assigned identity, not one biologically determined. The characters he embodies in film and on stage speak to that reality.

Douglas A. Cunningham's "Stalling Zion: Hegemony, Whiteness, and Racial Discourse in the *Matrix* Phenomenon" examines the way in which *The Matrix* science fiction phenomenon reaches far beyond its film genre trappings to probe deeper questions about the social construction of racial identity and the recent successes and failures of critical race theory. Cunningham exposes the film trilogy and its spin-offs (*The Animatrix,* the video game *Enter the Matrix,* and *The Matrix* comics) reconstructions of images from twentieth-century racial conflicts and the impact of those conflicts on Western, late capitalist societies. In particular he focuses on imagistic allusions to African-American history and literature (the *Dred Scott* decision, *Native Son,* the Million Man March, and the Los Angeles white police beating of African American Rodney King) as well as the reimaginings of highly media-lized images from abroad (scenes from Fritz Lang's *The Metropolis,* Eddie Adams's photograph of a Vietcong fighter being summarily executed in the streets of Saigon, the Tiananmen Square massacre, and the ethnic cleansing in Rwanda and Bosnia) to explain the phenomenon's warnings about the dangers of fascist rhetoric and the "whitewashing" effects of cultural assimilation. Ultimately, Cunningham argues that *The Matrix* phenomenon invites viewers to ponder a genuine Zion in which racial proscriptions and categorizations fall to the wayside in favor of a collective humanity united in a common cause.

At Home and Abroad seeks to historicize the complicit role nonwhites and ethnic whites have played and still play in (re)securing whiteness as dominant and superior since biological or sight whiteness founded the complicatedly shifting hierarchy of whiteness. The belief in a genetic or human superiority attached to individuals possessing white skin, now relegated to myth but still alive and thriving in numerous sectors of the world, has fed centuries of self-loathing in those lacking it and a false sense of self in those possessing it. Dismantling the mythical lynchpin of racial whiteness on which all other manifestations of whiteness have been founded opens up the possibility for recovering the humanity of those stripped and those stripping others of the common factor that ties us all and for forming a collective humanity commonly united. Preempting and revisioning past individual and national identity formations that have been toxic to present nation-building unity projects and to the constructions of a truly diversified body politic may also be realized. Exposing the preoccupation those outside the upper rung of whiteness have in keeping whiteness in the ascent may raise a consciousness that resists reifying and (re)securing whiteness, especially since its occupation of ascendance militates against twenty-first-century human equality and survival.

NOTES

1. Eric Lander, director of the Whitehead Institute at the Massachusetts Institute of Technology Center for Genome Research, spoke at the Eighth Millennium Evening at the White House on October 12, 1999.

2. Stoddard titled his book *The Rising Tide of Color Against White World-Supremacy* (1920). Madison Grant authored *The Passing of the Great Race* (1918) and penned the introduction for Stoddard's work.

3. From an American perspective, the case of John Punch in Jamestown, Virginia, historicizes the evolution of inequality based on skin color by the English in order to supply a dependent, easily identifiable, free labor force for the British colony. In 1619, ten years after the colony's settlement and one year before the founding of Plymouth Plantation in Massachusetts, a Dutch man-of-war arrived with a cargo of twenty Africans that it had obtained through trade with a Spanish vessel. Because Christians could not be enslaved, converting to Christianity would entitle the Africans to free status. They accepted Christianity and were baptized.

Because the British colony needed an inexpensive labor force to plant and harvest it crops, Englishmen and others who wanted to come to the colony and lacked a method of paying for their passage entered into a contract of indentured service. At the end of service each man would receive one hundred acres of land, a suit of clothes, and a bushel of corn. In 1640, three indentured servants, Victor, a Dutchman; James Gregory, a Scotsman; and John Punch, an African, broke their contracts and fled to Maryland. They were captured, returned to the colony, brought before a court, found guilty of breaching their contracts, and sentenced. An extra year was added to the indenture contracts of the Dutchman and the Scotsman and after that they were required to serve the colony for an additional three years. "But, as the court put it, 'the third being a Negro named John Punch shall serve his master or his assigns for the time of his natural life'" (Zinn 30). Punch's inequitable sentence established a British colonial legal precedent: in mid-seventeenth-century America, one's race now determined one's freedom or one's bondage. Perpetual servitude was no longer determined by non-Christian status but by nonwhiteness.

John Punch's fate stand in stark contrast to an Angolan named Anthony who had arrived in the British colony in 1621, twenty years earlier, and whose name appeared on the 1625 census with the surname Johnson added. Anthony Johnson married a Negro woman named Mary, had four children, five servants—some of whom were white—and ultimately owned 250 acres of land. Property ownership established identity and Anthony Johnson had the rights of an Englishman. See "Part I: 1450–1750, 'The Terrible Transformation,'" *Africans in America*.

4. See "Swahili Coast."

WORKS CITED

Africans in America: America's Journey through Slavery. "Part I: 1450–1750, 'The Terrible Transformation.'" WGBH Boston Video, 2000.

American Anthropological Association. Statement on "Race." 17 May 1998. American Anthropological Association. 29 Sept. 2006 <http://www.aaanet.org/stmts/racepp.htm>.

Bernal, Martin. *Black Athena: Afroasiatic Roots of Classical Civilization.* Vol. 1, *The Fabrication of Ancient Greece, 1785–1985.* New Brunswick: Rutgers UP, 1987.

———. *Black Athena: Afroasiatic Roots of Classical Civilization.* Vol. 2, *The Archaeological and Documentary Evidence.* New Brunswick: Rutgers UP, 1991.

———. *Black Athena: The Afroasiatic Roots of Classical Civilization.* Vol. 3, *The Linguistic Evidence.* New Brunswick: Rutgers UP, 2006.

de Gobineau, Arthur. *The Inequality of the Human Races.* Trans. Adrian Collins. New York: Putnam, 1915.

Du Bois, W. E. B. *The Souls of Black Folk.* 1903. New York: Penguin, 1989.

Dyer, Richard. *White.* New York: Routledge, 1997.

Grant, Madison. *The Passing of the Great Race.* New York: Scribner's, 1918.

Stoddard, Lothrop. *The Rising Tide of Color Against White World-Supremacy.* New York: Scribner's, 1920.

Sullivan, Shannon. *Revealing Whiteness: The Unconscious Habits of Racial Privilege.* Bloomington: Indiana UP, 2006.

"The Swahili Coast." *Wonders of the African World with Henry Louis Gates, Jr.* Dir. Nick Godwin. BBC/PBS, 1999.

Wills, Christopher. "The Skin We're In." *Critical White Studies: Looking Behind the Mirror.* Ed. Richard Delgado and Jean Stefancic. Philadelphia: Temple UP, 1997. 12–15.

Zinn, Howard. *A People's History of the United States, 1492–Present.* New York: HarperCollins, 2003.

PART I

LITERATURE

Argentina White

AMY KAMINSKY

Not entirely unlike Columbia Red, Mexican Brown, and Acapulco Gold, which find their primary buyers in the United States and Europe, Argentina White is a Latin American product marketed and sold to the industrialized nations of the North—and within Argentina as well. Argentina White is not a consciousness-altering drug, however, or at least not the kind that eager users smoke. It is, rather, a myth, a story of racial superiority made not only in Argentina but also in the complicit discourses of Europe, whose own racial anxiety it expresses and mirrors.[1]

Argentina White is a product of the deliberate extirpation of non-White bodies, Indigenous and Black, from the national territory. Historically, this ethnic cleansing consisted of a two-pronged policy of national Whitening that was attempted through material and discursive means. Successive post-independence governments both encouraged European immigration and waged wars of aggression against Native populations fought in part by soldiers of African descent. The elites who determined how history would be written, and whose poetry, stories, music, and visual representations counted as culture, manipulated the population by expunging the Black and Indigenous presence from the nation's historical and cultural consciousness. They put in place the myth of a monocultural Argentina early in the history of the Republic that continues to the present day. Their production of Whiteness, along with the myth of a monocultural Argentina that issues from it, endorses Cheryl Harris's eloquent argument in "Whiteness as Property" that while Whiteness is an intangible good, it renders tangible benefits to its owners.

Nevertheless, Argentina White is not quite the same racially engineered drug as its U.S. counterpart. Whiteness in Argentina is not thought of or marketed as exclusively an individual good, but rather is sold as a societal good. The European-descended founding fathers of Argentina believed that Northern Europeans were superior to people from Southern Europe, as well as to Jews (understood at the time as a separate racial category), Africans, and Asians.[2] By reiterating its Whiteness, Argentina would enter into modernity alongside its European exemplars. The racialized "other" would be blotted out, materially and discursively, rather than be constituted as a recognized "other" within. One of the ways to achieve homogeneity would be to absorb Blackness and Indigenousness, diluting them to the point of disappearance.[3]

Ironically, an understanding of the fluidity of race inherited from the practices of racial naming during the colonial period in Latin America—when an elaborate system of racial identity was put in place—enabled the adoption of a homogenous formula. The Spanish Empire first embraced a policy of Hispanicizing its colonies under the rubric of Hispanidad, which covered racial, cultural, religious, and linguistic identity.[4] In the eighteenth century, the penchant for scientific taxonomy destabilized racial categories by demonstrating how the various mixtures of three racial groups could result in a multiplicity of types. These groupings, called castas, sometimes misleadingly translated as "castes," were established to name the offspring of a kaleidoscopic mix of peoples and their descendants. The original categories were European, African, and Native American; the variations after several generations seemed endless.[5] A visual pedagogy of this racial taxonomy was carried out in part through a system of family portraits representing the father, who belonged to one racial group; the mother, who belonged to another; and one or two children, who belonged to still a third. Typically, these family portraits were arranged in a grid of sixteen paintings, four down and four across, each of which depicted a different racial combination or casta.[6]

The portraits were produced and disseminated primarily in colonial Mexico, which included what is today Central America. A much smaller number were painted in the Viceroyalty of Peru, headquartered in Lima. Although scholars debate the reason for the origin of these paintings, they seem to have been intended primarily for consumption by the elite Creole society, those born in the colonies of European descent, and by Spaniards living in Spain. Their original aim appears to have been educational: to display the "natural variety" of the Americas. Although the abundance of racial types was just one example of New World variety, it is the one privileged in the casta paintings. As Fermín del Pino Díaz points out, these works also provided a venue for depicting native flora—almost all the family portraits include careful renderings of native fruits and vegetables and, in the case of the Peruvian paintings, flowers. The Enlightenment's proclivity toward scientific exegesis, classification, and naming that was so effective in producing the scientific racism that justified slavery and the differential legal treatment of Whites, Blacks, and Indigenous people was codified for the Spanish Empire and the world it created in part by means of these paintings and rendered as part of the natural world.[7]

As a part of the viceroyalty whose seat of government was located in Peru, colonial Argentina was implicated in the casta hybridization system, even though the paintings themselves were primarily a northern phenomenon. Of the approximately one hundred sets of casta paintings that have been documented in the last decades, only one can be traced to Peru. Collections of these family portraits can still be found in provincial and national museums in Mexico, as well as in Spain and the United States. What they demonstrate, apart from the anxiety about fixing, naming, and thereby controlling racial difference, is the fluidity of racial categories. Only very rarely does the offspring of a "mixed" couple carry the racial name of either one of his or her parents; every generation spawns a new set of castas. The names applied to the different castas, as the generations multiplied the possibility of combinations, became ever more fanciful and varied.

Nevertheless, after several generations White blood could "redeem" itself. That is, the descendants of Blacks and/or Indians could eventually, over the generations, produce a White child by diligently reproducing with Whites. Nothing better suggests the instability of race. Moreover, far from the one drop of African blood that, under Jim Crow laws, constituted a person as Black in the United States, or the one-sixteenth Native ancestry that legitimizes enrollment in the bureaucratic apparatus of the tribe, it is Whiteness that, by its "strength," can reassert itself. Combination, not distillation, of ancestry determined an individual's casta. Casta, as a function of race, color, and ancestry, with assumptions about class encoded in the portraits, blurred the lines between the categories with every added generation.

Argentina's racial system, derived from the same assumptions about racial production that are so strikingly encoded in the casta images, is, of course, every bit as racist as the North American one. In both, Blackness has a negative valence; Whiteness has a positive one. Being Indigenous places one somewhere in between. These two equally racist systems differ in that one deems Blackness so powerful that it will inevitably erase the purity of the White and the other supposes that the natural superiority of Whiteness will eventually assert itself over incursions of the Black.

Whiteness itself is not absolute in the casta system. The most prestigious racial category in colonial Spanish America was "español," 'Spaniard,' and it was understood that the purity of Spanish blood was weakened as a result of geographical displacement. A child born in the Americas of two native-born Spaniards was not the equivalent of one born in Spain. Nevertheless, it is not clear from most of the portraits themselves if the español classification refers only to Spaniards born in Spain or if it includes Creoles, that is, individuals born in the Americas to European-born parents. In one example, discussed in more detail below, the child of an español and a mixed-race woman is labeled "español," indicating that at least in one set of paintings "español" refers to Creoles as well as to those born in Spain.

Most casta paintings contain captions painted onto the canvas itself, racially naming the couple and their child or children. The verbs most frequently used by the casta painters to express interracial reproduction are "producir" 'to produce,' "salir" 'to come/or turn out,' and "nacer" 'to be born.' For example, a caption may read, "Mestizo con India Producen Cholo" 'Mestizo with Indian Produce Cholo' or "De Español e India, nace Mestiza" 'From Spaniard and Indian a Mestiza is born.'[8] In one set of Mexican casta paintings, however, the caption reads, "De Español y Castiza torna a Español" 'From Spaniard and Castiza [one-quarter Native and three-quarters Spanish], the child goes back to being Spaniard.' In this painting, the verb choice "tornar," whose first meaning is 'to go back' but can also mean 'to render,' suggests that Whiteness reasserts itself if the non-White racial heritage becomes small enough over the generations.

In the Peruvian paintings, the classification of "gente blanca," literally 'white people' was applied to the child of an español and a "requinterona de mulato" whose own parentage was one-sixteenth African and the rest Spanish.[9] Gente blanca was only one category of Whiteness, however. In the next generation a gente blanca and an español produce a "casi limpio de origin," literally, a person 'almost pure/clean of origin,' a person who is White enough.

As might be expected, gender is far more stable in these paintings than race. Gender, perceived as a simple, natural binary, is called into action in the production of Spanish colonial racial ideology. In the vast majority of the casta paintings that I have seen depicting the mix of Spaniard and an "other," it is the man who is typically the Spaniard.[10] The recurrence of the Spaniard as male in these unions suggests that, as in the United States, there were cultural sanctions against sexual relations between European women and men of other races. The relatively few Spanish women who came to the Americas would have equally exacerbated the low probability of European females entering into mixed-race conjugal unions. Starting from the time of exploration, the men who made the journey vastly outnumbered the women; and although the ratio of women to men migrating to colonial Spanish America tended to become more even over time, men continued to outnumber women. Since there were fewer Spanish women available for procreation, it is not unreasonable that fewer would be depicted having done so. However, much more important in a system that prized Whiteness, the dominant males would also attempt to keep White women as their exclusive sexual preserve.

The gendering of the casta paintings also functions on a symbolic level. The images reinforce the racial superiority of Europeans and their descendants over those of African or Native ancestry by depicting the dominant race as a member of the dominant gender. In the case of racial admixing between African and Native peoples and their descendants, the gender distribution is relatively equal. In these paintings, where racial dominance is not the issue, and where gender

difference must be present (after all, the paintings are mapping reproduction), gender is not called into play to signify other relations of
domination.[11]

Argentina, like the rest of Latin America, inherited its Spanish
colonial understanding of the working of race, finding in it a means
to produce Whiteness out of a racially ambiguous past. A jumble of
reproductive possibilities was reflected in the multiplicity of names,
which, in the later generations at least, were hardly uniform. The
classification system reflected in and disseminated by the casta paintings predated, but also presaged, Mendelian genetics. The idea that
certain characteristics were dominant and others weak or recessive
made it possible for the early racial theorists of Latin America to create a system that would engender Whiteness. After independence,
the Argentine cultural and political elite drew on its understanding
of dominant and recessive race production and reproduction to draw
the color line around the nation rather than through it.

Argentina's Color Line

When W. E. B. Du Bois pointed out presciently that "the problem
of the twentieth century is the problem of the color-line" (1), he was
speaking specifically about a society in which the color line divides
the nation. In the United States, the color line is an internal (and
internalized) border for which no passport can be issued. As a result,
crossing that border has always been a clandestine act. It has meant
abandoning a deep sense of self or falsifying what one knows to be
most true about one's being in order to enter a space of danger in
which discovery and successful concealment alike carry heavy penal-
ties. From the popular twentieth-century melodramas of passing such
as *Imitation of Life*, which was first a 1933 novel by Fannie Hurst and
then adapted into movie versions in 1934 and 1959, and *Pinky*, directed
by Elia Kazan in 1949, to Cheryl Harris's wrenching account of her
grandmother, for whom the psychic price of passing (which involved
journeying daily across the unmarked but very real border between
her own neighborhood and the White part of town in order to work
at a job that would allow her to provide for her family), narratives of
passing construct leaving one's Black home as a physical and psychic

journey of identity border crossing. It means leaving what is most socially constructed but also what is most deeply felt about oneself behind.[12] In the United States, the Whiteness assumed through passing is by definition also socially constructed, in part because of the one-drop rule that the dominant culture institutionalized to enforce its particular version of race.

In the Latin American context, of which Argentina is one variant, performance of White identity, ratified by historically determined cultural codes of Whiteness (speaking Spanish rather than an Indigenous language, economic status, job category, and formal education within the dominant system), and certain visible markers of Whiteness (primarily light skin color, rather than, say, hair texture), make for White identity. Art historian Ilona Katzew reminds us that in eighteenth-century Mexico, wealthy descendants of slaves and Indians could buy official certificates conferring Whiteness upon them. In Latin America, even more than in the United States, Whiteness is performed and received as the counterpart not only to Blackness but also to Indianness. Black/White and Indigenous/White function as two separate but interrelated binaries.[13] In both cases, the binaries collapse into what, for most countries, is an uneasy acknowledgment of "mestizaje" or racial mixing.[14] The primary difference between Argentina and most of the rest of Latin America is that Argentine cultural consciousness disallows racial diversity or difference instead differentiating itself from the rest of the continent by claiming a White, European identity.[15] A perhaps startling example is that of Argentina's first president, Bernardino de Rivadavia. The Marcus Garvey web site lists Rivadavia as one of its "great people of color," yet in Argentina, Rivadavia is constructed as White. His social, economic, and political status and that of his parents guarantee his racial status within the nation.[16]

Argentina's attitude toward race is available to outsiders primarily through the voices and writings of Whites, including those who have assimilated into Whiteness by means of intermarriage, education, economic advancement, and the establishment of long and deep roots in Argentina. The dearth of self-identified Black Argentine literary voices is due in part to the fact that the equation "Argentine = White" is nearly ubiquitously accepted within Argentina itself. In addition, insofar as there are self-consciously nonwhite Argentine populations, they are overwhelmingly suppressed, marginalized, and impoverished and thus have very little access to public speech. They are thereby rendered invisible. When White Porteños, the name given to residents of Buenos Aires because of the city's important port, are asked to explain the presence of Blacks in Buenos Aires, they will usually respond that Blacks in the city are not Argentines, but Brazilians or Uruguayans. In other words, Argentineity itself confers Whiteness, and by definition Blacks are not Argentine but from somewhere else. A short and painful anecdote illustrates this assumption.

In 2002, María Eugenia Lamadrid, an Afro-Argentine whose family has lived in Argentina for five generations, was stopped at the airport as she tried to board a plane out of the country.[17] Lamadrid, founder of Africa Vive (Africa Lives), an organization that promotes knowledge of Black history and identity in Argentina, had been invited to an event in Panama honoring Dr. Martin Luther King Jr.[18] The Argentine immigration police detained her for six hours, refusing to believe that she, a Black woman, was Argentine. They asked if she spoke Spanish (one sign of Whiteness/citizenship in Argentina) and told her quite simply that her passport could not be real. Lamadrid is Black, and Blacks cannot *be* Argentine. The myth of Argentine Whiteness trumped the evidence of a legitimate passport carried by a living, breathing Black Argentine woman. The anecdote renders literal the metaphorical color line that Blackness cannot cross with a passport, illustrating vividly the color line Argentina draws around, not through, the nation.

This policing of the racial border suggests that the trope of Argentine Whiteness is a sign of uneasiness, a concern that Argentina's Black and Indigenous histories will assert themselves. For that history exists. Some of the Africans whom Europeans brought as slaves to the Americas became the property of Argentines; slavery was codified into law and eventually abolished, also by law. Marvin Lewis shows how vital Black men and women were in developing Argentine culture in the early nineteenth century, when one in every three Buenos Aires residents was of African origin.[19] But by the late 1880s less than 2 percent of the population was Black. A combination of a yellow fever epidemic that disproportionately struck poor urban

Luis de Mena's *Las Castas* (c. 1750) depicts the Virgin Mary presiding over the Spanish colonial project, with two historic scenes, one on either side of her, eight casta images below her, and below them a still life of native fruits and vegetables. Like the historical scenes and the fruits and vegetables, the casta images depicting racial lineage are labeled. *Top: left to right: De española y indio nace mestizo.* Of a Spanish woman and an Indian man, a Mestizo (mixed-blood) boy is born; *De española y mestizo nace castiza.* Of a Spanish Woman and a Mestizo man, a Castiza (in Spain, culturally pure) girl is born; *De castiza y español nace española.* Of a Castiza woman and a Spanish man, a Spanish girl is born; *De negra y español nace mulato.* Of a Black woman and a Spanish man, a Mulatto boy is born. *Bottom: left to right: De española y mulato nace morisca.* Of a Spanish woman and a Mulatto man, a Morisca (in Spain, a Christianized Moorish) girl is born; *De morisca y español nace albino tornatrás.* Of a Morisca woman and a Spanish man, a Throwback Albino boy is born; *De mestiza y indio nace lobo.* Of a Mestiza woman and an Indian man, a Lobo (literally "wolf") boy is born; *De india y lobo nace indio.* Of an Indian woman and a Lobo man, an Indian boy is born. Courtesy of the Ministerio de Cultura, Museo de America, Madrid, Spain.

neighborhoods, including those where many Blacks lived; the death of large numbers of Black soldiers during the Conquest of the Desert (the war waged against Native people); the deliberate undercounting of Blacks by the state; intermarriage with Whites; and emigration to Brazil and Uruguay effectively reduced the numbers of Afro-Argentines at the same time that immigration from Europe boomed. George Reid Andrews points out that Blacks were deliberately removed from the state's census reports and were, because they did not officially exist, denied necessary social services, which made them especially vulnerable. Jonathan Brown comments on multiple reasons for the undercounting of the Black population in the nineteenth century as well, including self-identification as some form of White and the lack of information concerning the number of Blacks in the provinces. Susana Rotker, arguing that the removal of Blacks from official discourse only partly explains why Argentina is perceived as a White country, notes that "if there are no Blacks in Argentina today it is because they mixed in to such a degree that *they are no longer noticed*" (22; original emphasis). Historian Seth Meisel believes that there was a deliberate shift in the official Argentine attitude that occurred sometime between the moment of independence, when the liberation of the nation was compared to the emancipation of enslaved Blacks, and the end of the nineteenth century, when the suppression of Blackness was well under way.[20]

The premeditated erasure of Indigenous and Black presence from the Argentine cultural consciousness is a textbook example of discursive and material practices reinforcing each other. Official immigration policy designed to bring the Whitest of Europeans to Argentina, under the rubric *gobernar es poblar*, 'governing is populating,' was meant not just to increase the number of Europeans whose labor, skills, knowledge, and capital would help develop the country but also to Whiten the nation. The tactic of disproportionately sending Black troops to kill Indigenous peoples, making their lands safe for the ever growing number of Whites, was a stroke of diabolic genius, though one that is not entirely unfamiliar to the history of U.S. soldiering in the twentieth century. The resulting brutal elimination of Indigenous and Black bodies from the Argentine national territory was accompanied by discursive practices that erased people of color from the collective historical and cultural consciousness of the nation.

If Rotker, Andrews, Brown, and Meisel are correct, Blackness is part of Argentina's very fiber, but it has been deliberately obscured, only to emerge obliquely. Certainly, Blackness is associated with that most Argentine of urban phenomena, the tango. Urban Black culture was instrumental in the making of the tango; thus tango itself is a sign of the historical presence of Argentine Blacks in the capital.[21] In what Marta Savigliano calls "a chain of jumpy, imprecise associations" that links tango, Blacks, sexuality, and primitivism (33), Afro-Argentines are both credited with important contributions to Argentine popular culture and framed in profoundly racist ways.

The abolition of slavery in Argentina began as a shift from agricultural and domestic servitude to military conscription, for men at least. José de San Martín, known as Argentina's liberator, believed that Blacks made the most valiant soldiers, and in 1816 he required all male slaves between fourteen and forty-five years of age to present themselves for military service. He thereby rounded up 710 Black men to fight in Chile and Peru (Paso et al. 142). Later, Blacks were disproportionately conscripted to fight and die in the euphemistically named Conquest of the Desert, the war waged to take control of the frontier by eliminating its Indigenous inhabitants. In the nineteenth century, both liberals and conservatives agreed on the subject of the elimination of the Indigenous population.[22] The conservatives' strategy was to subdue the Indians militarily and, apparently, to kill as many of them as they could. The liberals' strategy was to outnumber them through immigration and assimilate them through education, but they also approved of the outright extermination of Indians.

The dispute between opposing political camps over what constitutes the "authentic" Argentina began around the time of independence. The conservative Federalists believed in an "organic" Argentineity that, they thought, naturally occurred in the gauchos, whom they considered the autochthonous men of the pampas. Their political rivals, the "Unitarios" 'Unitarians' (who should not be confused with the religious group), believed that the nation could only succeed as a White, European country. When they came to power, the Unitarians set out to manufacture such a reality. Both Federalist and Unitarian views have a race-based concept of nation, but of different sorts. The Federalists claimed an autochthonous Argentine and a natural form of government arising from the land. The Unitarians, in contrast, believed in social constructionism. They held the liberal notion that the nation was made by men (gender intentional), not sprung from nature, and their plan was to sculpt a superior, White nation through a process of education and immigration. Importing its Whiteness from abroad, Argentina was not, on this view, naturally connected to, or produced from, the race/nation. The "natural" Whiteness and, therefore, the natural superiority of Europe would inhere in a populace that would *become* Argentine by virtue of its transplantation to Argentine soil.

Both Federalists and Unitarians might have made space for an Indigenous presence, but they did not. The Federalists could have found in its Native population a more "natural" inhabitant of the land than the gaucho. The Unitarians, building on the liberal French view of a socially contracted political entity that could represent a multiplicity of groups and interests, might well have included Indians among the represented groups. Neither did so. On the contrary, both parties were intent on removing the native population from Argentine territory and historical consciousness. The rhetoric of the Unitarians eventually carried the day, and its contemporary consequence is the national myth that holds that Argentina, unlike most of the rest of Latin America, is a White country. Ironically, because the Europeanized racism of Argentina is not entirely dependent on ideas about natural differences, it is, to a certain extent, right in step with contemporary social construction theory. The race of the nation is malleable. However, the underlying belief in a natural hierarchy among naturally occurring human races places us smack in the middle of very old, discredited ideas about race as a natural category.

The long history of native people in Argentina, which includes cultures going back thousands of years, was effectively obliterated in a nation that wanted to be part of the modern world. The Indigenous population of Argentina today, while by no means small in number with estimates ranging from 450,000 to 1.5 million out of a total population of approximately 39 million, is marginalized and impoverished. Despite the fact that Argentina has worked hard to establish itself as European and Western through a carefully fashioned discourse of Whiteness, popular culture provides a space for an Indigenous presence. One of the most widely read comic strips in twentieth-century Argentina was *Paturuzú*, whose eponymous hero is a fabulously wealthy Patagonian Indian with a ne'er-do-well Porteño godfather named Isidoro who is always stealing Paturuzú's money.[23] Despite what a North American sensibility today would characterize as a racist depiction of the Indigenous characters in the strip, Paturuzú is clearly the hero, and the reader's sympathy lies with him. For decades, *Paturuzú* made a space for acknowledging both the Indigenous presence in Argentina and the rapacious greed of urban, White Argentina in relation to its Indigenous past and present. Even so, its low-culture, comic format makes it possible to not take the critique entirely seriously.

Isidoro's selfish commandeering of Paturuzú's wealth offers a counternarrative to the formal accounts of the Argentine nation that recall the wars against native peoples to clear the land for White settlement and that construct exploitation as noble and heroic. Significantly, Indigenous groups are rendered present in these official histories even as the plot line is about their eradication. They remain a threat to national identity, a presence that predates the European founding of the nation, a difference within that threatens to destabilize identity. The continuing presence of an Indigenous Argentina is like a flickering light in the consciousness of the urban, largely European-descended population.

The earliest identification of nation with the now discredited idea of biological race still persists today in European countries such as Germany and Sweden that link citizenship to ancestry. The same foundationalism that focuses on physical characteristics like "blood" and "skin" and renders them symbolic is inevitably connected to parentage. In newly constructed or declared nations, like those within Africa, where traditional boundaries were redrawn by colonialism, or in the Americas, where people from different parts of the globe came or were brought to settle and build colonies and later nations, it is obvious that the racial singularity of the nation is problematic. In 1925, the Mexican thinker José Vasconcelos proposed the idea of the "cosmic race" as one way to deal with this conundrum. Vasconcelos asserted that a new blended race in the New World was emerging with the best features of those that comprise it.[24] However, fifty years earlier, the theory of racial mixing, or mestizaje as Vasconcelos would conceptualize it, did not have much currency in Argentina, where Domingo Faustino Sarmiento, its liberal president from 1868 to 1874, hired agents and took out advertisements in European newspapers to recruit immigrants. He cultivated an enticing image of Argentina, already White and becoming Whiter. By the end of the first decade of the twentieth century, Argentina was projecting itself as racially distinct from the rest of the South American continent.

Argentina White is, in part, an appeal to Europe to accept Argentina as an equal. In the mind of Europe, however, Argentina remains a Latin American nation and, therefore, racially other, even as Europe recognizes something of itself in that nation.[25] To the extent that Argentina wants to appeal to Europe not only as its equal but also as a bona fide member of the First World West, it projects itself to Europe as White. Moreover, insofar as Europe sees itself reflected in Argentina, it is telling that the purported racial homogeneity of the place surfaces as a point of uneasiness. The distinctions between nations and, therefore, races that predominated in late nineteenth-century Europe played into Argentina's project of racial self-construction. The most desirable Europeans were from the Protestant north, Englishmen and Germans whose work ethic would move the country forward. Less desirable were Southern Europeans whose poverty, lack of occupational skills, and illiteracy were thought to be naturally determined. Jews from Eastern Europe were, thanks to an imported anti-Semitism, at the bottom of the list. The discussions about which Europeans were the most desirable and, therefore, would be encouraged to resettle in Argentina dovetailed with the exclusion of Blacks and the discursive extermination of Indians that finished what the actual attempted genocide began.

The Black Gaucho and Martín Fierro

Although after emancipation the majority of Afro-Argentines resided in the city, there were also Blacks present in another prototypically Argentine sphere: the world of the gauchos. Some former slaves probably took up the nomadic life of the gauchos. Others, manumitted as a result of serving in the army, no doubt stayed on in the pampas. Yet the cultural representation of the nation invokes Blackness only to extirpate it. The Black gaucho is simultaneously evoked and destroyed in what is often taken to be Argentina's national poem, José Hernández's *El gaucho Martín Fierro* (1872, *The Gaucho Martín Fierro*).

In one of the most celebrated passages of Hernández's work, the usually sympathetic and sometimes even heroic protagonist Martín Fierro unnecessarily, and without provocation, insults a Black woman who arrives at a dance in the company of a gaucho who, like her, is Black. Fierro deliberately attacks the woman's dignity, with the expressed purpose of inciting a fight with her escort. As the quintessential gaucho, who is himself racially indeterminate, Fierro insults first the woman and then the man with taunts and epithets that are purely racial in content.[26] The scene ends in a duel in which Fierro kills the man he has insulted. Some critics have argued that the protagonist's murderous baiting illustrates how Fierro, as a symbol of the nation, has been contaminated by the violence that has been forced upon him, both as victim and perpetrator; he was one of the gauchos pressed into service in the Indian wars. One critic, Fermín Chávez, goes so far as to admonish the readers of his edition of *Martín Fierro* not to take race into account in the incident.

A handful of the poem's commentators, Nicolas Shumway among them, notes the racialized nature of the violence and attributes it to Fierro's own sense of marginalization, suggesting that he shores up his own masculinity by attacking someone who is lower on the social scale than he is. Dolores Aponte-Ramos openly challenges Fermín Chávez, arguing that race is a critical element of the episode, and she links it to other nineteenth-century representations of Black characters in Argentine literature.

It is most fruitful, however, to read this startling episode as a textualization of the overwrought response to Blacks by White Argentineans. There is simply no justification for Fierro's swaggering outburst. It is nothing more or less than an expression of racial braggadocio, a claim to superiority and a provocation to fight, with the result of extirpating Blackness from the space of the quintessential Argentine, that is, the world of the gaucho. If *El gaucho Martín Fierro* is the song of Argentine national identity, then the elimination of the Black man, also a gaucho, also making a claim to occupy the same social space as Fierro, is a fair mirror of Argentine society's rhetorical and real suppression of its Black population.

The unprovoked extirpation of Blackness in Argentine society expressed in this key episode has the effect of creating its own after-image. The passage from *El gaucho Martín Fierro* in which the hero provokes and kills his Black counterpart is one of the most frequently commented upon and most commonly anthologized sections of a poem that otherwise exalts the humanity of its protagonist. Many readers know little of the poem but this incident, which may well be Fierro's most ignoble moment. Hernández depicts Fierro throughout as an honorable, loyal, long-suffering true Argentine, yet in his baiting of the Black gaucho he behaves despicably. The author's position is unclear regarding his protagonist's behavior in this episode. Unlike other parts of the poem, where the reader sympathizes with Fierro's actions when he is brutally treated by the government, the reader is given no justification for the gaucho's behavior here. In recounting the episode, Fierro, as narrator of his own deeds, acknowledges that he is looking for a fight and indicates that the object of his generalized rage is not predetermined. Race is not the starting point of the violent interchange, but it is the vehicle that Fierro uses to provoke the fight:

> Como nunca, en la ocasión
>
> Por peliar me dió la tranca.
> Y la emprendí con un negro
> Que trujo una negra en ancas.
> (Hernández, stanza 194)
>
> *Then, more than ever before*
> *booze made me want to fight*
> *and I picked one with a black*
> *who came riding in with his woman*

The Black man becomes the object of Fierro's desire to fight almost by chance, but once he chooses him it is the man's race, and that of the woman who accompanies him, that is their most salient characteristic for Fierro. Nor does Fierro attack the man directly. Instead he provokes him to fight by taunting the woman he escorts. First he insults her directly, but not before noting that she herself pays no attention to anyone; that is, she is self-assured and uninterested in having anything to do with the other people present at the dance:

Al ver llegar la morena,
Que no hacía caso de naides,
Le dije con la mamúa:
Va . . . ca . . . yendo gente al baile.
(Hernández, stanza 195)

As she came in I saw
she wasn't lookin' at nobody,
so being drunk I said,
"Cow . . . ming to the dance?"

The above remark is the first of two that compares the Black woman to an animal—here the wordplay, which the woman quickly understands, likens her to a cow. "'Va cayendo gente al baile" means 'lots of people are showing up at the dance'; but a subtle shift in emphasis in the first two words, from "va cayendo" to "vaca yendo" changes the meaning from '[people] are showing up' to 'a cow is going.' She is quick to respond, insult for insult. The woman's sharp wit does not save her from further degrading comparisons to animals: After her partner's death, she "brays like a she-wolf" (stanza 217). Fierro uses animal imagery to describe and to belittle the Black gaucho as well, likening him to a squealing pig when he cuts him in the fight. The Black characters are, on the one hand, repeatedly besmirched by Fierro's invective. On the other hand, the Black gaucho is proud and brave, and the woman is quick-witted and loving. Fierro first wants to hit her to stop her crying after he has killed her partner, but he thinks better of it—out of respect for the dead.

The Conquest of the Desert, to use the Argentinean euphemism, sets the action of *El gaucho Martín Fierro* in motion: the poem documents the inhuman methods used to conscript and keep gauchos like Fierro in the army. The Black man in *El gaucho Martín Fierro* is also a gaucho; as such he is a man of honor, vulnerable to insult. His relationship to the woman is chivalrous, and his opponent uses his chivalry to provoke him. Because he is a worthy opponent who fights well, after killing him, Fierro thinks one day he will go back and give him a decent burial. Moreover, even though the Black woman is compared to a series of animals in an overt effort to render a human subject contemptible and ridiculous, she is still a fully human subject. She is quick-witted and loyal; she appropriately expresses grief when her man is killed. Finally, in Part Two of the poem, written several years later, Fierro encounters the brother of this man, whom he engages not in a knife fight, but in a singing contest traditional among gauchos. Unlike the murdered gaucho who is labeled "negro" 'black,' Fierro refers to the brother as "moreno" 'dark.' Moreno is also a racial label meaning Black, but it can also refer to someone with dark hair or eyes. As a mark of difference, it is a little less absolute.

Unlike the Black characters who are "othered" partially, Indians in the poem are the total other. They are wholly bestialized, represented as bereft of any moral or ethical understanding, brutal not only to their captives but also to the women of their own community, and incapable of exemplifying loyalty, honor, or friendship. In *El gaucho Martín Fierro*, Fierro and his comrade, Cruz, reject "civilized" society—which in Argentina, as in the United States, is associated with cities, education, and the socializing effects of women—by lighting out to Indian country where they encounter nothing but brutalizing savagery. The savagery of the Indians is considered self-evident once the supposedly naturally noble gauchos have seen evidence of their mistreatment of both White women whom they have taken captive as well as their own women.[27]

In contrast to the antisocial behavior of the Indians, gauchos, Black and White, demonstrate love, friendship, and loyalty that go beyond death and unto the generations. (This love tends to be of the homosocial sort among the White gauchos: there is little place for women in the lives of Fierro and Cruz beyond the production of sons that will allow for the perpetuation of friendship into the second generation.) Fierro and Cruz soon learn that there is no freedom with the Indians—only suffering, and in Cruz's case, death. *El gaucho Martín Fierro* can be taken as one instance of a discourse of othering that made it seem not only possible but also just and necessary to destroy the Indians in their person and in their culture. That their presence was blocking the White privatizing of land and constraining the development of property made it seem all the more justifiable to exterminate them. Any profit made by those members of the elite as a result of the elimination of Indigenous people from the land they wanted to claim was—from the elite's point of view—only for the good of the nation.

Blacks and Indians are rendered absent from Argentina, both from the city, which insists on its European origins both racially and culturally, and from the countryside, where the Indian is first incorporated into the gaucho and then extirpated from him. Blacks, Indians, and gauchos are all marginal figures, alternately criminalized, romanticized, and "disappeared." Insofar as the gaucho is the quintessential Argentine, it is not surprising that Indians and Blacks, repressed in the historical consciousness of the nation, oscillate between being and not being assimilated to the gaucho. The Black gaucho who is eliminated in the foundational text, *El gaucho Martín Fierro*, may have been historically present, even making his appearance in the poem, but the nation will have no part of him. The mestizo gaucho kills off the Indian in the process of participating in the wars of the desert into which he was pressed.

The foundational myth of the gaucho is that he is the child of a Spanish father and an Indian mother, but the maternal, the Indigenous, is fully excised when Martín Fierro and Cruz ride into Indian lands. They know they are going into the land of the absolute other. Theirs is a homosocial world that has little room for the feminine, whether in the form of actual woman or the mythic mother. The Indian mother withers away in the gaucho, whom deeply conservative and patriarchal Federalists hail as the autochthonous Argentine.[28] Just as they balk at the suggestion that Argentina is an Indian country, they deny that it is a feminine one, or an immature one. Masculinity, Whiteness, and virile adulthood are the threads that will be woven together into the fabric of Argentine nationality.

Europe and the Marketing of Argentina White

In Argentina, the Indigenous people were discursively removed from the realm of the human and physically displaced from their land. Afro-Argentines were drastically reduced in numbers, and the remaining old families and new arrivals, mostly from Brazil and other parts of Latin America, were quietly ignored, their very existence repeatedly denied. Yet it is never self-evident that Argentina is White. On the contrary, Europe always raises the question of race: Aren't there Blacks there? Isn't the place full of Indians?

The architects of Argentina's pavilion at the 1900 international exposition in Paris went to great lengths to efface any sign of Indigenous presence in Argentina in their representation of their nation. Europeans, however, not only expected but also desired evidence of Argentine racial difference. They had read about the plumed savages of the Americas in the adventure stories of Salgari and Karl May. They remembered that Darwin had brought Fuegian Indians back from his voyage of scientific exploration and paraded them before British royalty. They wanted the thrill of the exotic, a personal contact with the undifferentiated Latin America from which Argentina was trying to extricate itself.

The international expositions in which, according to Anthony Alan Shelton, Europe achieves "the most cogent expression" of empire (157) were the very places Argentina was trying to insert itself into the family of nations, as civilized as the nations of Europe and on equal terms with them. Europe was inclined to relate to the non-European world as the site of exoticism and barbarism (in the civilization/ barbarism dyad that haunts Argentina to this day), the colonized or colonizable other. This tendency collides with Argentina's desire to project itself as European. Thus when folkloric artifacts are solicited for display in the Argentine pavilion at the 1889 Paris exhibition, or when a Frenchwoman asks to see the natives there, it is not simply in recognition of a multicultural society to which the Argentine elite is too proud to admit.[29] It is also, and more importantly , a gesture that reinforces Europe's right to make use (and meaning) of the rest of the world. It is not surprising that the Argentine elite, desiring parity with Europe, refuses to capitulate to this version of its culture but instead insists on self-representation as a forward-looking, industrializing, literate, liberal nation. Both the European insistence on extracting the exotic other from Argentina for its own consumption and the Argentinean elite's refusal to embody the exotic other are racist, colonizing gestures. They both partake in the belief of European superiority, but there is a difference. Europe is distant enough from Argentine otherness and sure enough of its own preeminence that it longs to consume the Indigenous, exotic other, a tasty morsel for a jaded palate.[30] Argentina's elite class suppresses the very existence of the threatening other within in order to establish itself as the rightful owner and just ruler of a precariously "European" nation.

Europe projects its own racial anxieties onto Argentina, which in turn claims that it, too, is a European country. In both the Old and New Worlds, only the fabricated evidence of racial otherness makes the fiction of racial purity viable. The nations of Europe need their racialized others to satisfy their own sense of identity as racially pure. Argentina, among the many colonial sites onto which Europe deflects its racial anxiety, refuses to be so othered, choosing, rather, to engage in the same pretense of Whiteness. European texts uneasily collaborate with Argentina's claim, but not before demonstrating how shaky it is by questioning its very premises.

Argentina's racial anxiety mirrors Europe's. If Buenos Aires is the Paris of the Americas, then Paris is the gold standard of culture and refinement. Glory redounds to both, and the standard of racial purity needs to be upheld at both ends of the equation. Paris's own status as a city of Whites, challenged by the former colonials who have moved to its suburbs, is emblematic of the familiar disquiet of postcolonial Europe. Moreover, faced with the physical presence of its former colonial subjects pressing in on its borders, concerned with its own racial boundaries, Europe is confronted by still another challenge from an Argentina that claims that it, too, is European. Europe wants its others to be different, but Argentina insists that it is same. As if it were not enough that Europe's own countries are besieged by racial difference, here is a Third World nation that is refusing to be non-White. The boundaries are being blurred from all sides.

One of the ways White anxiety plays out in European literary texts is by Argentina's racial makeup surfacing as an issue to be questioned and clarified. Naïve Europeans assume Argentina is racially different from Europe, sometimes Black, sometimes Indigenous, and other times mestizo, but the more knowledgeable among them sets them straight. Over and over, European authors collaborate in the production of Argentina as a White nation. There is an oblique connection between Europeans' expectation of Argentine racial otherness and the suppression of that otherness among the Argentine elite that emerges. In texts by European writers, for whom Argentina and Africa sometimes evoke each other, such juxtapositions generally cast Africa as even more primitive and exotic. One French writer, Raymond Roussel, details the crass, showy, and spectacular wealth of the Argentine upper class in the prologue of his Africa travel book. His trip to Africa from France is preceded by a request by a young Argentine baron, "an enormously rich Argentine who, for many years, has led a life of crazy spending and continuous ostentation in Paris" to create a fireworks display to celebrate his wedding.[31] This Argentine, who has a "castle" near Buenos Aires, stands in stark contrast to the Africans the narrator will soon meet but to whom he is symbolically linked as Europe's other.

The veiled relationship between Argentina and Africa, rendered as negation, is amply presented in Dominique Bona's 1984 novel *Argentina*, in which the characters who have never been to Argentina express their belief that it is a multiracial society, only to be contradicted by the upper-class Argentines they meet on board the ship that takes them to Buenos Aires. The upper-class characters go out of their way to proclaim Argentina so White a country that implausibility may be figured by the odds that one might ever see a Black person there: "[W]hat terrible nonsense . . . all that has as much chance of happening as you or I have of running into a Black person on the streets of Buenos Aires" (Bona 38).[32] In his reply, a newcomer reveals his naïveté precisely in his vision of Argentina as a mestizo country full of Indians, a supposition that provokes the exaggerated protestations of his dinner companions.

> "I have been assured on the contrary," he said, "that Argentina was the strangest and most multiple mix of peoples. Will we be met at the dock by Indians with feathers?"
>
> Campbell choked in his glass, Lady Campbell raised her delicate shoulders, the large man laughed like a barbarian, and Robert de Liniers, for that was the name of the French aristocrat—responded, sardonically,
>
> "We are a White country, sir. The only perfectly White country south of Canada." (38)[33]

The European newcomer is disabused of his beliefs about the racial complexity of Argentina by a table full of his social superiors. Although this totalizing picture of Argentina as perfectly White (which itself depends on a disquieting view of a Canada equally bereft of its Native and Black populations) does not go unchallenged, that challenge is barely whispered.

Although material reality belies the idea that Argentina is a White nation, the Argentine elite has managed to project its country, and then see it reflected back, as the most European of Latin American nations. In contrast to Cuba or Brazil, whose African heritage is central to its national identity, or Mexico, where after the revolution the elite strove to create a mestizo culture into which its indigeneity could be incorporated, Argentina expunges all visible evidence of racial complexity.[34] Mexico's ideal ancestors, the Indians, would be integrated into its ideal citizenry as mestizo. In contrast, Argentina's ideal ancestor is the European immigrant. His descendant, assimilated into Argentine society linguistically, religiously, and culturally, is the ideal citizen, a product of the precarious discourse of melting-pot Whiteness. On such uncertain grounds Argentina continually shores up its shaky story of racial purity, selling and reselling Argentina White.

NOTES

1. Capitalization in English marks proper nouns, but in capitalizing "White" I would rather think of it as marking an improper noun. I have capitalized "White" throughout this study as a visible sign of its naming a race, a cultural construction. The symbolic meaning of capitalization is complicated, and I am not entirely happy with a notation that also seems to impart particular importance to the sign "White," whose signified is already overly self-aggrandized. By capitalizing "White" when it refers to the racial construct, I hope to indicate that White, like Black, marks the presence, not the absence, of race. The very fact that we have only belatedly come to study the production of Whiteness suggests how successful the discourse of racism has been at projecting "White" as "norm" and "Black" as "race" in big and small ways, including through the conventions of grammar. Moreover, I understand "Black" and "White" (as well as the rest of the racial color wheel—Red, Yellow, Brown) as metaphors rather than metonyms.

2. See Brodkin for a discussion of the shifting racial categorization of Jews that neatly demonstrates the culturally constructed nature of race.

3 Disappearance is a fraught word in Argentina where the military government, from the mid-1970s until it was removed from power in 1984, kidnapped, tortured, and killed approximately thirty thousand people who collectively are known as "los desaparecidos" 'the disappeared.'

4. See Kaminsky, "Gender, Race, Raza" for a fuller discussion of the phenomenon of Hispanidad.

5. Latin American "casta" is thus very different from Hindu "caste," which is reinforced, not undone, from generation to generation. "Casta" refers to those of mixed heritage.

6. In her excellent essay for the exhibition catalogue, Katzew describes the paintings, places them historically, and gives an overview of the workings of Spanish colonial racial classification.

7. To a certain extent the casta paintings are still used in this way. Just a few years ago, in the provincial museum in Guadalajara, Mexico, I observed a father explaining the casta images and captions to his small son, not as a lesson in history but as if these categories still had social and even scientific meaning.

8. These and subsequent examples are taken from the catalogue of the exhibit, *Frutas y Castas Ilustradas.*

9. The term "mulato" refers to an individual with one Black and one White parent. A "requinterona de mulato" would be the child of one White parent and one parent who was of one-eighth African and seven-eighths European ancestries. The word "requinterona" has a numerical root ("quinto" = 'fifth'; the prefix "re" and the suffix "ona" are both intensifiers), implying a mathematical precision that is belied by the confusion of the racial vocabulary overall. These terms signify the slippery, invented categories of race, and they are often inconsistent. Translation under such circumstances is at best tricky and at worst a reification of racial categories.

10. A caveat: I have seen only four sets of castas, plus individual paintings reproduced in various venues, so my observations here are tentative and based on a very small sample.

11. The children depicted in all the casta portraits are as likely to be girls as boys, which means that not just offspring but also representative offspring are as likely to be female as male. The cultural tendency to submerge the female in the normative male is undercut in these images to the extent that girls and boys, if not adult women and men, equally represent the human species.

12. Interestingly, these stories are gender specific. It is expressly the mother-daughter bond that is tested, as one member of the dyad—sometimes the mother, sometimes the daughter—clandestinely crosses the border of color, leaving them both, at least for a time, painfully separated.

13. In this, the system of racial classification is again different from the U.S. classification, in which the primary racial distinction is between Black and White backed up by a secondary system of color-coded racial difference. For a fuller discussion in the context of the racialization of the category "Hispanic," see Kaminsky, "Gender, Race, Raza."

14. The reason I call the acknowledgment uneasy is that racism persists in these societies; the mestizo identity of the nation often means absorbing Indigenous people into the dominant culture, and race is still determinant of social and economic mobility. José Vasconcelos's pronouncement in *The Cosmic Race* that Latin America owes its strength to combining the best characteristics of the races that

come together there is the positive face of mestizaje, but even Vasconcelos deteriorated into stark racism toward the end of his life.

15. Chile and Uruguay are closer to Argentina in identifying themselves as (primarily) European. Nevertheless, Argentina attributes part of the current presence of Blacks in its territory to migration from Uruguay.

16. My own admittedly limited reading on Rivadavia made no mention of the statesman's racial background. To check my outsider's knowledge, I asked poet Noni Benegas, who was born and raised in Argentina, what she knew of Rivadavia's racial heritage. She in turn asked two other well-educated Argentines. None thought of him as Black. Benegas did point me to a web site she discovered on Bernadino Rivadavia, Historia Colonial Argentina, that suggests once again how culturally and historically specific racial labeling is. The anonymous author of the site relates how the future Pope Pius IX met Rivadavia and commented that "poseía rasgos de mulato de tipo israelítico" 'he had the features of a mulatto of the Israelitic sort.' The point here is not that Rivadavia was or was not Black, or White, or "Israelitic" but that these racial categories, while deeply consequential, are also unsettled. For a more in-depth discussion on Rivadavia's racial heritage see *Afroargentinos*, directed by Jorge Fortes and Diego Ceballos. I am grateful to La Vinia Delois Jennings for telling me about this film.

17. Pérez Martín cites the *El Clarín* newspaper report on Lamadrid's experience with the Argentine immigration authorities in the web magazine *El Muro*, a weekly guide to Buenos Aires.

18. Obviously, the very existence of Lamadrid's organization demonstrates that the hegemonic view of race in Argentina is not universal. Similarly, there are Argentine organizations devoted to claiming Indigenous rights that by their very existence help make the Indigenous population visible. These counternarratives serve as a small wedge interrupting the dominant discourse.

19. One Black person in every three is the number most often quoted, but Emilio Ruchansky suggests that as much as 60 percent of the population of early and mid-nineteenth-century Buenos Aires was Black.

20. Meisel, personal correspondence.

21. The documentary film *Afroargentinos* (2005) also traces the African roots of the tango.

22. As Balderston points out, David Viñas shows in *Indios, ejército y frontera* that by 1870 "the Argentine intelligentsia, both liberal and conservative, agreed on the desirability of the removal or extermination of the pampas Indians" (87).

23. The character Paturuzú, drawn by Dante Quinterno, first appeared in a newspaper comic strip in 1928. By 1930 the comic strip was renamed for the character, and in the 1930s it became a monthly and, finally, a weekly publication of its own. I am grateful to Noni Benegas for telling me about Paturuzú and for providing me with copies of some of the Paturuzú comic magazines from the early 1960s.

24. It is important not to romanticize the notion of the cosmic race. In his later writings Vasconcelos expresses deeply racist attitudes.

25. In *Argentina: Stories for a Nation*, I engage in an extended discussion of Argentina as Europe's "uncanny other," similar yet different.

26. Gramuglio and Sarlo note that the gaucho is, on the one hand, hero and civilizer of the pampas, and on the other, a racial inferior condemned to disappear himself. The early-twentieth-century writer Leopoldo Lugones maintains that gauchos never believed they could be the political and social equals of Whites.

27. See Rotker for an excellent analysis of the figure of the captive and the construction of the savage in Argentine culture.

28. My sketchy discussion here only begins to scratch the surface of the complex myth of the gaucho in Argentine culture. For an excellent analysis of the cultural meanings of the gaucho figure, see Ludmer.

29. See Fey for a discussion of the Argentine pavilion at the 1889 Paris fair.

30. The Europe I evoke as a seamless whole here is, of course, internally fractured as well. The European elite organized the Paris expositions, but the working class as well as the bourgeoisie attended them.

31. "[R]iquísimo argentino que, desde hacía muchos años, llevaba una vida de locos gastos y continua ostentación en París" (Roussel, cited in Ferrari 230; the translation is mine).

32. "No! . . . Terrible non-sens! . . . tout cela a autant de chances de réussir que vous et moi en avons de croiser un negre dans les rues de Buenos Aires" (Bona 38; this and all subsequent translations from *Argentina* are mine).

33. "'On m'affirmait au contraire,' dit-il, que l'Argentine était le plus étrainge et le plus multiple bouillon de peuples. Serons-nous accueillis au port par des Indiens a plumes'?"

Campbell s'étrangla dans son verre, lady Campbell haussa ses minces épaules tandis que le gros homme chauve riait comme un barbare, et que Robert de Liniers—c'était le nom de l'aristocrat francais—réprondait, sardonique: "'Nous sommes un pays blanc, monsieur. Le seul pays parfaitement blanc au sud du Canada'" (Bona 38).

34. See Saldaña-Portillo for a cogent analysis of the process.

Works Cited

Afroargentinos. Dir. Jorge Fortes and Diego Ceballos. Filmagem Producciones, 2002.

Andrews, George Reid. *The Afro-Argentines of Buenos Aires: 1800–1900*. Madison: U of Wisconsin P, 1980.

Aponte-Ramos, Dolores. "Cuando la pampa se colorea: Los negros en la Argentina decimonónica." *Revista Iberoamericana* 65.188–89 (July–Dec. 1999): 733–39.

Balderston, Daniel. *Out of Context: Historical Reference and the Representation of Reality in Borges.* Durham: Duke UP, 1993.

"Bernardino Rivadavia." *Historia Argentina Colonial.* 11 Apr. 2005. <http://usuarios.lycos.es/historiaargentinacol>.

Bona, Dominique. *Argentina.* 1984. Cher.: Mercure de France, 1986.

Brodkin, Karen. *How Jews Became White Folks, and What That Says about Race in America.* New Brunswick: Rutgers UP, 1998.

Brown, Jonathan C. "The Bondage of Old Habits in Nineteenth-Century Argentina." *Latin American Research Review* 21.2 (1986): 3–31.

Chávez, Fermín. Introduction. *El gaucho Martín Fierro: La vuelta de Martín Fierro.* By José Hernández. Buenos Aires: Hércules di Cesare y Floreal Puerta, 1955.

Du Bois, W. E. B. *The Souls of Black Folk.* 1903. Boulder: Paradigm, 2004.

Ferrari, Roberto A. "El país motorizado: La Exposición Internacional de Ferrocarriles y Transportes Terrestres." *Buenos Aires 1910: El imaginario para una gran capital.* Ed. Margarita Gutman and Thomas Reese. Buenos Aires: Eudeba, 1999. 229–40.

Fey, Ingrid E. "Peddling the Pampas: Argentina at the Paris Universal Exposition of 1889." *Latin American Popular Culture: An Introduction.* Ed. William H. Beezley and Linda A. Curcio-Nagy. Wilmington: SR, 2000. 61–85.

Frutas y Castas Ilustradas: Museo Nacional de Antropología, Madrid, 25 Feb.–29 Aug. 2004. Madrid: Ministerio de Educación, Cultura y Deporte, 2003.

Garvey, Marcus. "Bernardino de Rivadavia." 2005. *Great People of Color.* Marcus Garvey. 5 Apr. 2005 <http://www.marcusgarvey.com/wmview.php?ArtID=525&page=1>.

Gramuglio, María Teresa, and Beatriz Sarlo. "José Hernández." *Historia de la Literatura Argentina.* 2 vols. Buenos Aires: Centro Editor de América Latina, 1980–86.

Harris, Cheryl. "Whiteness as Property." *Harvard Law Review* 106.8 (1993): 1709–91.

Hernández, José. *The Gaucho Martín Fierro.* UNESCO Collection of Representative Works, Latin-American Series. Ed. Carrino, Frank Gaetano, Alberto J. Carlos, and Norman Mangouni. Albany: State U of New York P, 1974. <http://www.gutenberg.org/etext/14765>. Originally published as *El gaucho Martín Fierro.* Buenos Aires: Imprenta de la Pampa, 1872.

———. *El gaucho Martín Fierro: La vuelta de Martín Fierro.* Buenos Aires: Hércules di Cesare y Floreal Puerta, 1955.

Hurst, Fannie. 1933. *Imitation of Life.* Durham: Duke UP, 2004.

Imitation of Life. Dir. John Stahl. Universal Pictures, 1934. Dir. Douglas Sirk, Universal Pictures, 1959

Kaminsky, Amy. *Argentina: Stories for a Nation.* Minneapolis: U of Minnesota P, 2008.

———. "Gender, Race, Raza." *Feminist Studies* 20.1 (Spring 1994): 7–31.

Katzew, Ilona. *Casta Painting: Identity and Social Stratification in Colonial Mexico.* Catalog for the exhibit "New World Orders: Casta Painting and Colonial Latin America." Americas Society Art Gallery, 26 Sept.–22 Dec. 1996.

Lewis, Marvin. *Afro-Argentine Discourse: Another Dimension of the Black Diaspora.* Columbia: U of Missouri P, 1996.

Ludmer, Josefina. *The Gaucho Genre: Treatise on the Motherland.* 1988. Durham: Duke UP, 2002.

Meisel, Seth. E-mail to the author. 9 May 2005.

Paso, Leonardo, Enrique Palomba, María Litter, and Pedro Calderón. *Compendio de historia argentina (desde la colonia hasta 1943).* Buenos Aires: Ediciones Directa, 1982.

Pérez Martín, Norma. "Los negros de hoy en Buenos Aires." 2002. *El Muro: La Guía Cultural de Buenos Aires.* El Muro. 3 Apr. 2005 <http://www.elmurocultural. com/Columnistas/cperezmartino9.html>.

Pinky. Dir. Elia Kazan. Perf. Jeanne Crain, Ethel Barrymore, and Ethel Waters. 20th Century Fox, 1949.

Pino Díaz, Fermín del. "Historia natural y razas humanas en los 'cuadros de castas' hispanoamericanos." Catalog for the exhibit, *Frutas y Castas Ilustradas.* Coord. Pilar Romero de Tejeda. Museo Nacional de Antropología, Madrid, 25 Feb.–29 Aug. 2004. Madrid: Ministerio de Educación, Cultura y Deportes, 2004.

Rotker, Susana. *Captive Women: Oblivion and Memory in Argentina.* Trans. Jennifer French. Minneapolis: U of Minnesota P, 2002.

Roussel, Raymond. *Impressions de l'Afrique.* Paris: Pauvert, 1963.

Ruchansky, Emilio. "¿Negros en Buenos Aires?" 2 Feb. 2003. *Agencia de Informacion Fray Tito para América Latina.* ADITAL. 31 Mar. 2005 <http://www.adital. org.br/site/noticia.asp?lang=ES&cod=5606>.

Saldaña-Portillo, María Josefina. *The Revolutionary Imagination in the Americas and the Age of Development.* Durham: Duke UP, 2003.

Savigliano, Marta. *Tango and the Political Economy of Passion.* Boulder: Westview, 1995.

Shelton, Anthony Alan. "Museum Ethnography: An Imperial Science." *Cultural Encounters: Representing "Otherness."* Ed. Elizabeth Hallam and Brian V. Street. London: Routledge, 2000.

Shumway, Nicolas. *The Invention of Argentina.* Berkeley: U of California P, 1991.

Vasconcelos, José. *The Cosmic Race; La raza cósmica.* 1925. Los Angeles: Centro de Publicaciones, 1979.

Viñas, David. *Indios, ejércitos y frontera.* Mexico D.F.: Siglo XXI, 1982.

A Dream of a White Vienna after World War I: Hugo Bettauer's *The City Without Jews* and *The Blue Stain*

PETER HÖYNG

Four years after the end of World War I, the then-popular Austrian journalist and author Hugo Bettauer (1872–1925) published two novels in which racist ideologies in Vienna are put to the test. Bettauer utilizes satirical means in *Die Stadt ohne Juden* (*The City Without Jews*, 1922) to prove that anti-Semitism in Vienna is not viable because the burgeoning metropolis presumably cannot afford to exist without its Jewish population. In *Das blaue Mal* (*The Blue Stain*), also published in 1922, he agitates again for a politics of ethnic diversity, only this time outside of Vienna and with an ironical inversion. Whereas in *Die Stadt ohne Juden* anti-Semitism informs the Viennese sociopolitical landscape, Bettauer portrays racism as absent in the Vienna of *Das blaue Mal* and instead "exports" it to the United States.

Rather than shrug off this apparent contradiction between the two narratives as simply authorial prerogative or caprice, the dichotomy can be read as a discursive symptom of a divided society in crisis. After all, the first Republic of Austria was founded upon the disillusionment of a lost war and the demise of the multiethnic and multinational Austrian-Hungarian Empire. Specific as the following discussion is in terms of history and topography, its locus centers on post–World War I Austria in which Bettauer's two narratives present, above all, an exemplary understanding of Vienna's Jewish minority and their mediation of a specific discourse of whiteness. Bettauer, in the midst of condemning anti-Semitism and racism in general, dreams unconsciously of a white Vienna and thus is not free of the racist ideology that he decries. Furthermore, Bettauer's own unconscious contradictions in regard to his liberal positions help to unveil what otherwise remains invisible: the powerful politics of whiteness in the age of anti-Semitism prior to the Shoah. A general historical comprehension of post–World War I Austria is essential to understanding and positioning Hugo Bettauer and his novels within the context of whiteness to which they accede.

Disillusionments and Lingering Anti-Semitism in Post–Word War I Austria

After four years of men killing each other on the battlefields of Western and Eastern Europe, and after ten million soldiers had died for no particular "cause" other than nationalistic chauvinism run rampant, the end of World War I became a catalyst for fundamental changes in the Orient and Occident. What had once seemed stable for centuries collapsed within weeks in November 1918. Three major European monarchies—the Hohenzollern, the Habsburg, and the Romanovs—that had ruled the German, the Austrian-Hungarian, and the Russian Empires respectively were either ousted into exile or, as in the case of the Romanovs, murdered. The implosions of these three empires brought about manifold, unforeseen social consequences for individuals and societies at-large in Central and Eastern Europe.

The first Republic of Austria was founded upon disillusionment because the vast territories of the dual monarchy of Austria-Hungary were split into several nation-states. Citizens of the much smaller Austria had to learn to step out of the shadows of the patriarchal society so strongly embodied by the figure of Franz Joseph I, who reigned over Austria-Hungary for no less than sixty-eight years, from 1848 to 1916. In "his" parliamentarian dual monarchy, he presided over a large but fragile state with as many as twelve ethnicities and/or nationalities—Czechoslovakians, Moravians, Slovakians, Poles, Russians, Romanians, Hungarians, Croatians, Serbians, Slovenians, Italians, and Germans. Jews and Gypsies constituted the two ethnic groups that were not considered "nationalities" since the determining factor for being of or from a discrete "nation" was language. But Jews within the Austrian-Hungarian Empire spoke the language of their "host" nation, or, depending on their Jewish identity, Yiddish, Hebrew, or German—or a combination of all three.

Establishing the first Republic of Austria meant not only downsizing its former territory but also transforming it into a seemingly monoethnic democratic state with a German ethnicity, language, and culture more dominant than ever before. According to Marsha Rozenblit, nation reformation caused "the most complicated identity crisis" for the Jews in Vienna:

> The dissolution of the Habsburg Monarchy and the creation of German-Austria called into question all the fundamental assumptions on which the identity of the majority of Vienna's Jews rested. They no longer lived in the capital of a large, multinational empire that was not obsessed with its German identity, but in a city that seemed too big for the small German nation-state over which it presided. They would no longer enjoy the comfort of their old Habsburg tripartite identity that allowed them to be Austrian by political loyalty, German by culture, and ethnically Jewish. (*Reconstructing a National Identity* 155–56)

Thus Rozenblit concludes that "most of them chose to mourn the collapse of the Habsburg Empire" and "continued to behave as if Habsburg Austria still existed, at least in an abstract sense" (158).

Yet the immediacy of the traumatic rupture of post–World War I Austria coincided and overlapped with a deeper historical layer of the Habsburg Empire, that of anti-Semitism. After centuries of various discriminations, in 1867 Franz Joseph I granted Jews constitutional rights. For the first time, Jews had the opportunity to experience an unprecedented integration into the dominant culture, though they still were excluded from higher positions in the civil service and military. These equal rights allowed many Jews to embrace the dominant German language of the political and cultural center of Vienna. As historian Robert Wistrich concludes, "Thus Vienna, unlike other provincial capitals in the Empire, continued to expand and maintain its hold after the 1860s as a magnet for Habsburg Jewry, and in this respect was rivaled only by Budapest" (43). Approximately 90 percent of all Austrian Jews lived in Vienna; however, no more than one-tenth, or about 170,000, Viennese residents were considered Jewish.[1] Having the freedom to either practice or ignore their religious beliefs while potentially integrating fully into a predominantly Catholic society allowed the manifold Jewish identities that Rozenblit mentions. An ethnic Jew, for example, could be politically loyal to the Habsburg monarchy, embrace German language and culture, and simultaneously be proud to be a Hungarian.

The process of Jewish emancipation, however, was anything but harmonious, as the aforementioned example of identity fusion might imply. Rather, the gradual acculturation and eventual assimilation of a large group of Jewish citizens created an intensifying split among the Jewish populations. While there was a significant Germanized Jewish elite in Vienna, there was also an even larger number of "Ostjuden" 'Eastern Jews,' who were by and large poor, Orthodox, and loyal to century-old traditions. "The *Ostjuden*," Wistrich notes, "were widely seen to be loud, coarse and dirty, immoral, and culturally backward in the eyes of their more modern Westernized brethren—a symbolic construct that was particularly widespread among German and Austrian Jews by the end of the nineteenth century" (51). The immigration of Eastern Jews, mainly from Galicia,[2] which began in the late nineteenth century and resumed following pogroms immediately after World War I, seemed to threaten the acculturation and assimilation of many Viennese Jews who feared that traditional Jews would only stir more anti-Semitism and thus weaken their own process of integration into the dominant culture.[3] Therefore, a number of Jewish and Zionist organizations tried unsuccessfully to gentrify the Jews from the eastern parts of the empire and to blend them into the dominant culture, that is, to make them as invisible as possible as Jews.[4]

The forced course of acculturation and assimilation over three generations among a significant number of Jews in Vienna came at a high price. Many Jews faced uneasy issues of identity among themselves, while at the same time finding themselves in a precarious situation within the multiethnic, multinational empire. These conflicting identity issues ultimately resulted in a double-bind for those willing to assimilate: either one assimilated with the dominant (German) culture so as not to be recognized and stigmatized as Jewish or faced disrespect from one's own ethnic group, resulting in forms of self-hatred.[5]

The competing and conflicting identities of many Jews in Vienna, those who enjoyed civil rights and the freedom of social mobility while being continually marked as the "other," are reflected poignantly in Theodor Herzl's biography (1860–1904). Herzl moved from Budapest to Vienna in 1878, opting for the assumed supremacy of German "Kultur" 'Culture' with its "achievements" in literature, music, philosophy, and modern science. Due to his extensive intellectual gifts, Herzl became a respected journalist of the widely circulated and liberal newspaper *Die Neue Freie Presse* (*The New Free Press*).[6] While later becoming their star "feuilletonist" 'culture critic,' he was fully aware of and at times commented on the anti-Semitism that began to increase in the 1880s.[7] However, it was his reporting from Paris about the Dreyfus affair in 1891 and his reaction to the anti-Semitism he witnessed in France that prompted his full identification as a Jew. As a result, he wrote *Der Judenstaat* (*The Jewish State*) (1896), in which he argues that the only solution to overcoming structurally deep-seated anti-Semitism is to create a nation-state for Jews:

> The nations in whose midst Jews live are all either covertly or openly Anti-Semitic. . . . We are what the Ghetto made us. . . . We are one people—our enemies have made us one without consent. . . . The Jews who wish for a State shall have it, and they will deserve to have it. (88, 92, 72)[8]

When Herzl published his political vision for his fellow assimilated Jewish citizens in the Austrian-Hungarian (and German) Empire it was, however, considered de rigueur by the majority of gentrified Jewish citizens in Vienna and elsewhere. Stefan Zweig summarizes this publishing event in his autobiography, *Die Welt von Gestern* (*The World of Yesterday*):[9]

> I was still in the *Gymnasium* when this short pamphlet [*The Jewish State*], penetrating as a steel shaft, appeared; but I can still remember the general astonishment and annoyance of the bourgeois Jewish circles in Vienna. What has happened, they said angrily, to this otherwise intelligent, witty and cultivated writer?

What foolishness is this that he has thought up and writes about? Why should we go to Palestine? Our language is German and not Hebrew, and beautiful Austria is our homeland. Are we not well off under the good Emperor Franz Josef? (103)

In retrospect, however, Herzl's firm position and self-confidence in regard to his idea of fighting anti-Semitism by starting a Zionist movement with the goal of establishing a state for Jews[10] seems prophetic since the Shoah became the worst-case scenario of acting out deeply rooted anti-Semitism, though in scale and monstrosity unimaginable for anyone, including Herzl.

Only twenty-six years after *Der Judenstaat* and four years after World War I, Hugo Bettauer imagined the unimaginable when he wrote *Die Stadt ohne Juden.* Though he, too, could by no means predict or envision the Shoah, he nevertheless anticipated in his satirical novel many racist acts of the Nazis once they annexed and ruled Austria in 1938. While Herzl's vision of a nation-state for the Jews became a reality *because* of the Shoah, Bettauer's literary imagination of Vienna without Jews became a reality *despite* his intentions to prove its Jewish citizenry was indispensable to Vienna and thus counteract persistent anti-Semitism. With the benefit of hindsight, Herzl's pamphlet became visionary, and Bettauer's fictitious political tour de force remains an uncanny daydream because he could not have envisioned that his own sardonic fantasy underestimated yet forecasted the dangers of perennial—and after World War I—increasingly latent anti-Semitism. It is, however, not Theodor Herzl but Hugo Bettauer and two of his novels—the abovementioned *Die Stadt ohne Juden* and *Das blaue Mal*—that provide astute glimpses into post–World War I Austria and its efforts to reconfigure Viennese society and create a new national identity buttressed on a racist ideology of anti-Semitism entangled in a discourse of whiteness.

Invisible Whiteness and Its Power

According to Richard Dyer, to become aware of and "to see whiteness" means to realize that white people create "standards of humanity," even if not necessarily "deliberately and maliciously" (9).[11] Looking at whiteness, therefore, initiates a learning process for white people whose goals are to "dislodge it from its centrality and authority" (10), to return autonomy to those who are considered not to be white, and to allow those ethnic groups to create an identity independent of white notions for and by themselves.

Dyer shows not only how pervasive the concept of whiteness is but also how intricately it is played out in various discourses. He argues that while nonwhites in white cultures are reduced to their bodies and thus to race (14), Christian thought, with its dichotomy of mind and body, structures the notion that different bodies have "different spiritual qualities" (17). As a result, white Christians establish a hierarchy where the "white" spiritual quality is valorized over the "dark" one. Along with this binary notion, white is conceptualized as "pure" and black is seen as "impure" and "dirty" (25). To underscore this bias against nonwhite people, Dyer argues, "Whites must be seen to be white, yet whiteness as race resides in invisible properties and whiteness as power is maintained by being unseen" (45).

The paradox of conceptualizing whiteness as corporeal and visible on the one hand, and powerful but invisible on the other becomes even more evident, according to Dyer, when looking at the "unclear and unstable" process of signifying who is considered white (20). It is, after all, the diverse ethnic groups of Jews who "have constituted the limit [sic] case of whiteness" (53). While Dyer refers to Jews as being considered nonwhite, he does so only fleetingly and by relying mainly on the substantial work of Sander L. Gilman, who argues that the "Jews became the white Negroes. . . . This image of the Jews as black is, however, not merely the product of the racist biology of the late nineteenth century. . . . For the association of the Jews with Blackness is as old as Christian tradition. Medieval iconography always juxtaposed the black image of the synagogue . . . with the white of the church" (Jewish Self-Hatred 7).[12] Gilman further observes, "It is . . . not only the color of the skin which enables the scientist to see the Jew as black, but also the associated anatomical signs, such as the shape of the nose" (Jew's Body 174).

Not only could Jews be perceived as nonwhite, but as the historian Klaus Hödl describes, in scientific discourse the Ostjuden were correlated to African Americans. He analyzes the medical discourse of the late nineteenth and early twentieth centuries where Eastern Jews and African Americans were both seen as predisposed to mental

illness and scientists thought that both groups had a disproportionately higher risk for disease because of their biological inability to
adapt to the dominant culture.[13]

Hödl substantiates Gilman's assertion that the Jewish body was
perceived as "dark" since the pseudoscientific discourse of a hundred
or more years ago, idolizing masculinity, interpreted the Jewish body
as generally pathological and, in particular, as "feminine." He emphasizes that the dominant German educated groups in Austria also
viewed the Yiddish language, mostly spoken by Eastern Jews, as "feminine."[14] Another strategy of effeminizing the Jewish male was to in-
sinuate a correlation between his proboscis and genitals. As Hödl
shows, some scientists interpreted the supposedly widespread nose
bleeding among Jewish males as menstruation[15] and, therefore, incontrovertible proof of their femininity. In short, the dominant white
culture saw in the Jewish man the opposite of a white man who was
typed as masculine, powerful, energetic, and spiritual.

The prominence and power of the image of a supposedly typical Jewish nose within pseudoscientific and anti-Semitic discourse
in medical journals or caricatures[16] becomes evident when reading
Herzl's 1903 *Neue Freie Presse* essay titled "Neue Nasen" 'New Noses.'
In it the fictional character "Kommerzialrat" 'Distinguished Business-
man,' Goldstein carries all the signs of a rich Jew since he "drives an
automobile and owns a yacht."[17] Goldstein's economic success is all
the more impressive because it also translates into his social success
of *looking* like a noble white man:

> He feels happy if one thinks that his descendants do not have any
> signs of looking Jewish ['nichts Jüdisches an sich haben']. So far
> this was difficult to achieve. Usually the nose was the hindrance,
> the nuisance to happiness ['Freudenstörer']. The new method [of
> Prof. Gersuny's nose surgery] provides the solution. From now
> on it will be possible to provide for the family of Mister Privy
> "Kommerzialrat" Goldstein not only a title of nobility but also a
> nose which will perfectly match the acquired ancestors.... For the
> race ['Geschlecht'], however, the successful nose surgery won't be
> of lasting help. Because a more than thousand year old experience
> teaches that an artificially corrected deficiency cannot be inherited,
> so that a circumcision of the nose has to take place for each new

Goldstein until the day where one will realize in the house of Privy "Kommerzialrat" Goldstein that of all the possible ancestors those are the best who are of one's own. (60–61)

While the dominant white culture employed the nose as a negative marker for Jews in general, its nexus to sexuality and the penis in particular made the negative connotations even more bewildering and thus all the more potent for abuse. Not only did the anti-Semites perceive the Jewish body as "darker," but because the nose of a Jew was judged ugly and therefore "sick," they also projected their own anxieties of sexuality onto Jews. Their anxieties confirm Dyer's assertion of sexuality being projected onto dark races on the whole, with the problematic consequence that "[n]ot to be sexually driven is liable to cast a question mark over a man's masculinity—the darkness is a sign of his true masculinity, just as his ability to control it is a sign of whiteness—but there can be occasions when either side discredits the other. . . ." (28).

Yet there is another layer of complexity that Dyer and Gilman only imply but that Hödl makes explicit: whereas the Jewish body in general was conceived as darker or black by being, for example, more pathologically prone than the white body, it was in particular the Jews from the Eastern parts of Europe who embodied most, if not all, the negative stereotyping of the Jewish body.

In this context one, therefore, has to differentiate the dynamics of Jewish acculturation and assimilation. Regardless of Herzl's hatred of the new nose for "Kommerzialrat" Goldstein, the successful Western Jew in Vienna potentially had the means not only to assimilate in language and so on but also to look like other "white" Viennese by having rhinoplastic surgery. Thus anti-Semitism in Vienna generated a triangle of interdependent social positioning: a politically significant group in Vienna tried to define their whiteness by marking the Jews in general as a contrasting race that was less white, less pure, and less masculine.

Simultaneously, a small yet highly influential number of Jews in Vienna attempted to integrate into and assimilate with the dominant culture while being aware of their insecure position. It was the larger number of unassimilated Orthodox and mainly Eastern Jews who reminded the assimilated Western Jews in Vienna of their fragile, racialized position. As a result, the more the assimilated Jews tried to be "white" and shed the cultural heritage of the "darker" Jew, the more they hoped to escape the humiliation of anti-Semitism. They in fact, however, continued to encounter anti-Semitism in subtle or overt forms of ostracism. After all, as Gilman argues, "the more the Jew desires to become invisible [as a Jew], the more the Jew's invisibility becomes a sign of difference" (*Jew's Body* 192). From this point of view, Herzl's move to political Zionism as a reaction to persistent anti-Semitism seemed not to be an option but the only viable solution since not even assimilation stopped Jews' ostracism. One can see and document this divide in the social topography of Vienna. Whereas the assimilated—secular and/or religious—Jews lived to a great extent along the neighborhoods of the famous and elegant Ringstrasse Boulevard, in particular the Ninth District, traditional, Orthodox Jews lived in the Second District on the other side of the Danube-Canal in the so-called Leopoldstadt.[18]

One also can observe this inner-Jewish conflict vis-à-vis persistent anti-Semitism in Sigmund Freud's biography. He, like Herzl, was an assimilated Jew, but unlike Herzl, he remained ambivalent about his Jewish identity throughout his life. Both Freud and Herzl had moved from the Second to the Ninth District, thus marking their upward mobility and desire to integrate into "white" Vienna. In the case of Freud, however, one can see how much he tried not to play into the anti-Semitic stereotypes by attempting to prevent them from seeing his psychoanalysis as a Jewish science.[19] Needless to say, Freud's emphasis on the importance of sexuality made it all the easier for anti-Semites in Vienna and elsewhere to project their "fears and insecurities onto the Jew." These fears were further amplified when, after World War I, the white Austrian male was no longer "the all-powerful hegemon of [the Habsburg] empire . . ." (Noveck, "Hugo Bettauer 1925" 444).

Hugo Bettauer's Desire and Failure to Be an Invisible Jew

It is in Hugo Bettauer himself, in his life and work, that all of the above-mentioned strains of conflict merge: the trauma of life after World War I, the economic and social conflicts of the first Austrian Republic, a conflicting Jewish identity, and the battle against anti-

Semitism and for a liberal and democratic society. Bettauer's biography reads to some extent, especially when one considers his startling murder in 1925, like one of his twenty-three sensational novels of which nine were adapted for the silver screen. Even before his tragic demise, Bettauer's life was turbulent. A case in point was his expulsion from Berlin because of his relentless editorials against police corruption in the emerging metropolis. Shortly thereafter, he lived for a number of years in New York City (1904–10), where at the age of thirty-two he became a well-known journalist and the author of several serial novels for newspapers printed in German.[20] Dynamic as the course of his American life was, it is, however, his life in Vienna that deserves attention within the context of whiteness or nonwhiteness, as it were.

Maximilian Hugo Bettauer was born in 1872, the first son of a Jewish family, in the small but posh spa town of Baden, a half-hour train ride from Vienna. The year and place of his birth is particularly significant in so far as Bettauer grew up during the period of Jewish emancipation. The fact that at age eighteen Bettauer converted to Christianity by joining the Lutheran Church points to his desire to erase his visibility as a Jew and demonstrates his attempt to blend into the dominant Christian culture. However, joining the Lutherans instead of the dominant Catholic Church can be understood as an act of political defiance. In other words, Bettauer's conversion is paradigmatic in that it demonstrates, in part, a resistance to the pressure that the dominant social and Catholic groups exerted on Jews to either assimilate to their standards or run the risk of being treated as the inferior "other."[21] Regardless of the willingness of many Jews to submit to the pressures of the dominant "white" culture and to change their faith, habits, language, or looks, they still encountered continued stigmatization as evidenced by Herzl's essay on the new fashion for wealthy Jews to look as "white" as possible by having rhinoplastic surgery.

One might return to Sigmund Freud as a paradigm of an assimilated, secular Jew because Hugo Bettauer helped to popularize some of Freud's tenets on sexuality by publishing two short-lived but highly significant and successful journals: *Er und Sie: Wochenschrift für Lebenskultur und Erotik* (*He and She: A Weekly for Life-Style and Eroticism*, 1924) and after legal battles over censorship, *Bettauers Wochenschrift: Probleme des Lebens* (*Bettauer's Weekly: Problems of Life*, 1924–27). In both journals, Bettauer endorsed the rights of homosexuals and agitated for legalized abortion. Furthermore, he openly promoted sex education for adults, which was as uncommon for the times as running indecent personal ads that contained erotic/sexual subtexts.[22] Bettauer's audience was unaccustomed to his journals' open discussions of sexuality, but nevertheless welcomed them all the more.[23] Conservative and legal authorities, however, were as opposed to his provocative and popular journals as they had been to the staging of *Reigen* (*Rondel*, 1921), a scandalous play by prominent, assimilated Jew Arthur Schnitzler a few years earlier. Bettauer's liberal, economically successful, and innovative form of addressing sexual issues unfortunately had dire consequences for him: Otto Rothstock, a twenty-year-old Nazi enraged by Bettauer's liberal point of view which he branded as "Jewish," fatally shot Bettauer in his office in March 1925.[24]

Bettauer's assassination highlights two crucial and interrelated aspects of anti-Semitism that had permeated Vienna's dominant culture since the 1880s. First, despite the law of Jewish emancipation in 1867, which was extended and improved in 1918, Jews continued to be ostracized. Second, despite Bettauer's conversion and attempts to be invisible as a Jew, he continued to be perceived as one. Furthermore, Bettauer's journalistic endeavors largely illustrated the ideological link that anti-Semitism had cultivated: the fear of sexuality was projected onto the hatred of Jews, ergo, being Jewish became a mark of the sexually threatening. The traumatic downfall of the Austrian-Hungarian Empire in 1918 created, especially for many Austrian males, a strong sense of insecurity and instability, followed by increasingly anti-Semitic notions whereby Jews functioned as the "perfect" scapegoat for the dominant culture's insecurities. These projections become all the more powerful if one considers that anti-Semitism seemed, as in the case of Bettauer, not to differentiate between assimilated and Orthodox Jews. Effectively, the dominant culture of ethnic Germans in Austria managed to "blacken" the Jews in order to buttress their own identity as pure, white, and male.

It should be evident by now that Hugo Bettauer, unknown in literary circles today, was one of the key figures in Austria's capital after the downfall of the empire. He did not pursue modernism but reflected modernity in two ways: he popularized Freud by disseminating his psychoanalytic views in groundbreaking journals, and he was an author who was unashamed of writing for a mass audience that craved plot-driven, accessible literature that reflected their daily and unconscious concerns.[25] In both of these professional venues, Bettauer understood how to combine capitalistic forms of publishing and entertainment with socially relevant and progressive ideas. His keenness in selecting controversial issues that were thinly disguised in public discourse is apparent not only in his frankness on sexuality but also in his open address of anti-Semitism in his 1922 satirical novel, *Die Stadt ohne Juden: Ein Roman von Übermorgen*,[26] or in its 1926 English translation, *The City Without Jews: A Novel of Our Time*.

Bettauer's Dream of a White Vienna in *A City Without Jews*

The City Without Jews is temporally structured in two parts.[27] It begins during the shockwaves following World War I as economic deprivation forces the conservative Austrian chancellor and parliament to pass a racial bill that expels all Jews from Austria: "the law requires that before the New Year all Jews—including baptized converts and the children of mixed marriages—must leave Austria" (Noveck, "Hugo Bettauer 1925" 441). The fictitious chancellor, Karl Schwertfeger,[28] justifies this racist law with the following personal disclosure that ends in an ironical rationale: he himself has a number of Jewish friends, and he assures his fellow politicians that he likes Jews, even admires them for their "native virtues . . . , their extraordinary intelligence, their strivings for higher things, their model family life, their internationalism, and their ability to adapt themselves to any environment" (Bettauer, *City Without Jews* 10). In contrast, the chancellor claims that "we Austrian Aryans are no match for the Jews" (11), because in comparison the Austrian Aryans are "simple and sincere people, dreamy, playful . . . upright and pious" instead of intelligent, clever, and ambitious like the Jews (11). Schwertfeger continues his essentialized claims by employing the metaphor of the body being under attack by a virulent force in order to make his objections against Jews in Austria understood: "We, however, cannot digest them; with us they always remain a foreign element that spreads over our entire body and finally enslaves us" (11). In opposition to historical reality, Schwertfeger's chop logic reverses oppressor and victim by stating, "[W]e are ruled, oppressed, and violated by a small minority" (11). His assertion seems reasonable because the Jews appear to dominate the print media, the economy, theater, literature, and the luxurious life-style and nightlife of Vienna (12).[29] After the chancellor's speech legitimizing his anti-Semitic politics and portraying himself as the "liberator of Austria" (22), representatives of other political groups second the racial politics that knows "no exception, no pity" (17). Of these factions, it is worthwhile to single out the Zionists who endorse the law, since it reflects their goals; they hope that half of the Jewish population compelled to leave Vienna will become Zionists (21). The first part of the novel ends on New Year's Eve as the majority of Viennese jubilantly celebrate the absence of approximately five hundred thousand Jews who have departed Austria by special trains, leaving behind their wealth. Austria is "liberated" of the "foreign element;" it is "finally" exclusively "white" and Christian: "Now . . . [the Austrian Aryans left behind] are alone, a single family" (59).

In the second part of the novel, events turn out quite differently than the Austrian Aryans anticipated, as "[g]radually Vienna, once the great cultural metropolis, becomes little more than a village without its Jewish playwrights, poets, and patrons of the arts" (Noveck, "Hugo Bettauer" 442). Both the luxurious and mundane life-styles are diminished, and the economy dives into a recession:

> [The Nazi party] has to fold for lack of a scapegoat. . . . Concurrent to the political satire, Bettauer weaves a love story between Lotte Spineder, the Christian daughter of a civil servant, and Leo Starkosch, a Jewish artist forced into exile [in Paris]. The human dimension emphasizes both the ludicrousness and tragedy of the expulsion of the Jews. Out of love for Lotte, Leo smuggles himself in disguise back into Austria, where he incites the people against the government, helps in the founding of a new liberal party that demands the repeal of the anti–Jewish Law, and sabotages the vote in the parliament to assure the success of the repeal of the law and the return of the Jew to Austria. (442)

This being a satirical comedy, the ending both unsettles and reaffirms the status quo, before the racial conflict begins to take its course.

Bettauer's novel instantly became a best-seller, published in more than thirteen editions and over a quarter-million copies sold (Hall, "Nachwort" 106; Noveck, "Hugo Bettauer 1925" 441).[30] The fact that it was adapted into a film in 1924 by Hans Karl Breslauer supplies further evidence for the popularity of the novel, although the film did not enjoy near the same success of the book.[31] The popularity of Bettauer's novel rested upon the novel's provocative fantasy of acting out latent anti-Semitism, a concept very much alive in Austrian society, and of interest to some Jews and non-Jews alike.[32]

Bettauer attempted to prove in his words and with a "cinematographic picture of Vienna" that Austria's capital could not, either economically or culturally, thrive without Jews (Hall, *Fall Bettauer* 171). Therefore, Bettauer picked up the anti-Semitic arguments and fears of his day, hoping to counter them by proving them ridiculously wrong and dangerously illogical.[33] The literal translation of the novel's subtitle, *Ein Roman von Übermorgen* (*A Novel of the Day after Tomorrow*) implies two future prospects, both of them "un-heimlich" 'eerie.' The plot at the beginning of the novel with its successful implementation and execution of racial laws, including the banning of marriage between interethnic couples, the expelling of the Jews by trains, and the confiscating of Jewish belongings, anticipates almost exactly the future racial politics of Hitler after his Nazi regime assumed control of Austria in March 1938. Whereas the first part of the novel is "un-heimlich" because it seems prophetic in regard to Nazi politics, the second part is uncanny because even the Shoah and current politics in Austria prove Bettauer wrong: many Aryan Austrians not only wanted Jews to disappear from the national landscape but also thought that they and the country would be better off without any Jewish presence.[34]

In 1933, the year Hitler was made chancellor of Germany, Hans Tietze published a classic text on the Jewish history of Vienna. He critiques Bettauer's novel as follows: "One can read this shallow satire, which was meant and perceived as a sassy mocking of the 'Aryan' Vienna, also as a distorting caricature of Jewish Vienna" (Tietze 279; translation mine).[35] For Tietze, the novel is a caricature because it does not portray the complexities within the Viennese Jewish population. The plotting of the novel is oblivious to the broad spectrum of the city's Jewish population that stretches from the assimilated, secular, and

reformed and/or Zionist Western Jews to the unassimilated, Orthodox, traditional Eastern Jews. Here, Tietze correctly hints at a blind
spot in Bettauer's Jewish Vienna: the traditional Ostjude is almost
completely absent.

Although Bettauer claimed to have written his novel without any
prejudice (Hall, *Fall Bettauer* 172), his narrative fantasy is also "un-
heimlich" for a reason beyond the two mentioned earlier. His novel
implies a dream of a white Vienna, a Vienna in which Orthodox and traditional Jews do not play any significant role. To put it bluntly, Bettauer,
as if in psychic denial, physically expunges the Second District of
Vienna, the Leopoldstadt. The Vienna of his novel is that of the center
marked by the elegant Ringstrasse with its adjacent gentile districts.

When the novel begins on the day of the chancellor's speech,
"white" Vienna, "[b]usinessmen and laborers, fashionable ladies and
women of the people," gather around the parliament, located on the
Ringstrasse, eager to shout, "Throw out the Jews!" (3). The white mob
assembles in the street, and "not a Jew was in sight." Under normal
circumstances, there would be "people with hooked noses or conspic-
uously black hair" (5). Thus Bettauer begins his narrative by using
the full-blown negative stereotypes of Jews: the physiognomy of "the
Jew" is darkened and in stark contrast to "white" non-Jews, like the
British journalist Holborn, a "blond, pink-cheeked young man" who
has come to Vienna in order to report on the unfolding political event
(6). Obviously, Bettauer is fully aware of using the negative clichés
against Jews that permeate so many discourses in Austrian society.
However, he negates the appearance of these anti-Semitic stereotypes
by having the Orthodox Jews absent not only on that fateful day but
also ever after.

In the first part there appears only once, and only fleetingly, an
old, poor Orthodox Jew with a caftan "and with cork-screw curls," a
person who survived a pogrom in Lemberg, once the eastern outpost
of the Austrian-Hungarian Empire, located in present day Ukraine
(28). When the narrative's intellectuals, all based on real-life, prominent, assimilated Jewish writers, discuss their fate in light of the
forced anti-Jewish law, the author Herbert Villoner (alias Arthur
Schnitzler) compares his to that of a Galician refugee. Yet Galician
refugees who, for the most part, lived in the Second District and were
the largest contingent of Viennese Jews are simply absent throughout

the novel. The publisher Pinkus, who has "unmistakably Jewish features," ensures his intellectual friends that despite his looks his family has been Christian for three generations (33). As at the beginning of the novel, Bettauer subtly alludes to negative marks of Jewishness that he employs ostensibly to undermine them as social constructs yet affirms them simultaneously. Bettauer otherwise carefully avoids describing traditional Jews in any realist mode that goes beyond utilizing the cliché-ridden and negative images that figure the Jew as non-white. The last Jews who leave the city are assimilated Jews, bank directors, and journalists who bear no negative epithets (57). And young Austrian men who, in an act of solidarity convert to Judaism, primarily have in mind to be like the Jews who are physically and culturally nearly indistinguishable from the gentile population (38).

Bettauer's own blind spot with regard to the majority of Orthodox Jews in Vienna is most obvious in the figure of Leo Strakosch, who becomes the hero during the second part of the novel by orchestrating the amusingly contrived plot of repealing the racial laws and bringing the Jews back to Vienna. Bettauer introduces him first by his physical appearance: he is "slender, dark-haired, and smooth-shaven" (52). In other words, his slim frame and shaven face cancel out his dark hair and he is introduced with neutral physicality rather than his Jewish physiognomy. Leo bears no phenotypic mark of Jewishness; in fact, one would not know he is Jewish if it were not mentioned in passing: "The fact that Leo was a Jew did not in the least perturb Herr Spineder" (53). More important than his religious or ethnic background is his fair success as an artist (53). Without being given any concrete details, the reader has to assume that he, like Bettauer himself, is a secular, assimilated Jew. The marked absence of "Jewish" traits makes Leo the ideal candidate for reversing the racial laws, because he poses no "threat" to non-Jews and their desire for a uniform, "white" society. He does not "perturb" them in any way so that they can easily identify with him. In short, Bettauer accomplishes an early version of literary ethnic cleansing.

It is this mixture of the rejected "ugly duckling" transformed into an acceptable "swan" and the ideal of an assimilated Jew that gives Bettauer's novel a subtext that contradicts his attempt to mock anti-Semitism. It is also this second layer that suggests the notion that if all Jews were like Leo, a wonderful carbon copy of a gentile white

Austrian, then there would be no reason or room for any racist politics against Jews. Once all Jews are "whitened," their intelligence and talent for commerce would make Vienna a utopia: a tolerant, multiethnic metropolis. In other words, Bettauer leaves no place in his utopia for Orthodox Jews. Their heritage and mentality defy assimilation to a "white," monoethnic Catholic society. By erasing the "other," Bettauer not only ignores the cultural clash between a traditional and modern culture within Vienna but also whitewashes the Jews. The absence of the "other" feeds Bettauer's desire to have the racially framed discourse against Jews disappear. In the end, the sad irony is that Bettauer truly underestimates the dangers of racist and intolerant politics in Austria that he imagines in his own text.

Bettauer's whitewashing of the Jews problematizes his ostensible intent to reify them as necessary contributors to the Viennese cityscape. Was his unintentional or unconscious whitewashing an extreme case of self-denial or self-hatred? Could it be that Bettauer himself internalized racist views while simultaneously imagining that he was challenging them? The plot of Bettauer's novel *Das blaue Mal*, published within months of *Die Stadt ohne Juden*, underscores his ambiguities toward Jewishness and hidden validation of whiteness in his quest to challenge anti-Semitism.

Be(come) Black as Long as You Stay White: Bettauer's Hidden Desire for Whiteness in *Das blaue Mal*

To date the novel *Das blaue Mal* has neither received any scholarly interest nor been translated into English.[36] Yet with racial conflicts as its main theme, it illuminates the theme of whiteness initiated in *Die Stadt ohne Juden*. The novel is divided into three parts, "Georgia," "Carletto," and "Der farbige Gentleman" 'The Colored Gentleman,' whose titles may be easily exchanged, respectively, with "A Mulatto Born," "A White Dandy in Vienna," and "The Long Path to Accepting His Black Identity." It is a novel that follows the inherent laws of a Bildungsroman, in which a male protagonist finds, through the course of hardships and unusual circumstances, his "true" identity—in this case his "blackness."

In the first and shortest part of the novel, "Georgia," Bettauer introduces Rudolf Zeller, a "blond haired, blue-eyed, and impeccably elegant" well-known professor of botany from metropolitan Vienna who travels to provincial Irvington, Georgia, in order to meet a like-minded botanist Colonel Wilcox, a plantation owner and a resolute racist (3).[37] While being welcomed in the house of the genteel southerners, Zeller soon feels alienated, primarily because of the overt racism of his host family.

Zeller not only feels pity for the African-American slaves whom the whites torture but also is attracted to the housemaid's daughter, the beautiful, sixteen-year-old Karola Sampson, who despite her slave status wishes to be a "white lady" (31). Zeller manages to constrain his sexual desire for Karola and treats her paternally as an Edenic child of nature whom he wishes to take to Europe. After witnessing a lynching in town, Zeller and Karola manage to flee to New York City. During their first sexual encounter in Atlanta en route to the North, they conceive Carletto, the story's protagonist. In New York City, Zeller becomes aware that Karola cannot be his equal partner not only because of their age difference and cultural gap but also because of the laws restricting interracial cohabitation. Yet the "mulatto girl" fulfills his sexual dreams and desires perfectly (51), while she adores the white man as her "savior" (46). Karola embraces "whiteness" by dressing conservatively and learning German. On Christmas Eve, Zeller discovers that Karola is pregnant with Carletto and that she wishes that the child "not be a negro, not a mulatto, not a terzerone but a completely white human being" like him (52). When months later Rolf Caro "Carletto" Zeller is born and his mother dies from delivery complications, Zeller immediately decides to return to Vienna.

Bettauer sets the second part of the novel, "Carletto," many years removed from the first part, in the altered cultural space of Vienna. The reader encounters Carletto, long after his father has died. He is now a handsome law student with an "olive-colored complexion," "black eyes, sensual mouth, and beautiful teeth" (54)—foreign features that make him look like a "Spaniard or South-American" (55). Carletto frequents cafés and has affairs with married women of the upper bourgeoisie. One of these affairs leads to a duel that, following his victory, raises significantly not only his social prestige among his friends but also his debts. His circle of friends believes that like them he can afford the carefree life of a dandy, while Professor Wendrich, Carletto's guardian after his father dies, reluctantly and only partially provides the necessary financial means to do so. The rest Carletto borrows from a profiteer. After his various mundane and expensive love-affairs, after his guardian dies, and after he abandons his studies and taking the law exam, Carletto becomes engaged to Lisl who embodies the proper and truly affectionate virgin, but who is of a lower class. His precarious financial situation makes it imperative for Carletto and Lisl to leave Vienna for New York with the hope of succeeding in the New World.

The novel's third and longest part, "The Colored Gentleman," starts in New York City, which functions both as the mythical space where anyone may succeed by hard work and the homeland of Carletto, a return to his place of birth. Carletto is, however, unprepared in more than one way to go back to the site of his nativity. For it is in New York that he is, for the first time in his life, defined as a "colored" person and that the southern "elaborate tabulations of degrees of blackness (mulatto, quadroon, octoroon)" are at once applied to him. He falls within the racial category of black because, as Dyer reminds us, "even as much as one drop of black blood was enough to make a person black. These measures focused on blackness as a means of limiting access to the white category" (25). Carletto experiences this "limit of access" literally, in various degrees in New York. Here, the handsome, well-educated, well-mannered man who in Vienna was accustomed to women turning their heads to look at him is shocked when, due to his skin color, he is not allowed to stay in a fancy hotel. In New York, he is a mulatto gentleman, "a half caste" (143), someone whom whites hate because they "intuitively sense that he wants to break the (color) barriers" (143). He poses more of a threat than a black person who can easily be delineated as the quintessential "other." Being of refined character also marks him as naïve, or at the very least, inexperienced, in a rough New York environment. In a short period of time, a thief steals his money, and he loses Lisl and everything familiar to him. Gone are his easy and high-class life-style, his luck with women, the familiar social and cultural codes, and his financial means: all the privileges that he had access to as a white man. These losses and a series of humiliations force Carletto to question who he is and what he wants.

When finally he is penniless, Carletto ends up in a black neighborhood close to the harbor and experiences acceptance for the first time after months in New York. Yet he resists being considered black, insists on his whiteness and wishes nothing so much as to be back in the white world of Vienna where there is supposedly no form of racism. In order to obtain money to return to Vienna, Carletto joins a group of woodchoppers, and on a train ride to Alabama, he joins a group of German men who tease him because of his apparent origin. It is only then that Carletto turns to his black co-workers who live in a segregated barrack. Although he enjoys "negro" music after a day of hard work (187) and is curious to learn more about his fellow black workers and "how they thought and felt and what they wanted and hoped for in life" (189), he clings proudly to his European whiteness, a whiteness that his black co-workers affirm in him as well. Carletto begins to teach them basic skills of hygiene, geography, and history and in return they call him "professor" (194). With his whiteness and desire to return to Vienna still intact, Carletto finally saves enough money for travel but meets a woman on his way from Birmingham to Atlanta. Jane Morris is a beautiful, educated African-American woman who teaches orphaned girls, works for the premier African-American publication, the *Crisis*, and reads the works of the Viennese author Arthur Schnitzler. An activist in the National Association for the Advancement of Colored People (NAACP), founded by W. E. B. Du Bois, she compares her race work to that of the emancipation of Jews and argues that Negroes should develop pride in their own race.[38]

Jane becomes the catalyst for Carletto to accept his "black" identity. Bettauer draws out Carletto's inner resistance to his blackness against the backdrop of the place where he was conceived, in Atlanta. Only after Carletto witnesses a brutal fight between blacks and whites in which he is ultimately wounded, and only after Jane has saved Carletto does his racial conviction assert itself and he decides not to return to Vienna after all. Instead, he assists a black activist group in fighting racism in the South. Thus the imposed personal crisis of racial identity resolves itself in the end with that of a political and public fight against racism.

Bettauer's narrative of the continuous conflict of accepting blackness within a racist society may be read in three ways. First, Bettauer unconsciously provides a prime example of whiteness and blackness as being first and foremost cultural constructions; that is, they function independent of skin pigment. As long as Carletto has control over his life in Vienna, he is white—a social status that is primarily determined by education, behavior, mentality, and economic status. Once deprived of his white and economic agency, others consider him black. While Carletto's physical appearance remains the same, the social value ascribed to his body changes due to whether the given society sees him as white or black. The reader is well into the novel— Carletto has returned to New York—before the plot bears out the blue stain on his fingernails, the sign of a "terzerone" that gives the novel its title. Although Carletto is a mixture of Anglo-Saxon and African ancestries, Anglo-Americans in the United States treat him as black because of racist views such as Wilcox's "one drop of a black's blood makes one a negro! . . . To mix [races] means to kill the white man in you and to create a cursed race!" (24). Like an assimilated Jew in early twentieth-century Vienna, the "terzerone" finds himself in a triangular position; while Carletto culturally assimilates to the dominant culture, the dominant majority does not allow full integration because of the sign of his body. At the same time, the minority culture sees him as "other" because of his cultural assimilation. This is the reason Carletto refuses to accept a black identity: both Anglo and African ethnic groups in the United States treat him as the "other," while in Vienna he is only seen as "white" and thus as part of the dominant, Viennese culture.

Second, it is noteworthy, if not surprising, that Bettauer projects racism outside of and not in Vienna and Europe. In fact, the novel's first sentence highlights one of the central themes of the following narrative. A fellow traveler of Zeller proudly asserts, "Good country you're going to, Mister, only too many damned negroes! If only we had one Dutchman of your blond sort for every ten of the black devils, it would be paradise!" (3). Thus from the novel's beginning, the Anglo-European reader assumes a superior position vis-à-vis the racially regressive U.S. society. While American society is sharply criticized for its race-based hate crimes in the South and the palpable racist discrimination in the North,[39] Bettauer implicitly insinuates that Vienna is a place that is free of racial intolerance and inequity. Zeller is incensed to observe how disrespectfully Wilcox treats African Americans by calling them "nigger" and to learn that Wilcox's friends do not see them as human beings since they "have no past, no history, no tradition, they are . . . like the baby that has just started crawling" (16, 21). In contrast, Zeller is the enlightened, educated, and ostensibly racist-free European who conveys to his white European readers that U.S. society is everything but enlightened, tolerant, and modern.

While witnessing a lynching in the American South, Zeller poses to himself the rhetorical question whether the United States in the late nineteenth century is, in fact, not unlike the Middle Ages, during which pogroms of Jews and witch hunts took place. Thus Bettauer insinuates that the discrimination against Jews is something of the Old World past, and therefore no longer an integral part of modern Vienna or Europe. Bettauer must have been aware how contrived this implicit notion was since he has Carletto make not only a comparison between forms of racism against Jews and blacks but, moreover, has Carletto's mother, Karola, die in New York, so he does not have to write a mulatto woman into Vienna society. After all, Zeller asks himself, "Should he take Karola with him, have her admired like a wondrous animal ['Wundertierchen,'] and get himself into a precarious and uncomfortable social position?" (47). Therefore Bettauer must erase Karola from the narrative prior to Zeller's European return in order to spare her the role of the quintessential exotic "other." Karola's erasure is proof that Bettauer knew all too well that his prejudice-free Vienna is hardly a reality. This is also evident when Jane reminds Carletto that his fantasy of a racist-free Europe is just that, a fantasy. She hypothetically imagines, "Oh, I know that one does not hurt the negro [in Europe] or the negro-like people ['Negerstämmling']. Not a bit! Because there are so few of them they are a curiosity! But bring ten thousand Negroes to Vienna or Berlin, then suddenly they will have to face hate . . ." (218).

Third, when Bettauer introduces Carletto, he reduces his "blackness" by describing his skin as an olive complexion that makes him look like a Spaniard, a level of exoticism that is amenable to the European context. From then on, there is no further description of any of Carletto's physiognomic features. Bettauer fabricates a narrative that negates the bodily signs of "otherness" for the sake of his antiracial intentions. Like Starkosch in *Die Stadt ohne Juden*, who does not "look" or "behave" like a Jew, Carletto in *Das blaue Mal* does not "look" or "behave" like a "black"; therefore he rejects self recategorization for an extensive length of time.

Bettauer's reprisal of whitewashing after first unconsciously featuring it in *Die Stadt ohne Juden* is all the more puzzling since he is fully aware of anti-Semitism and racism in Vienna and throughout Austria. After all, the anti-Semitism in his homeland urged him to write a satirical novel that exposed the damaging effects racist politics had on Vienna and Austria. Thus *Das blaue Mal* evokes the following question: Why does Bettauer project racism as absent in Vienna/Austria/Europe yet portray it as a distinction that exists between Old World and New World cultures, those of Europe and America?

Arguably, by creating a cultural fault line between the two societies, Bettauer manages not only to suppress the existing problems of racism within Viennese society but also to uphold whiteness as the invisible dominant culture. Carletto's final acceptance of black identity is a disguised form of white validation since it is only acceptable when blacks become, like Carletto or Jane, as "white" as possible. Both are culturally colonized. Zeller's view on racial politics implies a paternal, colonial attitude. Via an analogy between the natural world of flowers and the human races, Zeller, the botanist, sees every plant as legitimate and against which one cannot discriminate; thus "for him negroes were human beings with a different skin color but of no less value" (14). Yet Zeller maintains the notion that the other race is "on a lower level of civilization from which the white gardener could elevate them through care and love" (9). Like his father, Carletto argues that the emancipation of blacks can and will take place by the "systematic education of the American negro . . . until he has reached the level of the mature nations of Germans, Anglo-Saxons, Romans, and Slavs" (222). Carletto, the "professor," does his teaching with the assumption that blacks all have the "desire to grow up to be white people ['emporzuwachsen'] and become like them" (197). He paternalistically sees them as children and treats them as such.

It is here that Dyer's notion of whiteness can help explain the psycho-racial paradoxes encoded in Bettauer's two narratives. For Bettauer, whiteness serves as both an invisible and visible force. To be more precise, it is a dialectical relationship between the manifestations of two forces. Only after he has established whiteness as a superior concept in the name of enlightenment and tolerance is Bettauer committed to making Carletto's whiteness invisible. White visibility fades as soon as socially constructed whiteness reigns invisibly. Atlanta marks for Carletto both his place of conception and his belated but "true" identity as a black person. However, from the moment Carletto fully accepts his black identity, he implements whiteness among his black counterparts. The message is that whiteness is superior; therefore, it is in the best interest of blacks to assimilate successfully into its realm. Restated: blackness is acceptable only if one looks black but acts white.

To answer the questions posed earlier, Bettauer's whitening of the Jews in *Die Stadt ohne Juden* can be understood as a case of his self-denial and the unconscious internalization of a racist view despite his thinking that he was satirically challenging it. Once *Das blaue Mal* enters into the discussion, Bettauer, as exemplified in *Die Stadt ohne Juden*, unconsciously implies a subdued layer of racism by privileging the politics of whiteness. In both novels, Bettauer expresses a desire to reify white values while resisting different forms of racism. Whereas Bettauer ethnically cleanses Jews into gentiles, thus visibly whitewashing Vienna in *Die Stadt ohne Juden*, he tries to "whiten" those with African ancestry via Western education and social constructs in *Das blaue Mal*. Thus Bettauer embraces and promotes assimilation and homogenization to the point that ethnic differences become indistinguishable. Thus Bettauer's utopian dialectic of enlightenment means that while whiteness causes despicable racist attitudes, it simultaneously provides the tools for abolishing them.

Ultimately, Bettauer's narratives must be read in the context of the traumatic events of World War I and thereafter as a humanistic effort to minimize difference(s) between races. He does so by upholding a rational discourse within the project of enlightenment. As much as Bettauer's practice of and desire for a rational, civilized, tolerant discourse can be understood as attempts at redefining whiteness, it can also be understood as (self-)denial of ethnic differences and identities. As a person of Jewish origin who converted to Christianity, he tried to make himself an invisible Jew to blend seamlessly with the white dominant culture. Retrospectively, Bettauer's utopian hope that race and ethnic identities would no longer matter as long as non-whites subscribe to white ideals seems hopelessly naïve today. The politics of radical whiteness that Bettauer did not see or did not want to see enabled Vienna to indeed become the city without Jews.

NOTES

1. Cf. figures of Jewish populations in Rozenblit, *Jews of Vienna* 17.

2. Galicia was the eastern province of the Austrian-Hungarian Empire, and its territory today comprises southern Poland, Ukraine, and Romania.

3. Cf. Hödl, *Als Bettler in die Leopoldstadt* 9.

4. Cf. Hödl, *Als Bettler in die Leopoldstadt* 188–92 and 285. Joseph Roth's *Die Juden auf Wanderschaft* (*The Wandering Jews*) is one of the few texts that speaks on behalf of Eastern Jews, albeit from a Western—that is, assimilated—perspective.

5. See Gilman, *Jewish Self-Hatred* 2–4. Cf. Wassermann *My Life as German and Jew* 187–90; Hamann, *Hitler's Vienna*. Gilman not only argues that the history of Jewish self-hatred is identical with the concept and issue itself (1) but also entertains in his chapter "The Invention of the Eastern Jew" the idea that at the turn of the century the Eastern Jew became the "good" Jew, whereas the assimilated Western Jew was then viewed as "decadent" and inauthentic (270–86). As much as this argument holds true for intellectuals and writers such as Martin Buber, and to a certain extent for Franz Kafka, Alfred Döblin, Arnold Zweig, and Joseph Roth (Gilman refers to none of the last three popular authors), by and large the Eastern Jews continued to be viewed negatively by both Western Jews and non-Jews alike as Wistrich's and Hödl's historical studies show. See Wistrich, *Jews of Vienna* 62–97; Hödl, *Als Bettler in die Leopoldstadt* 188–92.

6. According to Stefan Zweig's nostalgic autobiography, *The World of Yesterday*, "[T]here was really only one journal of high grade [in Vienna], *Die Neue Freie Presse* [*The New Free Press*], which, because of its dignified principles, its cultural endeavors and its political prestige, assumed in the Austro-Hungarian monarchy a role not unlike the *Times* in England or the *Temps* in France" (99). If one were able to publish "Unter dem Strich" ("Below the Unbroken Line") from the ephemera of politics on page one, in the so-called feuilleton, that is, essays on poetry, theater, music, and the arts, one "had his name hewn in marble, as far as Vienna was concerned" (101). However, as prestigious as this position was, Theodor Herzl himself was disappointed that he did not succeed in being a respected writer and dramatist.

7. Herzl resigned his membership in the Albia fraternity after it openly demonstrated anti-Semitism in 1883. Cf. Wistrich 430–31. Hamann summarizes the rise of anti-Semitism in Hitler's Vienna: "In the 1880s Schönerer's struggle 'for the German people' turned into a bitter fight against 'the Jews,' initially mainly

the Russian Jews, who had been fleeing the pogroms in the Czarist empire since 1881" (241). Besides Georg Schönerer, Karl Lueger, the enormously popular mayor of Vienna from 1897 to 1907, promoted openly populist sentiments against Jews. Cf. Hamann, *Hitler's Vienna* 280–90; Wistrich 205–37.

8. I will pass over the question to what extent Herzl's political vision participated in the discourse of colonial imperialism. He reflects his idea of a Jewish state as a clear hierarchical order—"The poorest will go first to cultivate the soil" (93–94)—and exhibits an imperialist attitude when discussing where to locate the Jewish state, in either Argentina or Palestine, arguing for Palestine because it "is the ever-memorable historic home" (96). Once the Sultan of Turkey would grant the land, Herzl imagines the Jewish state becoming "a portion of a rampart of Europe against Asia, an outpost of civilization as opposed to barbarism" (96). Before publishing his political pamphlet *Der Judenstaat* (*The Jewish State*), Herzl came up with the grand plan of a mass baptism of all Jews converting to Christianity in the Gothic St. Stephen Cathedral in the center of Vienna. Cf. Wistrich 435; Zweig 102.

9. The editors of *Die Neue Freie Presse*, Eduard Bacher and Moriz Benedikt— themselves assimilated Jews—made clear to Herzl that they did not want to be associated in any way with Herzl's Zionist movement. See Haller and Unterberger.

10. Herzl in *The Jewish State* writes, "I am absolutely convinced that I am right, though I doubt whether I shall live to see myself proved to be so" (70).

11. When I use the term "white," I will follow the concept that Richard Dyer has so persuasively outlined in *White*. Whereas the term "white" or "whiteness" neither translates into German nor shows up as an English term in the comprehensive bibliography for German studies, Germanistik, the category of racism ("Rassismus") is listed. The German word "Rassismus" implies some aspects of the term "white" as defined by Richard Dyer. As to be expected, the term "Rassismus" within the context of German studies and/or Germany is mostly seen and discussed in light of the Nazi period. In contrast, the term "gender studies" is listed as such, that is, in English, for the first time in 1997, thus documenting how scholarship in the United States continues to influence the humanities and social studies in German-speaking countries. Even before the English term "gender studies" was integrated into scholarly discourse in German-speaking countries, the German translation of it, "Geschlechterbeziehungen," had established itself as an independent category reflecting the strength of feminist studies within Germanistik.

12. Also see Gilman, *Jew's Body* 171 and "'Rasse ist nicht schön'" 62; and Belovari 23–44.

13. Hödl, "Was haben Ostjuden mit Afro-Amerikanern gemein?" 136. In his book-length study *Gesunde Juden—Kranke Schwarze* published two years later, Hödl concludes in comparing the medical-scientific discourses regarding Afro-Americans and Jews mainly concerning the mental diseases where the two groups were juxtaposed in the late nineteenth and early twentieth centuries (278).

14. Hödl, *Pathologisierung des jüdischen Körpers* 180–87. Cf. Gilman, *Jew's Body* 21.

15. Hödl, *Pathologisierung des jüdischen Körpers* 210.

16. Cf. Gilman, *Jew's Body* 179–93; Hödl, *Pathologisierung des jüdischen Körpers* 217.

17. Herzl, "Neue Nasen" 60–61. Herzl's text was published on 1 November 1903 in *Die Neue Freie Presse*. In 1898, Jacques Joseph performed the first modern cosmetic rhinoplastic surgery in Berlin. Cf. Gilman, "'Rasse ist nicht schön'" 65 and *Jew's Body* 181–88; Hödl, *Pathologisierung des jüdischen Körpers* 217.

18. There is a certain historic irony at work in that the majority of (Eastern) Jews moved to the Leopoldstadt in the late nineteenth century, since it was the emperor Leopold who expelled all Jews from this area in 1670. After the Jewish settlements were completely destroyed and the area renamed after the emperor, Jews resettled again in this area, thus defying the brutal attempt of annihilating all Jewish culture in Vienna. Thus, the name Leopoldstadt points to both the attempts to destroy the Jewish community and its resistance.

19. Cf. Sigmund Freud, "Die Widerstände gegen die Psychoanalyse," qtd. in Wasserman 185.

20. According to the *New York Times* article ("New Yorker Is Shot by Vienna Dentist" 4) that reported on Bettauer's assassination, he was "for many years the Vienna correspondent of the *New Yorker Staats-Zeitung*" and "the assistant Sunday editor of the *New York Morgen Journal*." The translator of the American edition of *Die Stadt ohne Juden*, Salomea Neumark Brainin, states in her introduction that Bettauer "spent twelve years of his life in New York" (vi). It is fair to say that to date we know very little about Bettauer's years and activities in New York.

21. Some of today's cultural icons of the Viennese fin de siècle, such as Karl Kraus or, more prominently, Gustav Mahler and Arnold Schönberg, felt compelled to convert either to Catholicism (Mahler) or Protestantism (Schönberg and Kraus).

22. The legal accusation against his journals focused on indecency and moral behavior that were presumably breached by personal ads that contained erotic/sexual subtexts.

23. Noveck, *Maximilian Hugo Bettauer* 101.

24. Otto Rothstock did not face any punishment but was set free because of empathy by the judges who sanctioned his argument that the murder was legitimate because of the taboo-breaking and indecent nature of Bettauer's journal. Cf. Hall, *Fall Bettauer* 110–33. This lackadaisical legal judgment gives a glimpse into how much the newly established democracy was still rooted in the conservative mindset of the vanquished and vanished empire. Today a plaque at the site of the murder commemorates the site of the 1925 shooting.

25. I suggest that Bettauer can be understood as a paradigm of an author of modern times and not of literary modernism, which such different Viennese authors as Hermman Broch, Karl Kraus, Robert Musil, and Elias Canetti represent.

26. Bettauer's subtitle might be borrowed from Nietzsche's popular *Jenseits von Gut und Böse: Vorspiel einer Philosophie der Zukunft (Beyond Good and Evil: Prelude to*

a Philosophy of the Future) published in 1886. In section 7, "Unsere Tugenden" ("Our Virtues"), Nietzsche refers to the "Europäer von übermorgen" 'Europeans of the day after tomorrow' (109).

27. All quotes are drawn from the English edition of *The City Without Jews* published in 1926.

28. The chancellor is a composite of the notorious anti-Semitic mayor Karl Lueger and conservative chancellor Ignaz Seipel. His name refers to his racist politics since it means in German someone who cleans with a sword.

29. Wassermann's observation in *My Life as a German and Jew* echoes this list of key professions that Jews dominated (187).

30. Brainin writes, "[I]n less than a year, a quarter of a million copies of the novel have been sold, an unprecedented figure in German modern literature. The translation for the American edition was made from the fifty-fourth edition . . ." (viii). The U.S. edition is worthy of mention since it can be seen within the context of anti-Semitism in American society and racial issues in general. After all, Brainin, who tried to promote the novel, found it "symptomatic of our time" (v) with the "race problem that still torments the world—now more than ever" (vii). Her view might explain why she decided to translate the subtitle *Ein Roman von Übermorgen* or "A Novel of the Day after Tomorrow [or the Future]" more simply as *A Novel of Our Time*.

Die Stadt ohne Juden shares with the characteristics of a roman à clef that some of the novel's protagonists correspond to famous public figures like the fictitious chancellor Karl Schwertfeger with that of the anti-Semitic mayor Karl Lueger, and the writer Herbert Villoner with Arthur Schnitzler. Therefore, one might speculate that the American capitalist and pronounced anti-Semite Jonathan Huxtable refers to the outspoken anti-Semite and American icon Henry Ford.

A reviewer at the *New York Times* paid attention to the novel because of the sensational and political murder of Bettauer, and thus expected something highly provocative. Instead the reviewer found Bettauer's fictional Vienna dated, since the economic crisis was over by the time of the translation, thus implying that the assumed anti-Semitism in the novel is without any real base. The reality of pervasive anti-Semitism, however, seems not to have caught the reviewer's interest. The unsigned review expressed disappointment with the novel: "On the whole [. . .] it seems sad that Mr. Bettauer gave his life for something so cheap" ("Semitic Polemics" BR 9).

31. The movie was assumed to be lost until it was rediscovered in Amsterdam's film museum in 1991 and was later digitally restored. Originally the movie made it to the United States, where it was shown in Chicago but censored in New York City in 1928. See "Bans German Films on Jewish Theme" 10. According to the *New York Times*, there were plans to stage a theater adaptation, prepared by one of Hugo Bettauer's sons in December 1938 ("Dunning Arranges Theatre Novelty" 22). Hanns Saßmann adapted the novel for the stage in 1922.

32. Most recently the novel has been adapted for the stage by Helmut Peschina and was performed at the Volkstheater in Vienna during its 2005–6 season.

33. In a comment on his book, Bettauer repeated an argument that he makes in his novel that only Vienna, and no other metropolis to its degree, is in need of having Jews in order to make it as vital and vibrant as it used to be. Bettauer qtd. in Hall, *Fall Bettauer* 172. Hans Tietze echoes this notation in his canonical book on the history of Jews in Vienna. In it, he claims that in the Western Hemisphere, the Jews of Vienna are the most "fruitful.... Without Jews Vienna would not be what it is, as much as Vienna would lose its proudest aspect if they would lose their presence of past centuries" (282; translation mine). These notions are in contrast to Brainin's assumption that the novel could also take place in New York or London (v), which she might have simply forwarded in order to promote the novel to an English-speaking audience.

34. For the longest time Austria repressed and denied its active involvement in the Shoah and continues to be, if not openly anti-Semitic, ambivalent toward its Jewish citizens. These two attitudes can be explained by the fact that official Austria embraced the comfortable notion that—contrary to fact—it was the first victim of Hitler's Nazi Germany, as the Soviet Union had officially declared in 1945. In the summer of 2003, the Israelische Kultusgemeinde 'Israeli Religious Community' of Vienna faced a growing deficit that the conservative Austrian government was hesitant to cover. The final financial arrangements only came about after an intense public discourse about persistent anti-Semitism.

35. Tietze's German reads, "Allerdings kann man diese seichte Satire, die als freche Verhöhnung des 'arischen' Wien gemeint und empfunden wurde, auch als nicht minder verzerrende Karikatur des jüdischen lesen" (279).

36. All translations of *Das blaue Mal* are mine.

37. Like the name "Schwertfeger" in *Die Stadt ohne Juden*, "Zeller" is an obvious allusion to his profession in which cells determine the genealogy of plants.

38. The fact that Bettauer refers specifically to the *Crisis*, the NAACP's monthly journal founded and edited by Du Bois in 1909, supports Bettauer's familiarity with the contemporary political issues of African Americans in the United States.

39. See Berlin and Harris.

Works Cited

"Bans German Film on Jewish Theme." *New York Times* 1 July 1928: 10.

Belovari, Susanne. "Wie wir zur 'idealen weißen Rassen' kamen: Eine kurze Geschichte Des bilogoischen Rassenbegriffs." *Der schejne Jid: Das Bild des "jüdischen Körpers" in Mythos und Ritual.* Ed. Sander L. Gilman, Robert Jütte, and Gabriele Kohlbauer-Fritz. Wien: Picus, 1998. 23–44.

Berlin, Ira, and Leslis M. Harris, eds. *Slavery in New York.* New York: New, 2005.

Bettauer, Hugo, ed. *Bettauers Wochenschrift: Probleme des Lebens.* 1924–25. Wien.

———. *Das blaue Mal: Der Roman eines Ausgestoßenen.* Wien: Gloriette Verlag, 1922.

————. *The City Without Jews: A Novel of Our Time*. Trans. Salomea Neumark Brainin. New York: Bloch, 1926.

————. ed. *Er und Sie: Wochenschrift für Lebenskultur und Erotik*. 1924. Wien.

————. *Die Stadt ohne Juden*. Drei Akte von Hugo Bettauer und Hanns Saßmann. Wien: Vertriebsgesellschaft Theaterverlag Otto Eirich, 1922.

————. *Die Stadt ohne Juden: Ein Roman von Übermorgen*. Bühnenfassung by Helmut Peschina. Wien: Thomas Sessler Verlag, n.d.

Brainin, Salomea Neumark, trans. Introduction. *The City Without Jews: A Novel of Our Time*. New York: Bloch, 1929. v–viii.

Breslauer, Hans Karl. Adapt. *Die Stadt ohne Juden*. 1924. Ed. Film Archiv Austria. Wien: Filmarchiv, 2000.

"Dunning Arranges Theatre Novelty." *New York Times* 17 Aug. 1938: 22.

Dyer, Richard. *White*. New York: Routledge, 1997.

Gilman, Sander L. *Jewish Self-Hatred. Anti-Semitism and the Hidden Language of the Jews*. Baltimore: Johns Hopkins UP, 1986.

————. *The Jew's Body*. New York: Routledge, 1991.

————. "'Die Rasse ist nicht schön.' 'Nein, wir Juden sind eine hübsche Rasse!' Der schöne und häßliche Jude." *Der schejne Jid: Das Bild des "jüdischen Körpers" in Mythos und Ritual*. Ed. Sander L. Gilman, Robert Jütte, and Gabriele Kohlbauer-Fritz. Wien: Picus, 1998. 57–74.

Hall, Murray G. *Der Fall Bettauer*. Wien: Löcker, 1978.

————. "Nachwort." *Die Stadt ohne Juden: Ein Roman von Übermorgen*. By Hugo Bettauer. Frankfurt a. M.: Ullstein Verlag, 1988. 101–9.

Haller, Günter, and Andreas Unterberger. "Unter dem Strich." *Die Presse* June 26, 2004, Spectrum: I–II.

Hamann, Brigitte. *Hitler's Vienna: A Dictator's Apprenticeship*. Oxford: Oxford UP, 2000.

————. *Hitlers Wien: Lehrjahre eines Diktators*. München: Piper, 1996.

Herzl, Theodor. *The Jewish State*. Mineola: Dover, 1988.

————. *Der Judenstaat*. 1896. Berlin: Philo, 2004.

————. "Neue Nasen." 1903. *Die treibende Kraft: Feuilletons*. Ed. Marcus G. Patka. Wien: Picus, 2004. 54–61.

Hödl, Klaus. *Als Bettler in die Leopoldstadt: Galizische Juden auf dem Weg nach Wien*. 2nd ed. Wien: Böhlau, 1994.

————. *Gesunde Juden—kranke Schwarze: Körperbilder im medizinischen Diskurs*. Innsbruck: Studien-Verlag, 2002.

————. *Die Pathologisierung des jüdischen Körpers: Antisemitismus, Geschlecht und Medizin im Fin de Siècle*. Wien: Picus, 1997.

————. "Was haben Ostjuden mit Afro-Amerikanern gemein?" *Jüdische Identitäten: Einblicke in die Bewußtseinslandschaft des österreichischen Judentums*. Ed. Klaus Hödl. Innsbruck: Studien-Verlag, 2002. 121–40.

"New Yorker Is Shot by Vienna Dentist." *New York Times* 11 Mar. 1925: 4.

Nietzche, Friedrich W. *Beyond Good and Evil: Prelude to a Philosophy of the Future.* Trans. and ed. Marion Faber. New York: Oxford UP, 1998.

Noveck, Beth Simone. "Hugo Bettauer 1925." *Jewish Writing and Thought in German Culture, 1096–1996.* Ed. Sander L. Gilman and Jack Zipes. New Haven: Yale UP, 1997. 440–47.

———. *Maximilian Hugo Bettauer: Sexuality, Politics and the Political Culture of the First Republic in Austria.* Diss. Universität Innsbruck, 1994.

Roth, Joseph. *Die Juden auf Wanderschaft.* Köln: Kiepenheuer & Witsch, 2000.

———. *The Wandering Jews.* Trans. Michael Hofmann. New York: Norton, 2001.

Rozenblit, Marsha. *The Jews of Vienna, 1867–1914: Assimilation and Identity.* Albany: State U New York P, 1983.

———. *Reconstructing a National Identity: The Jews of Habsburg Austria during World War I.* Oxford: Oxford UP, 2001.

"Semitic Polemics." *New York Times* 7 Feb. 1927: BR9.

Tietze, Hans. *Die Juden Wiens: Geschichte, Wirtschaft, Kultur.* 1933. Wien: Wiener Zeitschriftenverlag, 1987.

Wassermann, Jakob. *My Life as German and Jew.* London: Allen & Unwin, 1933.

Wistrich, Robert S. *The Jews of Vienna in the Age of Franz Joseph.* Oxford: Oxford UP, 1990.

Zweig, Stefan. *The World of Yesterday: An Autobiography.* 1943. Lincoln: U of Nebraska P, 1964.

From "Yélida" to Movimiento de Mujeres Dominico-Haitianas: Gendering Resistance to Whiteness in the Dominican Republic

DAWN DUKE

While there are no direct and visible links between Tomás Hernández Franco's celebrated poem "Yélida" (1942) and Movimiento de Mujeres Dominico-Haitianas (MUDHA), the grass-roots movement and organization for Dominican-Haitian women, there are definite connections between literary representation and social reality, especially as they relate to the intersection of female racialized experiences. The poem and movement are connected in the way they address the broader paradigms of race and racism in the Dominican Republic. The deeper historical reality impacting the poetic characters, Madam Suquí and Yélida, on the one hand, and women activists such as Sonia Pierre of MUDHA, on the other, is the reflection of a greater contemporary dilemma: Dominican-Haitian socio-racial tensions. Moving through these figures and beyond on the island of Hispaniola, where Haiti and the Dominican Republic comprise its western and eastern nations respectively, one observes in the latter country a national self-identification that is historically constructed, aesthetically imagined, and often self-imposed as a result of individual and collective multiracial trauma. In relation to the literary and cultural productions of the Dominican Republic, the construction of a historically traumatized subject is particularly ubiquitous. Shaped by a Spanish colonial experience and a precarious political relationship with Haiti, the Dominican Republic's cultural and aesthetic representations have become entrenched largely in issues of separations and distinctions based on race and border identity. The country's intractable problems of assimilation, miscegenation, and whitening are reminiscent of other Latin American colonial and postcolonial experiences recorded in the nineteenth and early twentieth centuries in Brazil, Venezuela, and Colombia. The continuing marginalization of peoples of African descent in Brazil and Venezuela attests ostensibly to irresoluble racial problems. Today, historical and literary research focuses on the Dominican rejection of Negritude as a possible paradigm for its national existence. The accepted paradigm of whiteness, to which the country clings well into the twenty-first century, acts as a point of clear national reference that underpins the long-term social implications of existing forms of self-definition that are nationally revered.

While scholarship in the Caribbean has neither focused on nor endorsed theoretical conceptualizations of whiteness, undoubtedly the theories and practices of whiteness are a part of the region's historical and cultural legacies. Penelope Ingram speaks of the ennobling of whiteness as part of the discovery and colonizing experience depicted literarily as a historical and imagined, albeit natural, part of mankind's progress.[1] It projects itself as pure, courageous, and civilizing: qualities much needed in a hot, diseased, and dangerous island world void of Christianity. Whiteness represents the expansion and salvation of civilization, epitomized in the European conquistador sailor-settler. Blackness, on the other hand, relegated primarily to a literary space that deposits it historically in the body of the enslaved African, has been doomed to occupy the traits of negativisms, symbolic of all that is dark, anti-Christian, unrestrained, and unknown. These are the racialized literary codes that mark Dominican national literature to the present day.

Tomás Hernández Franco's poem "Yélida," written during the Trujillo era (1930–61), reveals connections between poetics and the politics of race that have long existed in the Dominican Republic. Even today, media and museum exhibitions of the Dominican people as the product of three distinct and mutually exclusive ethnic groups that historical upheaval brought together are destabilized by a premeditated erasure of a founding African identity. Owning that founding identity is problematic because of its approximation to Haitian identity. In the Dominican Republic, what one is not, in this case not Haitian and therefore not African, normalizes the national identity. The national fabrication of a "white," social identity by denying its African ancestry has opened a void that today can no longer be filled by the description "white," given the fact that many Dominicans are neither of fair complexion nor of primary Anglo-European ancestry. The filling of that void requires plucking from the ashes of the distant past the figure of the rustic Indian of the original nations now decimated. It is not by chance that the greatest nineteenth-century Dominican novel, Manuel de Jesús Galván's Romantic saga *Enriquillo* (1876), finds inspiration in the heroic Taíno, Enriquillo, who waged armed resistance against the invading Spaniards between 1519 and 1533.[2] It is a literary manipulation of history that psychologically informs the national consciousness. The linguistic reference "indio," which many pro-Indigenous scholars and activists largely reject, continues to serve as the preferred term of racial classification for the majority of Dominicans.

Peter Kolchin's "Whiteness Studies," drawing upon the ideas presented in Matthew Frye Jacobson's *Whiteness of a Different Color* (1998), extends the idea of whiteness or being white as an identity developed within a newly "discovered" land in which the European subject settled permanently, thereby provoking cultural transformations. An increasing self-perception as white combined with dislocations in the cultural functioning of whiteness in that new land produced a "variegated whiteness" (163). The imported, monolithic sense of Caucasian whiteness contrasts sharply with the system of difference in force within the Dominican Republic. The infinite body shades and features that self-define some Dominicans as "white" only serve to drive home the incompatibility of the term with the visual presentation of many Dominicans. Racial identity remains unresolved in an ambiguous limbo that suits the national preference for the way it promotes distancing the body politic from contemplations of its African heritage. What is important is not the fact that Dominican whiteness is nonwhite but the fact that many Dominicans whose skin displays the darkness of melanin perceive themselves as white.

Politics in the Poetics of Tomás Hernández Franco

Tomás Hernández Franco (1904–1952), who was a major poet in the literary movement "los independientes del '40" 'Independents of the 1940s' that preoccupied itself with social issues, is considered today one of the prominent Dominican literary voices of the twentieth century.[3] His intellectual and poetical works revolve around the treatments of the mulatto, the sailor, and eroticism and clearly display his vision of the Caribbean as the historical site of prodigious racial admixture. His propaganda in favor of miscegenation connects first with his ultimate vision of Spanish culture as a refined, civilizing influence on the region and second with his political allegiance to the ruthless dictator Rafael L. Trujillo Molina. Because Hernández Franco was known as "un intelectual trujillista" 'a pro-Trujillo intellectual,' there is debate over the extent to which Trujillo cultivated the opinions and productions of the writer, perceiving in him strategic possibilities as an authentic representative of the language of power for his own regime.[4] From 1930 onward, the connection between literature and reality became more important in light of the ever-increasing absolutism of Trujillo's rule. According to Julián Fernández Muñoz, the writer, intellectual, and later president Joaquín Balaguer commented on the positive impact the Trujillo government had on Dominican letters. By drawing parallels between education and democracy in his political speeches, Trujillo opened up the intellectual panorama of the country by encouraging singular ideas and original, progressive doctrines. It is a discourse in which Hernández Franco invested fully: "Hernández Franco, ve en Trujillo, el símbolo del alma dominicana" 'Hernández Franco sees in Trujillo the symbol of the Dominican soul' (Fernández Muñoz 21).[5]

The intense national sentiment visible in Dominican letters during the Trujillo era served as a justification for the unfolding of extreme state policies and measures that would mark some of the most tumultuous years in Dominican history. Bernard Vega and Lauren Derby have studied this moment that, together with the early nineteenth-century Haitian occupation, was deemed the most crucial in the country's formation. They confirm the vigor with which Dominican identity has been contrastively defined in relation to Haiti as the dichotomy of whiteness and blackness. The Haitian control of the island from 1822 to 1844 set the scene for political rivalry and cultural rejection, the remnants of which are in operation today. The Haitian's status in the Dominican Republic as invader, tyrant, and archenemy continues to propel the rejection of all blackness and Haitianisms visible in the culture and laws of the Dominican Republic. The nineteenth century's "movimiento indigenista" 'Indigenous Movement,' the national denial of self as African and Spanish and replacement of both with a new idyllic sentimentalism of the state of mulattoness and/or Indianness, initiated the rejection. The new, ideal, racial state now rests on the figure of the Indian who paradoxically had vanished centuries before from the Dominican landscape. To date, the abhorrence of "black" as a term of racial identification is widespread. It is an abhorrence that the long period of Trujillo reign and his clearly racist politics fueled through contrast when "the Dominican state became most emphatically committed to promoting Eurocentric and white supremacist views of Dominicanness . . ." (Torres-Saillant, "Tribulations of Blackness" 132).

Within a discussion of race, identity, and historical relations with Haiti, Rafael L. Trujillo Molina's cultivation of the ideology of "hispanidad" 'Hispanic identity' and the 1937 Haitian massacre define the dictator's reign. The river called "El Masacre" 'Massacre,' defining the border between the two countries, derives its name from that terrible period when the water was said to have turned red, transformed by the blood of the thousands of Haitians Trujillo's soldiers executed with machetes. The sequence of historical events that led up to the massacre confirms the process of transformation in race relations that resulted under Trujillo's rule and beyond in the establishment of systems of racial classification and geographical distinctions between the Dominican and the racial Other, the body of the Haitian that embodied everything African. The planned campaign of demonizing Haiti is one that loses its intensity in the post-Trujillo era; however, the echoes of anti-Haitianism since the dictator have been felt by each subsequent generation of Dominicans. Anti-Haitianism diverges from traditional models of racism, and according to Derby, seems to be more a feature of "a species of racialized nationalism" (496). Persisting into the twentieth century, it distributes itself as class-based prejudice, "a rejection of the sub-stratum of Haitian cane cutters who are seen as patently subhuman" (493). Issuing from the Dominican state is a discourse of Haitian rejection that may seem less intense today given cultural border crossings at the familial and communal levels, but the signs of racial division and distinction remain painfully visible.

Literature has also played a role in constructing a discourse of Haitian rejection. Even as Tomás Hernández Franco's poem plays into Dominican abhorrence of things Haitian, his clear delegation of superior whiteness and inferior blackness is also rooted in history. His dual approach to the issue of Dominican racial composition clearly reveals influences of the region's historical experiences rooted in slavery. With the expansion of slavery in the Caribbean came a new way of determining differences, one predicated on phenotypic traits—the hair, skin, and facial features of those who were clearly of African ancestry.[6]

Madam Suquí as Dominican Imagery

Tomás Hernández Franco's poem, "Yélida," provides an important literary text for reflecting on contemporary issues of whiteness, women, and identity in the Dominican Republic. It is today acknowledged as one of the great accomplishments of Dominican literature. The poem has particular value given the way it brings a series of colonial and contemporary issues—gender, religion, and Eurocentrism—to the forefront. Important among these are the Dominican and Haitian historical interconnectedness, the contrast of the Haitian woman to a Dominican ideal of whiteness, the politics of race and religion in the Caribbean, and the Dominican valuing of European ancestry over African/Haitian ancestry.

To what extent does "Yélida" reproduce the contemporary concerns of race and the accompanying geopolitical relationship with Haiti? The reality of Hernández Franco's poem cannot be dismissed given the implications of its final message of Dominican identity as a miscegenated race. It appears to be intensely conformist in the way it holds rigidly static the patterns of racialized relationships developed initially by way of Europe's first contacts with and subsequent colonization of the Caribbean. Within the saga of New World discovery, whiteness appears as an integral part of those inaugural transatlantic voyages made by ambitious European sailors. Gary Taylor argues that the construction of whiteness needs to be gendered given the way it connects to the "white male voyaging, much more than [the] white female" (52–53). Taking his argument further, blackness later emerges with the inclusion of black femaleness, necessarily completing the Caribbean myth of harmonious cultural contact through sexual contact and procreation. True to form, the roots of miscegenated regional ethnic identity are laid firmly with Hernández Franco's Erick, the roving European sailor, and Madam Suquí, the Haitian witch-temptress who fascinates him. Yélida, their offspring, embodies the psychological trauma of the collision of cultures even as she symbolizes the island's hybrid identity.

The fact that Hernández Franco bypasses the Spanish-Hispanic racial composite (glorified in the concept of hispanidad) that plays a large role in the Dominican historical trajectory, in favor of a Nordic one, seems to confirm a greater poetic objective of original, ethnoracial perfection. His poetry strives to confirm origins that are purer as well as superior to Hispanic identity in an apparent quest for even greater Eurocentric connection. Erick's pure Nordic ancestry appears symbolically as one of the two important strains of Hispaniola's ethno-social formation. The Other, depicted in Suquí's dark, unforgiving, Haitian body, produces sharp contrast open to various levels of aesthetic and ideological interpretation. At one level, the traditional literary pattern continues in the figures of the imported, white, colonizing male and the native, black, accommodating female. At another level, contrast is crucial for sustaining the hierarchical distinction and conflict between the Nordic and Haitian heritages. The privilege the poem chooses to bestow on Yélida's European ancestry serves as a reminder of the poet's political alliances. Of Hispanic descent, Hernández Franco occupied a privileged place in the autocratic hierarchy of the Trujillo regime known for its extreme acts of violence and anti-Haitian sentiment. His privileged place sets the stage for questioning notions of the national, racial subject in the Dominican Republic.

Nordic demise is the result of the powerful, conniving forces of the tropical, Africanized island and the supernatural powers of the Voudun priest and priestess that Erick's Haitian lover invokes. The subsequent destruction the island wreaks on Erick's Aryanism is one of the more forceful messages of the poem. Indeed the symbolic power of the writing lies in the extreme development of contrastive binaries— European Norwegian man/African Haitian woman, white man/black woman, white Christian purity/black Voudun impurity, and Europe continent/Caribbean island. The perfection and tranquility that grace the words used to describe the unadulterated, serene, Scandinavian life-style to which Erick belongs will clash with the mystery, suspicion, and somberness that characterize the descriptions of Suquí, her culture, and her spiritual beliefs. The ongoing effects of the binary perceptions of white versus black and good versus evil within and beyond literature will play itself out in the realities of the modern age.

With epic-like grandeur, Hernández Franco's poem tells the story of Erick, born into a Scandinavian family from a humble fishing community who, lured by stories of far away places, departs his homeland and sails to the hot tropical islands teeming with lush vegetation and sensuous dark-skinned women. Upon arrival, he abandons the mariner vocation of his lineage and becomes ardently devoted to Haitian Suquí, a bewitching, sensual Voudun practitioner, who visits her spiritual guides and makes offerings to the Haitian divinities. With the help of the intermediate gods, she captivates Erick, severing his homeland link and binding him emotionally to her forever. Tragedy strikes quickly, for Erick, unacclimitized to the searing temperature and lacking immunity to tropical diseases, falls gravely ill and dies. His displaced soul takes flight, returning to his Norwegian homeland. A pregnant Suquí, in the meantime, gives birth to their daughter, Yélida, the product of two very strong wills and drastically different racial legacies. The stylistic beauty of the poem peaks here for it is in describing Yélida that the embodiment of whiteness and blackness intersect. Hernández Franco deposits in the mulatto female body traumatic coexistence even as he makes explicit the greater vulnerability associated with it. He thereby increases the impact of the internal racial collision while creating a superb allegory that extends itself outward to encounter the Dominican concept of self as white and the idealizing of a whiteness that is taken beyond Hispanism. Inevitably, with the Dominican idealization of whiteness comes rejection of the Haitian legacy of blackness and its spirituality expressed through Voudun.

Erick hails from a fishing community, yet his value in this poem is not based upon the socioeconomic but the ethnoracial worth that white skin gives him. His European stock is pure, for he is from Norway where the national body is known for its superior physique, blond hair, and blue eyes. While on the one hand the poet places great emphasis on the fishing heritage of which Erick is proud, on the other hand, his mythological, Adonis physicality sets him apart as a superior human specimen. Even as Hernández Franco cultivates classical notions of racial superiority, he abides by traditional versions of the historical trajectory of the European explorer by converting Erick into the seafarer dispatched to tropical lands, seeking adventure and fortune. While there is never a clear mention of the island to which he goes, it is clear from references to Legba and Ogun, loa (divinities) of the Voudun pantheon, that it is an imagined Haitian setting:

> Esta no es la historia de Erick al fin y al cabo que a los treinta
> años no era marinero y vendía arenques noruegos en su tienda de
> Fort Liberté mientras la esposa de Erick madam Suquí rezaba a
> Legbá y a Ogún por su hombre blanco rezaba en la catedral por su
> hombre rubio. (Hernández Franco 112)[7]

> *This is not all there is to Erick's story who, at thirty, was not a*
> *sailor and sold Norwegian herrings in his shop in Fort Liberté while*
> *Erick's wife, Madam Suquí, prayed to Legba and Ogun for her white*
> *man prayed in the cathedral for her blond husband.*

His sexual union with Madam Suquí obeys traditionalist conceptions of the imagined conquistador effect whereby the white European male copulates with the black African/Haitian female, thereby reproducing perfectly all imagined and historical notions of the colonizing process at the roots of the formation of Caribbean racial identity. Critic Claudette Williams draws attention to the "attribution of dichotomous moral values to black and white" clearly embodied in these two figures (39). It is a concern that she forwards in light of the belated appearance of this poem after the famous Hispanic Caribbean negrismo movement's conclusion and in spite of the fact that a regional consciousness of Negritude in a different dimension informs the 1940s.

The second part of the poem reenacts their intimate relationship as a contest between good and evil. It is one in which evil, personified in the Voudun that Madam Suquí practices and that the speaker-poet clearly presents as witchcraft, overcomes Erick's unsuspecting white purity and innocence. The success of Eric's portrayal lies in the power of white innocence. Poetic bias in favor of white male innocence connects to matters of race as these imply the ideas of innocence and defilement. The very contrast between his whiteness and her blackness is symbolic of the poetic message of the violation of white male purity by black female sorcery. Even as poetry cultivates the theme of white innocence, poetic emphasis deposits all culpability in the black female body, freeing the pure white male from any responsibility in his own demise. In this way, white innocence feeds on the cultural, religious, and sexual themes that abound in the poem. It will feed on the black female body and the subsequent female mulatto body it engenders.[8] The final effect is a dramatic narration that points back to the Dominican Negrophobia that sustains a poetic discourse of whiteness. There is remarkable similarity between the color-based religious tones and images used in the poetic construction of the black female character in this mid twentieth-century work and the current Dominican demonization of Haitianness that continue to determine national attitudes today. Williams establishes a relationship between the poem's argumentation and national experience:

> "Yélida" also exemplifies the xenophobia that compounds racial attitudes in the Dominican Republic, where [Dominican] blacks are considered less African and therefore superior to blacks from Haiti and other areas of the Caribbean. The racial prejudice implied in the poem is also evidence of the historical antipathy felt by Dominicans for Haitian blacks. (40)

The vilification of Madam Suquí confirms the psychological anxiety directed toward blackness that will later absolve itself in a belated celebration of mulattoness, the latter being the final moment of absolution of the historical legacy of whitening, whiteness, "hispanidad" 'Hispanic identity' and "dominicanidad" 'Dominican identity.' The poem conjures up sexual myth in the passionate relationship between these two. The Othering of the black female figure greatly aids the sustaining of the hypothesis of whiteness given the extent to which contrasts work in this poem. Her depreciation is crucial for promoting cultural fantasies often aligned with the tropical Caribbean isle. It is an aesthetic technique that appears here as a continuation of a deliberate strategy whose origin lies in the negrista poetic aesthetic of the 1920s and 1930s, a genre criticized for its static, often stereotypical representations of the black female figure.[9]

What ensues is a battle for Erick's soul. The success of Madam Suquí's prowess rests exclusively on her religion and sexuality. The message that Voudun is evil and so is she denotes her character, and there is clear indication that her supernatural connections enhance her sexual control over Erick. His rather ineffectual attempts to free himself from her sexual grip intensify the idea of the weakness of his white flesh, an idea introduced earlier in the apparent inability of white Norwegian sailors to resist the rum, the heat, and the dark, alluring flesh of the women of the tropics. The celebration of whiteness takes place indirectly, for, as Williams indicates, the "myth of the Afro-Caribbean woman's sexual virulence creates the fiction of white male innocence" (72). Erick's apparent sexual naïveté is distinct from the darker kind of sensual passion associated with Madam Suquí's possessive passion. It is a force that Erick's physical strength cannot withstand. Comforting memories of his homeland provide some relief, yet they are obliterated by her fiery desire that the poet describes in close conjunction with the dense, heavy, tropical landscape. The archetypical contest between light and dark continues, only this time internally, for Erick is emotionally defenseless and physically weakened. Any culpability is less his since he is now a victim of malevolent manipulation, an uncontrollable circumstance, and a virulent environment. Even as his disease ravaged body collapses, under Suquí's invocations, nature and the Voudun priest act as a spider's web, drawing him to his doom:

> y muy pronto los casó el obispo francés
> mientras en la montaña papaluá Luipié
> cantaba el canto de la Guinea y bebía la sangre de un chivato blanco
>
> En la noche sudaba de fiebres y marismas
> Erick sin sueño marinero varado sobre la carne fría y nocturna
>   de Suquí

71

fue dejando su estirpe sucia de hematozoarios y nostalgias
en el vientre de humus fértil de su esposa de tierra
y Erick murió un buen día entre Jesucristo y Damballá-Queddó
apagado el pulso de viento del velero perdido en el sargazo
su alma sin brújula voló para Noruega
donde todavía le quedaba el recuerdo
de un pie de mujer blanca que hacía frágiles huellas en la arena
    Mojada. (Hernández Franco 113–14)

and very soon the French bishop married them
while in the mountains Papalwa Luipie
sang the chant of Guinea and drank the blood of a white baby he-goat

At night he sweated from fever and nausea
Erick, no longer a sailor's dream, sunken in Suquí's cold night flesh
Gradually abandoning his unhealthy legacy of disease and nostalgia
in the fertile mass of his wife's earthy belly
and Erick died one good day between Jesus Christ and Damballa-
    Queddo
snuffed out like the wind's pulse of the sailing ship lost in the Sargasso
without a compass his soul flew back to Norway
where memory reminded him still of the foot
of a white woman that made small prints in the wet sand.

The religious clash referred to in the phrase "Jesucristo y Damballá-Queddó" 'Jesus Christ and Damballa-Queddo' (114) intensifies the idea of Madam Suquí's evil manipulations even as it glorifies the notion of Erick's body as the eternal victim. In the end, feeding on the powerful imagery of Christ's resurrection, it is his soul that will be salvaged, freed, and returned to its native location and original state. The final mention of a white woman walking along the beach of Norway serves as confirmation of the privileging of whiteness along with the caution to others of Erick's hue to remain faithful to safe, untainted sexual shores. What is ultimately valued is the Northern European world, made to appear more attractive and sincere than the trauma and manipulations associated with the heat and complexity of its antithesis.

Madam Suquí is a passionate and aggressive woman whose body and spiritual beliefs ascend to hegemony. She represents African ancestry, slavery, Haitianism, and paganism, aspects socially disparaged in the Dominican Republic and associated with the lower classes and unsavory groups. Her character conjures up poetic images of witch-craft and the demonic. Historian Barbara Bush confirms that the ten-dency of displacing the responsibility for white male impropriety onto the female slave has its roots in white assuagement and white imposi-tion. The transference of culpability for his carnal behavior onto the bewitching influences of the nonwhite woman thereby exonerates the white male entirely (18). The African female's relegation to the sta-tus of sexual animal serves to reify Western ideals of sexual purity, morality, and social order. Within colonial society and beyond, abject poverty, enslavement of Africans, and the Eurocentric vision of Afro-descendants as barbaric were responsible for the accepted view that the Caribbean was a world quite apart from the aesthetic beauty and moral correctness of European culture. Sander L. Gilman confirms modes of defining the essence of woman in terms of her genitalia, even as Western notions—"race," sexuality, and pathology—assist in defining the white male's method of coping with his concerns about power and control. Self-assuredness is a constant only by projecting his loss of physical and sexual control onto those subordinate to him: "the 'white man's burden,' his sexuality and control, is displaced in the need to control the sexuality of the Other, the Other as sexual-ized female" (107). Gilman's views reference those of the postcolonial theorist Homi Bhabha who argues that by associating black subjec-tivity with barbarism, anarchy, and lust, sustaining the oppression of peoples of African descent becomes justified.

Yélida's Mulattoness as National Anguish

negra un día sí y un día no
blanca los otros
nombre de vodú y apellido de kaes
lengua de zetas
corazón de ice-berg
vientre de llama.
(Hernández Franco 114)

> *black one day but not the next*
> *white the others*
> *first name from voudun and last name from k's*
> *from the languages of z's*
> *heart of iceberg*
> *flaming womb.*

Locked within Yélida's body and mind are remnants of two heterogeneous identities. Yélida is the Dominican Republic, imagined in a symbolic, hybrid, female existence that now appears as a synthesis of the island's history and signified by cultural confrontation, opposing spiritual formations, and conflicting human expectations. Concurrently she appears the perfect fusion of Caribbean and Dominican identities imagined as the result of cultural encounters and miscegenation. Her mixed heritage and deep psychological instability confirm the battle raging within her between the white, Nordic nation's colder, Christian heritage and the intense fierceness of black, hot, Haitian, Voudun ancestry. In the poem, the racial-cultural polarization shifts from the mystical-spiritual imagery of her parents' union to imagery that is heavily naturalistic, creating associations between the black female body and extreme elements of the tropical environment. Her very being concentrates the collision of forces between her parents, making it an irresoluble quest to save Yélida from herself.

Descriptions such as "nórdico viento preso en el subsuelo de la noche" 'Nordic wind imprisoned in the subsoil of the night' (114) and "hermafrodita en el principio del mundo" 'hermaphrodite at the beginning of the world' (115) attest to the portrayal of dual identities brought together by force of circumstance. At first, her mother Suquí does all she can to discover what her child's destiny will be. She connects to no avail with the forces of nature, the beings and spirits that determine night and day, good and evil, life and death. Here, language becomes heavily ornamental, for the poetic imagery used to describe Suquí's connections with the spiritual world contrasts with language that refers to Yélida's paternal heritage that still seeks to claim her. The imagery "Los liliputienses dioses infantiles de la nieve" 'The child-like gods of the snow' (115) contrasts with "al dios negro del atabal y la azagaya / comedor de hombres constelados de muertes" 'the black god of the kettle-drum and the spear / consumer of men marked by death' (116) in a poetic vision that privileges one spiritual and cultural form over another. There is no celebration of the fact that Yélida is in her mother's care, for Suquí's influence and maternal control confirm the triumph of Voudun identity. Its triumph highlights Yélida's estrangement from her father's heritage: "pacto roto de la costilla de oro / traición hembra del tiempo libertada" 'pact broken with the rib of gold / female treachery of a licentious time' (115). The speaker-poet employs language of purity and innocence throughout in the depiction of Yélida's white heritage. This linguistic strategy conforms to Hernández Franco's own biased convictions about the positive contributions of Nordic culture in contrast to his racially compromised nation. The link between whiteness and European perfection later contributes to the iconization of the Indigenous figure that, in the national imagination, replaces the European figure as the Dominican racial ideal. The substitution is especially important for comprehending the ambivalent attitude toward mulattoness as the national ideal, a popular sentiment confirmed in the ambiguities present in the portrait of Yélida.

Yélida is not a tranquil figure for she is the product of an irreconciled legacy in conflict with itself. The message is that her internal chaos is the result of her estrangement from that vital part of her legacy, described with great intensity in language that refers to aspects of Northern life-style, landscape, and the imagined world of European myths and legends. "Las árticas auroras" 'Arctic dawns' (115), "los dioses de algodón y de manzana" 'the gods of cotton and apple' (115), and "los hiperbóreos duendes del trino y del reno" 'hyperborean elves of the trine and the reindeer' (116) create notions of a world that is lost to her for she is a prisoner in a fiery island: "perdida iba a quedar para Noruega / en las islas de fuego condenada" 'She was to remain lost to Norway / Condemned to the islands of fire' (116). Travelers beg for her soul, seeking out all the dark spirits and gods of death and Voudun such as Wangol (Shango), god of the cemetery and thunder; Badagris, dictator of the stab and venom; Agoue, the pot-bellied god of the water; and Ayida-Queddo, the spirit who makes the red lamp of rape burn, but to no avail. The intense descriptions of these divinities seemingly confirm their associations with evil and the underworld. They appear invincible, insidiously sapping the last drop of Erick's Scandinavian blood and innocence. The gods of Norway beg for his life in vain. Ayida-Queddo dances to the chant of the rooster and "la sangre se les iba haciendo de plata derretida" 'his blood flowed away from them like melted silver' (117). Yélida sustains her connection with the tropical world of heat, nature, sweat, sex, Voudun, and the drumbeat. In the end, she mirrors her environment, fierce and merciless, consuming and manipulating. She will have her first sexual experience from which she emerges "alma de araña" 'soul of a spider,' "asesina" 'murderess,' and "vegetal y ardiente" 'burning vegetable' (118) but no less controversial with respect to love and identity. The mysteriousness of her mixed sensual nature deepens, for now she will never escape the extremes from which she emerges:

> por éxtasis de blanco y frenesí de negro
> profunda hacia la tierra y alta hacia el cielo
> en secreto de surco y en místico de llamas.
> (Hernández Franco 118)

> *ecstasy of white and frenzy of black*
> *deep towards the earth and high towards the heavens*
> *secretly by furrow and mystically by flames.*

Indeed she will always represent the conflicting origins responsible for her genetic state of being to which she is eternally connected.

Black female identity varies little from the traditions of poetic description associated with the Caribbean negrista literary movement. Nature and sensuality combine to categorize the female figure and at the same time reaffirm the moralizing values associated with the European human type. The island within which these two female characters appear is taken to an extreme as the utopia of African-originated spiritual belief that is suspect, even as it is partly responsible for that zone of resulting miscegenation that leads to a permanent instability of mind and body. Tomás Hernández Franco's *Apuntes sobre poesía popular y poesía negra en las Antillas* (1999) on popular black poetry in the Antilles confirms his awareness of the literary movement known as Negrismo and the paradigm of Negritude. However, he cultivates the paradigm only so far as it allows him to invoke miscegenation as the synthesis of regional and national identity. The poetic trend of demonizing "lo haitiano" 'Haitianness' while glorifying an imagined white Northern masculine subjectivity lays the cornerstone for the continuity of cultural paradigms of racial superiority. The latter persists firmly entrenched in the Dominican psyche and clearly manifests itself today in the Dominican's insistent referral to himself as the offspring of an Indigenous ideal that had become extinct centuries earlier.

Dominican "Whiteness" Today: A Sign of the Times

There are trajectories of cultural operation today that counteract the continuing mainstream discourse of Dominican national whiteness. They provide the space to debate and negotiate all terms and situations connected to issues linked to race and identity. Of importance here are literary works, cultural essays, and other written scholarship that express pride in and reverence for the African legacy that, together with the Hispanic heritage, is one of the major components of contemporary Dominican racial identity. Noticeably there are a greater number of studies and literary works circulating, an important and very recent development in scholarship, that effectively works as a counterbalance to the wide cultural trend of Dominicans' self-identifying as "indio," the term chosen by the vast majority to account for their darker hue. The country has neither a recent broad black activism nor a past postslavery legacy of Dominican black activism as occurred in other nations of the Americas such as Cuba and Brazil. Several important cultural studies, however, do exist that analyze the colonial and postcolonial roles Africans and their Dominican descendants played in key moments of national history and cultural formation. These important moments include the Haitian Revolution (1791–1804), the subsequent Haitian occupation of the Dominican Republic (1822–44), and ensuing independence campaigns, the Trujillo dictatorship (1930–61), the April 1965 movement, and ongoing abhorrence to Haitian presence on the island and in the Dominican Republic itself. Notable intellectuals and writers have contributed to the accumulation of substantive discourses that question current paradigms of national identity. Important here is

Afro-Dominican cultural icon and poet Blas R. Jiménez, whose literary production and cultural activities identify him as a central point of reference in matters relating to race, identity, and literature on the island. An important voice on the topics of racism, Afro-Dominicans, and the Dominican Republic's problematic relationship with Haiti, he hosts a weekly television talk show, *Página Abierta* (*Open Page*), which directly addresses Dominican identity, history, politics, and literature.[10] The development of a celebratory discourse of Negritude, however, remains limited in an environment known for its intense preoccupation with a whiter version of self.

Juan M. Rodríguez, curator of Santo Domingo's Museo del Hombre Dominicano, 'Museum of the Dominicans,' backs the very prominent voice of Blas R. Jiménez. Rodríguez laments the way in which electronic and print media publicly project a white-skinned majority in a country whose population of that pigment is clearly the minority. In an August 2005 interview in Santo Domingo, Rodríguez decried the manipulations of *Listín Diario*, the major local newspaper, and central museum exhibitions for their concerted promotions of, first, a national, mestizo Dominican race; second, a self-identification with the now extinct Indigenous people, the Taíno; third, the journalistic cultivation of an almost Nordic phenotype; and fourth, a fervent hostility to any serious naturalization of Haitian culture on national soil. Striving to reclaim the contributions of Africans to Dominican history at the Museo del Hombre Dominicano, Rodríguez works toward centralizing permanent exhibits that celebrate the African/Haitian legacy. Notable among these is the "Voudun Sala," an exhibit that contains Dominican-Haitian Voodoo-Santería artifacts. A second permanent installation in the museum pays homage to "La hermandad del Espíritu Santo de los Congos de Villa Mella" 'Brotherhood of the Holy Spirit, the Congos of Villa Mella,' the oldest known African brotherhood in the country. UNESCO (United Nations Educational, Scientific, and Cultural Organization) recognized the brotherhood in 2001 as an important part of Dominican heritage.

Museo del Hombre Dominicano's permanent exhibits celebrating Haitian contributions serve as a direct contrast to the commemoration of the Republic's African influences at the Centro Cultural Eduardo León Jiménez, popularly known as the León Museum, a heritage museum located in the city of Santiago, the country's second largest city. As part of the exposition titled "Signos de Identidad" 'Signs of Identity,' the exhibit of African contributions to the nation's cultural development emphasizes musical artifacts, thereby reproducing stereotypical notions regarding music and entertainment as the most salient retentions of the enslaved Africans that Europeans forcibly brought to the Americas. Partitioned from the other exhibits, instruments and a few vestments are arranged behind a white wall with small rectangular peepholes through which visitors peer to view the display. Rodríguez critically indicts the León Museum's approach to mounting the installation, stating it amplifies the current popular but unfortunate perception that African heritage in the Dominican Republic is shameful and therefore should be hidden, shrouded behind an impenetrable wall of whiteness.

To what extent has the Dominican Republic of today distanced itself from the legacy of racialized, colonial conflict so intensely referred to in "Yélida"? How far has the country come from the Haitian massacre and the ideology of hispanidad that the era of Trujillo spawned? Today, as studies indicate, the country has not fully freed itself from that legacy; indeed, there is still a profound slippage between self-perception and historical fact. The racial designations of "white" or "indio" are the preferred, which is particularly disconcerting in light of the fact that biological markers inherited from their African forebears are clearly visible in Dominican facial features, hair texture, and skin color, while Indigenous markers are not. The 1993 documentary *Mirrors of the Heart: Race and Identity (Bolivia, Haiti, the Dominican Republic)*, discusses this social contradiction. The film opens with a beach scene, a panoramic view of Caribbean people in a tropical setting of sand, sun, and sea. Every person captured on camera has some discernible African characteristic. The images highlight their contradictory definition of racial self-identification, a contradiction that North Americans' clear distinction between "white" and "black" further complicates.

The ever-increasing contact of Dominicans with North American culture via tourism and migration has contributed immensely to a greater questioning of formerly sacred patterns of Afro-Indio racial representations. The nonexistence of the identity categories "indio" and "mulatto" in the United States as official racial markers, and the very clear "white" versus "minorities" distinction that Dominicans are subjected to upon arrival in Miami or New York, create psychological and cultural challenges to a nation known for its unyielding anti-Haitian stance, and by extension, total lack of pride in its African heritage. From an international perspective, the Dominican population finds itself labeled as predominantly "black," given that the category of "mestizo" or "mixed race" is unacknowledged in the United States. The distance between what one is perceived to be and what one perceives as his or her racial identity is a personal and national experience that is not new to the Latin American region. What makes the Dominican case unique is the extent to which the perception of self as "white" or "indio" is staunchly affirmed. The mania of labeling oneself something one is interpreted as not being from the European and North American perspectives come across as an anomaly in the structure of racial divides that predominates. To this end, Paul Gilroy maintains, "Where racist, nationalist, or ethnically absolutist discourses orchestrate political relationships so that these identities appear to be mutually exclusive, occupying the space between them or trying to demonstrate their continuity has been viewed as a provocative and even oppositional act of political insubordination" (1). While Gilroy's description of the broader Latin American condition is appropriate, the Dominican case veers slightly from the regional pattern in terms of the element selected to serve as "the space between" given its insistence on undermining the predominantly traditional structure of racial divides by merely indicating that what one sees is not always what is. As noted in "Yélida," internal human turmoil results, especially for the person who is of mixed heritage. In *Mirrors of the Heart*, an inner psychological state is visible in various individuals and families and described as an ingrained feeling of denial. Gilroy indicates that trying to be "both European and black requires some specific forms of double consciousness" (1). In the Dominican context, with the double sense of self comes a clear rejection of the blackness of self manifested in the still existing cultural imperative "mejorar la raza" 'to improve the race,' or in other words, become whiter, more Spanish, less black.

The national white perception presently remains intact; indeed, any undermining of it is fairly recent and stems from travel to the

United States and the shock Dominicans receive when, upon their arrival, they are categorically labeled as a "minority," "Latino/a" or "black," followed by racialized treatment that enlightens them to what it means to be nonwhite in the United States and the Dominican Republic. In the documentary *Mirrors of the Heart*, the mulatto taxi driver interviewed perceives himself significantly enlightened by travel in the United States. Declaring all North American whites "racist," he takes a more aggressively nationalistic stance. Yet he does not define himself as "black," opting instead for the designation "mulatto." Furthermore, he is unaware of his own predisposition for placing clear demarcations between "us" (Dominicans) and "them" (Haitians), a division that is exclusively based on physical appearance and inspired by the complicated political and historical experiences that all previous generations have also nurtured. Today the shift from whiteness in the pure sense intensifies the problem for now the national distinction of Haitian versus Dominican is one that can be classified as "mulatto" (the Dominicans prefer to say "indio") versus "black." Very dark skin, "African" facial features, and Haitian identity configure the latter. The reduction of the historical to the socio-physical finds expression in the popular statement, "All Haitians are black, and all blacks are Haitian." The purpose is to make a specious syllogism between black people and Dominicans. Physical criteria continue to be basic: "pelo malo" 'bad or kinky hair' versus "pelo bueno" 'good or straight hair' is an important one. The hours and money spent in the cosmetic straightening of hair testify to the deep psychological impact of "white" cultural thinking. The taxi driver's mother prefers him to marry a light (or lighter) complexioned woman, with good (or better) hair to ensure her son's continued prosperity and happiness, which will in turn ensure the prosperity of his light-skinned offspring.

Afro-Dominican poet Blas R. Jiménez refers to his personal experience of being labeled "mulatto" even though he insists he is not. He explains in *Mirrors of the Heart* that self-ascribed mulattoness is commonplace in his country where most people will say that they are not racist even as they treasure those physical attributes or cosmetic transformations that promote greater proximity to whiteness. The film documents the reign of a national white pigmentocracy by focusing on a mixed-race marriage between an Afro-Dominican doctor and his Hispanic wife from a traditional, elite family. The disparate marital union sends the message of the continued miscegenated status of the country. Indeed the optimistic tone of the film indicates the possibility of future national harmony through racial amalgamation. Presently, however, one cannot help but be suspicious of the total value of an interracial relationship which, in Dominican terms, is still more the exception than the rule. Moreover, the absence of an Afro-Dominican female voice—the three black Dominican interviewees in the documentary, the taxi driver, Jiménez, and the doctor, are all male—complicates understanding the color line in it totality since it excludes a feminized perspective, silences Afro-Dominican female discourses on the issues of racism, classism, sexism, whiteness, and anti-Haitianism.

Women's Writing: Consciousness or Apathy?

Since the 1980s, there has been an ever-increasing awareness among Afro-Dominican women of the complexity and injustice of race relations. In a culture where blackness and Haitianness come together in continued defiance of the preferred mainstream discourse of white and Hispanic identity, the dual pursuits of women's writings, on the one hand, and women's and feminist-based activity, on the other, mirror the culture's affirmation of Dominicanness (whiteness, European/Hispanic identity) and the negation of its counter-identity (African/Haitianness).[11] While there are some ideological connections between women's writings and women's activism, the prevailing shared restraint observed in scholarship and the few literary works pertaining to race make it difficult to establish direct correlations between female literary creation and socio-ethnic reality.

There are contemporary Afro-Dominican women whose activities in the areas of writing, publishing, politics, and social activism have established greater connections with revolution and resistance to political oppression than with opposition to the racial divides that exist. Scholars Celsa Albert Batista and Ochy Curiel, the late educator and journalist Petronila Angélica Gómez (d. 1971), feminist activists Sonia Pierre and Sergia Galván, the late land-reform martyr

Florinda Soriano known as Mamá Tingó (d. 1974), Miriam Ventura, Aurora Arias, and Mercedes Mota are all national icons. Their status as Afro-Dominican women is less celebrated than their social achievements. In a context where national allegiance overrides all else and is strongly protected, defended, and visualized in opposition to Haiti, their efforts in organizations, politics, and writings have more value as symbols of their intense patriotic commitment to preserving the sovereignty of the nation.[12]

In *Mujer y esclavitud en Santo Domingo*, Celsa Batista leads the attack against derogatory, racist language directed toward nonwhites in the social sphere. She closely examines the linguistic expression engrained in national speech patterns and widely used and cultivated in the media. An expression such as "bien parecida" or "buena presencia" 'good appearance' implies that there are those who are not of good appearance racially; many Dominicans regard being of darker skin as unattractive and having a bad physicality. The term appears in newspaper employment advertisements as a necessary requirement for prospective job seekers. Individuals lacking it need not apply. The use of the term confirms the existence of a color hierarchy, the cultivation of an ideology of racial preference, and a covert move to shut out those of Haitian ancestry from white-collar jobs. Individuals with dark skin are referred to as "sucio" 'dirty,' while the preferred expression of "indio lavado," literally 'washed Indian,' suggests one has an acceptable pigment (Batista 157). Batista reports limited celebration of Negritude seen in the way she refers to Dominicans as a mulatto race that cultivates Western cosmetic trends of whitening. Her words reveal disapproval of contemporary methods of personal transformation, confirmed by "el alaciarse el pelo desde la edad de infancia y en el uso exagerado de cremas blanqueadoras por doloroso que sea este proceso" 'the straightening of hair from childhood and the exaggerated use of whitening lotions regardless of how painful this process may be' (158).

Various derogatory words used to refer to the nonwhite female figure confirm the high level of cultural concern with and condemnation of her approximation to Afro-origins. References to dark skin color, "grampa, greña, pimienta, negra, prieta, haitiana" (158), point toward a broader distaste that is the fruition of an artificially constructed desire to imagine the national feminine body in a whiter state of being. Statements including "no te cases con negra/o que atrasas la raza" 'don't marry black or you'll pull the race down' and "yo soy negra y fea, pero de mí nadie se burla" 'I am black and ugly but no one makes fun of me' (158, 162) associate with cultural backwardness and underdevelopment. At the same time, they confirm the constant dialogue between the social gaze that produces the process of self-degradation and the effect of Othering. Other statements reinforce the widespread inability to accept achievement as coterminus with blackness, even when faced with supporting evidence: "Negra pero Licenciada" 'She is black but with a university degree' or "Es una negra que ha llegado donde no han llegado blancas" 'She is a black woman who has arrived (succeeded) where white women have not' (163).

The private sector and the media, especially television and newspapers, largely project the Dominican sphere as white. The positive currency placed on having a fair hue and Hispanic or "white" features has clear economic advantages and determines the select criteria of who is physically the most acceptable at the national and international levels. The pressure the predetermined criteria for whiteness places on the female to uphold the select standard is even greater, given the extent to which the cult of beauty often weighs more heavily on the female psyche. The reign of Santo Domingo, the Dominican Republic's capital and largest city, as the country's urban trend setter, together with the vision of Haitians, children of Haitian and Dominicans, Afro-Caribbean immigrants, and the frontier populations as existing outside these prescribed aesthetics, necessarily implies the continuance of the present status quo of whiteness as the only physically and socially acceptable one.

Counteracting Whiteness: MUDHA's Campaign

Acknowledging that racialized identities are taught, learned, or constructed is crucial for studying the Caribbean and Latin America, where racial boundaries, especially in comparison to the United States, are radically unstable. Yet race as a social construction proves at best indeterminate in the Dominican context, given that the national discourse has been historically infused with biased ideas about differences between social classes, genders, and races—biases now so firmly entrenched that they prove unassailable, forcing culturally disenfranchised groups to seek alternative ways of penetrating or dismantling them.[13] In Santo Domingo today, there is one unique and important movement of female resistance to the national model of whiteness. Created in July 1983, MUDHA is a nongovernmental organization entirely operated by Afro-Dominican and Haitian women. Its primary goal is to defend all legal and social interests of Dominicans of Haitian descent who currently compose probably the only community of people native born but denied the rights of citizenship that is legally theirs. Under the direction of Sonia Pierre, MUDHA continues to dedicate all its resources to combating injustice and inequality with special attention given to women and children in the hope of improving their quality of life. Particularly beneficial are the projects it coordinates and supports in the areas of health and education in the predominantly rural and primarily Haitian-Dominican poverty stricken communities known as bateyes, shanties originally belonging to sugar plantations. Once the dwelling places of the enslaved, bateyes continue to be the homes of many dark-complected Dominicans and Haitians. The film *La Rue Cas-Nègres* (*Sugar Cane Alley*), originally released in 1983 and set in the Caribbean island of Martinique, portrays their legacy. That these set apart communities continue to exist in the Dominican landscape is a clear testimony to the persistence of outdated paradigms of race, class, and economics that have yet to be dismantled.

As its mission statement indicates, MUDHA's specific purpose is "para enfrentar la situación de maltrato y agresión a que son sometidas las mujeres en esta sociedad, especialmente las mujeres de descendencia haitiana" 'to confront the mistreatment and abuse experienced by women in this society, especially women of Haitian descent' (Gallardo 15). Its objectives are very practical and immediate—to intervene in any way possible to effect improvements in the areas of health, education, and legal and human rights for all women. Moreover, its primary strategy is to educate for community organization and participation. Depending on its own fund-raising efforts and local and international financial aid, MUDHA has established community centers that serve as storm shelters, health clinics, and schools. One important center is located in the batey community of Palmarejo.

Now in its twenty-second year under the very efficient guidance of Sonia Pierre, MUDHA has carved out a very specific site for itself in a difficult socio-ethnic backdrop that continues to express overall hostility to its efforts to empower the local Haitian population.[14] Ongoing projects, discussion forums, pamphlets, and books have solidified MUDHA's activism in the national sphere making it the only organization dedicated to women of African descent that transcends hostile geographical and ideological boundaries firmly instituted on the island.[15] Its advocacy for Haitian-Dominican women over the years has made it a constant target of public ridicule and criticism. The combined forces of officialdom and the heavy hand of the army, in support of an ideologically racialized policy that sells itself as nationalistic and the epitome of patriotism, have continued to hold Haitians and their successive generations of Dominican descendants in a constant state of socioeconomic siege. For the good of the nation, Haitian persecution, officially initiated and legitimized by the Trujillo-mandated massacre of 1937, continues intact. It feeds on a politics of nationhood, self-rule, and territorial protection even though the very population it protects cannot help but recognize its greatest flaw: the inhumane treatment of the more than one million Haitians who currently reside in the Dominican Republic. MUDHA treads carefully yet firmly in precarious political waters for the essence of Dominicanness lies in its ability to sustain its discourse of racial uniqueness, a discourse constructed primarily on the notion of ostensibly what it states it is not—not African or Haitian. By insisting on the rights of immigrants to affordable health care, public education, proper nutrition, and equal employment and housing, the women's organization continues to operate in the zone of national consciousness and guilt, for it forces the realization of the damaging internal contradictions that continue to play themselves out in the national psyche. The consistent demonization of everything Haitian is yet at an all-time high, well above the 1822–44 era, when Haiti controlled the island. Modern excuses as to why ethnicity-based distinctions continue today seem to be primarily economic; however, cultural attitudes and rigid codes of separation that are visible elsewhere in the region are in place and this means that visible Afro-Dominican and Haitian presence in prosperous or key socioeconomic positions will never come to fruition given the privileging of Hispanic-indio identity.

A process of Haitian erasure is in operation, one that stems from government policies enforced by acts of aggression on the part of the army and sustained by the lack of a strong social movement's opposition. Dominican women of Haitian descent live and suffer in circumstances of total invisibility, exclusion, and marginalization. They lack the necessary documents that would legitimize their "existence" in a national system that places human value on the possession of identification cards for the mothers and birth certificates for the children born there (S. Galván 17). Now more vulnerable to poverty and sexual exploitation given their undocumented status in the country, they are women on the margins of Dominican society. They are condemned to remain in silence, cast aside by officially sanctioned processes of segregation that seem archaic even as they serve the interests of those in political power, in their desire to stem the flow of Haitian immigrants, as well as those in economic control, in their exploitation of Haitians as cheap labor. It is in this context that MUDHA constructs its raison d'être, for by its very existence it stands apart from Dominican society, offering itself as a refuge, but more important, as a stronghold of resistance to the injustices of the color line that are officially sanctioned and socially tolerated. Today, the organization is a very important voice and presence in the legal system, litigating on behalf of those without the means to do so, and in the spheres of government, protesting existing legislature that continues to block Haitian access to mainstream society.

To what extent does the Dominican-Haitian female experience, both symbolic and real, mirror the broader complexities surrounding whiteness? How is it a reflection of the deeper state of indeterminacy that characterizes what it means to be Dominican, that is, white? Although a racialized state of being is one that is historically and socially constructed, Dominicans' conception of themselves is one they are taught and in which they believe. A continuing racialized indoctrination is visible in Tomás Hernández Franco's poetic construction of Yélida and in the contemporary moment. Hernández Franco makes a clear distinction between Madam Suquí and Yélida. The inability to divorce the former from notions of the fantastic operations associated with the spiritualism of Voudun highlights the Dominican mentality that exoticizes and fears Haitian culture. Ostracizing fear and hatred are conditions of the official Dominican national character and cultural education; thus there is a need for major revamping of socio-racial values and precepts in order to integrate the Dominican-Haitian figure into mainstream society. In the case of Yélida, her poetic description is intensely ritualistic in the fantasized battle for her being. Her mulattoness seems less a biological fusion and more a tug-of-war between two national and genealogical identities that splinter her psychically and irreconcilably.

The way the Dominican tourist industry markets the national identity of indeterminacy evidences the bifurcation of Yélida's and the nation's racial psyche. There are primarily two kinds of souvenirs that vendors sell to tourists visiting the Dominican Republic, "Haitian" paintings and faceless Dominican ceramic dolls. Many Haitian-Dominican paintings that appear to celebrate a pseudo–Haitian/African identity line the market stalls in the sections of Santo Domingo that tourists frequent. The mass production and marketing of Haitian stylized art seems most paradoxical in a nation that takes pride in distinguishing itself from its western neighbor in all aspects, especially the racial one. The mass marketing of female ceramic dolls that come in various sizes and shapes is also a racial paradox. These dolls are customarily tall, elegant, slender figures wearing Eurocentric dress, and they are always faceless. Their lack of phenotypic traits is particularly telling in the way those absences suggest an unstable, indeterminate national self without a legitimate, fixed identity. For Dominicans, fixating on forms of racial whiteness seems the least conflictive state possible, a rather problematic position to assume as the Haitian trauma continues.

NOTES

1. See Ingram 157–58.

2. For the English translation of Galván's *Enriquillo*, see Robert Graves's *Enriqullo: The Cross and the Sword*.

3. The poetry of the Trujillo era, which was in decline by the late 1950s, is associated with the rise of three very important poetic movements or generation of the 1940s: "la poesía sorprendida" (1943–47), "los independientes del '40," and the "generación del '48." The awards, homage, and recognition that poetry received during this time sparked a celebration of the culture of literary art. See Fernández Muñoz.

4. Important Dominican studies on the politics of Hernández Franco's poetics can be found in Mateo; Del Cabral; and Hernández Franco, "Política de cultura" and "Síntesis."

5. A few months after his pro-Trujillo conference speech in the Ateneo Dominicano in 1943, Tomás Hernández Franco was appointed Minister of Haiti. He supported Trujillo's anti-Haitian campaigns of the 1940s, as confirmed in his essay "Síntesis, Magnitud y Solución de un Problema" 'Synthesis, Magnitude and the Solution of a Problem.' In it, he clearly indicates the need to stem the flow of the undesirable African element into the Dominican Republic: "de raza netamente africana, no puede representar para nosotros, incentive étnico ninguno" [...] clearly an African race, it cannot represent any ethnic incentive for us' (qtd. in Fernández Muñoz 26).

6. See Brewer 20–21.

7. All translations of "Yélida" are mine.

8. See Ross 263.

9. For expanded reading on the development and implications of the negrista poetic aesthetic on the black female figure, see Mansour; Young; Kutzinski; and Branche.

10. For further details on literary and contemporary interpretations of experiences in relation to race, ethnicity, Negritude, and Haitian culture, see Stinchcomb, Howard; Handelsman; and Jiménez, *Caribe africano; Exigencias; Nativo;* and *Aquí.*

11. The literary works of Aída Cartagena Portalatín, the literary critique of Pura Emeterio Rondón, and the historical and ethnographic studies of Celsa Albert Batista and Ochy Curiel stand out as written productions that exist at the intersection of race, literature, and Afro-Dominican women. Simultaneously, two key organizations that have found themselves at the junction of national identity, women's rights, and the Haitian-Dominican dilemma are Casa por la Identidad de la Mujer Afro (Center for the Afro-Women's Identity) and the Movimiento de Mujeres Dominico-Haitianas (Dominican-Haitian Women's Movement).

12. Cocco de Filippis; Nacidit-Perdomo; and Collado and Romero have written detailed essays on important trends in Dominican women's writings.

13. Garner contains a chapter on whiteness in Latin America and the Caribbean.

14. Pierre, personal interview.

15. MUDHA has over the years been carefully documenting and publishing on aspects of its community projects and political agenda. See Féliz Féliz; Gallardo; Guerrero C.; Torres-Saillant; and Lespinasse and Pierre.

Works Cited

Batista, Celsa. *Mujer y esclavitud en Santo Domingo*. República Dominicana: INDAASEL, 2003.

Bhabha, Homi. "The Other Question—Homi K. Bhaba Reconsiders the Stereotype and Colonial Discourse." *Screen* 24.6 (1983): 18–36.

Branche, Jerome. "Negrismo: Hibridez cultural, autoridad y la cuestión de la nación." *Revista Iberoamericana* 65.188–89 (June–Dec.1999): 483–504.

Brewer, Mary F. *Staging Whiteness*. Middleton: Wesleyan UP, 2005.

Bush, Barbara. *Slave Women in Caribbean Society, 1650–1838*. Bloomington: Indiana UP, 1990.

Cocco de Filippis, Daisy. *Desde la diáspora: A Diaspora Position*. New York: Alcance, 2003.

———. "Introduction." *Bilingual Anthology of the Poetry of Aida Cartagena Portalatín*. Santo Domingo: Taller, 1988. 9–17.

———. "Introduction." *Documents of Dissidence*. New York: CUNY Dominican Studies Institute, 2000. vii–xvi.

Collado, Miguel, and Rafael García Romero, eds. *Ensayos críticos sobre escritoras dominicanas del siglo XX*. Santo Domingo, República Dominicana: CEDIBIL, 2002.

Curiel, Ochy. "Aproximación al análisis de estrategias frente al racismo: La lucha política desde las mujeres." *Rebelión*. 19 May 2005 <http://www.rebelion.org/mujer/030408curiel.html>.

Del Cabral, Manuel. *10 poetas dominicanas: 3 poetas con vida y 7 desenterrados*. República Dominicana: Publicaciones América, 1980.

Derby, Lauren. "Haitians, Magic and Money: Raza and Society in the Haitian-Dominican Borderlands, 1900 to 1937." *Comparative Studies in Society and History* 36.3 (July 1994): 488–526.

Féliz Féliz, Gerardo E., ed. *El nombre y la nacionalidad como simbología de la existencia*. La República Dominicana: MUDHA, Grafo-Caribe, 2000.

Fernández Muñoz, Julian. *Joaquín Balaguer y Tomás Hernández Franco, francamente atrujillados*. Santo Domingo: Valdez, 1997.

Gallardo, Gina. *Camino a construir un sueño*. República Dominicana: MUDHA, Grafo-Caribe, 2001.

Galván, Manuel de Jesús. *The Cross and the Sword*. Trans. of *Enriquillo*. 1876. Robert Graves. Bloomington: Indiana UP, 1954.

———. *Enriquillo*. Santo Domingo: ICM, 1988.

Galván, Sergia. "Las mujeres domínico-haitianas." *El nombre y la nacionalidad como simbología de la existencia*. Ed. Gerardo E. Féliz Féliz. República Dominicana: MUDHA, Grafo-Caribe, 2000. 13–23.

Garner, Steve. *Whiteness: An Introduction*. London: Routledge, 2007.

Gilman, Sander L. *Difference and Pathology*. Ithaca: Cornell UP, 1985.

Gilroy, Paul. *The Black Atlantic: Modernity and Double Consciousness*. Cambridge: Harvard UP, 1993.

Guerrero C., Pedro L. *Informe de investigación: Incidencia de las políticas públicas y actitudes de la población, en edad reproductiva, de las comunidades bateyanas, en relación con el VIH/SIDA. Período sept. 2003–julio 2004*. República Dominicana: Mediabyte, Sept. 2003–July 2004.

Handelsman, Michael. "Balaguer, Blas Jiménez y lo afro en la República Dominicana." *SECOLAS Annals* 29 (1998): 85–91.

Hernández Franco, Tomás. *Apuntes sobre poesía popular y poesía negra en las Antillas*. 3rd. ed. Santo Domingo: La Trinitaria, 1999.

———. "Síntesis, Magnitud y Solución de un Problema." *Cuadernos Dominicanos de Cultura* 1 (Sept. 1943). Santo Domingo, R.D. s.d.

———. "Una política de cultura." *Ateneo*. Santo Domingo, 1943.

———. "Yélida." *Poesía afroantillana y negrista (Puerto Rico, República Dominicana, Cuba)*. Sel., Intro., Notas, Glosario Jorge Luis Morales. San Juan: Editorial Universitaria Universidad de Puerto Rico, 1976. 111–18.

Howard, David. *Coloring the Nation: Race and Ethnicity in the Dominican Republic*. Oxford: Signal, Lynne Rienner, 2001.

Ingram, Penelope. "Racializing Babylon: Settler Whiteness and the 'New Racism.'" *New Literary History* 32.1 (2001): 157–76.

Jiménez, Blas R. *Aquí . . . Otro Español: Poesía*. República Dominicana: Manati, 2000.

———. *Caribe africano en despertar*. Santo Domingo: Nuevas Rutas, 1984.

———. *Exigencias de un cimarrón (en sueños)*. Santo Domingo: Taller, 1987.

———. *El Nativo (Versos en cuentos para espantar zombies)*. Santo Domingo: Búho, 1996.

Kolchin, Peter. "Whiteness Studies: The New History of Race in America." *Journal of American History* 89 (June 2002): 154–73.

Kutzinski, Vera M. *Sugar's Secrets: Race and the Erotics of Cuban Nationalism*. Charlottesville: U of Virginia P, 1993.

Lespinasse, Colette, and Sonia Pierre. *En busca de vida: Una investigación sobre las mujeres haitianas implicadas en la migración en la República Dominicana*. República Dominicana: GARR—MUDHA, 2005.

Mansour, Mónica. *La poesía negrista*. Mexico, D.F.: Era, 1973.

Mateo, Andrés L. "Prólogo: La mulatidad de Tomás Hernández Franco." *Apuntes sobre poesía popular y poesía negra en las antillas.* República Dominicana: La Trinitaria,1999.

Nacidit Perdomo, Ylonka. "Fragmentos del discurso pronunciado por la secretaria de estado de la mujer, Dra. Yadira Henriquez de Sánches Baret, en el acto de homenaje a las mujeres destacadas del siglo XX." *Mujeres* (July 2003): 36–37.

Pierre, Sonia. Interview with author. 19 July 2005.

Portalatín, Aída Cartagena. *Escalera para Electra.* Santo Domingo: Universidad Autónoma de Santo Domingo, 1970.

———. *Tablero.* Santo Domingo: Taller, 1978.

Rodríguez, Juan M. Interview with author. 5 Aug. 2005.

Rondón, Pura Emeterio. *Estudios críticos de la literatura dominicana contemporánea.* República Dominicana: Búho, 2005.

Ross, Thomas. "White Innocence, Black Abstraction." *Critical White Studies: Looking Behind the Mirror.* Ed. Richard Delgado and Jean Stefancic. Philadelphia: Temple UP, 1997. 263–66.

Stinchcomb, Dawn. *The Development of Literary Blackness in the Dominican Republic.* Gainesville: U of Florida P, 2004.

Taylor, Gary. *Buying Whiteness: Race, Culture, and Identity from Columbus to Hip Hop.* New York: Palgrave Macmillan, 2005.

Torres-Saillant, Silvio. "Situación legal, política, cultural y socioeconómica de los/as inmigrantes en los Estados Unidos." *El nombre y la nacionalidad como simbología de la existencia.* Ed. Gerardo E. Féliz Féliz. República Dominicana: MUDHA, Grafo-Caribe, 2000. 25–36.

———. "The Tribulations of Blackness: Stages in Dominican Racial Identity." *Latin American Perspectivas* 25.3 (May 1998): 126–46.

Vega, Bernardo. *Trujillo y Haití.* Vol. 1, *1930–1937.* Santo Domingo: Fundación Cultural Dominicana. 1988.

Williams, Claudette. *Charcoal and Cinnamon: The Politics of Color in Spanish Caribbean Literature.* Gainesville: U of Florida P, 2000.

Young, Ann Venture. "The Black Woman in Afro-Caribbean Poetry." *Blacks in Hispanic Literature: Critical Essays.* Ed. Miriam DeCosta. Port Washington: Kennikat, 1977. 137–42.

Romancing Whiteness: Popular Appalachian Fiction and the Imperialist Imagination at the Turns of Two Centuries

EMILY SATTERWHITE

> The ancestry of our mountain folk is ... almost wholly Revolutionary and British.... [T]he "leading families" of the mountains are clearly sharers in the gracious influences which formed the English and Scottish people....
>
> [The mountaineer] certainly belongs to the category of the "native born." ... And while in more elegant circles American families have ceased to be prolific, the mountain American is still rearing vigorous children in numbers that would satisfy the patriarchs. The possible value of such a population is sufficiently evident.
>
> —William Goodell Frost, 1899

Appalachia, a region of the United States often understood as coterminous with the southern portion of the Appalachian mountain range, has served as both a symbol of quintessential American whiteness and as a proxy for understanding and managing "group-based difference."[1] In the geographical imagination of middling and elite white Americans at the close of the nineteenth century, Appalachia represented a bounded, isolated reservoir of racially "pure" white Americans whom William Goodell Frost observed were oddly "behind the times" (311). Anglo elites understood true "Americanness" as linked to whiteness and British ancestry. When northeastern urban elites feared immigrants from Eastern and Southern Europe would overrun "their" country, they looked to Appalachia as a source for native-born Americans of "creditable" Revolutionary War–era ancestry purportedly uncontaminated by contact with foreigners, Negroes, or the institution of slavery (315). The supposed existence in the southeastern mountains of a pool of desirable "Saxon" stock served to reassure elites that their vision of America could be replenished thanks to prolific white mountain people who, according to Frost, sustained a respectable "pioneer" way of life in the face of modernity.[2]

Popular stories and novels in Frost's time embraced this vision of simultaneous Appalachian whiteness and otherness. John Fox Jr. (1862–1919), author of the best-selling novel *The Trail of the Lonesome Pine* (1908), was one of the most popular early twentieth-century writers to articulate mountaineers' group difference through racialist constructs. In popular novels published a century later, representations of Appalachia again served as both a celebration of white folkways and a case study for readers dealing with group difference understood as exotic but nonthreatening. Trade paperback novels from the latter era that linger on ethnicized Appalachian whiteness include Charles Frazier's *Cold Mountain* (1998) and Silas House's *Clay's Quilt* (2002). In parallel ways, popular fiction set in the region offered readers at both the turn to the twentieth and twenty-first centuries a vision of a safely white domestic space. At the same time, Appalachia proffered the comfort or discomfort of a differentiated whiteness. White American readers might see themselves as rightful rulers or innocent victims, or both, depending upon the degree to which they identified with mountain characters or intervening outsiders in Appalachian novels.

Beginning with the local–color literary movement (c. 1868–1910), stories and essays published in middle- and highbrow periodicals constructed and drew upon an imagined geography of Appalachia as a region of preindustrial white folk. Popular fiction played a crucial role in perpetuating and molding assumptions about the supposedly irrevocable correlation between American nativity, American character, whiteness, frontier self-sufficiency, and national superiority. At the same time, popular fiction reflected and shaped elites' conflicted attempts to articulate mountaineers' precise social and class status. Concerns about mountain residents' supposed ignorance, crudeness, and violence confounded elite observers' hope that white mountain people might be models of unsophisticated salvation from modernity. Writers cast about for the appropriate language to describe mountain whites' perceived difference. In actuality, that difference was one of class disparity wrought by the uneven development of capitalism in the postbellum southeastern mountains. But writers adopted a more ready-to-hand racial vocabulary to explain mountain distinctiveness.[3]

In their efforts to pinpoint Appalachia as a resource for national whiteness yet distinguish Appalachian Americans from sophistica-ted, elite, white readers, commentators like William Goodell Frost utilized racialized language that associated mountain residents with the barbarian tier of civilization according to cultural evolutionism. As "barbarians," Appalachian residents were considered just one step above "savages," who were generally understood as nonwhites. Frost worried over "whether the mountain people can be enlightened and guided so that they can have a part in the development of their own country, or whether they must give place to foreigners and melt away *like so many Indians*" (319; emphasis added). According to Gilded Age commentaries, mountaineers were both "us" and "them."[4] From per-spectives like Frost's, mountaineers were surely one of "us" in their raw hereditary and racial "potential" for uplift. But to live up to this poten-tial, mountaineers had to be managed as one of "them"—"ward[s] of the nation" like nonwhites, including "Negroes," Native Americans, and, beginning in 1898, Cubans and Filipinos (319).[5] Hence, even as commentators praised Appalachian people for being of sound British stock, their discomfort with differences rooted in class and geography led writers to racialize mountaineers in a manner that undermined the label of "white" that initially instigated commentators' fascination with and admiration for them.

Late-nineteenth-century anxieties regarding immigration, group difference, and the maintenance of Anglo power nationally and glob-ally reverberated forcefully in the late twentieth century. The post-Vietnam era witnessed a revival of wealth disparity, corporate influence, nationalistic fervor, and xenophobia reminiscent of the Gilded Age. During this "second Gilded Age" or "neo–Gilded Age," as recent jour-nalists, scholars, and activists have described it, fiction set in a mytholo-gized rural Appalachia once more served as a figurative place through which Americans envisioned a safely white interior homeland.[6] Even as Americans continued to imagine the region as populated entirely by whites, confusion over the social and class status of mountain resi-dents resulted in ethnicized constructions of mountain distinctiveness; Celtic and Native American "blood" were the most frequently proffered explanations for group difference in recent fiction set in southern Appalachia. Mountain characters understood as racially nonthreatening yet ethnically and culturally distinct from "mainstream" Americans permitted readers of Appalachian fiction to negotiate postmodern anxieties regarding identity, including the specters of generic, undifferentiated whiteness and fragmented metropolitan selfhood.[7]

Beginning in the 1990s, a spate of best-selling novels demonstrated the widespread appeal of high-middlebrow writing about Appalachia.[8] Successful trade publications, including Charles Frazier's *Cold Mountain* (1998), Silas House's *Clay's Quilt* trilogy (2001–4), Jan Karon's *At Home in Mitford* series (1994–2005), Adriana Trigiani's *Big Stone Gap* trilogy (2000–2002), and Barbara Kingsolver's *Prodigal Summer* (2001), reassured white high-middlebrow readers of the presence of Appalachia as a refuge for "real" American values, folkways, and racial homogeneity.[9] In an era of Anglo-American discomfort over the riot that followed the 1992 acquittal of the California police officers who beat African American Rodney King, with the rise in racially charged anti-immigrant hysteria like that emblematized in 1994 by California's Proposition 187, and with a newfound enemy in the chimera of the post–September 11, 2001, brown Arab, representations of Appalachia offered an imaginative space of whiteness and safety from global processes and conflicts.[10]

Turn-of-the-twentieth-first-century best-sellers' homage to close-knit white community represented a departure from mid-twentieth-century representations of Appalachia. All-too-familiar stereotypes of Appalachia depicted the region in a Gothic vein, emphasizing violent and degenerate hillbilly characters; this Gothic representation was popularized most dramatically by director John Boorman's 1972 film *Deliverance*, the cinematic adaptation of James Dickey's best-selling novel of the same title published in 1970. Novels published after 1990 reasserted the rural nature of Appalachia but reconfigured it as pleasant, neighborly, eccentric, and quaint. By configuring Appalachia as wholly rural and largely homogenous, neo–Gilded Age novels implicitly promised their primarily white readers the possibility of retreat from the diversity of races, creeds, and nationalities often associated with urban places. Simultaneously, post-1990 novels set in Appalachia reassured readers about the value of nonthreatening and assimilable cultural differences that might stave off the fearsome sterility of standardized suburban landscapes.

Furthermore, twenty-first-century readers' designation of white, mountain folk life as the root of "real America" constructed Appalachia as "home" in contrast not only to heterogeneous domestic cities but also to "sinister" foreign places that seemed to threaten "home" figured as the (innocent white) nation. In the process of identifying with Appalachian protagonists, well-to-do white American readers could project themselves into a purportedly embattled but innocent minority group besieged and victimized by outsiders who do not understand or appreciate it. At the same time, the nonnormative cultural or "ethnic" qualities of white Appalachian characters offered readers the opportunity to negotiate fears of racial and global others by substituting more intimidating racial difference with the proxy of rural mountain people as a "home-grown" variety of ethnic curiosity. In both instances, readers used a white ethnic Appalachia as a means to cope with exotic and menacing difference abroad.[11]

The post-Vietnam era witnessed the efforts of white ethnic revivalists to assert their victimization as ethnoracial minorities and to demand privileges they believed belong rightfully to whites. While Eastern European ethnic revivalism surged during the 1970s, the 1990s saw a parallel trend in the rhetoric of white Americans supposedly disadvantaged by their "Celtic," Scottish, Irish, and/or Scots-Irish ancestry.[12] Popular Appalachian fiction folded into a larger discourse about ethnic whiteness that drew upon and fed readers' ambivalence. On the one hand, readers embraced whiteness as safe; on the other hand, readers rejected whiteness as generic and incapable of offering a grounded identity. Neo–Gilded Age folk-life festivals, "Highland games," radio programs, scholarly texts, and movie adaptations of novels set in the southeastern mountains drew upon and constructed ideas of Scottish, Scots-Irish, Celtic, or other ethnicity-based constructions of race.[13] Scholars, commentators, and white ethnic celebrants combined reclamation of ethnic heritage with a spatial component that collapsed personal ethnic disadvantage with regional discrimination and turned a blind eye to class formation. Examples include writings as diverse as "redneck" manifestos like Britney Bultman's *Redneck Heaven* (1996) and monographs such as Grady

McWhiney's *Cracker Culture* (1988). While these particular examples linked ethnic revivalism and *southern* sectional identity, many texts designated southern Appalachia as the cultural, historical, and biological homeplace of Celtic, Scottish, and Scots-Irish descendants in the United States. American readers' reactions to best-selling novels set in Appalachia occasionally verged upon a kind of blood-and-soil nationalism grounded in readers' enchantment with America's supposedly white rural Anglo-Saxon and Celtic essence. Late-twentieth-century celebrations of Celtic, Scots-Irish, southern, and Appalachian heritage, nourished by popular fiction, increasingly followed a neo-conservative logic in which the embrace of race colored as white could be rewritten as ethnic expression, not racism.

Fox and the Not-Quite-White Whites in Appalachia

Writers of antebellum travelogues commented upon a wide variety of activities and peoples in the southern mountain region, including industrial enterprises and slavery.[14] After the Civil War, however, local-color writers and commentators constructed Appalachia as antislavery, homogeneously white, and primitively nonindustrial. Early local-color stories enacted a tourist's delight in unthreatening and simple white rural people living in a world that seemed remote from metropolitan life. In the 1880s, for example, Mary Noailles Murfree's quaint characters appealed to readers concerned with Anglo Saxon superiority and immigrants' seeming threat to the authority of WASPs.[15] The assumed whiteness of Appalachian characters often went unmentioned.

With the popularity of stories by John Fox Jr., beginning in the 1890s, came an important shift in the national construction of Appalachian regional character.[16] As industrialists began to secure mineral rights and build mines and railroads for the extraction of coal and iron, and as conflicts surrounding industrialization erupted into violence, some Americans began to see people living in Appalachia not as picturesque imaginative resources but as sometimes dangerous obstacles to the collection of natural resources. Now perceived as

partly threatening as opposed to wholly charming, mountain characters' racial status was up for question in new ways.

Fox, a member of a family of industrialists seeking its fortune in
coal in southern Kentucky and southwestern Virginia, was the most
successful author to provide early twentieth-century readers with an
opportunity to feel both great loss and great relief at the industrial
modernization of the mountaineers. His 1908 novel *The Trail of the
Lonesome Pine*, one of the most popular novels in the first quarter of
the twentieth century, describes the intervention of "civilization" in
a feud-ridden territory on the border of Kentucky and Virginia. Fox's
novel reconstructs the boom development in 1880s southwestern Virginia, taking as its primary setting the town to which the Fox family
had relocated: Big Stone Gap, referred to simply as "the Gap" in the
novel. The first visionary to arrive is protagonist John Hale, a young
mining engineer from the Bluegrass region of Kentucky. Hale meets
a precocious mountain child named June Tolliver and quickly finds
himself taken with her guileless charm. Their introduction initiates
a conventional love story founded on the meeting of two supposedly
incompatible, irreconcilable worlds. From the outset, the structural
demands of the romance novel's form require that the resolution of
Trail of the Lonesome Pine entail the consummation of Hale and June's
love. Before this outcome is possible, however, readers must experience both the titillation and the horror of June's transformation from
innocence to decadent refinement and Hale's transformation from
reserved sophistication and urbane professionalism to manly bold-
ness and near-animalism. Furthermore, the couple's union must first
be threatened by cousin Dave Tolliver's jealous hatred of Hale, by the
interloping "law and order" for which Hale stands, by the events of
the murderous Tolliver-Falin feud, and by June's regression into blind
loyalty to age-old family animosities.

Anxieties about the precise social and class make-up of Appalachian residents led to conflicting representations of mountain people
at the turn of the twentieth century. Elites desirous of attracting capital investments and, in the case of Berea College president William
Goodell Frost, wealthy donors, insisted upon the "possible value"
of mountain people thanks to their pure Anglo-Saxon racial ancestry. John Fox Jr., on the other hand, was not quite so sure about the

mountaineers' racial credentials. A Bluegrass Kentucky southerner and apologist for slavery, Fox thought of mountaineers as a "strange brown-eyed race" whose "prolific" nature was more disturbing than valuable to American prowess (qtd. in Wilson 13–14).[17] According to cultural historian Darlene Wilson, early drafts of Fox's work, including *Trail of the Lonesome Pine*, depicted mountain characters as Melungeons, or members of a "tri-racial isolate group"—part European, African American, and Native American.[18] In published versions, however, Fox capitulated to the assessments made by ac- quaintances who were agents for industrial capitalism, by his corre- spondent Frost, and by longtime fan Theodore Roosevelt who was then at the U.S. Civil Service Commission. All favored emphasizing the Anglo and British origins of mountaineers.[19]

Nonetheless, Fox's suspicion regarding Appalachians' racial in- tegrity seeps into his stories. As Wilson argues, "Fox's impact . . . has been to racialize the 'southern mountaineer' . . . as 'almost-white,' a regional 'other' historically bound to pathological, under-class status" (Wilson 8). In *Trail of the Lonesome Pine*, Fox tries to hew the line of dominant theories of scientific racists and industrialists regarding mountaineers' pure Anglo stock. Yet Fox places such proclamations in the monologues of minor characters like lawyer Sam Budd without ever quite embracing them himself. Instead, he returns repeatedly to racist cues to signal mountain characters' inferiority.

Whenever Fox intends the reader to interpret a character in *The Trail of the Lonesome Pine* in the most positive light possible, he refers to the character's pioneer spirit or blood, which becomes in the novel shorthand for white, Anglo-Saxon, American, and masculine virility. The brave members of the Volunteer Police Guard who bring law, order, and civilization to the Gap are newcomers, "strong, bold young men with the spirit of the pioneer and the birth, breeding and educa- tion of gentlemen" (98). "The pioneer spirit" in protagonist John Hale's blood "would still out" (41). All of the women and men who arrive in Big Stone Gap during the boom, including Hale, have blue eyes. Although June's eyes are on occasion described as "black" (178), they are usually "dark"—in contrast to her dangerous cousin Dave's "black" eyes. June is the only one of her mountain brethren to have blonde hair—always described as "gold" or "bronze" rather than blonde, which has the effect of associating her with natural treasures and of tinting her hair darker than the yellow implied by "blonde." June's "brown" hand initially underscores her wildness although there is no mention of the color of her skin once she begins her education (21). June is a wild creature, tamed. The extent of her capacity for domestication relies on the degree to which Sam Budd's theories about the origins of the mountaineer are true. Are mountain people of good blood but poor environment? Can they learn, like June, to be refined and wear fashionable clothing? Part of the explanation for June's special ability to rise above the status of her birth is biological. The narrator directly states, "The Tollivers were of good blood" (101). For Fox, "good blood" had a particular history; like the Foxes, the Tollivers "had come from Eastern Virginia," further testimony to their worthiness. Finally, and tellingly for Fox's usually submerged ideological commitments, the narrator's testament to June's venerable lineage is that "the original Tolliver had been a slave-owner" (101).

The contest between savagery and civilization in the novel reaches a climax in the trial of June's uncle, Bad Rufe Tolliver. Fox represents "objective" commitment to law and order over personal affiliation as the defining and most necessary feature of civilization. The now-sophisticated mountain lass June must choose between loyalty to clan (which the book claims mountaineers inherited from their primitive Scottish ancestors) and the impartiality of "modern" justice. Just as the blue-eyed, flaxen-haired, rosy-cheeked doll that Hale gives June symbolizes the "outer world" and represents a brighter future for June in refined society, the conflict between savagery and civilization comes down to the power of "the black eyes of Rufe Tolliver and the blue eyes of John Hale." June's ability to choose the blue eyes of Hale proves that some mountain people have enough "good blood" to overcome their environment and surpass the destinies of their black-eyed neighbors and kin.

Ultimately Fox's novel both praises mountain potential and purity and advocates benevolent imperialism to save mountaineers from their degenerate selves, as June had been saved by her education in supposedly aristocratic Bluegrass Kentucky and New York. Little wonder Fox's novels appealed to "strenuous life" advocate Theodore Roosevelt, who embraced stories by Fox, Mary Noailles Murfree, and Owen Wister, frequently recognized as the author of the first

Western. Roosevelt's preoccupation with "the strenuous life" was not merely a concern with masculinity and "overcivilization" but was also intricately bound up in his belief in the racial dimensions of civilization. Perhaps in part due to his desire to offer leadership to and demonstrate dominance over "primitive" peoples, Roosevelt frequently wrote to praise Fox on his most recent publication and to hail Fox's contributions to American literature and to the nation itself.[20]

In part due to his relationship with Roosevelt, Fox hungered to participate in the expansionist Spanish-American War when it broke out in 1898 and eventually secured a coveted position as a *Harper's Weekly* magazine correspondent in Cuba. On a publicity tour upon his arrival home, Fox explicitly linked for his readers the quest for empire abroad with the quest for industrial domination in the Appalachian mountain range. In response to the interviewer's loaded question about "the capacity of the Cubans for self-government," Fox called the Cubans he had observed "an irresponsible lot." But, Fox noted, the "Cuban war was nothing in comparison with" his experience working for the industrialists' Volunteer Police Guard in putting down the rebellion of mountain outlaws who threatened industrial interests in Virginia ("Talk with John Fox, Jr." 3). Fox's linkage of Cuba with Appalachia allowed readers the impression that the mountain-born were as unruly, as exotic, and as questionably white as they thought the enemy in Cuba. His assertion suggested that Americans' experience with ruling unruly mountain people could be readily parlayed into the practiced governance of non-Americans of color.[21]

Popular Appalachia, Again

On the cusp of the twenty-first century, commentators began to remark upon a return to the Gilded Age in the United States. Extreme disparities in wealth approached late nineteenth-century levels and unchecked corporate power again inspired calls for greater government intervention. The blatant imperial aspirations of the 1898 efforts to bring nations of brown people under U.S. sway returned full-force in the mid-twentieth century, although attention had shifted from the Caribbean and the Philippines to Southeast Asia in the 1950s and

1960s, to South America in the 1970s and 1980s, and to the Middle East beginning in the 1940s and intensifying in the 1990s. Surging fears of alien immigration belied a new but equally virulent nativism. U.S. readers turned once more to Appalachia, as it was constructed in the country's geographic imaginary, as a reassuring vision of a national homeplace. The popularity of fiction set in the region soared.

Fiction set in Appalachia provided turn-of-the-twenty-first-century readers with a sampling of the ethnically tinged difference of characters perceived primarily as safely white—a kind of multiculturalism "lite"—without confronting them with the unresolved racial conflicts that they associated with black-white and immigrant-native relations. By the close of the twentieth century nearly 40 percent of all Appalachian residents lived within a metropolitan area.[22] In defiance of this demographic reality, many readers turned to Appalachian-set fiction as a refuge from postmodern society. By configuring Appalachia as rural and white, the novels offered their primarily white readers the possibility of retreat from the diversity of races, creeds, and nationalities often associated with urban places—even as they reassured readers about the value of nonthreatening and assimilable cultural differences. Anglo-American fantasies of nongeneric whiteness and white American desires for exploring their own nonracialized ethnic identity helped fuel the renewed popularity of fiction set in Appalachia.[23]

White characters whose difference is described in terms of ethnic particularity populate the two recent novels set in Appalachia under consideration here: Charles Frazier's *Cold Mountain* and Silas House's *Clay's Quilt*. Both novels draw upon and reinforce visions of Appalachia that appealed to readers seeking "down home," "salt of the earth" white innocence.

Cold Mountain (1998) spent sixty-one weeks on the *New York Times* hardback best-sellers list and twenty-nine weeks on the *New York Times* paperback best-sellers list. By the summer of 2005, the novel had sold well over a million copies in hardcover and over a million in Vintage paperback. Although rarely identified in the popular press as "Appalachian fiction," *Cold Mountain* emerges from and reiterates a number of Appalachian tropes, from fiddlers to corn whiskey drinkers, to hog-skinning, ballad-singing, bare-footed, reclusive natives. Frazier peoples the novel with conventionally craven poor white trash southerners, mountain laze-a-bouts of the Snuffy Smith variety—"[a]ll they wished to do was hunt and eat and lay up all night drunk, making music" (287)—and ignorant but noble, simple, God-fearing, self-sufficient mountain people living off the land "pure and apart" from society (279).

Frazier depicts the small Blue Ridge Mountain town to which the heroine Ada Monroe and her minister father move as an isolated and humble retreat, "a good place to hide" from the materialism and snobbery of Old South Charleston (36). The journey of Inman, a deserter from the Confederate army, repeats this movement of escape from the corrupt, slave-owning lowland Old South with its ugly flat land and "mean towns" toward the purportedly slaveless, "thinly settled" mountain ideal of home and "homeland." The community of Cold Mountain, North Carolina, represents simplicity, family, and intimacy with the land.

As a Civil War novel, *Cold Mountain* rewrites the reason for the war, asserting (as did John Fox's 1903 novel, *The Little Shepherd of Kingdom Come*) that the war was not about slavery. Without offering an alternative rationale, Inman ridicules the notion that "the Federals are willing to die to set loose slaves" (275). Inman, like many characters and historians before him, describes mountain residents' relationship to the war as distinct from that of lowland southerners' and repeats assertions of mountain people's desire for self-sufficiency and seclusion (85, 261). He explains, perhaps justifies, mountaineers' participation in the war as resistance to "every feature" of "the big cities" of the North (275). In Frazier's novel, Appalachia represents justice and egalitarianism in the face of imperialist northern power.[24] Readers' identification with Appalachian characters enabled them to sidestep questions about their own relationship to U.S. imperialism. The supposed racial innocence of the mountains is underlined by Inman's easy childhood friendship with the Cherokee boy Swimmer, who serves (as is conventional for Indian characters in Westerns) both as Inman's teacher and as proof of Inman's lack of racist prejudice and his spiritual connection to place and the past. The dwindling number of enslaved or escaped African Americans Inman encounters as he approaches home further underscores Cold Mountain residents' racial innocence.

Although whites populate the Appalachia of Frazier's novel, several distinctions mark mountain characters' whiteness. Throughout the novel, Frazier weaves in descriptions of the mountaineers' purported "Celtic" ancestry. The missionary Reverend Monroe interprets one of the locals as someone without any religion "other than a worship of animals and trees and rocks and weather." Monroe concludes that "Esco was some old relic Celt . . . ; what few thoughts Esco might have would more than likely be in Gaelic" (57). Frazier indicates that Monroe's opinions about locals are often unreliable and condescending, yet in other places the narrator reinforces the notion that Celtic ways have been transmitted through generations. The locals' whiskey "differed only in minor particulars from the usquebaugh and poteen of their Celt forebears" (342). A local boy performs a "dance of great mystery; ancient Celtic jerk and spasm such as might have been performed after any number of defeats in battle against Roman and Jute, Saxon and Angle and Brit" (333). A Celt here is explicitly contrasted with normative whiteness of Romans, Germanic Jutes, Saxons, Angles, and Brits.

Frazier also distinguishes mountain people's brand of whiteness by both twinning them with and contrasting them to Indians. When Reverend Monroe uses the word "mission" in reference to his purpose as a preacher, the locals take offense because they believe that Monroe perceives his congregation to be composed of "benighted savages." Cold Mountain residents had "put up cash money to send missionaries among true savages, folks they pictured in skins of various dim colors living in locales they conceived of as infinitely more remote and heathen than their own" (79). The narrator also describes Charleston residents' belief that mountaineers are "but one step more advanced in their manner of living than tribes of vagrant savages" (55). Although such "outsiders" decry mountaineers' hopeless ignorance, they envy mountaineers' supposed freedom from material desire made possible by their primitive way of life.

The novel reinforces the purported distance between mountain people and Charleston outsiders in racial, social, and chronological terms. This insistence on mountain particularity enables the novel to proffer its readers a lesson in cultural relativism, tolerance, and admiration of mountain difference as Ada and Monroe learn to appreciate mountain residents' simple existence without "need nor wish to travel"

(244).²⁵ At the same time, *Cold Mountain's* construction of worthy, humble Appalachian people caught up in a whirlwind not of their own making enables its readers to identify with/as the rooted and innocent victims of outsiders' misunderstandings about their homeland rather than view themselves as agents of imperial power in the world. Readers could imagine themselves, like Cold Mountain residents, as desiring only the "right to exist unmolested somewhere" (85).

Clay's Quilt takes the romance and fascination with Appalachian whiteness to a new level of ubiquity and centrality. While the novel did not make the *New York Times* or *Publishers Weekly* best-sellers lists, it was a surprise hit whose success with Algonquin Books led Ballantine, a division of Random House, to purchase the paperback rights to the novel.²⁶ Ballantine released *Clay's Quilt* as a "Ballantine Reader's Circle" trade paperback that appended questions for discussion and an interview with the author. The novel received widespread praise in *Booklist* and in newspapers across the country, including *USA Today*.²⁷

The novel is set in fictional Crow County in southeastern Kentucky. Its protagonist, young Clay Sizemore, is a young man who begins to feel an emptiness in his daily routine and a yearning for something he cannot quite name. Falling in love with Alma, who initially resists his charms, and learning more about his mother, Anneth, and her untimely death when he was four years old satisfy his free-floating yearning. House's novel includes major touchstones of Appalachian fiction, including coal mining, which is Clay's occupation, and fiddling, Alma's calling. It displays the Appalachian icons of patriotism, Pentecostalism, and clannishness and showcases the obligatory mountain activities of boozing, gambling, shotgun hunting, clogging, quilting, and gospel singing. The novel exhibits aspects of the previous century's local-color writing in other ways as well. The narrator explains that driving to Free Creek, Kentucky, is like "driving back in time" (House 106). In the current style for regional prose, House depicts dialect without phonetic representation, relying instead on vocabulary, phrasing, and grammatical construction. For example, Clay, referring to the prospect of Alma's having a child, states that she is not "fixing to bear a youngun" (103).

House's romantic, nostalgic vision of Appalachia is set within a strikingly white and silvery landscape. In the remembered scene of

Clay's mother, Anneth's, death on a wintry night many years ago, five travelers move through a world of whiteness. The car windshield is frosted, with young Clay's breath forming a "white fist" upon it. The highway and cliffs are covered with snow and ice, as are the pine trees with limbs "like jagged bones with damp, yellow ends bright against the whiteness." Anneth's white scarf, which she wraps around Clay's frostbit hands "like a bandage," becomes "a fat white ball" (1–4). The first and penultimate chapters emphasize winter whiteness, with "a light dusting of fine, sugarlike snow" and spring petals "caked with ice" from the last freeze (287). Two bloody scenes with snowy backdrops bookend the novel. In between, July burns "hot and white"—a change in temperature but not color (12). Throughout *Clay's Quilt*, House dwells upon white light (276), a white glow (284), white leaves (267), a looming white cross (258), snow like wet paper (260), snowflakes (245), and more snow (247).

Toni Morrison asserts that whiteness in canonical white literature figures as "mute, meaningless, unfathomable, pointless, frozen, veiled, curtained, dreaded, senseless, implacable." Snow is a "wasteland of unmeaning, unfathomable whiteness" (58–59). Gendering its usage, Patricia Yaeger, in *Dirt and Desire: Southern Women's Writing 1930–1990*, states that "in southern women's fiction . . . white is always the color of danger" (xv). Its ubiquity signals a crisis of whiteness. "Uncanny" white surfaces and "white detritus" provide an "almost present structure of feeling that has not yet emerged as a structure of thought." Whiteness is so pervasive that it is "as if these writers are hyperconscious about trying to thematize something about whiteness that passively resists articulation" (20, 105).

In House's novel, snow is what Yaeger would call "so 'natural' a part of this environment that it is nearly invisible as a signifier" (105). Whiteness seems to function both in ways that Yaeger identifies with canonical men and those she identifies with noncanonical women writers. White is a signal of implacable danger. The most violent and bloody scenes of the novel occur in what Morrison refers to as landscapes of "frozen whiteness" (59). The dreaded conflicts are pointless and unnecessary, in Morrison's language of whiteness. At the same time, white floats unpredictably and uncontrollably through *Clay's Quilt* just as Yaeger says it does through women's writing: white leaves, snow that darts into Clay's collar, where it does not belong, and snow that sticks like wet paper appear randomly in the narrative. This unruly, uncanny whiteness is suggestive of what Yaeger might classify as a near-successful attempt to thematize the romance with whiteness that lays at the heart of popular fiction set in Appalachia.

Whiteness, though seemingly all pervasive, is also marked, or threatened, in curious ways in the novel. In the opening scene, the man driving the car carrying Clay and his mother predicts they will not make it down the mountain without wrecking and dying. At this point in the scene "black trees and gray cliffs" break or disfigure the white landscape and imagery. The marring of whiteness begins in other ways as well. One of the travelers' lipstick is "smudged across her straight white teeth" (House 5). "Dead vines" wrap the "white guardrail" and create "brown places through the thick snow." From that night on, Clay "sometimes dreamed of blood on the snow, blood so thick that it ran slow like syrup and lay in stripes across the whiteness, as if someone had dashed out a bucket of paint" (6–7). As the novel progresses, black coal dust threatens to smother clothes, faces, bodies, and trucks.

Against this landscape of whiteness and disfiguring, grimy threats to whiteness, House evokes characters that are visually white. The icicles, Anneth notes, "look like the faces of people we know": Clay's Aunt Easter, his Uncle Gabe, and the president (3). Yet phenotypically white characters have hidden ethnic identities that, as in late nineteenth-century regional writing, explain personality through bloodline. Clay is "filled with a wild blood that he was always conscious of. . . . Maybe it was the mixture of his Irish and Cherokee blood" (65). His mother explains, "You know that my mommy was full of Cherokee blood and from this I have always been filled up with life" (119–20). Clay's surname, Sizemore, is one of many popularly linked to Melungeon ancestry.

House attributes not only individual character but also Appalachian culture to not-quite-white ethnic strains. Clay traces indigenous mountain music to Irish roots, referring to the ballad "Barbara Allen" as the product of Ireland (95) and to a fiddle tune as "something that Clay's Irish ancestors might have played as they danced about these mountains celebrating their newfound freedoms" (97). These variations on whiteness are not presented as threats or blights, like black dust or blood on snow. They are indicators of unpredictable but pleasing difference, romanticized ethnicities. *Clay's Quilt*, then, proffers an inchoate grappling with these two interpretations of marked whiteness. Whiteness is dreaded implacable sameness. Yet alternatives to whiteness both offer relief from monotony and are fraught with peril.

Whether Appalachian distinctiveness is attributed to "Celtic" blood, as in Frazier's *Cold Mountain*, or to the protagonist's Irish and Cherokee roots, as in House's *Clay's Quilt*, recent trade novels attempt to describe the largely economic and social differences of white Appalachian residents in terms of variations on whiteness. Even when all the characters are "white," race and racial alterity are undeniably present. As did the fiction at the turn of the last century, popular novels set in Appalachia promised an identifiable rural hinterland as synonymous with innocent white nationhood. In this guise, an Appalachian-identified American nation could see itself as simple and benevolent. The novels provided white readers with spaces of nonthreatening exoticism (the virtual space of the novel, the imagined space of the region) that staved off fear of the homogenization and standardization of postmodern landscapes and hegemony. Inhabiting these spaces allowed readers to appreciate, and simultaneously anticipate the need to control nonwhite elements.

Post-1990 regional fiction promoted cultural sensitivity and appreciation of the Appalachian region. The fiction suggested to some readers the values of tolerance and respect for group difference. It also allowed some readers to criticize the presumptive superiority of metropolitan cosmopolitanism and the presumptive inferiority of places where capital accumulation has failed due to uneven development.[28] The revaluation of Appalachian distinctiveness as a homology for the authentic rural roots of the nation, however, had a cost. Whatever the novels' delight in nonthreatening difference and authenticity, they reinforced a spatialized notion of virtue, where family, home, faith, and true Americanness reside primarily with simple (mostly) white country folk. Fiction of this tenor served to reassure readers of a soothingly safe ancestral home for the nation imagined as white community. This imagination of nation both naturalized and satiated white longing for safe homogeneity and belonging without acknowledging that such a selective nationalism required the active exclusion of other races.

At the same time, an ethnicized vision of Appalachia (and America) also promised assimilation without annihilation of difference. Novels constructed the ethnic particularity of Appalachia as that of "pure" Anglo-Saxon America whose blandness was tempered by the masculine energies of Cherokee, Celtic, Scottish, or Scots-Irish blood. Thanks to the assumption of the historical, submerged influences of those peoples upon American identity and culture, this vision of a "not-quite-white" Appalachia helped explain and celebrate Appalachian alterity without dismantling the dominant understanding of the region as essentially white.

Beginning in the 1980s, celebrations of Celtic, Scottish, southern, and Appalachian heritages gained considerable momentum. A wave of interest in Scots-Irish genealogy inspired library workshops, "heritage tours" of Ireland and Scotland, "Scots-Irish Month" in Georgia and South Carolina, a cultural heritage route in Maine, and simplistic radio and newspaper articles that attributed George W. Bush's 2004 reelection to voters' Scots-Irish cultural traits.[29] Most treatments of Celtic and Scots-Irish Americans emphasized their status as "underdogs" in a way that rendered class exploitation in terms of ethnic discrimination.[30] Claiming an ethnic version of whiteness has allowed many Americans to identify as victims rather than oppressors. Paradoxically, this very claim to victimization has been a critical component of white Americans' pursuit of global leadership and domination.[31] Similarly, fiction readers' willingness to romanticize and identify with a "victimized" white Appalachia—yet simultaneously insist upon the privileges of whiteness—likely bolstered an aggressive American imperialism undergirded by assumptions of innocence.[32]

In each case, in fact, novels that imagine nation as white community, novels that imagine Appalachia as ethnically tinged, and novels that combine the two to imagine white America as embattled and oppressed have served as models for imperialist political agendas. The vision of Appalachians as infused with the "wild blood" of Celts or Indians helped rationalize "Appalachia-as-*governed-by*-America," a ward in need of protection. Novels that indulge in such a cultural evolutionism model, wherein less developed societies deserve the intervention and aid of a benevolent civilization, have suggested the appropriateness of benign imperialism at home *and* abroad. Appalachia-as-ward has promoted the United States as a nation experienced in legitimate governance over culturally and ethnically defined others.[33]

The ethnically tinged whiteness of Appalachia characters has also suggested to readers a "colors-of-Benetton" multiculturalism, a comforting vision of American diversity. The ideal of the United States as a diverse multicultural society in turn legitimated its project of white imperialism in the guise of overseas peacekeeper for diverse nations and divided countries.

Finally, the novels' vision of America as homologous with an ethnic white Appalachia allowed high-middlebrow white readers to project themselves imaginatively into the position of an embattled minority. Particularly following the events of September 11, 2001, these readers' identification with mountain characters may have encouraged them to feel misjudged by outsiders and justified in protecting themselves from racialized outside threats. High-middlebrow white readers of fiction set in Appalachia could sympathize with characters from a misunderstood region, since they, like Cold Mountain residents, merely desired the "right to exist unmolested somewhere."

NOTES

The epigraph appears in Frost 315, 318. Appalachian scholar Allen Batteau argues that Frost, president of Berea College in Kentucky from 1889 to 1920, played a central role in defining the Appalachian region in the popular imagination due to his frequent and eloquent fund-raising efforts in national periodicals (64).

1. See Elliott's discussion of late-nineteenth-century literature's interest in "group-based difference" (xiii) and its representation of "rural culture" as "authentic but not threatening in its difference" (xxi).

2. See Frost 313, 312, 316; Silber; and Whisnant.

3. See Wilson. Racial vocabularies were not simply more "ready-to-hand" but also less threatening to Americans' preferred understanding of their nation as one without class stratification. See Lang's discussion of the ways in which "Americans displace the reality of class into discourses of race, gender, ethnicity, and other similarly 'locked-in' categories of individual identity" (6) as a consequence of Americans' anxieties surrounding the task of "naming . . . and containing the effects of class difference" (4).

4. See Blee and Billings 119.

5. Frost 319. See Greeson; Jacobson, *Barbarian Virtues*.

6. William H. Gates Sr., father of Microsoft mogul Bill Gates, referred in a *Sojourners Magazine* article to "the first Gilded Age" and to the present moment, when, he argued, "the gap between the very rich and everyone else is once again at historic levels." See Gates and Collins 36–39. Examples of more predictable liberal comments equating the present moment to the Gilded Age include media scholars McChesney and Nichols's 2003 description of the current era as one "when the influence of corporations on government decision-making rivals the power of the trusts in the Gilded Age." See also Goodman; the *Nation* editors' assertion that we are "[i]n a gilded age" in "Bush's Gulf of Credibility"; Dionne; Thompson; and Walsh. Juliet Schor, an economist at Harvard University, states, "Whether measured by wages, income or wealth, for 25 years the share of the privileged has increased, and everyone else (a roughly 80 percent majority) has become relatively worse off. We are truly in a second Gilded Age" (in Collins, Leondar-Wright, and Sklar). See also Foote 4.

7. Cheng discusses the premise that "modern and contemporary cultures—especially First World cultures—are increasingly marked by an anxiety over authentic cultural identity" as a means to "replace . . . seemingly vacated identities" (3).

8. The term "high middlebrow" is from Lutz and Collins, who derive it from the hierarchies constructed by Bourdieu, Levine, and Smith.

9. For his discussion of the ways in which nationalism necessarily posits a homogeneous "community" in the face of heterogeneity, see Anderson. Additional recent popular trade fiction releases set in the Appalachian region include Gail Godwin's *Evensong* (1999) and *Father's Melancholy Daughter* (1991) and two Oprah Book Club selections, Robert Morgan's *Gap Creek* (1999) and Gwyn Hyman Rubio's *Icy Sparks* (2001). Mass marketed popular fiction set in the region includes Sharyn McCrumb's East Tennessee ballad novel series and David Baldacci's *Wish You Well* (2001). Many of Lee Smith's novels enjoy continued sales success and popularity with readers, although no single Appalachian-set novel reached best-seller lists. The first novel in the Christian-themed frontier series *Spirit of Appalachia* was released in 1997. The above novels are only the most visible and financially successful of Appalachian-set fiction. Gretchen Laska's novel *The Midwife's Tale* (Dial, 2003) and balladeer Sheila Kay Adams's *My Old True Love* (Algonquin, 2004) are but two examples of the well-received Appalachian-set fiction released by smaller presses. Alongside these fictional works are a number of nonfiction releases by major publishing houses, including Bill Bryson's best-seller, *A Walk in the Woods* (1998), NPR personality Noah Adams's *Far Appalachia* (2001), and Homer Hickam's best-selling memoir, *Rocket Boys* (1998). Academic and small presses have published memoirs, including *Creeker* (1999) by Linda Scott Derosier, *Appalachian Mountain Girl* (1998) by Rhoda B. Warren, and *Cogan's Woods* (2001) by Ron Ellis. All these fiction and nonfiction releases, plus a spate of children's books set in Appalachia, indicate broad audience interest in Appalachian settings at the turn of the twenty-first century.

10. See Menand; Lovato; and Shorris. California's Proposition 187 passed by a margin of three to two on November 8, 1994. The measure was intended to deny

social services, including education, welfare, and nonemergency medical treatment, to undocumented immigrants and would have required education and health officials to report suspected illegal immigrants to immigration authorities. See Ayres, "Court Blocks New Rule" and "Anti-Alien Sentiment"; and Dunn.

11. See Greeson.

12. See Jacobson, *Whiteness of a Different Color*; and Webb.

13. See Goldfarb and Satterwhite, "'That's What They're All Singing About.'" A musical written by John Anderson, *On Eagle's Wing*, opened in 2004 with the promise to do for the Scots-Irish what *Riverdance* did for the Irish.

14. See, for example, "A Winter in the South" by Porte Crayon (the nom de plume of David Hunter Strother), published in multiple installments in *Harper's New Monthly Magazine* between 1857 and 1858.

15. See Satterwhite, "Reading Craddock."

16. Fox's first mountain story, "A Mountain Europa," appeared in the *Century* in 1892.

17. Fox used the phrases in letters to his brother James, Sept. 1882, his father, n.d., and his brother Oliver, 16 Feb. 1883, Fox Family Papers.

18. Anthropologists consider the Melungeons one of many small groups of "tri-racial isolates" in the eastern half of the United States. The largest concentration of Melungeons is thought to be in Tennessee along the Virginia border. In 1994, Brent Kennedy's influential and controversial study *The Melungeons* argued that Melungeon ancestry included Portuguese, Spanish, and Turkish people as well as Moors, Jews, Native Americans, Africans, and other Europeans. His book sparked widespread interest in Melungeon identity and genealogical research.

19. See Darlene Wilson 28. Letters from Theodore Roosevelt to John Fox Jr., 14 June 1894 and 23 Oct. 1894, Fox Family Papers.

20. See Wilson, 25. Theodore Roosevelt and John Fox shared an interest in the "strenuous life" that would invigorate American manhood and nationhood and commended each other's writings as advancing their shared ideology. Roosevelt wrote from the Civil Service Commission as "a fellow-Harvard man" to praise Fox on the first installment of his second mountain story, "A Cumberland Vendetta." See York 72–74, 98, 101, 104; letter from Roosevelt to Fox, 4 June 1894, Fox Family Papers. In 1908, Roosevelt expressed his admiration for Fox's latest novel, *The Trail of the Lonesome Pine*. Fox wanted to join Roosevelt's Rough Riders in Cuba and was disappointed when Roosevelt invited him only as journalist. Fox praised Roosevelt's *Winning of the West* (implied in a letter from Roosevelt to Fox, 23 Oct. 1894, Fox Family Papers).

21. The South after the Civil War, Greeson argues, served the nation as a means of practicing both the rhetoric of and the skills for governing a subordinated territory. The South's new material subordination (versus its previous conceptual subordination) "facilitated a major transformation of U.S. nationalist ideology in the last decades of the nineteenth century—from the ideal of a republican nation defined by consensus, to the emergent imaginary of an imperial nation rightly aggrandized by its superior

strength." Having such a visible colony enabled U.S. cultural producers to envision the nation as an imperial power on par with European colonial giants (272–73).

Fox's white imperialist understanding of the world continued to inform the assignments he sought and the novels he formulated while participating in overseas ventures. In 1904, Fox traveled to Japan to cover the Russo-Japanese War. During his stopover in Hawaii, Fox found himself offended by the mix of races there. The title of one of his installments from the front, "Trail of the Saxon," and his comment upon boarding a British ship bound for the United States suggest his level of race consciousness. He and his companions were immensely grateful to be finally able to wear "the white man's clothes and [eat] his food and [drink] his drink." Despite the United States' alliance with the Japanese, when Fox encountered a Russian prisoner he immediately identified with the captive, who had "skin like ours" as opposed to the "yellow faces" of his nation's allies. Fox sympathized with the Russian for the humiliation he must feel to come suddenly upon "white men" like himself. Whatever his government's commitments, Fox observed, "[b]lood is thicker than water." Fox began planning *The Trail of the Lonesome Pine* while in Japan, and his racist ideology regarding rightful global power underpins the best-selling novel. See York 183, 210.

22. See Satterwhite, "Seeing Appalachian Cities."

23. The renewed popularity of fiction set in Appalachia was part of a broader return of interest in regional fiction nationally. As during the local-color movement, the prevalence of regional fiction was due not only to reader interest but also to changes in the publishing industry that led to a demand for new high-middlebrow authors. During the late 1800s, the publishing trend, so welcoming of debut authors, was driven by the need for short fiction unencumbered by new international copyright laws to fill the pages of budding middlebrow and highbrow magazines like the *Atlantic Monthly* and the *Century*. During the late 1900s, debut authors found entry into publishing via the trade paperback format—popular with publishers because of its greater profit margins and embraced by the burgeoning book club movement. The larger, handsome trade format allowed publishers to risk releases by unknown authors whose products would not have been profitable in hardback or mass market paperback. See Satterwhite, *Locally Colored* 156–60.

24. I am indebted to Barbara Ellen Smith for her assistance with the formulation of this point.

25. For Ada and Monroe's initial prejudgment and growing understanding of mountain residents, see Frazier 55, 79.

26. Brodart Company.

27. Leber; Minzesheimer; Eyman; Meiman.

28. See customer reviews of *Clay's Quilt* on the web sites of Internet booksellers Amazon.com and Barnes and Noble.

29. See Satterwhite, "'That's What They're All Singing About.'"

30. See Jacobson, *Whiteness of a Different Color*; and Bultman's paean to Celtic America, *Redneck Heaven*. Webb's *Born Fighting* (2004) shares with other

white ethnic revivalist treatises a complaint against perceived marginalization by WASPs.

31. Historian Patricia Limerick has shown that white Americans' claims to unfair persecution often accompany their pursuit of personal and group advancement, including in the midst of colonial and imperial conquest.

32. See Satterwhite, "'That's What They're All Singing About.'"

33. See Greeson.

Works Cited

Anderson, Benedict. *Imagined Communities: Reflections on the Origin and Spread of Nationalism.* New York: Verso, 1991.

Ayres, B. Drummon, Jr. "Anti-Alien Sentiment Spreading In Wake of California's Measure." *New York Times* 4 Dec. 1994, late ed., sec. 1: 1.

———. "Court Blocks New Rule on Immigration." *New York Times* 17 Nov. 1994, late ed.: A16.

Batteau, Allen. *The Invention of Appalachia.* Tucson: U of Arizona P, 1990.

Blee, Kathleen and Dwight Billings. "Where 'Bloodshed Is a Pastime': Mountain Feuds and Appalachian Stereotyping." *Confronting Appalachian Stereotypes: Backtalk from an American Region.* Ed. Dwight Billings, Gurney Norman, and Katherine Ledford. Lexington: UP of Kentucky, 1999.

Bourdieu, Pierre. *Distinction: A Social Critique of the Judgement of Taste.* Trans. Richard Nice. Cambridge: Harvard UP, 1984.

Brodart Company. "Algonquin Books." *GEMS* [industry newsletter]. 31 Mar. 2005 <http://www.gems.brodart.com/publishers/algonquin.htm>.

Bultman, Bethany. *Redneck Heaven: Portrait of a Vanishing Culture.* New York: Bantam, 1996.

"Bush's Gulf of Credibility." *Nation* 17 Feb. 2003: 4.

Cheng, Vincent J. *Inauthentic: The Anxiety over Culture and Identity.* New Brunswick: Rutgers UP, 2004.

Collins, Chuck, Betsy Leondar-Wright, and Holly Sklar, eds. *Shifting Fortunes: The Perils of the Growing American Wealth Gap.* Boston: United for a Fair Economy, 1999.

Deliverance. Dir. John Boorman. Warner Bros., 1972.

Dionne, E. J., Jr. "Revolution in Reverse: In Solidifying Its Power, the GOP Is Loosening Its Ethics." *Washington Post* 19 Nov. 2004: A29.

Dunn, Ashley. "In California, the Numbers Add Up to Anxiety." *New York Times* 30 Oct. 1994, late ed., sec. 4: 3.

Elliott, Michael A. *The Culture Concept: Writing and Difference in the Age of Realism.* Minneapolis: U of Minnesota P, 2002.

Eyman, Scott. "Mountain-Style Survival." *Palm Beach Post,* 5 Aug. 2001: 8I.

Foote, Stephanie. *Regional Fictions: Culture and Identity in Nineteenth-Century American Literature.* Madison: U of Wisconsin P, 2001.

Fox Family Papers. Special Collections and Archives. Margaret I. King Library, University of Kentucky.

Fox, John, Jr. *The Little Shepherd of Kingdom Come.* New York: Scribner's, 1903.

———. *A Mountain Europa; A Cumberland Vendetta; The Last Stetson.* New York: Scribner's, 1912.

———. *The Trail of the Lonesome Pine.* New York: Scribner's, 1908.

———. "The Trail of the Saxon." *Following the Sun-Flag: A Vain Pursuit through Manchuria.* New York: Scribner's, 1905.

Frazier, Charles. *Cold Mountain.* New York: Vintage, 1998.

Frost, William Goodell. "Our Contemporary Ancestors in the Southern Mountains." *Atlantic Monthly* (Mar. 1899): 311–19.

Gates, William H., Sr., and Chuck Collins. "Tax the Rich?" *Sojourners Magazine* (Jan.–Feb. 2003): 36–39.

Goldfarb, Michael. "A Southern State of Mind." WBUR, Boston. Inside Out. 7 Nov. 2004 <http://www.insideout.org/documentaries/southernstate>.

Goodman, Ellen. "Taxing Our Children." *Boston Globe* 13 Mar. 2005. D11.

Greeson, Jennifer Rae. *The Figure of the South and the Imagination of Nation in the United States.* Diss. Yale University, 2001.

House, Silas. *Clay's Quilt.* New York: Ballantine, 2002.

Jacobson, Matthew Frye. *Barbarian Virtues: The United States Encounters Foreign Peoples at Home and Abroad.* New York: Hill and Wang, 2000.

———. *Whiteness of a Different Color: European Immigrants and the Alchemy of Race.* Cambridge: Harvard UP, 1998.

Karon, Jan. *At Home in Mitford.* New York: Penguin, 1994.

Kennedy, N. Brent. *The Melungeons: The Resurrection of a Proud People: An Untold Story of Ethnic Cleansing in America.* Macon: Mercer UP, 1994.

Kingsolver, Barbara. *Prodigal Summer.* New York: Harper Collins, 2000.

Lang, Amy Schrager. *The Syntax of Class: Writing Inequality in Nineteenth-Century America.* Princeton: Princeton UP, 2003.

Leber, Michele. "Clay's Quilt." *Booklist* 97.13 (1 Mar. 2001): 1226.

Levine, Lawrence W. *Highbrow/Lowbrow: The Emergence of Cultural Hierarchy in America.* Cambridge: Harvard UP, 1988.

Limerick, Patricia Nelson. *The Legacy of Conquest: The Unbroken Past of the American West.* New York: Norton, 1987.

Lovato, Robert. "Fear of a Brown Planet." *Nation* 28 June 2004: 17–21.

Lutz, Catherine, and Jane Collins. *Reading National Geographic.* Chicago: U of Chicago P, 1993.

McChesney, Robert W., and John Nichols. "Media Democracy's Moment." *Nation* 24 Feb. 2003: 16+.

McWhiney, Grady. *Cracker Culture: Celtic Ways in the Old South.* Tuscaloosa: U of Alabama P, 1988.

Meiman, Karen. "Author Dispels Appalachian Stereotypes in Book." *Kentucky Post* [Covington] 3 Dec. 2001, BC cycle.

Menand, Louis. "Patriot Games: The New Nativism of Samuel P. Huntington." *New Yorker* 17 May 2004: 92–98.

Minzesheimer, Bob. "House Letter-perfect with His First Novel." *USA Today* 19 Apr. 2001: 5D.

Morrison, Toni. *Playing in the Dark: Whiteness and the Literary Imagination.* Cambridge: Harvard UP, 1992.

Satterwhite, Emily. "Locally Colored: Popular Appalachian Fictions and Geographies of Reception." Diss. Emory University, 2005.

———. "Reading Craddock, Reading Murfree: Local Color, Authenticity, and Geographies of Reception." *American Literature* 78.1 (2006): 59–88.

———. "Seeing Appalachian Cities." *Appalachia: Social Context Past and Present.* Ed. Phillip Obermiller and Michael Maloney. Dubuque: Kendall/Hunt, 2002. 104–7.

———. "'That's What They're All Singing About': Appalachian Heritage, Celtic Pride, and American Nationalism at the 2003 Smithsonian Folklife Festival." *Appalachian Journal* 32:3 (2005): 302–38.

Shorris, Earl. "A Nation of WASPs?" *Nation* 31 May 2004: 21–22.

Silber, Nina. "'What Does America Need So Much as Americans?': Race and Northern Reconciliation with Southern Appalachia, 1870–1900." *Appalachians and Race: The Mountain South from Slavery to Segregation.* Ed. John Inscoe. Lexington: UP of Kentucky, 2001.

Smith, Barbara Herrnstein. "Contingencies of Value." *Critical Inquiry* 10.1 (1983): 1–35.

Strother, David Hunter [Porte Crayon]. "A Winter in the South." *Harper's Monthly* 16 (Jan. 1858): 167–83.

"A Talk with John Fox, Jr., Author and Correspondent." *Sentinel* 10 Dec. 1900: 3.

Thompson, Bob. "Sharing the Wealth?" *Washington Post Magazine* 13 Apr. 2003: W08.

Trigiani, Adriana. *Big Stone Gap.* New York, Random, 2000.

Walsh, Joan. "Plutocrats to the Rescue!" 15 Feb. 2001. Salon.com. 12 Apr. 2005 <http://archive.salon.com/politics/feature/2001/02/15/buffett>.

Webb, James. *Born Fighting: How the Scots-Irish Shaped America.* New York: Random, 2004.

Whisnant, David E. *All That Is Native and Fine: The Politics of Culture in an American Region.* Chapel Hill: U of North Carolina P, 1983.

Wilson, Darlene. "The Felicitous Convergence of Mythmaking and Capital Accumulation: John Fox Jr. and the Formation of An(Other) Almost-White American Underclass." *Journal of Appalachian Studies* 1.1 (1995): 5–44.

Yaeger, Patricia. *Dirt and Desire: Southern Women's Writing 1930–1990.* Chicago: U of Chicago P, 2000.

York, Bill. *John Fox, Jr., Appalachian Author.* Jefferson: McFarland, 2003.

The Threat to Whiteness: White Women's Marital Betrayals in Colonial Settings

SUZANNE LEONARD

The role of the white woman, and specifically the white wife as the cultural standard-bearer of her respective nation and protector/reproducer of the white race, has been tacitly fixed in the psyches of whites and nonwhites since the nineteenth century. But only recently has her socio-sexual role been explicitly scrutinized, and some of the most useful scholarship theorizing it has been published under the rubric of whiteness studies.[1] In an effort to apprehend how the white woman's racial and gender identity informs her cultural significance, scholars have pointed out that although she is often subject to varying attributions, one of the white wife's most unsettling potentialities is the threat of a hidden "blackness." As Lewis Gordon explains in "Bad Faith and Antiblack Racism," "Unlike the black woman, out of whom only black children can be born, she [the white woman] can bear *both* white and black children. Because of this, the white woman ultimately stands on the same ontological level as slime in an anti-black world." The white woman is so reviled, Gordon suggests, because hidden in her whiteness "is the antiblack's suspicion of her blackness. She stands as a white blackness, as a living contradiction of white supremacy" (305). Located within a complex ideological web, white women historically exist as sites onto which masculine Western cultures project their insecurity over the possibility of miscegenation;

they are likewise implicated in white culture's desire to forestall the differentiated social organization that would be the inevitable result of racial crossing. White patriarchal systems thus need white women, on whom they maintain a tortured reliance to ensure the continued hegemony of the white race. Part of the threat of the white woman, then, inheres in her vulnerability as a gateway, both literally and metaphorically, for the "other's" penetration into the closed community of whiteness.

As much as the white woman's command over biological reproduction situates her as a threat to the propagation of whiteness, it is essential to understand the "reproduction" of whiteness more generally. That is, although white women literally reproduce whiteness by giving birth to white babies, they are also often called upon to reproduce the white race socially, culturally, and ideologically, in effect bearing responsibility for exhibiting behaviors and beliefs that contribute to sustaining systems of racial dominance. This latter requirement becomes all the more salient in a colonial context, since imperial societies are often founded on the organizing principles of fixed racial identities and racial separation, which are then used as ideological justifications for economic exploitation and cultural and political oppression. While regulations outlawing interracial marriage and miscegenation in the racial past of the United States (a reality well documented in Werner Sollors's impressive compendium, *Interracialism: Black-White Intermarriage in American History, Literature and Law*) reinforced the desire to protect whiteness and police racial-sexual boundaries, similar prohibitions were perhaps even more necessary and unyielding in British colonial contexts, wherein authorities staked their claims to economic and cultural superiority on racial grounds. Thus although the white woman's presence in the colonies might rightly serve a "civilizing" function, her perceived sexual vulnerability nonetheless threatened to compromise the colonial mission. Richard Dyer explains:

> The coming of white women to the empire was often seen as the beginning and end of British domination, a notion especially inclined to be voiced in sexual imagery. Women, by their very presence, introduced the fact of sexuality; unwittingly, they enflamed

the already overheated desires of native men; they sapped their own men's energies, or . . . were liable to wind up betraying them. (186)

If one extends Dyer's contention that in colonial contexts the danger presented by the white woman inheres in her sexual identity, this danger might be further articulated and understood by analyzing the white woman's gendered role in sustaining systems of colonial whiteness. Variations of the threat posed by white women's sexuality appear, interestingly, in three otherwise unrelated female-authored British novels of the twentieth century: Doris Lessing's *The Grass Is Singing* (1950), Jean Rhys's *Wide Sargasso Sea* (1966), and Ruth Prawer Jhabvala's *Heat and Dust* (1975). Although set in different contexts— colonial Rhodesia, Jamaica, and India—respectively, each novel exposes the sexualized and genderized mechanisms that manufacture and safeguard "white" ideology and hegemony specifically by examining the white wife's role in sustaining the imperial mission at large. All three novels are nonetheless marked by a failure in this regard, for each narrates the story of a white wife whose real or imagined marital breach figuratively and imaginatively destabilizes her whiteness and imperial whiteness at large. In each case, a white woman becomes "racialized" as a result of her connection with, or proximity to, a colonized subject and their closeness, whether sexual or not, jeopardizes her whiteness. These novels thereby make pivotal acknowledgment of the discursive construction of whiteness and suggest that patriarchal constituencies rely on enforced racial identities in order to ensure and protect colonial dominance. Likewise, the novels confirm white marriage's political implication in and inextricable linkage to the impulse to stabilize and fix racial difference, an imperative that hinges on the sexual and reproductive behaviors of the white wife.

Each of these novels therefore attempts to interrogate and to assess the colonial project, an investigation that turns on the figure of the "unfaithful" white wife who somehow neglects to protect or to maintain designated racial boundaries and thus hierarchies. Her failure to safeguard white domination, however, is not necessarily an ethical or intentional flouting of colonial ideology: female protagonists are rarely, in fact, inoculated from or resistant to the logics of colonialism. As Samina Najmi and Rajni Srikanth contend, the white wife is "at once racially privileged and sexually marginalized" (8) and the aforementioned novels admit to this conflict, for the white wife simultaneously benefits from and is injured by the logic of white privilege. Similarly, while these novels expose the gendered mechanisms that construct racial and sexual hierarchies, they do not offer rubrics for change or individualized occasions for blame or resistance. They do, however, call on us to understand the retribution visited on the "darkened" white wife as a result of her perceived attachment to (or similarity with) the dark other as an act of cultural protection. Her symbolic punishment is exacted not in response to a real transgression but in order to protect the larger systems of racial, economic, and class privilege on which the colonial order relies.[2]

Whiteness as Learned Behavior in *The Grass Is Singing*

Doris Lessing's first novel, *The Grass Is Singing* (1950), has been alternatively praised as offering a powerful indictment of colonial racism in Africa and accused of reproducing precisely the sorts of racially pernicious attitudes it claims to critique. While the text in many ways straddles these two positions, Lessing's novel is perhaps unparalleled in its exposition of the machinations that create whiteness as a category, a mandate that ultimately destroys a white wife not sufficiently vigilant of the imperative to "protect" her whiteness. The novel begins with a cryptic journalistic report. Titled "Murder Mystery," it describes the death in the 1940s of Mary Turner, a white, British farmer's wife found murdered by her black "houseboy" who confessed to the crime. Mary cuts a controversial figure in this opening scene, for in many ways she sits on the fault line of the racial axis that divides her community. To wit: the white townspeople in Ngesi, Rhodesia (now Zimbabwe), do not mourn the dead woman but sympathize with her white husband, Dick Turner, whom they pity "with a fine fierce indignation against Mary, as if she were something unpleasant and unclean, and it served her right to get murdered" (Lessing 3). The genesis of her dirtying, or rather, Mary's process of becoming "unclean," informs the unfolding plot of Lessing's novel, which travels back in time in order to explicate Mary's gradual mental and physical breakdown and to uncover the disciplinary logic of her colonial community, wherein her murder is regarded as a symbolic and legitimate punishment for the breaking of racial taboos.

Mary's whiteness is an embattled category, yet its instability is made salient only after she marries. An only child of a poor alcoholic father and an embittered mother, Mary appears as an immature and even infantalized woman who nevertheless enjoys her single life working as a secretary in town and living in a "girls' club" (34). In her thirties, social displacement moves Mary to wed Dick Turner, a man she does not know, after inadvertently hearing herself gossiped about by friends who characterize her as a woman unfit for marriage. The social shaming perpetrated in their assessment impels Mary to a hastily conceived union with Dick Turner, a poor farmer who lives in the bush and employs native blacks to work on his land. Prior to her move to Dick's farm, however, Mary has little cause to consider her race or that of others: "'Class' is not a South African word; and its equivalent 'race,' meant to her the office boy in the firm where she worked, other women's servants, and amorphous mass of natives in the streets, whom she hardly noticed. . . . She had nothing to do with them really. They were outside her orbit" (32–33). Mary has nevertheless been brought up to fear the black natives and is made especially uncomfortable by the sight of black women nursing their babies, a reaction which suggests that in her cultural lexicon black bodies are associated with a corporeality she both fears and rejects. The confrontation with black bodies indeed structures her arrival on Dick's remote farm in the sweltering Rhodesian countryside, wherein the regimented racial division between black laborers and white owners requires the practical daily enforcement of white ideology if only to separate out Mary and Dick, poor whites living in virtual squalor, from their supposed inferiors, the natives whom they employ. As Mary quickly learns, even to acknowledge the Turners' economic limitations would be a betrayal of colonial ideology: "To do that would be letting the side down. The Turners were British, after all" (3).

As convention dictates, no matter how impoverished, Mary must have a black house servant to cook and clean for her, in part to uphold the class and racially inflected designations that maintain the appearance of white racial superiority. As Eileen Manion observes, "Women's responsibility for the private space of home and housework takes on a unique character in the colony. No matter how poor Lessing's colonial housewives are, no matter how small their houses, they must have African 'houseboys'" (441). At the mercy of the conflicting requirements of gender and race, Mary's domestic role requires her to care for the home, yet as a *white* woman in a colonial context, she is expected to delegate domestic labors to a servant.[3] This contradictory requirement renders Mary aimless, for she lacks a function within the space of her home and, more generally, her life. Furthermore, the marital contract has quite clearly conferred a racial identity on her, forcing her to become or regard herself as "white." Mary's shifting self-designation thus demonstrates how racial identity becomes constructed within the colonial context and, specifically, within the white marital institution.

Mary gets the opportunity to "try on" her whiteness and specifically her white authority in her dealings with black laborers, behaving in a way that is nothing short of maniacal. Prone to issuing verbal invectives and other methods of psychological abuse, Mary cycles through a quick series of house servants—all of whom eventually quit—and Mary physically assaults Moses, the man who later will kill her, when she supervises the workers in the field on one occasion. However, while one might read her domestic tyranny as overcompensation for feeling otherwise powerless, it seems important to point out that Mary is besieged with the economic and social requirements of being a "white wife." Mary's racist actions are partially a learned behavior gleaned from years of living in a racially segregated country and a somewhat hysterical expression of her confrontation with the hierarchical systems of race and gender, a condition also brought on by the sexual acts requisite within marriage.[4] In comparing her town life to her life on the farm:

> She felt, rather, as if she had been lifted from the part fitted to her, in a play she understood, and made suddenly to act one unfamiliar to her. It was a feeling of being out of character that chilled her, not knowledge that she had changed. The soil, the black laborers, always so close to their lives but also so cut off, Dick in his farm clothes with his hands stained with oil—these things did not belong to her, they were not real. It was monstrous that they should have been imposed on her. (107–8)

The above passage illustrates Mary's discomfort with her place in the farm's gender and racial hierarchy, specifically by figuring white wifehood as a "monstrous" role in which Mary has arbitrarily been cast. A sexual subtext brews beneath the surface as well, since Mary's engagement in a conflicted psycho-sexual drama is underlined by the image of her husband "Dick" (pun intended) with his dirty black hands. Mary's horror of having sex, which in the novel's lexicon is coded in racial terms that are meant to evoke the image of the "dark" other, clearly mediates her encounter with the horror of farm life. Her sexual paranoia is not, however, a recent pathology; prior to her marriage, Mary runs away from a man who attempts to make love to her, a scene that highlights her sexual naïveté. Therefore, it is perhaps not an overreach to apprehend Mary's name in biblical terms, as an ever-enduring virgin. Further, her psychological collapse of darkness with sexual desire is later literalized by the repetitious compulsion that Mary adopts with respect to Moses, her physically imposing black servant with whom she becomes locked in an obsessive cycle of hate and desire.

Because Mary's trauma exists as an amalgamation of racial, sexual, and gender conflict, one symbolic remedy for this conflict, Lessing suggests, would be for Dick to reinforce his own racialized subject position. Were he to shore up his commitment to whiteness by acting strong, successful, and imposing rather than dirty, weak, and "dark," Mary would be better able to mediate against what she ascertains as the farm's encroaching "blackness." Dick's assertion of white masculinity thus figures as a stance necessary to keeping their faltering marriage intact:

> She needed to think of Dick, the man to whom she was irrevo-
> cably married, as a person of his own account, a success from his
> own efforts. When she saw him as weak and goalless, and pitiful,
> she hated him, and the hate turned in on herself. She needed a
> man stronger than herself, and she was trying to create one out of
> Dick. If he had, genuinely, simply, because of the greater strength
> of his purpose, taken the ascendancy over her, she would have
> loved him, and no longer hated herself for being tied to a failure.
> (143–44)

The couple's ideological effort to protect their vulnerable status as "whites" in many ways relies on the maintenance of idealized notions of femininity and masculinity.[5] As Jeanette King argues, "The individual's failure thus threatens the myth of white superiority, according to which black men are poor because they lack the ability and willingness to work which have made the white man rich" (8). If the myth of the white man's superior work ethic ensures his racial and economic privilege, such mythologies require Dick to demonstrate that he is, indeed, worthy of his whiteness. Dick's failure to produce wealth thus threatens to expose the shaky foundations on which racial divisions are erected, divisions which rest tenuously on the understanding that white men are entitled to, and deserving of, the economic successes they enjoy. This ideology, in fact, impels Dick's rich white neighbor, Charlie Slatter, to offer to buy Dick's failing farm: "It was not even pity for Dick that moved him. He was obeying the dictate of the first law of white South Africa, which is: 'Thou shalt not let your fellow whites sink below a certain point; because if you do, the nigger will see he is as good as you are'" (205). Charlie's law is lent the weight of religious conviction, a slippage Lessing's deliberately heavy-handed rhetoric exposes, except that his "god," so to speak, is a figment of white superiority.[6]

Mary's sexual obsession with Moses, who becomes her house servant, operates therefore as a perverse recodification of the taboos put in place to protect whiteness. Culturally, black men are constructed as potent sexual predators, in part to ensure that white women fear rather than desire them.[7] Mary in some ways internalizes this dictum too thoroughly, in that the more erotically attracted to Moses she becomes, the more immobilizing is the obsession that he is going to harm her. She thus reenacts the logic of white superiority which demands the sublimation and redirection of outlaw emotions: put simply, Mary has no other rubric by which to understand her heightened sexual desires except as an instance of sexual panic. As her attraction to Moses mounts, so too does her hysteria: "She was fighting against something she did not understand. Dick became to her, as time went by, more and more unreal; while the thought of the African grew obsessive. It was a nightmare, the powerful black man always in the house with her, so that there was no escape from his presence. She was possessed by it, and Dick was hardly there to her" (191). Mary's desire intermingles with a maniacal terror, which suggests how wholly indoctrinated she is within an ideology of colonial whiteness. Acutely aware that as a white woman she must not, or cannot, desire a black man, she internalizes a fear of miscegenation so thoroughly that she descends into madness.[8] This psychological unraveling can be explained in part by Mary's confrontation with the ideology of whiteness: because she occupies the subject position of the "white wife," madness is Mary's only possible response to her errant attraction.

Furthermore, as Mary's physical and mental condition deteriorates, she grants Moses increasing access to her body, allowing Moses to dress her, for example, which in turn only intensifies her erotic obsession. Her desires are thus allowed expression only in sadomasochistic fantasies wherein Mary is alternatively victim and perpetrator. Her compulsion leads to increased physical and spiritual self-abjection, which ultimately results in what has been read as her death wish fulfillment. As Sheila Roberts notes, "Mary foresees her killing and does not try to save herself from it: in fact, she goes walking out into the night as if to greet it" (79). Similarly, Lynne Hanley observes that Mary "conflates Moses with her father and invites her annihilation at his hand" (498).

Moses's subjectivity and his reasons for killing Mary, unfortunately, are left largely unexplored in the novel, as are the details of their intimate relationship. Although the narrative gives Mary's lurid fantasies vivid description, the novel withholds an explicit confirmation or denial of a sexual consummation brought about as the result of those fantasies. Thus following her death, the Rhodesian township exacts her symbolic punishment in response to what is only an assumed or inferred violation. The community nevertheless looks on her dead body with "bitter contemptuous anger" and "profound instinctive horror and fear" (14). The racial imperative that they assume Mary transgresses in life is maintained with a compulsive exactitude after her death. Town authorities, for instance, prohibit Moses from riding in the same van with Mary's body for "one could not put a black man close to a white woman, even though she were dead" (19). Such a practice is customary according to the town's racist social organization "which will never, never admit that a white person, and most particularly, a white woman, can have a human relationship, whether for good or for evil, with a black person" (21). Were such a relation acknowledged, racial hierarchies (and implicitly colonial civilization) would promptly fall apart. Lessing's novel also offers an instructive account of the process by which white authorities come together to assign meaning to black on white crime, wherein they invent a logical scenario—stating that Mary's murder was committed by a sexually predatory black man—that neither threatens their preexisting beliefs nor white society's claims to racial and intellectual superiority.[9]

Inevitably, Moses will be hanged for the murder of Mary, although in reality it is she perhaps even more than Moses who bears the brunt of the white Ngesi townspeople's hatred and fear. They demonstrate that the institution of whiteness may be compromised by little more than the suspicion that a white wife has voluntarily had a sexual relationship with a black man. A consensual, interracial relation, even in nascent form, thus has the potential to destabilize white privilege and white identity, which explains the unforgiving manner in which the male authorities apprehend Mary's murder and the police handle her dead body. Their racial behavior suggests that the maintenance of the mythology of white righteousness often unconsciously relies on its obverse, the image of the sexually threatening black male.

Despite the valuable perspective Lessing's novel provides regarding the creation and maintenance of colonial whiteness, it is perhaps worth concluding this section with some of the critiques leveled against *The Grass Is Singing*, wherein a largely faceless and dehumanized black man commits a senseless murder of a white woman. As Eve Bertelsman argues, Lessing relies on formulations of a savage and uncivilized Africa and thus Moses's brutal murder of Mary operates as a confirmation rather than a repudiation of colonial wisdom. Bertelsman writes that "the ending fulfills every fear and foreboding of the white imagination treated by Lessing so dismissively at the social-realistic level of her tale" (656). Bertelsman's censure is strong, but might be modulated with the suggestion that Lessing's text is problematic not because it unconsciously reinscribes the same racist ideology it seeks to condemn, but perhaps because it, much like the townspeople who refuse to hear Mary's story for fear it will destroy their illusions of white superiority, also fails to admit its own culpability in the construction of whiteness. This is to say, just as Mary has internalized the construction of her racial superiority and is ideologically unable to apprehend Moses as anything other than a black threat, the novel symptomatically reproduces this blindness through its own failure to humanize Moses, who appears only within Mary's hysterical projections. Although *The Grass Is Singing* exposes the need of white townspeople to silence Mary's story to contain the danger they feel she represents, Lessing may in fact deploy a similar racialized practice of evasion when she silences, neglects, or entirely avoids assigning Moses an interior humanity and perspective.[10] Lessing's single-minded focus on the white wife who is not only called upon to reproduce and maintain colonial hierarchies but also disciplined through the process does a thorough job of deconstructing white ideology yet sacrifices meaningful exploration of colonized black subjectivities.

Wide Sargasso Sea's "Darkening" of the White Wife

If Doris Lessing's *The Grass Is Singing* substantiates the white woman's threat to whiteness with a narrative of an assumed sexual and racial border crossing, Jean Rhys's *Wide Sargasso Sea* (1966), a now-classic rewriting of and imaginative prequel to the plot of *Jane Eyre*, offers a formulation whereby Antoinette Cosway (whom Charlotte Brontë represents as the madwoman in the attic) is vilified by her husband for precisely the same suspicions. Just as the townspeople in *The Grass Is Singing* symbolically punish Mary Turner posthumously for her alleged interracial sexual transgressions, in *Wide Sargasso Sea* Antoinette's husband, Mr. Rochester, enacts a similar disciplinary regimen by rhetorically darkening his allegedly licentious wife. Enmeshed in a marital situation that reenacts the colonial encounter, Antoinette's potential for transgression is thereby marked by her husband's racialized apprehension of her "dark" and errant sexual impulses, which succeed in confirming, for him, her symbolic association with and identification as the racialized other.

Of the three marriages discussed within this essay, Rochester and Antoinette's is the one an economic imperative most obviously determines. Rochester, a dispossessed second son from a disgraced British family, arrives in Jamaica to marry Antoinette Cosway, enticed by the dowry her stepbrother promises. The economic transfer calls Rochester's masculinity into question, in part because he assumes Antoinette to understand that she has bought him. Their transaction thereby disrupts the symbolic association made in the colonial context between whiteness, masculinity, and economic power. Because Rochester inherits money from his wife rather than through legitimizing, masculinized channels of inheritance or by his own work initiative, his marriage directly imperils his status as an independently solvent "white" male. From the start, Rochester views his marriage as a corrupting transaction, one that destabilizes his masculinity, his whiteness, and even his "English" identity.[11]

Faced with the subconscious need to protect his own tenuous economic and social standing and to distinguish himself from the impoverished, black former slaves who also reside in the Caribbean, Rochester relocates his own national and racial instability onto his wife's body. Rochester soon notices his wife's "sad, dark alien eyes" and assesses that "Creole of pure English descent she may be, but they [her eyes] are not English or European either . . ." (Rhys 39). Although technically a white West Indian, Antoinette is also a disinherited Creole and therefore embodies a nexus of competing racial meanings. Designated a "white nigger" or a "white cockroach" because of her family's lamentable social history—including her father's sexual relations with his slaves, her mother's madness, and her brother's sickness—such terminology evidences the extent to which class and cultural status become conflated with racial designations. Rochester's suspicion that Antoinette is neither ethnically nor sexually "pure," a doubt expressed in racialized terms, further underscores his cognizance of his wife's reduced social standing. Cataloguing her myriad failures to demonstrate a conservative, measured, "white" way of existing, Rochester notes of his wife: "I was watching her, hardly able to believe she was the pale, silent creature I had married" (52). Rochester's symbolic alignment of Antoinette with the dark and savage land of the Caribbean further extends her blackening: "it is a beautiful place—wild and above all untouched, with an alien, disturbing secret loveliness" (52). His anthropomorphizing gesture links the dark land to his wife's symbolically dark body, both of which he apprehends as strange and disquieting.[12]

Rochester's comments also convey his sense of the seductive and evil powers lurking in this Edenic setting, and he figures his wife as a vile temptress intent on luring him into the depths of hell. His invocation of the notion of "untouched" land nevertheless has a double meaning, for it connotes a biblical paradise, and serves as well as a euphemism for Antoinette's sexual history, since Rochester marries her as a virgin, but then promptly defiles her. This new specter of sexual availability nonetheless threatens assumed notions of British civilization and propriety and affords Rochester symbolic justification for questioning his wife's whiteness. Conveniently forgetting his part in introducing Antoinette to sex and likewise ignoring the fact that he frequently subjects her to sadomasochistic sexual relations, Rochester self-servingly recasts his wife as one who possesses a voracious sexual appetite: "Sometimes a sidelong look or a sly knowing glance disturbed me, but it was never for long. 'Not now,' I would think, 'not yet'" (52). A symbolic alliance is thereby forged between Antoinette's uncontrollable sexuality and her racial identity, such that her darkness is understood to have informed her excessive, insatiable appetites.

Also at risk is Rochester's ability to maintain his English civility, for the fear that he will become symbolically darkened along with his overly desirous wife panics him: "I was thirsty for her, but that is not love. I felt very little tenderness for her, as she was a stranger to me. . . . One afternoon the sight of a dress which she'd left lying on the bedroom floor left me breathless and savage with desire" (55). Because his wife elicits desires in him for which he feels ashamed, Rochester treats her violently, in an attempt to ward off his own corruption. Noting the "savage" desires that his wife incites, however, amounts to an admission that he, too, has been coerced into the "darkness." To quell this haunting self-doubt, Rochester continually searches for proof that his wife is more uncivilized than he, finding evidence in her willingness to hug blacks while he does not (54), in her description of herself as "lazy" like her black maid Christophine (51), and in her careless dispensing of money to their relatives and servants, whom he does not trust (53). Rochester's suspicion that he has been corrupted by dark or uncivilized desires further informs his exoticizing of his wife, whom he deems an encroaching white blackness.

That Antoinette's supposedly shifting racial categorization so unsettles Rochester has much to do with the colonial project of protecting whiteness, a fear literalized when two biracial characters, Amelie and Daniel, inform him that Antoinette had a sexual relationship with her cousin Sandi, who is also part black. Having finally acquired evidence of his wife's symbolic blackness, a confirmation that arrives via the suggestion that she had indiscriminate and even incestuous relations with a man who is not white, Rochester promptly feels "disgust and rage" (76). Directly after he learns about Sandi, in fact, he notices that Antoinette looks "very much like Amelie" (76–77).[13] The suggestion that his wife has had sexual relations with Sandi only confirms Rochester's nagging suspicion that his white wife is not really "white" and further shores up his resolve to regard his wife as a sex-obsessed, indiscriminate dark woman: "She thirsts for *anyone*—not for me. . . . She'll loosen her black hair, and laugh and coax and flatter [a mad girl. She'll not care who she is loving]. She'll moan and cry and give herself as no sane woman would—or could. *Or could*" (99).[14] Antoinette's "othering" as dark and mad is underpinned by her implied sexual and racial instability—giving herself to "anyone" equals a transgression of the cultural and racial category of whiteness. Similarly, recasting his wife as "black" and sexually excessive allows Rochester to imagine a more purified, sanitized form of sexuality for himself, one more closely tied to white norms. In fact, after the revelation of his wife's supposed transgressions Rochester starts exhibiting more classically British or "white" behaviors: he turns "calm" and "self-possessed" and begins invoking the specter of a Christian God, all of which suggest that once he decides that Antoinette is "black," he can more easily shore up his commitment to being "white" (76).

Deciding that Antoinette's whiteness has been irrevocably compromised by her liaison with Sandi, Rochester fortuitously acquires a "legitimate" justification for his hatred of her, and he rejects her by renaming her "Bertha" and turning so cold and cruel that she eventually goes mad. Antoinette becomes reified and othered within Rochester's symbolic project of claiming his own whiteness and civility, and achieves a functionality whereby she serves as the scapegoat for *his* racial instability. In other words, once Rochester aligns Antoinette with Sandi, categorizing them both black and savage "others," he is able to escape his own implication in questionable or deviant sexual practices, which include a sexual affair with Antoinette's biracial maid, Amelie. Psychic displacement guarantees Rochester's absolution; in his symbolic schema, Antoinette becomes a repository for all the so-called darkness of the Caribbean land and people.

Ironically, in terms of sexual comportment, Antoinette Cosway is the least transgressive of the three female protagonist discussed here, yet she is perhaps the most vilified for allegedly crossing the color line. Because Rochester locates the darkness and the otherness within her, it becomes paradoxically irrelevant whether she actually transgresses racial boundaries or not. Although Rochester is *told* that Sandi has "defiled" her, much like the unconfirmed interracial consummation in *The Grass Is Singing*, Rhys's novel deliberately obscures validation of the white wife's sexual transgression. The rumor is repeated twice in part 2 of the novel, first by Amelie and then by Daniel, yet the only confirmation that Antoinette and Sandi shared more than a friendship appears in part 3, when Antoinette/Bertha is mad. She confesses that Sandi often came to see her while "the man" was away, but suggests that they embraced in a sexual way only once: "We had often kissed before but not like that. That was the life and death kiss, and you only know a long time afterwards what it is, the life and death kiss" (110). Although Antoinette's "confession" is an unreliable account at best, Rochester nevertheless reracializes his wife in a swift act of patriarchal imagining that characterizes Antoinette as a threat to whiteness and at once punishes her for that imagined transgression. Antoinette thus "becomes" the "other" since she has been defiled by the "other." According to the white husband, Antoinette's seeming refusal to police racial boundaries, to "remain white" and confine herself to white sexual partners, constitutes her sexual and ideological transgression of the tenets of whiteness.

Reproductive Refusals in *Heat and Dust*

In Ruth Prawer Jhabvala's critical exploration of British occupation in India, *Heat and Dust* (1975), Olivia, the protagonist and white wife of a colonial administrator, literalizes the fear that is at the heart of the ideological organization of whiteness as it relates to the figure of the white wife. Unlike Mary Turner and Antoinette Cosway, who only threaten or are imagined to blur the boundaries between their bodies and that of the dark "other," Olivia has an affair with and possibly may be impregnated by an Indian prince. Unlike Mary's or Antoinette's unsubstantiated transgression, hers is a validated sexual betrayal and reproductive risk, thus Olivia's story realizes the reproductive anxiety that circumscribes the figure of the white wife in the colonial context. Further, Jhabvala's novel demonstrates the extent to which "white" ideologies must be sustained within colonial European marriage in order to have an effect on reproductive choices. Only when Olivia begins to reject the racialized value system of the British colonial aristocracy does she commit a sexual transgression with a man who is not her husband and not of her race.

Olivia and her husband Douglas live in Satipur, India, in 1923 during his appointment as a British administrator of a small Indian province.[15] Theirs is a marriage of love, not convenience, and Olivia appears initially in awe of her husband, perhaps precisely for his ability to play the part of the strong, good Englishman. Conversely, he is equally enamored with her, ostensibly for her ability to embody seamlessly the character of a loving, helpless wife. Douglas takes pride in his wife's whiteness and demonstrates a clear investment in her performance of feminine passivity: "He looked at her golden head bent gracefully from her white neck: he loved to have her sitting there opposite him, sewing" (Jhabvala 38). Douglas's controlled but magnanimous masculinity also enraptures Olivia. She finds him "noble and fair" and to her his eyes are "the eyes of a boy who read adventure stories and had dedicated himself to living up to their code of courage and honor" (40). The fictions of romance, with its strong moral man and his demure female counterpart, here appear easily translatable to the colonial context, for it, too, is structured around the mythology of white male righteousness and female dependency.

Despite such fantasies of colonial benevolence, the imperial atmosphere nonetheless stifles Olivia: "She kept asking herself how it was possible to lead such exciting lives—administering whole provinces, fighting border battles, advising rulers—and at the same time to remain so dull" (15). A sign of the cracking façade of British manifest destiny, Olivia's fatigue registers the unstable ground on which colonial administrators stake their claims to racial and moral superiority. Although they speak with an air of objectivity, currents of condescension run throughout the British tendency to categorize the Indians as petulant children, who, despite years of colonial rule, will never become civilized. "And not only did they [the British administrators] keep completely cool, but they even had the little smile of tolerance, of affection, even enjoyment that Olivia was beginning to know well: like good parents, they all loved India no matter what mischief she might be up to" (58). A system of practices and attitudes that literary and critical theorist Edward Said characterizes as Orientalism informs these iterations, which center around an impulse to infantilize India and its people. According to Said, the "Oriental is irrational, depraved (fallen), childlike, 'different'; thus the European is rationale, virtuous, mature, 'normal'" (40). These characterizations reconfirm the colonialists' hegemonic belief that they are rational, logical, and civilized, whereby the Indians are impulsive, childish, uncivilized, and thereby inferior.[16]

Olivia's investment in this Orientalist narrative becomes increasingly untethered, however, thanks in part to her increasing skepticism of British reiterations of their racial and moral superiority. Douglas characterizes the Indians as up to "their usual tricks," noting "they think they are frightfully cunning, but really they're like children" a statement that suggests to Olivia that his attitudes are not fundamentally different from those of his condescending compatriots (38). Neither is Douglas shy about touting his own intellectual advantages. As Laurie Sucher perceptively writes, "His chivalry turns out, viewed through the close-up lens of a marriage, to be naïve and sentimental paternalism; his steadfast uprightness entails 'genuine respect' for his dull superiors" (111). Furthermore, the novel invites comparison between Douglas's treatment of Olivia and he and his friends' attitudes toward India; Douglas is fond, for example, of characterizing his wife as a passive, helpless child who is unable to make decisions and needs others to take care of her (39).

Olivia's disillusion with her husband, her marriage, and her life in general intensifies when she befriends the Nawab, a wealthy Indian prince with dismissive attitudes toward the British aristocracy. The Nawab derisively calls Douglas "a proper Englishman," and suggests that much of Douglas's power derives simply from his having had a privileged upbringing (43–44). Although Olivia is also a product of this system of privilege, her relationship with the Nawab in effect defamiliarizes the British colonial aristocracy. In some respects, Olivia merely transplants herself from one position of luxury to another, as evidenced by the fact that she begins to spend her long days lolling around the Nawab's palace while Douglas is at work. Nevertheless, under the Nawab's influence, she actively cultivates the desire to distance herself from the world of the British colonialists. Upon the Nawab's suggestion that the British "all are the same," Olivia is horrified: "Olivia had a shock—did he mean her too? Was she included? She looked at his face and was frightened by the feeling she saw so plainly expressed there: it seemed to her that she could not bear to be included in *these* feelings, that she would do anything *not* to be" (122). Obviously, Olivia dislikes being categorized within her national group because it separates her from the Nawab, for whom she has an increasingly concentrated attraction. Nevertheless, her chagrin conveys her interest in forging an intentional, if symbolic, separation from her British counterparts, and specifically, from their designations of racial and cultural superiority.

The complicated narratives that circulate around the issue of race and reproduction in the novel, however, trouble this transition. Despite her faltering marriage and the fact that she actively begins an extramarital affair with the Nawab, Olivia still desires a white baby: "She thought if she had a baby—a strapping blond blue-eyed boy— everything would be all right. She would be at peace and also one with Douglas and think about everything the same way he did" (107). The imagined baby thus becomes a means by which Olivia can rearticulate a commitment to whiteness and white ideology, so that she might again "think about everything" in the same way as her husband. The production of a white baby would therefore realign her with the racial imperatives of the British colonial aristocracy, and allow her reentry into an imperialistic epistemological regime from which she has voluntarily become estranged. Further, the desire for a boy rather than a girl suggests Olivia's continued investment in protecting the legacy of patriarchy; among other benefits, bearing Douglas a son would guarantee the perpetuation of his patronymic. Olivia's reproductive impulses therefore have a clear racial purpose, one perhaps even tainted with the hint of eugenics. Wondering why she has not yet gotten pregnant: "She was sure that a couple like herself and Douglas were meant to have children, to be the founders of a beautiful line" (105). Biological reproduction conflates here with a racial imperative, for surely blond-haired, blue-eyed babies populate Douglas and Olivia's "beautiful line."[17]

When Olivia does conceive, the baby's paternity is indeterminate, since the unborn child might be the product of a failing marriage or a clandestine extramarital affair. The fear of the "otherness" potentially growing within her, however, presents itself to Olivia as an immobilizing prospect. Conversing with Harry, a homosexual friend of the Nawab's, Olivia describes the christening robe that her husband, who believes himself to be the expectant father, plans to obtain from England:

> "He says it's awfully pretty. Cascades of white lace—very becoming to the Rivers' babies who are very fair. Douglas says they all have white-blond hair till they're about twelve."
>
> "Babies don't have hair."
>
> "Indian babies do, I've seen them. They're born with lots of black hair. . . . You have to help me, Harry. You have to find out where I can go." (162)

Olivia's anxiety concerning the legibility of the baby's race, and also the fact that white reproduction is associated with the reproduction of so-called Christian values is here crystallized in the image of a blond baby wearing a white christening robe. Equally possible, of course, is that Olivia will bear a nonwhite baby whose shock of dark hair will expose not only its illegitimate parentage but also Olivia's sin. The unborn baby thus represents the potential to corrupt whiteness, and to interrupt its claims to moral and ethnic superiority.

Thanks in part to the illegibility of the baby's race while in utero, Olivia's body exists as something of a floating signifier onto which both prospective fathers project the potential to reproduce his own race. Interestingly, both the Nawab and Douglas, each believing the baby to be his, ask Olivia, "[Y]ou would do this for me?" (152, 155), which suggests an intended co-optation of her body and confirms the extent to which, in this colonial context, biological reproduction serves the goals of patriarchy. For the Nawab, Olivia's consensual seduction and ensuing pregnancy represent a successful act of retribution against the British. Harry repeats to Olivia that the Nawab "said that when this baby was born, Douglas and all were going to have the shock of their lives" (161). In this context, the baby provides not only a rejoinder to British superiority but also trace evidence that the Nawab has quite literally penetrated the hegemony of white colonial power, a stealth act all the more potent because he instrumentalizes the white female body to do so. After receiving the news of her pregnancy, the Nawab strengthens his commitment to Olivia: "he sent for her every day and made no secret in the Palace of the relations between them. . . . He never for a moment doubted that the child was his. . . . As far as he was concerned, Douglas had already been dismissed" (153).

Clearly, both men have an interest in claiming paternity; for Douglas the baby codifies and propagates a racial hierarchy, whereas for the Nawab, the baby disrupts the British power structure. In laying claim to the unborn child, each engages in the symbolic gesture of either reifying or undermining colonial power structures, an entitlement frustrated only by Olivia's decision to abort the fetus. The decision, however, costs her her marriage, her position as a white wife, and perhaps even her national identity. Subsequent to the abortion, Olivia remains in India supported by the Nawab, occupying a marginal position in Indian society. As a result, she comes to be remembered not simply as a woman who betrayed her marriage vows, but as one who had "gone too far" and become emotionally entangled with India and its people. As Major Minnies, one of Douglas's colleagues, explains, "It is all very well to love and admire India . . . but always with a virile, measured *European* feeling. One should never . . . allow oneself to become softened [like Indians] by an excess of feeling; because the moment that happens—the moment one exceeds one's measure—one is in danger of being dragged over to the other side" (171). The rhetoric here is feminized not only because he refers to Olivia but also because the Indian "other" is figured as a force whose seductive power is nevertheless acknowledged as having a corrupting influence. While Major Minnies touts the importance of masculine control and resistance in order to protect whiteness, his statements also reveal the paradoxical position of white women, who are so frequently dismissed as being weak and ineffectual by virtue of their sex, but are unavoidably depended upon to perpetuate the legacies of patriarchal and colonial domination.

Heat and Dust makes salient the connection between the ideology of whiteness and its system of organizing marital behavior: once Olivia ceases to believe in the innate superiority of white ways of being and thinking, she no longer confines herself to a white sexual partner. She thereby interrupts the process of racially sanctioned reproduction on which the colonial order relies. Because Olivia cannot or will not reproduce whiteness, her decision underscores the tenuous role of the white wife; although frequently called on to protect racial hierarchies, she can, and often does, refuse this interpellation.

The three novels examined here, while set in disparate colonial contexts with admittedly separate histories and racial understandings, nevertheless all demonstrate the racial and reproductive imperatives surrounding the position of the white wife. In each text, the author renders the white female body as an unstable site on which racial meanings are made, and more saliently, racial boundaries are policed. In this strict racial order, the punishment for even an imagined transgression is swift: Mary Turner dies; Antoinette Cosway goes mad; and Olivia lives the remainder of her life in seclusion in the Indian mountains. As an ideological critique, these texts illustrate that there is a constant interplay between the constructs of white ideology and the female body, as evidenced by the fact that colonial systems aim to curtail women's sexual and reproductive choices in the name of racial purity and frequently racialize her body in order to do so. The danger need not be real or even realized to wreak cultural havoc; white women can compromise the dominant social order not only by having sexual relationships with nonwhite men but also by failing to recognize or respect the boundaries that separate the races. While Mary obsesses over Moses in *The Grass Is Singing*, the ideology of whiteness proves too strong to permit any literal transgression, yet she is still vilified for what in all likelihood was only an imagined racial crossing. Similarly, in *Wide Sargasso Sea*, Antoinette's racializing is imposed by her husband—her sin is "written" on her body: her husband comes to see her as black, and believing her to have coupled with a black body, he places her outside the sphere of true white womanhood. Finally, in *Heat and Dust* Olivia realizes the miscegenation that Mary and Antoinette only threaten; rejecting the colonial logic of whiteness, Olivia actively and intentionally breaks sexual taboos, and it would seem, unsettles the colonial project as a result. In each case, a socio-racial contract compels these white wives to produce and reproduce the values associated with whiteness. In failing to comply with its imperatives, they are sacrificed upon the altar of white marriage, an institution that, under the regimes of colonialism especially, func-tions as a racial, sexual, and economic contract. Indeed, in all of these novels marriage makes salient not only these women's racial identities but also their implication in the colonial project of reproducing white-ness. Likewise, this reproductive imperative takes remarkably similar forms across three otherwise unrelated texts, in that each white wife is expected—but fails—to contain the threat of her blackness. These women's inability or unwillingness to reproduce whiteness portends their spiritual and social falls, yet each text usefully reminds us that the reproduction of whiteness is contingent upon willing female par-ticipants. When women intentionally refuse to participate or fall victim to happenstance, the logic of marriage, with its implicit reli-ance on the reproduction of racial hierarchies, also falls apart. These fictionalized colonial treatments help to throw into relief the often invisible racial contract of marriage, which is perhaps more easily papered over in other less socially and racially segregated milieus.

Notes

1. See especially Frankenburg; Ware; Sharpe; Stange; and Najmi and Srikanth.

2. There is a certain parallel to be drawn in all three texts between colonialism and patriarchy, in the sense that the subject under colonialism might be linked to the wife who is colonized under patriarchy. In this analogy, marriage is understood as a dis-ciplinary regime under which the white wife exists as a colonized body. Although I find this paradigm suggestive, I fear it encourages uncritical associations between colonized peoples and white women, associations that obfuscate the power any white person has in a colonial or postcolonial setting. For an explication of the analogy between women and colonized peoples in *The Grass Is Singing*, see Gottlieb and Keitner.

3. The system of colonial organization actually provides the conditions for the very liaison that it prohibits, specifically by placing black men in close proximity to the white women they serve.

4. Roberts notes that Lessing's novel incorporates elements of the Gothic, wherein a sexually inexperienced heroine is often driven to paranoia upon her entry into an unknown space, usually a mysterious or otherwise suspicious home (77).

5. The social system under colonialism dictated rigid gender roles for men as well as women. Manion writes, "The constant necessity of keeping a whole race, who outnumber their masters, in subordination seems to require an exaggeration of the stereotype of masculinity. White men must really be *men*—strong, aggressive, sure of themselves, in command. The colonial venture elicits and exalts all the elements of machismo" (441).

6. The consolidation of white power is thus aligned with the forging and protection of national identity. See Babb for a reading of whiteness operating as a nationalistic, unifying device in early American society.

7. See Harris for a compelling explanation of how the creation of the myth of the sexually potent black man is a legacy of white male insecurity. Harris notes that "by maintaining that sexual contact between black males and white females is taboo, he [the white man] eliminates that mythic phallic symbol, which he himself created, from competition with himself; for there is always the realistic possibility that if black men are so favorably endowed, white women may prefer them as sexual partners. To prevent that, the white man tells his women that coupling with a black men is tantamount to coupling with an ape or some other subhuman species" (301).

8. The specter of female madness also occurs in *Wide Sargasso Sea*. According to Hogan, "It is no coincidence that so many literary protagonists who suffer madness in the colonies are women . . . patriarchy can be as powerful and pure a force against identity as is colonialism" (86).

9. In the text's lexicon, the act of maintaining silence about even the possibility of interracial attraction indoctrinates one into a position of "white privilege." The appearance of Tony Marston, a recent British arrival in South Africa who lives down the street from the Turners during the final three weeks of Mary's life, illustrates this point. Although Marston mentions Mary's poor treatment of Moses, and how "difficult" the murder is to understand, Charlie Slatter effectively prohibits him from offering any indications of the sexual relationship that may have existed between Mary and Moses. Interpellated by the conspiratorial act of protecting white privilege, Tony is in effect schooled in the necessity of confirming the racist assumption that black men are a constant and abiding threat.

10. Toni Morrison's argument in *Playing in the Dark: Whiteness and the Literary Imagination* inspires the observation that white writers use a metaphorical or allegorical Africanist presence as a foil against which to talk about their own fears and insecurities.

11. For an excellent reading of the novel as concerned with the making of "Englishness," and in particular as a negotiation of English womanhood and nationhood, see Ciolkowski.

12. That he believes there to be a correlation between the land and his wife is further reconfirmed at the end of part 2 when Rochester states in regard to the land, "I hated its beauty and its magic and the secrets I would never know. I hated its indifference and the cruelty that was part of its loveliness. Above all I hated her. For she belonged to the magic and the loveliness" (Rhys 103).

13. Although space prohibits me from exploring this point in detail, Rochester also darkens his white wife when he aligns her with her mother, Annette, whose whiteness is also questionable. When she goes insane, a black man violates Annette sexually, which only confirms for Rochester that there is no pure whiteness to be found in the Caribbean. In its place, he sees only deviant sexuality and rampant miscegenation.

14. Fayad aptly notes how in Rochester's estimation, Daniel's revelations make it "very easy for Antoinette to make the transition from temptress to whore" (445).

15. The name Satipur is significant because it translates as "city of the faithful wife" or "place of suttee," which is the practice by which a grieving widow throws herself on the flames of her dead husband's funeral pyre. Clearly, Jhabvala is using the designation ironically.

16. In her discussion of *Heat and Dust*, Newman also uses Said's theory to help elucidate the ideological underpinnings of colonialism; she writes, "The feminization of India goes to the heart of the colonial enterprise" (80).

17. For a detailed account of the strong ideological and historical presence of eugenics in the early twentieth century, and a reading of how it circulated especially in discussions of motherhood, see Doyle chap. 1.

WORKS CITED

Babb, Valerie. *Whiteness Visible: The Meaning of Whiteness in American Literature and Culture*. New York: New York UP, 1998.

Bertelsen, Eve. "Veldtanschauung: Doris Lessing's Savage Africa." *Modern Fiction Studies* 37.4 (Winter 1991): 647–58.

Ciolkowski, Laura. "Navigating the *Wide Sargasso Sea*: Colonial History, English Fiction, and British Empire." *Twentieth Century Literature* 43.3 (Fall 1997): 339–59.

Doyle, Laura. *Bordering on the Body: The Racial Matrix of Modern Fiction and Culture*. New York: Oxford UP, 1994.

Dyer, Richard. *White*. New York: Routledge, 1997.

Fayad, Mona. "Unquiet Ghosts: The Struggle for Representation in Jean Rhys's *Wide Sargasso Sea*." *Modern Fiction Studies* 34.3 (Autumn 1988): 437–52.

Frankenberg, Ruth. *White Women, Race Matters: The Social Construction of Whiteness*. Minneapolis: U of Minnesota P, 1993.

Gordon, Lewis. "Bad Faith and Antiblack Racism." *Black on White: Black Writers on What It Means to Be White*. Ed. David R. Roediger. New York: Schocken, 1998. 305–6.

Gottlieb, Lois C. and Wendy Keitner. "Colonialism as Metaphor and Experience in *The Grass Is Singing* and *Surfacing*." *Awakened Conscience: Studies in Commonwealth Literature*. Ed. C. D. Narasimhaiah. Hong Kong: Heinemann, 1978. 307–14.

Hanley, Lynne. "Writing Across the Color Bar: Apartheid and Desire." *Massachusetts Review* 32.4 (Summer 1991): 495–506.

Harris, Trudier. "White Men as Performers in the Lynching Ritual." *Black on White: Black Writers on What It Means to Be White*. Ed. David R. Roediger. New York: Schocken, 1998. 299–304.

Hogan, Patrick Colm. *Colonialism and Cultural Identity: Crisis of Tradition in Anglophone Literatures of India, Africa, and the Caribbean*. Albany: State U of New York P, 2000.

Jhabvala, Ruth Prawer. *Heat and Dust*. Washington: Counterpoint, 1975.

King, Jeanette. *Doris Lessing*. London: Edward Arnold, 1989.

Lessing, Doris. *The Grass Is Singing*. 1950. New York: Perennial, 2000.

Manion, Eileen. "'Not About the Colour Problem': Doris Lessing's Portrayal of the Colonial Order." *World Literature Written in English* 21.3 (Autumn 1982): 434–55.

Morrison, Toni. *Playing in the Dark: Whiteness and the Literary Imagination*. New York: Vintage, 1993.

Najmi, Samina, and Rajini Srikanth, eds. *White Women in Racialized Spaces*. Albany: State U of New York P, 2002.

Newman, Judie. "Retrofitting the Raj: Ruth Prawer Jhabvala and the Uses and Abuses of the Past." *British Women Writing Fiction*. Ed. Abby H. P. Werlock. Tuscaloosa: U of Alabama P, 2000. 70–89.

Rhys, Jean. *Wide Sargasso Sea*. 1966. Ed. Judith Raskin. New York: Norton, 1999.

Roberts, Sheila. "Sites of Paranoia and Taboo: Lessing's *The Grass Is Singing* and Gordimer's *July's People*." *Research in African Literatures* 24.3 (Fall 1993): 73–85.

Said, Edward. *Orientalism*. New York: Vintage, 1978.

Sharpe, Jenny. *Allegories of Empire: The Figure of Woman in the Colonial Text*. Minneapolis: U of Minnesota P, 1993.

Sollors, Werner, ed. *Interracialism: Black-White Intermarriage in American History, Literature, and Law*. Oxford: Oxford UP, 2000.

Stange, Margit. *Personal Property: Wives, White Slaves, and the Market in Women*. Baltimore: Johns Hopkins UP, 1998.

Sucher, Laurie. *The Fiction of Ruth Prawer Jhabvala: The Politics of Passion*. London: Macmillan, 1989.

Ware, Vron. *Beyond the Pale: White Women, Racism and History*. London: Verso, 1992.

PART II

Performance

The Suspect Whiteness of Spain

BALTASAR FRA-MOLINERO

With Spain's conquest of America in the sixteenth century and the extension of its military presence in the Netherlands and Italy, a political campaign in the presses of northern European countries against the legitimacy of the Iberian hegemony took the form of anti-Spanish political propaganda. One of the arguments northern Europe leveled against Spain and Spaniards was predicated on race. Northern Europeans charged that Spaniards were less than white, or in the words of Sir Edmund Spenser, they were a "mingled nation" (91). The mixture of Moorish and Jewish populations with Roman and Germanic peoples throughout the preceding centuries created a perception of Spain as religiously suspect, its Christianity different and strange. This perception was contradictory, because Spain had been criticized since 1492 for its racial politics of exclusion. Early in that year, Islamic presence in Spain came to an end with the conquest of Granada on January 2, and the Jewish minority was given the choice of forced conversion to Christianity or expulsion on March 30. The *annus mirabilis* of 1492 can be considered the starting date of the whitening of Spain, an act of erasure of its diverse past. And like all acts of erasure, political acts of historical denial leave lasting social consequences.

Spaniards have seen themselves as white since early modernity. The Atlantic slave trade that Spain and Portugal initiated in the middle of the fifteenth century received a decisive impulse after the conquest of the American territories and the exploitation of sugar cane and mining in the newly invaded lands across the ocean. With Spain's and Portugal's justification of slavery and conquest on religious grounds, a new concept of "race" developed in both countries that excluded from their native communities an ever-expanding number of other peoples. Statutes of "limpieza de sangre" 'purity of blood' spread in the sixteenth century with the foundation of the modern state, the first one in Europe. Blacks, mulattoes, and Indians were immediately marked as racially impure, together with Lutherans and descendants of Jews and Muslims. Since high office necessitated a thorough investigation into a candidate's ancestry—the "pruebas de limpieza" 'proof of purity'—being of old Christian stock and of a lighter skin became one and the same thing. Whiteness and Christianity were conflated. Race was religion turned biology. Whiteness became a default category in which one's personal history—ancestry—took a socially relevant value. Controlling one's ancestry became a national obsession, and erasing entire branches of one's family tree a generalized exercise in silencing the past. Purity of blood ceased to be a sociopolitical prerequisite in Spain only in 1869, when its empire was coming to an end. The loss of empire increased its sense of inadequacy as a "white" European country. The silence over personal ancestry was transferred to the Spanish colonial past with the early imperial losses of the nineteenth century. At the close of that century, the crisis of 1898—the Spanish-American War that resulted in Spain ceding Puerto Rico, the Philippine Islands, and Guam to the United States and abandoning all claim to Cuba— was for many a crisis of whiteness.

Given Spain's early relations to whiteness, the discussion that follows addresses the escalation and suspicion of modern Spanish whiteness. It then turns to the mechanisms by which Spanish filmmakers interrogate Spain's national-racial identity since the end of General Francisco Franco's dictatorship in 1975, Spain's instauration of a parliamentary democracy in 1978, and its 1986 incorporation into the European Union, the unofficial international club of white countries. Shaped from Richard Dyer's theoretical definition of whiteness, the assertions that emerge herein target three areas of representation and symbolic social practice that constitute the changing nature of Spain's national identity and its redefinition of whiteness. Spanish filmic exempla best illustrate three discernible social paradigms that define and contest the suspect whiteness of Spain. The first exemplum relates to Gypsy identity, the second to Latin American and African immigration, and the third to the new sexual politics of the Spanish state under democracy, with its shifting redefinition of Spanish whiteness.

The Oriental Within: Tourism, Flamenco, Gypsies, and *Carmen*

For African-American writer Richard Wright, who traveled extensively throughout Spain in the 1950s while expatriating in southern France, Spain was decidedly non-European. In his travel book *Pagan Spain* (1957), Wright depicts a poor, Moorish, Gypsy, Fascist, Catholic country enamored of bullfighting, practicing strict segregation along gender lines, and curiously lacking a racial definition for a person like him, a middle-class Black man with a disposable income. His literary exercise could be qualified as sweet revenge: the "other" was "othering" the "self."

In a recent essay on "Spanish Orientalism" Ignacio Tofiño-Quesada argues that Spain has lived with the contradiction of "orientalizing" others (mostly African peoples) and being "orientalized" by European and North American nineteenth-century traveling writers. From Washington Irving's *Tales of the Alhambra* (1832) to Théophile Gautier and Prosper Mérimée's *Carmen* (1845), an image was created of what Tofiño-Quesada calls "orientalism *à la carte*" (143) in which the Muslim Arab past was seen in the present of their travels and exemplified in Gypsy lore.[1] Created outside Spain by the post-romantic imagination, this image was shared to a large extent by intellectuals and writers within Spain for more than a century, although with a different emphasis. Classic composers of the magnitude of Albéniz and Manuel de Falla or writers from the Generation of 1927 like Federico García Lorca pursued what they called a Gypsy aesthetic in part of their work. After the Spanish Civil War ended in 1939, the Franco regime exploited the image of Gypsy Spain to develop its tourism industry through the promotion of a "Carmen-esque" series of advertisement posters and the popularization of a Gypsy-style or "folklórica" genre.

The film *¡Bienvenido, Mr. Marshall!* (1952) satirizes this tendency through the story of a typical Castilian town that "transforms" itself into an Andalusian-Gypsy enclave to attract U.S. investment capital at the time in which post–World War II Europe was benefiting from the Marshall Plan, which notoriously excluded Spain as a nondemocratic regime that had sympathized with Nazi Germany.[2]

During the Franco years (1939–75), Spain sold its Gypsy image outside its borders to promote its tourism industry while fiercely excluding Gypsies from the national agenda. Gypsies were at the core of the famous official slogan from the Spanish Ministry of Tourism: *Spain is different.*[3] Nevertheless, Gypsies were and still are the most racialized minority of Spanish society, the most marginalized and rejected ethnic group in Spain, the other within (Santaolalla 58). Historically, Gypsies have developed, within Spanish society, a true sense of what W. E. B. Du Bois calls "double consciousness" (5).

After the death of Franco in 1975, Spanish culture took a new interest in things Gypsy, particularly in flamenco. Appropriation of Gypsy culture in post-Franco Spain is slowly giving more space to Gypsy cultural agents.[4] For the first time in Spanish history, Gypsies are in charge of defining their own identity and their relation to the identity of the Spanish majority. Yet for "payos"—the term Gypsies call non-Gypsy Spaniards—Gypsy Spaniards represent a perpetual other of nonwhiteness, in spite of the fact that they perceive Gypsy culture as inherently Spanish. Payos logic asserts that Gypsies are "inherently" Spanish but "different," which makes them less Spanish. The frozen image of the Gypsy among the majority of Spaniards is connected to criminality of one kind or another, primarily drug trafficking and addiction, substandard living conditions in the outskirts of towns and cities, and unemployment and the lack of a "work ethic." All of these perceptions justify their exclusion as a group "disinterested" in participating in the majority culture. The payo majority has criminalized many forms of Gypsy existence—itinerant ways of life, commercial activity, even music and dance—creating a stigma that is relatively impervious to the profound transformation of the Gypsy minority during the last fifty years.

The payo majority needs to see Gypsies in essentialist terms in order to establish the "difference" that makes a payo white. This majority that needs to define the minority group as a marked category for exclusion rejects a dynamic sense of Gypsy identity as "un-Gypsy." The growth of Pentecostal Christianity among many Gypsies in Spain is a case in point, as Catholics, and even other payo Pentecostals, view with suspicion Gypsy conversion to the religion. They interpret the moral agency and autonomy of Gypsy Pentecostal groups as religiously illegitimate. They also dismiss the evolving Gypsy identity and social consciousness that these groups develop—an identity invested in social response to the problem of toxicomania among Gypsies and the promotion of women's education and economic autonomy—as "inauthentic" in their "Gypsiness" (Cantón Delgado 102). The rest of Spain sees in Gypsies what Europe sees in Spaniards, a lesser form of its own. In Spain today the word "Gitano" 'Gypsy' is still an insult among non-Gypsies in the way that "judío" 'Jew' and "judiada" 'a treacherous action' are negative terms. For the majority, Gypsies need to remain static in their ways in order to be recognized. In fact, there is a vested interest in cultivating a certain image of the Andalusian-Gypsy to execrate it. Whereas in 1983 Carlos Saura recreated Bizet's operatic version of *Carmen* to explore the nonwhite female version of the story, the white-male perspective is still the norm in the twenty-first century. The Spanish fixation with the French literary myth is an attempt to exorcise the nonwhite, dark, and female other within under the guise of making Carmen "more authentic" and "Spanish," as Saura declared in 1984 (Davies 8).

A Spanish, Italian, and English co-produced film with an international cast of actors and actresses, Vicente Aranda's *Carmen* (2003) defines Spanish whiteness as male by pitting it against the female "other," which in this case is also a racial "other," or ambiguously close to it. Aranda's film depicts French writer Prosper Mérimée, the original author of the 1845 novella by the same title, as the narrator/ witness of the seduction of a man from the north by a woman from the south. Many ironic forms and moments signify the white/nonwhite dichotomy, some of them hilarious. The casting of the leading actors is one example, with an Italian (Leonardo Sbaraglia) as Don José and a brunette non-Gypsy Spaniard (Paz Vega) as Carmen, the Andalusian/Gypsy seductress. The film plays with racial ambiguity, or rather, with the limits of whiteness. Don Próspero (Mérimée's name in Spain) defines an Andalusian woman as someone possessing three phenotypical qualities: black hair, dark eyes, and white skin. At the same time Don Próspero (his Shakespearean overtones should not be underestimated as master of the story) defines himself as an archaeologist and a historian in search of the origins of the Ummayad and Nasri dynasties of the Arab period of Spain.

The search beginning the film, while flamenco music sounds in the background at key scenes, serves as a frame to predicate the mysterious ethnicity of Carmen, as it is never fully revealed. Don José's Basque Navarre origin and his use of the Basque language that linguistically signals his racial purity, together with his deeply devout Catholicism— as it corresponds to a "Basque" in the imaginary of the Spanish spectator—articulate his whiteness. On the other hand, Carmen *also* speaks Basque, but one is suspicious of her fluency because she is a "witch" who has a pact with the devil. She is "irreligious"—mocking Don José's devotion to his hometown Virgin, the superwhite "Virgen de las Nieves" 'Our Lady of the Snow'—and profoundly "superstitious," paying constant attention to signs of good and bad luck and reading the tarot cards to know her future.

Don José possesses whiteness by default; he has a natural self-control and rationality that he will cast out under the spell of sexual passion, the dark force that threatens whiteness. He reaches his nadir of depravity when he asks Carmen to be the mother of his children since the ultimate threat to whiteness is interracial reproduction (Dyer 25). Carmen, illegitimately usurping the place of the Virgin Mary and Don José's mother, will make Don José divest himself of his whiteness through seduction and amorality. Unlike the Virgin, she is not one— her father, we are told, sold her virginity four times before she was fourteen years of age—and she accepts Don José's mother's wedding ring with indifference, unwilling to claim the female responsibility of motherhood that goes with marriage. She receives her just reward in the final love scene when the scorned Don José stabs her in the middle of an empty Baroque church, her blood staining for symbolic emphasis the tiles of a black-and-white checkered floor. Don José is sentenced to die by "garrote vil," an iron collar quickly tightened leading to strangulation, a new execution method for criminal commoners: those who were read as non-aristocratic and therefore racially impure. The subtextual message embedded in Aranda's *Carmen* is that the darker subject strips the nondark of his whiteness.

Immigrants in Spanish Cinema and the Affirmation of the (White) Self

Spain is white in as much as it receives nonwhite immigrants. Following this equation, the more immigrants it receives, the whiter Spain becomes. One out of ten children born in Spain in 2003 had at least one non-Spanish parent.[5] However, the geography of immigration shows marked differences in regional distribution, with a higher concentration of immigrants in southern and eastern Spain than in Old Castile or the Basque Country.[6] These regional concentrations demonstrate an eerie similarity to the historical division between Muslim and Christian Spain in the twelfth century, but it signifies a more complex reason, such as the existence of a plantation economy in the agricultural sector of these regions that employs large numbers of undocumented immigrant workers. The lands of Al-Andalus, so to speak, are also the site of acute social inequity. Ironically, these areas receive a large population of "nonwhites" coming from countries related to Spanish imperial history. By country or continent of origin, Africa and Latin America represent more than half of the immigrants, with Morocco and Ecuador being the two single countries composing almost a third of the total.[7]

This historical coincidence is generally met with an equal exercise in silence and in disavowal of the imperial past. In terms of immigration, Spain is not different from the other European countries in its social environment, and this demographic phenomenon would make Spain more European, rather than less.[8] However, this is not the way Spanish people tend to view this trend. Significant public figures such as Marta Ferrusola, the wife of former Catalan president Jordi Pujol, sounded the alarm in 2001 about the loss of Catalan identity due to the influx of immigrants—mostly from Africa and Latin America. Their alarm contrasts with the response from Catalan writer Juan Goytisolo, who reminded the public of the migratory past of the Spanish people a few decades earlier.[9] Basque nationalism, on the other hand, has been much more open in its policies toward immigrants, both from other parts of Spain as well as from African and Latin American countries. In fact, three Spanish films made in the last fifteen years that address immigration issues have Basque directors, screenwriters, or producers. Montxo Armendáriz, Icíar Bollaín, and Imanol Uribe, whose films I discuss below, are among the most visible.

Representing and defining whiteness in Spanish contemporary cinema is the ultimate agenda of a series of immigrant-themed feature films where the presence of a symbolic Black person brings about a crisis of conscience to the moral landscape of Spanish society. The transformation renders the non-Black spectator both morally uplifted and whiter. Four films—*Las cartas de Alou* (*Alou's Letters*, 1990), *Bwana* (*Lord*, 1996), *Flores de otro mundo* (*Flowers from Another World*, 1999), and *Poniente* (*West*, 2002)—exemplify a filmography that constructs and defines Spanish whiteness while espousing overt democratic and progressive agendas. The presence of Blacks in European and American history is fraught with the memory of slavery and its aftermath of colonization and other forms of violent disenfranchisement, actions in which Spain was a prominent agent. But as pointed out earlier, that history has been erased from the collective memory of Spaniards. Thus the influx of darker skinned immigrants to Spain since the 1980s is presented as something new and unexpected. Spanish films are complicit in this novel (re)construction of history.

James Snead's study of American cinema's treatment of Blacks as icons, *White Screens, Black Images*, offers a list of three "devices"— marking, mythification, and omission—by which Blacks "have been consigned to minor significance" (4). Blacks' treatment on the screen, from the use of makeup to specific roles and limitations to the scope of those roles, has permeated to the cinema of other countries such as Spain, both in the past and the present. Even when Black characters appear prominently or are the protagonists, their presence on screen does not receive the same treatment as white characters that tend to represent a nonracial universality. This difference, as Snead demonstrates, is codified, and audiences respond with pleasure even while they recognize these devices as morally and historically invalid.

James Snead defines marking as the series of coded elements present in a film that overemphasize the Blackness of a character. These can be extradiegetic drum sounds, recognizable African or Afro-Caribbean music, dress, speech patterns, or even the use of lighting to underline the darkness of the character's skin color.[10] Ultimately, these elements create in the viewer the expectation of a subordinate relation between white and nonwhite characters (Snead 6). In *Las cartas de Alou* (1996), directed by Montxo Armendáriz, the title's protagonist, (Mulie Jarju) is an African man—who is in fact a Wolof-speaking Sengalese, a detail that is passed over in favor of a generic continental identification—that writes letters back home telling about his experiences as an illegal immigrant in Spain.[11] Similar to Montesquieu's *Lettres persanes* (*Persian Letters*, 1721) or José Cadalso's *Cartas marruecas* (*Moroccan Letters*, 1793), Alou's letters home have the distancing effect of rendering unfamiliar a series of social mores the viewer may take for granted. The content of the letters, represented by Alou's disembodied voice-over, has the effect of positioning the spectator as the object of the gaze and as analyzer of the other. The separation, as Alou's race represents, is a degree of insurmountable difference. The background music is an important extradiegetic marker of Alou's Blackness and foreignness in contrast with the Spanish characters of the dominant culture.

The film narrates the complexity and variety of immigrant experiences, ethnicities, religions, and cultures, which the Spanish majority tends to ignore (Urioste 53). As the intended spectator sits in the comfort zone of whiteness, the process of sympathizing with the Black African protagonist begins. The plot advances to a point in which sympathy may turn into identification; scenes of economic exploitation suffered by the protagonist recall the not-so-distant experiences of Spanish migrant workers in northern Europe, especially those employed in seasonal harvests. In the logic of the mechanisms of identification within a narrative, the heterosexual character aims for a romantic climax, which signals reproduction of the self and the nation. Here is where the narrative progress of *Las cartas de Alou* comes to a halt. Alou had been displaying a contradictory mixture of wanderlust and nesting, the latter marked by his sexual self-control and his religious piety as a manly devout Muslim. When he and a Spanish white woman, (Carmen, ironically perhaps), fall in love, racism will raise its ugly head, and his arrest and expulsion from the country cut short the promise of a happy heterosexual ending. Although the state's racist policies are to blame for the interruption of the love story of this Black man and white woman, the narrative avoids addressing the question of what kind of nation would be built by the couple through preemption: a Spanish policeman's unfairness toward Alou forces him to bid good-bye to Carmen in what could be interpreted as the state's repression of an interracial relationship. The film, however, ends as it started, Alou on a "patera" 'boat' on his way back to restart his Spanish adventure.

In the narrative economy of this film, Alou is a bearer of gifts, one of the three Magi, and is referred to as "Baltasar," the African wise-man, by Carmen's father. Coming from a strange land he heralds to the spectator the new Epiphany at the end of the twentieth century, that Spain is somehow special, divinely chosen, in spite of its xeno-phobia and multicultural insensitivity. Alou, the writer of letters, is himself a gift that Spain would be foolish not to accept, because he bears the news that Spain is white. The problem remains in deciding what to do with the messenger after he has delivered the message.

If the protagonist of *Las cartas de Alou* is a messenger of Spanish whiteness, Imanol Uribe's *Bwana* (1996) is an exercise in "white" guilt reflected against the mirror of a Black body.[12] Of the three ele-ments outlined by James Snead in his essay on white spectatorship of the Black body, mythification applies to this film. Mythification of Blacks eliminates the need for historical analysis. In this case, a mysterious and apparently nameless Black man (Equatorial Guinean actor Emilio Buale) washes ashore on a Mediterranean beach. Found by a lower middle-class family of Spaniards, the Black man ends up being attacked by a group of white supremacist skinheads who previ-ously had harassed the taxi driver head of the Spanish family (Spanish actor Andrés Pajares). Several elements within the film that resonate with a Spanish audience signal the narrative of whiteness. The geo-graphic setting is a beach in Almería—the same location where Alou starts his Spanish experience—in the extreme southeast, across from the African coast, and an impoverished land of migrants itself in the 1950s and 1960s.[13] Stuck in the social practice of middle-class aspira-tions initiated during the later years of the Franco era, the (white) protagonists find themselves cornered in this desolate landscape between the presence of the group of skinheads and the Sphinx-like Black man, who is constructed as fixed, outside history, following the classical Hollywood code for the representation of Blacks (Snead 3). This Black man's inability to speak Spanish or any European language correlates to his silence and immobility. Even when he pronounces his name—Ombasi—at one point, his interlocutors do not understand him, and they will never address him by it. His silence and immobility are misinterpreted, and members of the family, whose lack of cultural sophistication is their class mark, misread his black body. These markers bar the spectator's identification with these "lesser-white" individuals. Instead, the audience sympathizes—not identifies—with the Black man, and its disidentification parallels the disidentification the character experiences within the plot at the film's end. Language here is an important factor of characterization—as it is in many recorded encounters between the colonizer and the soon-to-be-colonized in Spanish chronicles of the American conquest, from Columbus's *Diaries* to Inca Garcilaso's *Royal Commentaries*. Ombasi's incomprehensible, unidentified language in this case is Bubi, one of the languages spoken by actor Emilio Buale. Connected to the Spanish imperial past, the Bubi language of the island of Bioko, Fernando Poo in colonial times, is first disavowed, and then instrumentalized as a representation of the insurmountable communication divide between Black Africa and white Europe. The suspension of disbelief is strained at this point, as one can hardly imagine an African immigrant to Europe who does not speak at least one of the languages of the former colonizers. This Black immigrant is not a historical individual but an avatar of the eternal African other.

A parallel linguistic disability threatens the patriarch of the family. He is intimidated by the violent attitude of superiority of the skinheads, one of whom is a woman, symbolized by the languages they speak—German and English, both reminiscent of the Spanish working class's own history of migration to Europe. The difference is that German and English are identifiable to the audience, whereas Bubi is beyond the pale, in spite of its historical connection to Spain.

Indeed, each member of the family interprets the Black man in a fragmentary manner that amounts to a unified discourse. The young daughter of the family comes running to announce the presence of a Black man on the beach "who has killed another one" (his dead companion who drowned in the wreck of their makeshift vessel). Through the optic of the Tarzan movies, the patriarch's son names him "Bwana," 'Lord' in Swahili, in a not-so-innocent game of colonial role reversal.

Believing him dangerous, the father offers propitiatory gifts—money, a gas lighter, and his own food. His wife (Spanish actress María Barranco) reads the presence of the Black man through popular anthropology and raw stereotyping; he may practice anthropophagy, the gas lighter "is" a magic object for him, he will rape her, and he is the carrier of unknown diseases: "Estos negros están llenos de microbios. Lo dicen en la tele." 'These Blacks all carry diseases. They say so on television.' She projects a gendered discourse of whiteness. Under her initial fear lies an erotic desire for him expressed through a dream. She further follows him to the sea, where she contemplates his naked body in the water and fashions herself as white American actress Ava Gardner in the film *Mogambo:* "Ava Gardner se bañaba en la playa con unos negros. ¡Qué poderío!" 'Ava Gardner was swimming at the beach with Black men. Now that was power!' The naturalization/sacralization of the Black body climaxes with his naked silhouette in an attitude of prayer against the rising sun with his arms extended in the form of a cross, a foreboding of his impending death. The eruption of the skinheads who attack the Black man, shouting in English their wish to castrate him, precipitates his end. As the members of the family flee the scene by car, they witness the lynching of the naked Black man, now reduced to frightened humanity. The four family members watch from inside their car and refuse to open the door to give him sanctuary: "No puedo ayudarte, corre, no puedo. . . . Arranca por Dios, Antonio. . . . No puedo hacer nada por ti. . . . Los niños, nos matan a los niños, vámonos!" 'I can't help you, run, I can't. . . . Start the car, Antonio, for God's sake. . . . I can't do anything for you. . . . The children, they are going to kill our children, let's go!' In the next shot the skinheads surround the naked Black man, whose face, intensified with an extreme close-up, looks in the direction of the camera, the viewpoint of both the audience and the retreating Spanish family, made white in their flight and insolidarity. This Bwana, lord, dies for the sins of the white husband and wife, who are unable to confront their own inadequacies and the looming threat of fascism represented by the skinheads—practitioners of white supremacy who operate without the legitimacy of a state apparatus—a new fact of European history. In the case of the husband, the loss of patriarchal privilege fuels his sense of inadequacy, and in the case of the wife, an internalized frustration with her gender-sex role that includes the unsatisfied erotic desire for the Black body curtails her complete sexual freedom. The Black man the skinheads kill is no longer the mythified Bwana of the white family but a human being, helpless and naked. Whiteness is a violent religion whose Messiah is this Black man offered in sacrifice. The expenditure of sympathy by the film's intended white audiences is paid with the all too common currency of racialized films: death of the racialized object of sympathy.

Directed by Icíar Bollaín, *Flores de otro mundo* (1999) represents the feminist response of exorcising the public's bad conscience. Elucidating Snead's theory of omission with respect to white spectatorship in film, *Flores de otro mundo* is the substitution of an omitted story—the murder of Lucrecia Pérez Matos, an Afro-Dominican immigrant on October 13, 1992, the night of the emblematic date on which official Spain celebrated the five-hundredth anniversary of the Columbian expedition. After an extensive investigation, a report of the findings revealed that there was a shooting, an action taken by a white supremacist group, involving the local police. Matos's death caused a national outcry among progressive forces and immigrant organizations, drawing massive media coverage.[14]

According to the screenwriters, directors Bollaín and Julio Llamazares, the film is a "veridic documentary" of the experience of immigrant women in Spain, with the unstated assumption that the portrayal of immigrants in the media and the attitudes toward them from the (white) Spanish majority are neither truthful nor sincere (Martínez-Carazo 380). *Flores de otro mundo* presents the stories of three women, one white *and* from the Basque Country and two Afro-Caribbeans from Cuba and the Dominican Republic respectively. Each one is in search of a male companion in a small, mythical village in the middle of Castile and has been invited by its mayor as part of a campaign to stop the demographic drain, a pervasive depopulation problem in rural northern Spain due to the migration of young people to urban centers. If Almería symbolizes the outer extreme of white territorialization, Castile is its very center, now in danger of demographic emptying. The center of whiteness has fewer and fewer whites.

The gendering of immigration as female exposes a construction of whiteness by which one of the Black women, Afro-Dominican Patricia

(Lisette Mejía), decides to stay and settle with a local man, Damian (Luis Tosar), after a series of dramatic turns in their emotional involvement marked by her legal complications as an immigrant. Of the three women, she is the only one still raising a family. Her two children are the only Black ones in a sea of whiteness emphasized by a snow scene and a first communion episode, both of which visually underline—or "mark" in Snead's grammar of racial representation of Blacks in film—the Black/white contrast that is at the base of the tension in the film.[15] Marirrosi, the Basque woman, uses her white privilege of professional independence to return to Bilbao. Young and curvaceous, Black Cuban Milady (Marilin Torres) is penalized with a brutal beating for choosing to be a free spirit without being middle class and white. Her choice of attire, lycra pants with the stars and stripes of the American flag reminiscent of Cuba's historical intersection with the United States and Spain, symbolizes her historical predicament (Martín-Cabrera 46). Patricia, the Afro-Dominican woman, has to be saved by her homely, male Spanish knight from her younger and attractive blackmailing Afro-Dominican ex-husband who comes to represent male domestic oppression. This flower from another world will settle in a mythical rural Spain and cease to have a history. The movie ends with her acceptance of the mother and dutiful wife role in exchange for her children and herself. A key scene critics comment upon occurs between Patricia and her future mother-in-law in the cemetery as they both clean the tomb of her fiancé's father. Prior to this moment, the two women have had a strained relationship for reasons that mix motherly jealousy and cultural difference. Yet in the cemetery, they reach a truce as they realize that their lives are tied to two basically good men, one above ground and the other six feet under, son and father. The pleasure of the moment for the viewer obfuscates critical inquiry into the life Patricia has bought for herself and her children. The film predicates a triumph of integration through the economic subjugation of a Black woman, who receives the prize of marriage to the Spanish man. A good immigrant is a servant immigrant to a white master, a well-intentioned Spanish male. The marking devices of James Snead's grammar of Black representation come into focus at the film's end, which confirms the "goodness" of the Black woman's subordination to white male Spanishness, one that does not seem to have problems with race mixture, provided it is done with the Spaniard on top, as critic Jo Labanyi has demonstrated in the case of other racialized representations in the Spanish missionary films of the early Franco era (32).

After viewing only one-third of the film *Poniente* (2002), directed by Chus Gutiérrez, the Spanish spectator "knows" that she or he is being told another omitted narrative, that of the tragic events of El Ejido, a town in Almería where white supremacist elements, spurred on by the local mayor and the police, attacked the homes, businesses, and civil association headquarters of North African immigrants in December 1997. Much like Miguel de Cervantes did in the Ricote episodes of *Don Quijote* (2: chapters 54 and 63) with the expulsion of the Morisco population in what amounts to an exercise of a journalistic novel—the expulsion was taking place almost as he was writing in 1614—*Poniente* fictionalizes a repressed narrative of white oppression and violence that is in the historical memory of its intended audience. The film is also an indictment of Almería's recent past of nonwhiteness, as Juan Goytisolo reminded the readers of *El País* about his road trips through the province, one in the late fifties and a second in the early sixties, accompanied by Simone de Beauvoir.[16]

The title of the film is an intended translation from the Arabic word "Maghreb," the common term Arab geographers gave to the westernmost lands known to them, which included the Iberian peninsula. The word "poniente" means "west," yet it is a reflection on Spain's "eastern" or "oriental" roots. That the land, Almería, so cherished by the white protagonists in the film, has a name given in the language of the oppressed opens the dialogue between Curro (José Coronado), a Spaniard who is ill at ease with the capitalist transformation of the landscape into a sea of plastic, and Adbembi (Farid Fatmi), the enlightened Berber immigrant who educates the white Spaniard into divesting himself of whiteness: "Te he explicado mil veces que no somos árabes. Nuestro pueblo tiene cinco mil años de historia y se extiende por todo el África del norte" 'I have told you one thousand times that we are not Arabs. Our people have a five-thousand year history, and it stretches along all northern Africa.' Adbembi later reminds Curro of the common ancestry of Spaniards and Berbers in a rewriting of the philogenetic discourse of whiteness that has prevailed in Spain since the Middle Ages.

Whiteness in this film is feminized in the person of Lucía (Cuca Escribano), who returns to the town of her childhood to settle some traumatic events in her life—a difficult relation with her father whom she comes to bury and the death of her infant daughter who drowned at the beach years before. Almería, the easternmost province in southern Spain, acts as the site of trauma at the personal and national levels. Lucía performs her whiteness through a discourse of feminism and progressive politics in her resolution to become the dynamic element in the narrative of the film. The place of a woman in film, and in the narrative in general, has been that of "bearer of meaning, not maker of meaning" (Mulvey 7). As the product of a feminist aesthetic, *Poniente* makes Lucía address the trauma of the losses of her father and her motherhood, marked by her decision to leave family ties behind in order to attain modernity and economic independence as a school teacher in a big city. Her return as a landowner takes the form of enlightened reform in order to establish a feminist utopia in a sea of men. She improves the salaries of the migrant workers under her employment and appoints one of them a foreman—whose name, Chad, marks his visible Blackness—over the objections of Paquito, representative of the law of her late father. A male establishment embodies gender and racial oppressors whose politics are dictated by raw capitalist imperatives in the form of credits that must be paid in a plantation economy.

In *Poniente*, the other is fighting to occupy a space contiguous with the self without abandoning his identity. This other, in the persons of the migrant workers from Africa and Eastern Europe, is defined collectively as "Moor" and "Black" by the local majority of La Isla 'The Island,' as the enclave is known, with full intended, exclusive symbolism. Universal maleness, as far as the camera shows, and the marking elements of immigration—tomato greenhouse work, extradiegetic Moroccan music, discriminatory housing—freeze the possibilities of the few individualized nonwhite characters having salient roles in the narrative. The most prominent one, Adbembi, observes passively how his friend Curro becomes desperate about their common project of opening a chiringuito, a food and drink bar by the beach. He justifies his passivity with quotes from the Quran, his role being that of a prophet, mythical and ahistorical. As in *Bwana*, set also in Almería, white supremacist violence precipitates the end in the form of an anti-immigrant riot that climaxes tragically for Lucía and her love interest

Curro, whom an organized gang of male greenhouse owners kills with baseball bats. The last scene shows the ultimate white icon, a "pietà" scene, the image of cradling and death (Dyer 15). Lucía holds the dead body of Curro, the Christ-like dreamer of interethnic collaboration. Although the film's title promises a dialogue on the commonality of Maghrebi immigrants and local Spaniards, the last scene centers only on the fate of the Spanish participants, marked by the recourse to a (white) Christian iconographic tableau.

What's Gay Got to Do with It?
Europeanness, Movida, and Almodóvar:
Toward a (Re)definition of Spanish Identity

Using the Kantian distinction, Spain debates its white identity between a transcendent concept of Europeanness and an immanent definition of Europeanness. On the one hand it is an inheritor of the medieval religious-political idea of Christendom, and on the other it absorbs a series of ideas and practices closely tied to historical changes that impact its democratic form of government, popular sovereignty, secularism, and an expanding idea of human rights and equality. Legalized in July 2005, gay marriage, in the Spanish case, is an example of this immanent European practice. The philosophy behind this historical step is one that believes Spanish law needs to be more in tune with both public mores and what the Spanish Left considers progressive changes that leave behind, once and for all, the Franco era and its legacy of unenlightened conservatism through its doctrine of national Catholicism.[17] The Left plays down sexuality and erotic desire, two banners of the sexual revolution of the seventies in Spain, while the Church makes its stand against the destructive force of sexuality that excludes reproduction (of an unstated white community). The Left answers with adoption and the change of the patriarchal concept of the family.[18] At play is the state's maneuver to establish its primacy in regulating sexual desire over the monopoly of the Church on sexuality as a sphere of the sacred. In Spain, whiteness is losing its old connection with Christianity in favor of secularism, in an age where religious fundamentalism is associated with nonwhite people, Muslims in particular.

The legislation on gay marriage is the product, to a large extent, of the sentimental education of a generation of Spaniards who woke up in the 1980s to the sexual politics of hybridity, the ferocious critique of Spanish machismo, the calling into question of gender roles, and the conscious cultivation of some of the least white icons of Spanish popular culture, such as flamenco and bullfighting, but now suffused with a queer aesthetic. The "movida" was a cultural move away from the orthodoxy of the Left as much as it was the burial ceremony of cultural Francoism. Through a practice of impure forms in music, fashion, social mores, literature, and film, the movida finally conquered Spanish television, perhaps the most sclerotic of all official cultural institutions. By ignoring monocultural European/white narratives of identity and instead practicing multiple identities—sexual, gender, national, geographic, even racial—the movida offered something new and attractive to both Spaniards and cultural critics abroad. The movida gave Spain a sort of "Europeanness" insofar as it recalled former icons of Spanish culture like Luis Buñuel or Salvador Dalí. The international poster boy of this cultural phenomenon was filmmaker Pedro Almodóvar.

Like Miguel de Cervantes, the author of *Don Quijote*, Pedro Almodóvar, the most emblematic filmmaker Spain has produced to date, is an exception to the rule. Almodóvar is atypical among creative artists, and yet he has connected with the most critical intellectual traditions, the writers of the 1898 and 1927 generations, the ones that called into question the need for Spanish whiteness. Almodóvar's films bring the margins to the center: homosexuals, racial minorities (Gypsies, Latin Americans, Blacks) and the rural hinterland of La Mancha, from where some of his characters, like himself, come. Almodóvaresque themes, like those of Luis Buñuel, destabilize the conservative institutional pillars of Spanish society. The Catholic Church, the army, the patriarchal family, and normative heterosexism are constantly assailed in his work. The most "European" and emblematic of all Spanish film directors, Almodóvar ridicules the ersatz Europeanness and fake gestures of a Spanish bourgeoisie that is far from embracing the democratic principle of equality and the ethics of solidarity.

In *Todo sobre mi madre* (*All About My Mother*), the 1999 Oscar winner for best foreign-language film, an upper-middle-class Catalan woman (Rosa María Sardá), who lives in a house built by modernist architect Antonio Gaudí, makes a living painting fake Chagals while castigating her daughter Rosa (Penélope Cruz), an aspiring nun with a social conscience, for wishing to join a religious community in civil war–torn El Salvador. In *Todo sobre mi madre*, perhaps the most Christian of all the Almodóvar films, the suffering of the mother who has lost her young son increases her charity toward people with AIDS, including her ex-husband, a transsexual dying of the disease. Manuela (Argentinean actress Cecilia Roth) represents Almodóvar's homage to the generation of Latin American political exiles of the 1970s who fled a brand of murderous oppression eerily similar to the one Spain practiced after its Civil War. The Spain of *Todo sobre mi madre* is hybrid and decidedly democratic in spirit, aesthetically underlined in many scenes by the color red, the least of all white/ European colors. The film enshrines two gay, effeminate classic playwrights of the twentieth century—Tennessee Williams and Federico García Lorca—as the artistic response to any form of heterosexist masculinity, which can be read as a rejection of a sexual norm that generated white supremacy and purity of blood as its byproducts.

The urban tapestry against which the action of *Todo sobre mi madre* takes place is decidedly multicultural, not white or overwritten/overridden by whiteness. Barcelona's Barri Gotic (Gothic Quarter) with its European medieval architecture as landscape is now the haven of entire families of Black people. They represent the new Spain. As the upper-class Rosa visits an obstetrician to check on her pregnancy by HIV-positive transgendered Lola (Toni Canto), the camera shows in the background a couple of African descent, the woman also pregnant. The extradiegetic music that accompanies the iconic view of Barcelona at night is identifiably African, as African in origin as the slave labor that paid for Antonio Gaudí's emblematic homes for the Catalan slave-owning bourgeoisie.[19] In his representation of Spain, Pedro Almodóvar makes his actresses and actors invertedly perform whiteness by "raceing" the self as Gypsy, homosexual, a pregnant nun, a transsexual, a lesbian actress, a southern immigrant in northern Spain, or an exiled Argentinean nurse who specializes in dramatizing organ transplant donations. None of the protagonists of Almodóvar's films are "normative," their whiteness being suspect and contaminated. And they are celebrated for being so.

NOTES

1. The list of French writers who visited Spain in search of Gypsy culture includes Victor Hugo, Stendhal, Gustave Flaubert, Chateaubriand, Alexandre Dumas père, and others, followed by plastic artists such as Gustave Doré and Edouard Manet (Charnon-Deutsch 29).

2. In 1947, George Catlett Marshall, the secretary of state for the United States, proposed a solution to the disintegrating economic and social conditions that faced Europeans in the aftermath of World War II. European nations set up a reconstruction program with U.S. assistance that marked the official beginning of the Economic Recovery Program (ERP).

3. In 1960, *Los Tarantos* was an attempt to create an "authentic" Gypsy film very much in the style of the time. A story of passion, violence, and flamenco singing and dancing, *Los Tarantos* showed a stereotypical view of Gypsy life in its attempt to portray the transition of Gypsies from an itinerant into an urban life.

4. Film director Carlos Saura made his own version of *Carmen* (1983) with a decidedly Gypsy aesthetic and the presence of Gypsy artists as he had done in his 1981 flamenco dance version of García Lorca's *Bodas de sangre* (*Blood Wedding*). He continued this practice in *El amor brujo* (*Love the Bewitcher*, 1986) and in his two monographic films *Sevillanas* (1994) and *Flamenco* (1995).

5. "El 10% de los 416.518 bebés nacidos el año pasado fueron de madres extranjeras." 'Ten percent of the 416,518 babies born last year were of foreign mothers.' ("España alcanza por la inmigración su mayor cifra de nacimientos" 1).

6. According to the Instituto Nacional de Estadística, quoted in the daily newspaper *El País*, 28 Apr. 2005, eastern Spanish regions (Catalonia, Valencia, Murcia, the Balearic Islands) have immigrant populations that compose between 10 percent and 15 percent of the total inhabitants in those regions, together with Madrid and the Canary Islands. Andalusia and New Castille range between 4 percent and 5 percent, but with rates of increase among the highest in the country, with an increase of 28 percent and 29 percent in immigrant population in just one year. In contrast, northern Spain (Galicia, Asturias, Cantabria, the Basque Country, Old Castile, and León) have minimal rates, between 2.5 percent and 3.6 percent of its total population composed of "empadronados," locally 'registered immigrants' ("España ya alcanza los 44 millones de habitantes" 30).

7. The Secretaría de Estado de Inmigración y Emigración, quoted in "Los datos oficiales revelan que 1,5 millones de extranjeros viven sin papeles en España": "'Official figures reveal that 1.5 million foreigners are living in Spain without legal papers,'" reproduces a similar map of Spain that misleadingly shows the numbers of legal residents. It marks with a bold bar the word "Marruecos" 'Morocco' with almost 400,000 legal residents (31).

8. *El País*, 27 Apr. 2005, citing sources from the Observatorio Permanente de la Inmigración (Permanent Observatory on Immigration), announced that two million

foreigners were permanent residents in Spain, making them almost 5 percent of the total population. The newspaper distinguished between European Union citizens and citizens from outside the EU, which it calls "the true immigrants." The newspaper adds that Spain is "far from the percentages in countries like France (8%) and Germany (9%)" ("Los extranjeros con residencial legal superan ya los dos millones" 24). However, the following day *El País* gave figures that indicated a total foreign population of 8.4 percent out of a total of forty-four million. The source now was the Instituto Nacional de Estadística (Institute of National Statistics), which counts both legal and nonlegal residents ("España ya alcanza los 44 millones de habitantes 30).

    9. See Goytisolo, "Metáforas de la Migración" 13.

    10. Extradiegetic markers are those that do not have any visible or logical source within a scene. The terms "extradiegetic," as well as "intradiegetic," its opposite, are commonly used in narrative theory since structuralism.

    11. The film won the main prize at the San Sebastián Film Festival in 1990, and Mulie Jarju obtained the best actor award at the same venue (Urioste 59).

    12. The movie is a free version of Ignacio del Moral's play *La mirada del hombre oscuro* (1992).

    13. Goytisolo's *Campos de Níjar* is a well-known testimony of that moment. In his article published in *El País* he mentions that the town council of El Ejido declared him persona non grata ("De magrebíes y gente así").

    14. "Hoy se cumple el décimo aniversario del asesinato de Lucrecia Pérez" and "Una immigrante aróuima que se convirtió en mártir" 10. The song "Canción a Lucrecia," composed by Carlos Cano (1994), paid explicit homage to this victim of a rising tide in white supremacist violence against immigrants.

    15. Through this visual contrasts of Black and white, the director of photography is following a long tradition in Hollywood films of coding Blackness through the use of light, darkening the skin color of Black actors and making them wear white uniforms to indicate their perpetual adscription to the servant class (Snead 5–6).

    16. See Goytisolo, "¡Quién te ha visto y quién te ve!"

    17. "De la cárcel al salon de bodas": "Más de 5.000 personas fueron a prisión durante el franquismo por las leyes que perseguían la homosexualidad" (36). 'More than 5,000 people were imprisoned during the Franco period in application of laws that persecuted homosexuality.'

    18. "Alejandro Amenábar": "'Quiero adoptar. Me imagino con dos niños'" (34). 'I want to adopt. I imagine myself with two children.' Íñigo Lamarca/Ombudsman for the Basque People: "Me caso en octubre" (34) 'I am getting married in October.'

    19. According to Hughes, Antonio Gaudí's major patrons, Claudio López Bru (second Marquis of Comillas) and Eusebi Güell, derived their fortunes from the slave-traffic enterprises of their fathers in Cuba (332).

WORKS CITED

"Alejandro Amenábar: 'Quiero adoptar: Me imagino con dos niños.'" *El País* 24 Apr. 2005: 34.

Bwana. Dir. Imanol Uribe. Perf. Andrés Pajares, María Barranco, and Emilio Buale. Columbia Tristar, 1996.

Cano, Carlos. "Canción a Lucrecia." *Forma de ser.* Dalur Discos, 1994.

Carmen. Dir. Vicente Aranda. Perf. Pasión Vega and Leonardo Sbraglia. Star Line, 2003.

Las cartas de Alou. Dir. Montxo Armendáriz. Perf. Mulil Jarju. Connoisseur, 1994.

Charnon-Deutsch, Lou. "Travels of the Imaginary Spanish Gypsy." *Constructing Identity in Contemporary Spain: Theoretical Debates and Cultural Practice.* Ed. Jo Labanyi. Oxford: Oxford UP, 2002. 22–40.

"Los datos oficiales revelan que 1,5 millones de extranjeros viven sin papeles en España." *La Razón* 26 Apr. 2005: 31.

Davies, Ann. "The Spanish Femme Fatale and the Cinematic Negotiation of Spanishness." *Studies in Hispanic Cinemas* 1 (2004): 5–16.

"De la cárcel al salón de bodas." *El País* 21 Apr. 2005: 36.

Du Bois, W. E. B. *The Souls of Black Folk.* New York: Penguin, 1989.

Dyer, Richard. *White.* New York: Routledge, 1992.

"España alcanza por la inmigración su mayor cifra de nacimientos desde 1988." *El País* 18 June 2003: 1.

"España ya alcanza los 44 millones de habitantes, y los extranjeros superan el 8,4%." *El País* 28 Apr. 2005: 30.

"Los extranjeros con residencial legal superan ya los dos millones." *El País* 27 Apr. 2005: 24.

Flores de otro mundo. Dir. Icíar Bollaín. Perf. Lisette Mejía, Luis Tosar, Marilín Torres, and Elena Irureta. Alta Films, 1999.

Goytisolo, Juan. *Campos de Níjar.* Barcelona: Seix Barral, 1973.

———. "De magrebíes y gente así." *El País* 28 Feb. 2001 <http://www.elpais.es/articuloCompleto.html?d_date=20010228&xref=20010228 elpepiopi_7&type=Tes&anchor=elpepiopi>.

———. "Metáforas de la migración." *El País* 24 Sept. 2005: 13.

———. "¡Quién te ha visto y quién te ve!" *El País* 19 Feb. 1998 http://elpais.es/articuloCompleto/elpepiopi/19980219elpepiopi_5/Tes/opinion/Quien/ha/visto/quien/ve>.

"Hoy se cumple el décimo aniversario del asesinato de Lucrecia Pérez." *El País* ˙181 23 Nov. 2002: 10.

Hughes, Robert. *Barcelona.* New York: Knopf, 1992.

Labanyi, Jo, ed. *Constructing Identity in Contemporary Spain: Theoretical Debates and Cultural Practice.* Oxford: Oxford UP, 2002.

———. "Internalisations of Empire: Colonial Ambivalence and the Early Francoist Missionary Film." *Discourse* 23.1 (2001): 25–42.

Martín-Cabrera, Luis. "Postcolonial Memories and Racial Violence in *Flores de otro mundo.*" *Journal of Spanish Cultural Studies* 3.1 (2002): 43–55.

Martínez-Carazo, Cristina. "*Flores de otro mundo:* La pluralidad cultural como propuesta." *Letras Peninsulares* 15.2 (2002): 377–90.

Mulvey, Laura. "Visual Pleasure and Narrative Cinema." *Screen* 16.3 (1975): 6–18.

Poniente. Dir. Chus Gutiérrez. Perf. Cuca Escribano, José Coronado, Farid Fatmi, and Ana Huete. Olmo Films, 2002.

Santaolalla, Isabel. "Ethnic and Racial Configurations in Contemporary Spanish Culture." *Constructing Identity in Contemporary Spain: Theoretical Debates and Cultural Practice*. Ed. Jo Labanyi. Oxford: Oxford UP, 2002. 55–71.

Snead, James. *White Screens, Black Images: Hollywood from the Dark Side*. Ed. Colin MacCabe and Cornel West. New York: Routledge, 1994.

Spenser, Edmund. *A View of the Present State of Ireland. The Works of Edmund Spenser: A Variorum Edition*. Ed. Edwin Greenlaw, Charles Grosvenor Osgood, Frederick Morgan Pedelford, and Ray Heffner. Vol. 9. Baltimore: Johns Hopkins UP, 1949. 39–231.

Tofiño-Quesada, Ignacio. "Spanish Orientalism: Uses of the Past in Spain's Colonization in Africa." *Comparative Studies of East Asia, Africa and the Middle East* 23.1–2 (2003): 141–48.

"Una inmigrante anónima que se convirtió en mártir." *El País* 23 Nov. 2002: 10.

Urioste, Carmen de. "Migración y racismo en el cine español." *Revista Monográfica /Monographic Review* 15 (1999): 44–59.

Wright, Richard. *Pagan Spain*. New York: Harper, 1957.

The Myth of Whiteness and a Changing Italy: Historic Memory and Colonialist Attitudes in *Lamerica*

RENÉE D'ELIA-ZUNINO

A myth is defined as a story that is passed on from generation to generation; it tells how things were and how they continue to be. A myth does not really explain, or give motivation, but simply establishes. As the *Oxford English Dictionary* defines it, myth is a

> traditional story, typically involving supernatural beings or forces, which embodies and provides an explanation, or justification for something such as the early history of a society, a religious belief or ritual, or a natural phenomenon. Also, a widespread but untrue or erroneous story or belief; a widely held misconception; a misrepresentation of the truth.

The power of white domination, for example, founds itself on the myth of the superiority of white people: it forwards that whites are the best of humanity. In German philosopher Immanuel Kant's words, "The white race represents the greatest perfection of humanity" (316). The myth of whiteness tells us that white people have primacy, and that they have created the history, art, democracy, and future of all humanity. The myth reflects itself in the images people confront every day, not only through television and cinematic media but also, and especially, through Christianity. It is most evident in Christian churches, where Adam and Eve, the Virgin Mary, Jesus and God are predominantly represented as white. In other words, "Whiteness receives the halo of sanctity, goodness and divinity," as whiteness critic Richard Dyer argues in his discourse about Christianity (17).[1]

Within a Christian context, white bodies have a "special" relation to race, but the relation is rendered invisible because it cannot be specified. It is as if the archetype of Christian whiteness is so entrenched in the minds of people that few question whether the history that has been taught centuries ago needs to be reevaluated in the light of inaccuracies that emerge today. Linda Kintz, in "Performing Virtual Whiteness," explains, "Whereas people of color can be reduced to their bodies, whites, in this frame, cannot, because the very 'matter' of the Christian subject is the whiteness of the Spirit itself. This is a whiteness in the body but not of it" (341).

Dyer's analysis of whiteness does not pertain only to Christianity; for him, whiteness is paradoxical. As a hue, whiteness is the combination of all colors, and at the same time, no color at all. As a racial designation, white describes people whose skin color is not literally white, therefore " . . . [w]hites are not of a certain race, they are just the human race" (3). And the ultimate contradiction remains: "Whiteness as ideal can never be attained, not only because white skin can never be hued white, but because ideally white is absence: to be really, absolutely white is to be nothing" (78). Dyer thus reveals the countermythical quality of whiteness.[2]

While American scholars, in general, have been talking increasingly about the "disembodied embodiment" crisis of white people in reference to their "raceless" identity, and the longing to understand what it really means to be a white person in today's multicultural society,[3] in Europe, Italy in particular, the study of whiteness is very new.[4] Unlike English, the Italian word for "whiteness" is not translated literally as a noun "bianchezza" (from "bianco"); it is "bianchitudine," which means how white a person feels rather than how white she or he appears. These Italian terms could be compared to the English "whitening" versus "whiteness," although in English the former implies some kind of process to attain whiteness. Philology apart, Italian society is changing dramatically due to the recent increasing numbers of North African, Eastern European, and Asian immigrants arriving in the southern areas of the peninsula. However, as Italy transforms into a multicultural nation, as a reaction to the immigrant influx, racism now pervades the minds of many people. Racist affirmation comes from the sentiments of fear and discrimination that immigrants are witnessing today.

White domination is not typically terrifying within Italy; Italians have not known the "white supremacist terror" that literary scholar and social critic bell hooks talks about through an American lens.[5] The supremacy of whiteness enacts itself mostly among whites in Italy because, although the rising numbers of African and Asian constituents do not seem to represent a threat, the rising numbers of Albanians, Slovenians and Rumanians do.[6] In fact, the peninsula does not have a history of racism based on skin color but on provenience, and both combined have brought today more than ever an identity crisis to Italian people who now question themselves on issues of "Italian-ness" *and* racial superiority/inferiority.

We (and I use the collective form because I grew up in Italy and lived there for over twenty-seven years) are still very far from being conscious of our whiteness among a new multiethnic society, because the publicly acknowledged notion of a racialized society has emerged only in the last few decades. It is impossible to understand the phenomenon of privileged and underprivileged whites and the people and its paradoxes in Italy today without reflecting on the history of the country as a whole. Newly arisen aspects of the collective consciousness/imagination push some Italians to live "diversity" as a new form of culture and others to live it as an increasing form of identity loss. The current Italian society is already living a profound identity crisis; the individual white Italian is not yet ready to conceive his or her existence outside of whiteness. Through Italian cinema, and specifically in Gianni Amelio's film *Lamerica* (1998), historic memory assists Italians in living their recently argued "binary consciousness" and regaining a once fixed national identity. Italian cinema, as much as American cinema, uses the concepts of race and imperialism to define the (in)visibly white person.

Italy and Its Paradoxes

Italy is, in many ways, a paradox. It is geographically an isolated country, almost an island, contained by Europe's highest mountain chain to the north and by the sea on its remaining sides; yet it has always been an encounter and transit point between Europe, Africa, and Asia, via the Middle East. Given Italy's proximity to Africa, the question arises why an African presence is not as obvious in Italy as it has always been in France or England. Italy can truly be considered a bridge between Africa and Europe, yet not only have the Italians and Africans been remote neighbors, but also they have practically been strangers. Italian professor Sante Matteo, in considering the history and the culture of the peninsula and how it has been shaped by an old and strong contact with Africa,[7] reasons, "Racism based on skin color has not been an entrenched, institutionalized aspect of the Italian society" (5). In the Americas, particularly the United States, slavery completely obliterated Africans' identities because families were broken up and dispersed, resulting in the loss of personal and collective consciousness. Matteo asserts, "What remained of their Africanness was primarily the dark color of their skin, which became the sign of their status as slaves and which remains a sign targeting them for racist bigotry" (6–7).

In European countries such as France and England, a prior history of extensive colonialism in Africa explains the larger presence of Africans than in Italy, and since many Africans had learned French or English under colonial rule, it is only natural that they would immigrate to countries with a familiar language. In Italy, most of the African immigrants are not from former Italian colonies, such as the Italian East Africa (Somalia, Ethiopia, and Eritrea) or Libya, where colonization came relatively late and was short-lived.[8] They are rather from Senegal and Morocco, where the official languages are respectively French and Wolof, and Arabic and French.

Journalist and politician Livio Caputo shows in his most recent survey that, in fact, we cannot talk about racism toward Africans, or people of a darker hue in general, since there is no common instinct among Italians to preserve a "pure" race. Many may argue that the instinct existed, especially during the 1920s through 1940s of imperialist Fascism, when racial purity became, to a certain extent, popular among Italians.[9] Furthermore, there were few "black Italians" prior to the late 1980s, which shows how little the population mixed; but today they are becoming a reality for the first time. Nothing has been published on Italians and Africans as a mixed race; but statistics do show an increase in mixed-race weddings where Italian women predominantly marry North African men, while Italian men take as spouses primarily women from Eastern European countries ("Rapporto Annuale" 353–85).

A defining moment for Italian society that marked a change in national hues occurred as the new millennium approached. The country was caught by surprise when, in 1996 Denny Mendez, the daughter of a woman who had emigrated from the Dominican Republic to Italy and married an Italian man, was crowned "Miss Italy," the winner of the nation's televised beauty pageant. The event made news throughout the world. The pageant's judges and millions of voters at home unanimously chose Denny Mendez. After the event, Prime Minister Romano Prodi commented, "This is the changing Italy, the new Italy," while Enzo Mirigliani, patron of the competition, stated that her victory indicated "[t]ruly a revolutionary year for Italy. Just like when, in 1961, the first blond-haired Miss Italy was elected" ("La nuova Miss Italia" 8–11). As banal as the event may seem, it tells us about the changing society and the willingness of Italians to accept "other" versus self. Interestingly, the at-home viewers came together unanimously in the voting, forgetting, for once, the political and cultural differences that separate the country. In this particular context, their unanimous decision brings us yet to another paradox, the typical lack of "united-ness" in regard to Italian society.

For centuries Italy was the main crossroads in the Mediterranean and, therefore, has been visited and populated by a great variety of peoples who have contributed to the country's cultural diversity, richness, and development. However, Italy has always been a fractured country, eternally split by old and new mentalities and historically divided into different kingdoms with foreign rulers, which contributed to the feelings of national divisiveness. Although it is a country at the center of grand political and religious empires, as well as artistic magnitude, Italy's unification as a nation occurred only as recently as 1861 when it was a very poor and backward country, both economically and industrially, with a very high birth rate. The consequence was massive emigration, but today it has achieved a high standard of living, which encourages others to adopt Italy as their new home.

It remains a matter of fact that Italians are not united as a people. The country is that of disenfranchised societies, and there is a sense of strong "campanilismo" 'regionalism.' Socially, it is a land of people rooted in its communities, generation after generation, and for which political banishment was, historically, the worst punishment.[10] Yet it is also a land steeped in a history of wanderers and explorers[11] for whom travel represented adventure, gain, and liberation. Today the eternal separation between north and south is more than ever fermenting federalist tendencies that transpire through the politics of Umberto Bossi.[12] Psychologist Neil Altman, in *The Analyst in the Inner City*, parallels today's Italy to the United States of two hundred years ago:

> The racial situation in Italy is becoming, to a certain extent, similar to what has long been happening in the United States. On one hand, some Italians of the North, relatively privileged, are opposing resistance to a national identity that would include the relatively poor Italians of the South. On the other hand, Italians are experimenting today what Americans faced two or more centuries ago: waves of immigrants that meet prejudices, discrimination, fear, and resistance from being accepted as Italian citizens. (17)

Sociologist Michel Wieviorka warns, however, that although in many countries like Italy the theme of racism presents strong ties with those of immigration, and that in Italy today immigrants are the first to be victims of racism, no automatic correlation exists in the public consciousness. In fact, in his statistical study *Razzismo (Racism)*, one learns that in electoral colleges where the presence of immigrants is scarce, if nonexistent, a high percentage of votes by racist or xenophobic parties exist, whereas there is a very modest percentage where immigrants are in high numbers. Wierviorka argues that as immigration increases, it is not necessarily true that racism increases as well:

> It is intellectually incorrect to confuse, or to put too near, racism and immigration. The first is an internalized phenomenon, which

pertains the functioning of a society, and the relationship between different human beings. The second is a phenomenon that deals with international relationships, migrating waves, and is a result of the relationships established between the outside and inside of the society. (120)[13]

With so many ambivalences in mind, my consideration is that the negotiation of "otherness" has been forever an essential component in the Italian imagination. But Italy has a problem of nonexistent cohesion, where the "questione meridionale" 'southern issue' has made the South Italy's internal Africa. In Corrado Giustiniani's words, this was, however, part of a " . . . [q]uiet, monoethnic and monoracial past, chiseled only by the 'terrone' accent of the people of southern Italy, and of those who moved from their lands to the north, to become blue collar workers" (vii).[14] Today, the "other" is a reality. Italy is an overcrowded country, with nearly 190 inhabitants per square kilometer and a very high unemployment rate. What has changed? Waves of immigrants are arriving at the peninsula's shores every day, and not just to cross the country but to stay. Their immigration coincides with one of the worst economic crises the country has seen. Ironically, without immigrants, it is impossible to stimulate the economy.[15] The movement of people is global, just like the world's market, capital, and commerce. Although twenty-first-century Italian society is multicultural, the "extracomunitario" 'the foreigner or non-European' is the scapegoat for all ill-tempered Italians who accuse the foreigner of taking away jobs and being ignorant, uneducated, dirty, poor, and criminal. In this sense, it is difficult to avoid the racial confusion Wierviorka warns of above.

Are Italians Racist? "New Racism" and the Identity Crisis

While many Italian politicians, essayists, and journalists try to understand the new dynamics of a growing multicultural Italy,[16] scholars and historians find themselves divided by the tendency to affirm either that Italians have never been or always have been racist.[17] The sudden interest in this issue corresponds, ironically, to the realization that white, nonimmigrant Italians are on the road to extinction.

Most recent census data from the Istituto Italiano di Statistica (ISTAT) projects that unless the birth rate increases Italians are destined to be extinct in the span of 250 years.[18] Most demographers, however, argue this is unlikely, although the country's actual economic crisis does not help.[19] The situation is so alarming that Rocco Falivena, mayor of the city of Laviano, southeast of Naples, offered €10,000 in 2003—at the time the equivalent of $11,900—to every Italian family that had a baby by December 2004. Laviano is not alone in its fight to increase the number of future Italian descendants: Italian women in general are least likely to have babies among European women.[20] Therefore it is not a coincidence that feelings of resistance and prejudice are becoming particularly diffused among Italian people toward those who are now called the extracomunitari who inhabit the peninsula. The 2001 United Nations conference in Durban, South Africa,[21] addressed the issue of low birth rates in Europe, confirming that Europeans, who in 1950 represented 22 percent of the world's population, will be reduced to 9 percent by 2050.

At the same meeting, Spanish demographer Juan Salgado-Ibarra,[22] through provocative comments, discussed problems of race and came up with a "new" thesis for racism. His theory is that racism, in certain countries like Italy and Spain, is not to be considered in the traditional sense as a demonstration of hatred coming from one ethnic group that considers itself superior to another. It should rather be seen as a "defensive xenophobia," and he argues, "It is only natural that Italians, Spanish, Germans, English, with their ridiculous birth rate diminishing more and more, have started to fear the ethnic groups that are bound to replace them and to consequently be hostile to them" (Salgado-Ibarra 8).

In the context of a disappearing native Italian population crisis, Salgado-Ibarra's thesis seems fitting and comes across as new. However, if we accept the demographer's conjecture, then we might understand and justify those instincts that motivated the Kosovars to fight against the Serbians in 1999, or justify the Dayak's Borneo massacre of one thousand Madurese immigrants in 2001.[23] Arguably, Italy is manifesting itself through a form of defensive xenophobia where the instincts of self-preservation make people act impulsively and degeneratively. But the metamorphosis of white people's racism from an aggressive ideology to a defensive ideology sounds farfetched and may have contributed in making the borderline between racism and xenophobia invisible. The "new" theory of racism coincides with an identity crisis in this particular moment in history. The last twenty-five years have seen a country, well known for its citizens moving abroad, suddenly become a home for many. The confrontation with the "hordes of immigrants," as writer Gian Battista Stella calls them in *L'Orda: Quando gli albanesi eravamo noi* (*The Hoard: When We Were the Albanians*) has fed a rising xenophobia, and growing defense that "[w]hen we Italians were immigrants, we were 'different.' We were 'better,' more loved" (23). However, writers such as Stella, Wierviorka, Giustiniani, and Claudio Camarca, who have dug into the past of the Italian immigrant to show not only how Italians were mistreated but also how Italians today are forgetting about their mistreatment, challenge the defensive memory.

In Stella's introduction "Bel paese, brutta gente" ("Beautiful Country, Ugly People") the opening lines refer to Italian emigrants' reception in other parts of the world as the "[s]cum of the planet, this is what we were. Or better: this is how we were perceived" (7). In the United States and Australia, Stella affirms, not only were Italians considered the "non visibly Negroes," but they were lynched and mistreated; their children were sold; their women were prostituted; they were all considered criminals, exploiters, dirty, and second-class society (75). In short, according to Stella, Italians have forgotten and are starting to stereotype foreigners in the same way they were once stereotyped.[24] An example of foreigner intolerance is Europarliamentarist Mario Borghezio, from the political party "Lega Nord" 'Northern League,' who, when traveling on trains, disinfects his seat with sprays, claiming that "Nigerian women and their gigantic gigolos often put their dirty and stinky feet on the seats, and do operations of personal toiletterie, and devour foods, staining and infecting the whole compartment" (Stella 76–77). Another example is Giancarlo Gentilini, twice mayor of the city of Treviso in northern Italy, who is called the "Sheriff," or "Genty," or "Super G" and who wore the sheriff's star until the day he punched an extracomunitario in front of a McDonald's, accusing him of molesting the people passing by the food franchise. He became the infamous "custodian of the Piave race,"[25] when, during a press conference in October 1999, he proclaimed that "in order to allow hunters to practice, we should dress our *extracomunitari* as hares, and then *tin, tin, tin* (imitating the sound of a gun)" (Giustiniani 64). His chilling suggestion cost him an indictment, but he was soon absolved, because it was brushed off as a joke, and as if "the fact did not subsist."[26]

Once again, it is not the color of the skin that determines "otherness" and racism. In Italy, some "foreigners" are more welcomed than others, notwithstanding their hue. Albanians, Slovenians, and Rumanians, in particular, are the most targeted immigrants, although their skin color does not distinguish them from other Italians and they would also be racially categorized as white. Caputo argues, "If we look closely at Italy and its inhabitants, it never has had racist connotations, in the classic meaning. Demoscopic inquiries have shown that Italians are more diffident toward people from the former Yugoslavia and Albania, who are Europeans, and Rumanians, who are Latin, rather than Senegalese or Singhalese in general" (13). The refusal is, therefore, not commensurate to the degree of diversity, cultural distance, and ethnicity that separates Italians from immigrants but to the intensity of what a civilized cohabitation represents in the collective unconscious/imagination. The "Questione Albanese" 'Albanian Issue' offers an example that illuminates cohabitation.

To put into perspective the "Albanian Issue," some historical facts are necessary. Pre–World War II Albania had no university-level education, and all advanced studies were pursued abroad. The great majority of the students attended Italian universities because of their proximity to the peninsula and because of special relationships between the governments of Rome and Tiranë.[27] As a consequence, use of the Italian language was made compulsory in all Albanian secondary schools and Fascist ideology and orientation were then incorporated into the curricula. The "colonization-invasion" by Mussolini in 1939, and his use of Albania as a springboard to invade Greece during World War II, brought consistent Italian presence in the country until 1941, when guerrilla groups began to operate against the Italian forces, and the whole education system became paralyzed. Following World War II, a Soviet-supported Socialist dictatorship came into power, and nearly all communications with the Balkan nation were cut off. Few were aware of the staggering level of poverty that persisted until 1991, when the democrats overthrew the country; the borders opened, and the Albanians started fleeing to Italy. The immigrant crush was like the European influx into the United States earlier in the century, with forty thousand seeking a home (in contradistinction to the earlier migration) in a very small country.[28]

Albanian politicians Raymond Zickel and Walter Iwaskiew explain in *Albania: A Country Study* that by 1991 the Albanian government was making an attempt to break with the nondemocratic traditions of the past, announcing the birth of a National Information Service (NIS) that was to dismantle the notorious Sigurimi Albanian secret police.[29] Its dismantling coincided with a steep rise in crime, and a wave of Albanians fleeing to Italy. "The exodus was so great that the NIS was not able to stem it. The refugee problem reached epic proportions in August 1991, with 20,000 Albanians seeking asylum in Italy all at once; most were later returned to Albania" (Zickel and Iwaskiew 190–91). Italy's former foreign minister, Giulio Andreotti, was the first to declare the impossible cohabitation of 1991: "We are absolutely not in the condition to take in the Albanian people who are swarming the Italian coasts, and the government of Tiranë agrees with us that they must return to their country" (Andreotti-Bufi Agreement, September 1991).[30] Many of those who managed to remain had criminal pasts. Claudio Camarca, in *Migranti*, explains that many of those fleeing Albania had ties with the Sigurimi secret police or were criminals escaped from prison and argues, "The Albanians are not opposed because they are 'different,' but because among them, there is a particularly high rate of criminals, and of individuals who refuse our laws and abandon themselves to violence" (7).[31]

In light of these negative events, the mistrust and anxiety of the average Italian toward his Albanian neighbor are understandable. The agitation to enfranchise Albanians attests what David R. Roediger calls the move to achieve the "fluidity" of a social category (133–34).

The "privilege" of belonging to a particular category like whiteness depends on origin, historical past, and unconscious archetypes that society inflicts upon us. We can all agree that whiteness, like other social identities, is a communication phenomenon. However, the Italians' refusal to accept others, such as Albanians, does not stem from a conscious racial discrimination within a world of whiteness. While in countries like the United States, past laws prohibited marriages between whites and nonwhites or denied access to public spaces, this has never occurred in Italy, at least not based on differences of pigment.[32] On the other hand, although the phenomenon has nothing to do with skin color, it has everything to do with the sense that "invaders" and "undeserving foreigners" undermine and threaten social privileges.

Amongst an almost all white Italian society, the Albanians are certainly today's victims. They are stereotypically raced as an inferior, dirty, and criminal nation. Over forty thousand Albanians landed in Italy in 1991 in five different waves. Between the sixth and seventh of August of that year, Italy witnessed the landing of twenty thousand refugees on the coasts of the Puglia region, in Bari and Brindisi. Staggering images were broadcast live by the various Italian television networks of the refugees being transported to the old city stadium of Bari before being deported to their country. A witness to the misfortune and disaster was movie director Gianni Amelio who, a few days after the event, told reporters that he felt it was time to accomplish cinematically an old project, inspired by the emigration of southern Italians to the New World.[33] He embarked upon filming a movie that would offer an opportunity for the country to reflect upon the immigration occurring in Italy. From the remembrances of the past, contrasted with his impressions of the devastating reality of Albania, came the idea for *Lamerica*.[34] The film compares the present dream of the Albanians to come to Italy to make a better life with the earlier aspiration of many Italians to live the American dream, a myth that pushed many Italian immigrants to leave their families and lands in search of fortune. The combination of desires and illusions, of present and past, allowed Amelio to reflect not only on a dramatic immigration period in Italian national history, but also to interrogate his own family's immigrant past.

Besides personal reasons, Amelio, during an interview with actor Federico Pacifici, admits that he made the film for the "Italians that today have a short memory. The 1980s have given us a generation of people who are still in power but fail to remember the past of misery that many Italians went through" (Vitti 2).

Historic Memory and Colonialist Attitudes in *Lamerica*

Gianni Amelio's first on-the-scene investigations of the Albanian territory began right after the refugees' expulsion in 1991. He encountered a country of economic misery, and his observations brought back the memory of postwar southern Italy and his poor childhood in Calabria. In the film *Lamerica*, the Albanians view Italy as "their America," hence the title with the apostrophe omitted—as the grammatically correct spelling of "L' America" requires—to represent the semi-literacy of the Albanians (Cattini 131).

When Albania turned into a democracy after the fall of Enver Hoxka's communist regime, some of the first foreign investors came from Italy, and some of their proposals were illegal. *Lamerica* opens with the arrival in Tiranë of two Italian swindlers, Fiore (Michele Placido), a corrupt Italian entrepreneur, and Gino (Enrico Lo Verso), his young assistant. Both claim to be in the shoe-making business. As the story unfolds, the viewer learns that in order for the company to be "legal" Fiore and Gino must appoint a native resident as its head. They select at random a homeless former prisoner, Spiro Tozai, alias Michele Talarico (Carmelo Di Mazzarelli), whom they eventually discover is not an Albanian native but an Italian World War II deserter whom the Albanian police imprisoned after the end of the war. Born in Sicily seventy years ago but incapable of remembering the last fifty years he spent in jail, Spiro is convinced that he is only twenty years old. During their visit to what was once a prison in search of an Albanian who will meet their need, Fiore and Gino must confront those who, despite being free, still live incarcerated like zombies. The dark atmosphere, the dirty, old, and bearded faces of the men, and the narrowness of space suffocate Fiore who runs away in fear.[35] Viewers can empathetically share the impression of suffocation through the images of these souls forgotten by the preceding regime just like the appointed chief executive officer of the fictitious company who has lived there since 1941. However, the men also represent the souls of the forgotten in any time and in any place, hence Amelio conveys a universal message of social displacement and national disenfranchisement. As the film progresses, the police discover Gino's fraud, and he begins to lose his sense of national identity, becoming as "Albanian" as the hundreds of Albanians surrounding him.

"I'm Italian, don't you understand?" Gino emphatically asserts to dismissive Albanian policemen as he clings to his superior birthright after failing to pull off his company's scam. His car tires stolen, his passport taken with his clothes, and his arrogance weakened, Gino has no national identity and no will power. Overwhelmed, he questions, "How can I live without a passport?" and the Albanian official responds, "But none of us have passports." Fiore, who has returned to Italy, informs Gino that Italian funds are no longer available to bail him out of his predicament. Gino, identifying as an Albanian refugee, travels with Talarico to the port of Tiranë, hoping to board a boat with thousands of refugees that will transport him back to Italy.

In the final scene on the boat, the montage of the passengers' faces is memorable. Amelio states, "In that scene and throughout the film [I] was trying to show, in the relations between the Italians and the Albanians, that, in a symbolic sense, we're all Albanians. Even if today Gino is rich and can live the way he wants, he can't forget that at some point he could become a destitute and need help" (9). Gray Crowdus and Richard Porton maintain in "Beyond Neorealism: Preserving a Cinema of Social Conscience" that Amelio emphasizes the social racism and sense of national superiority that the older Italian Fiore embraces. He stands in contrast to the naïve Gino whose experiences as the Albanian "other" raise his national social consciousness and explode his biased perception that he as an Italian is exempt from personal destitution and social decline. Fiore, on the other hand, is morally dangerous because while he is older and has more life experiences he has less human compassion. At the beginning, he engineers all the cruel actions and games being played on the Albanians. His character does not change because he has no time and undergoes no stimulus to evolve. Soon after arriving in Albania, he returns to Italy where he will continue to control events in Albania from a distance. He becomes the true symbol of an arrivist mentality and a presumptive cultural and social racism. He definitely considers the Albanians, their history and their culture, as inferior. "The younger character, Gino, is really only guilty of being ignorant. Although he is the one that yells and appears like a racist, at the end of the film he's the one who undergoes a transformation and changes. Fiore, had he gone through the same experience, never would have changed" (6–13).

In an interview with *La Repubblica*, Amelio directly addresses this loss of a fixed Italian national identity because of immigration:

> Although post-war Italian cinema could be considered representative of a popular and national sentiment, and a primary connection between the image and the collective identity, today's historic response has become weaker because of the loss of a national image, and the multiplying cultural and regional fractures. In *Lamerica* the documentaristic discourse goes arm in arm with a political indictment, and the historic fresco of the journey, with an individual interior transformation: the reference of Italy and Albania becomes a larger metaphor on global immigration.[36]

Despite his attempt to expose in *Lamerica* the social and racial prejudice and superiority that Italians lord over Albanians, Amelio was accused of not doing enough. Leftists criticized the film, and Albanian writer and Nobel Prize nominee Ismail Kadaré especially regretted that the director gives no space to the important role the poor Albanian farmers played in saving, hiding, and feeding over twenty thousand Italian soldiers after September 8, 1943. Kadaré also criticized Amelio for not sufficiently illustrating the contrasting behavior between the Albanian farmers who, in 1943, instinctively forgave the Italians although they had devastated their land and the Italians who, in 1991 and 1992, locked up and deported a few thousand Albanians who were fleeing from the hunger and misery of their country.[37] When writer Emanuela Martini, during an interview, asked about the universal message of his film, Amelio observed that those closest to the ethnoracial issues that he interrogates are least able to comprehend them:

> Strangely, although many critics tend to underline the "Mediterraneanness" of my films, I realize that they are better understood by different cultures. They have had more success, in fact, in Scandinavian countries, rather than in France or Spain, for example. . . . It is obvious that in societies where certain problems are strongly rooted, one notices an estrangement. (4)[38]

The "estrangement" Amelio talks about is a tool of self-defense: the more one is complicit in a behavior, the less one wants to acknowledge his or her complicity. With two generations of immigrants in his own past—one of his grandfathers never returned from Argentina and his father and uncle returned physically wounded—Amelio parallels their experiences elsewhere to the plight of Albanians and other outsiders to Italian nationality and whiteness:

> They were the Rumanians, Moroccans and Albanians of today; we must not forget. Immigration is most necessary for our culture to survive and avoid extinction. I cultivate the utopia that one day no one will emigrate any longer, . . . and that the world of tomorrow will be multiracial. (7)[39]

His comment elucidates a problem of changing Italian society: Italy needs foreign peoples to join its communities in order to stimulate its economy and to create jobs. Yet the jobs offered to foreigners like the Albanians, who are treated in the same manner as groups who have historically been raced as "black," are the most menial and labor intensive that most native Italians refuse to perform.[40] An Albanian youth in *Lamerica* asks Gino, "Which is the best soccer team, Juventus or Milan? . . . Being a soccer player is the best profession in Italy; it gets you a lot of money. . . ." And Gino, who knows the reality of his country, replies: "Yes, you want to be a soccer player. . . . If you are lucky, in Italy you will be washing dishes! We already have Moroccans, Polish, all other blacks, but you just go ahead and come . . . come. . . ." His bitter reply receives the Albanian's optimistic response: "It's better to wash dishes in Italy than to die of hunger in Albania!"[41] Through Gino, Amelio reveals the perpetuation of whiteness as not an issue of racial hue but a racial tension within the social construction of whiteness itself.

Italian constructions of whiteness via Christianity, racial discourse, imperialism, gendered models of white behavior, the technology of photography and cinema, and sports' modern iconography are chapters in white studies that have yet to be written. While in the United States, for example, those working in white studies hope to make whites more responsible for their social interaction among citizens,[42] Italians are working to become more responsible in their social interactions with immigrants. Xenophobic theories and "new" racist theories notwithstanding, Italians need to first of all recognize their "new neighbor" as Italian, regardless of provenience, which for them means to realize that "Italian white" is, like any other form of white, not superior. The clash between native Italians and Albanian immigrants illustrates that one of the greatest social issues facing Italy is not predicated on racial hue but a whiteness construction that turns on the opposition and negation of the other, even though that other is neither an Africanized one nor visibly discernible from itself.

Finally, when the traditions, the historic memory, and the claims of a community's identity are treated with contempt and ignorance, with reason immigrants feel rebuffed and racialized. Italy cannot impose its own customs on immigrants and vice versa. However, the nation can make an attempt to avoid the tendency of "ethnicizing" or racializing social relationships to the point they become manifestations of racism. It is necessary to have political procedures that ensure democratic treatment and that are capable of detecting and eliminating not only the dictatorship of the majority but also of the minority. The first step will be to sensitize Italians to "working through" their notions of superiority and entitlement in opposition to labeling others who are unlike them inferior and undeserving.

NOTES

1. Discussing Christianity in *White*, Richard Dyer states that he is "not arguing that Christianity is of its essence white. Given that Christianity developed initially within Judaism, that one of its foundational thinkers was the North African Augustine, and that it is now most alive in Africa, South America and the black churches of Europe and North America, it is by no means clear that whiteness is constitutive of it. Yet not only did Christianity become the religion, and religious export, of Europe, indelibly marking its culture and consciousness, it has also been thought and felt in distinctly white ways for most of its history, seen in relation to, for instance, the following: the persistence of the Manichean dualism of black: white that could be mapped on to skin colour difference; the role of the Crusades in racialising the idea of Christendom (making national/geographic others into enemies of Christ); the gentilising and whitening of the image of Christ and the Virgin in painting; the ready appeal to the God of Christianity in the persecution of doctrines of racial superiority and imperialism" (17).

2. I use the term "whites" to refer to a racially dominant group of people of European descent and the word "whiteness" to refer to the processes through which they gain and perform social dominance.

3. Dyer begins his study on the matter of whiteness by stating, "Racial imagery is central to the organisation of the modern world" (1).

4. Maria Assunta Sozzi's "Un cuore grande per amare," and Elke Wollard's "Politica del corpo" are two of the few articles on whiteness.

5. In "Representing Whiteness in the Black Imagination," bell hooks describes her terror as a black child having to traverse a white neighborhood and the relief of seeing her dark-faced grandfather sitting on his porch waiting for her when she arrived home. She discusses how presenting a black perspective causes anger in some white people "because they believe that all ways of looking that highlight difference subvert the liberal conviction that it is the assertion of universal subjectivity (we are all just people) that will make racism disappear" (167) and believes that this suppression of difference, of not acknowledging widely varying responses to a situation, is yet another form of oppression. She quotes Richard Dyer's observation that "[p]ower in contemporary society habitually passes itself off as embodied in the normal as opposed to the superior" (340).

6. Foreigners represent only 2.2 percent of the population in Italy, which totals 57,679,955 inhabitants. The ISTAT (Instituto Nazionale di Statistica) released its data on immigrant presence in Italy for the year 2000: from 1992 to 2000, the Yugoslavian presence increased 28.5 percent; the Tunisian presence increased 23.3 percent; the Albanian presence increased 17.3 percent; the Senegalese presence increased 1.5 percent; and the Chinese presence increased 6.8 percent (1–6).

7. In classical times, for example, the Punic Wars between Rome and Carthage saw the conflict between the two cultures followed by the consolidation of Christian hegemony under the tutelage of great scholars like Athanasius, Origen, and Augustine, who were all African writers; further contacts resulted from the Crusades and then the colonial wars.

8. Italy conquered the African countries comprising Italian East Africa in the 1930s during Benito Mussolini's reign, and they remained under Italian control until the end of World War II. Italy conquered Libya in 1912; it regained its independence in 1951.

9. Italian Fascism was a totalitarian political regime based on totalitarian philosophies and ideas that had been twisted to suit the desires of a Fascist party. It was a controlling regime that survived by dominating the political system and the working-class population. Nationalism was an important concept in the context of Fascism. The upkeep and success of the country was highly valued. Violence and propaganda were used to exploit various nationalities and to help achieve fascist goals. One of Italian Fascism's main features was its racial overtones and association with anti-Semitism. Fascists saw the outbreak of war as a final solution to achieving superiority over all other nations.

10. Dante Alighieri, Ugo Foscolo, and Giuseppe Mazzini are famous political exiles.

11. Marco Polo, Amerigo Vespucci, Christopher Columbus, and John Cabot (born Giovanni Caboto of Genova) are all expatriate wanderers.

12. The Northern League was constituted in 1991 after the Leagues of North Italy had united at their first congress at Pieve Emanuele (near Milan). Umberto Bossi campaigned to create an independent northern Italian state called "Padania." The movement, founded by Bossi, does not interpret political struggle as a clash between social classes or categories but as a conflict between centralist states and the people who claim their right to self-determination and freedom. The Northern League has held anti-immigration rallies throughout northern Italy during election campaigns. The league's campaign pledges have included setting immigration quotas for each of Italy's twenty regions and measures to ensure that only immigrants with work permit are allowed into the country. These restrictions stand despite the fact that the north of Italy now desperately needs immigrants to fill growing labor shortages. See Smith.

13. The English translation is mine from the Italian: "É intellettualmente scorretto confondere o accostare troppo il razzismo all'immigrazione. Il primo é un fenomeno ormai interno, che riguarda il funzionamento della società, i rapporti fra gruppi umani diversi. . . . Il secondo é un fenomeno che rinvia ai rapporti internazionali, a flussi migratori provenienti dall'estero, ed é il risultato di rapporti che si stabiliscono tra l'estero e l'interno della società."

14. The English translation is mine from the Italian: "Quel tranquillo passato monoetnico e monorazziale, scalfito soltanto dall'accento 'terrone' degli operai trasferiti al Nord, é morto e sepolto."

15. The system appreciates immigrants for their flexibility and propensity to travel. Fewer and fewer Italians are willing to do jobs such as garbage collecting, house cleaning, and crop harvesting because social benefits supplement them a livable minimum wage (Giustiniani 56).

16. Among those who write about Italian multiculturalism are Zincone; Caritas; Diamanti; and "Rapporto sullo stato della sicurezza in Italia."

17. Territorial research from the Union of Hebrew Communities conducted in 2003, titled "Racism in Italy," shows that of the twenty-two hundred students interviewed between the ages of fourteen and eighteen and of 110 Italian communes, an equal percentage in the north and south feels threatened by "the foreigner" in general, 12 percent are in favor of multiculturalism, 22.7 percent do not trust Jews, 33.2 percent affirm that Muslims are invading Italy, 29 percent believe Muslims are enemies of progress, 32.8 percent assert immigrants in general take jobs away from Italians, 21.2 percent maintain they bring diseases, 50.9 percent state they create prostitution, and 46.5 percent are concerned that "if we go on this way, they will be more than us" ("Il razzismo in Italia" 12).

18. See Cini 66.

19. In a *La Repubblica* interview, Rosario Trefiletti, of Federconsumatori 'Consumers' Federation' states, "There is a large scissor that separates Italy in three parts: a third of the country is taking advantage of the actual economic crisis and continues to get rich with the increase of prices; there is another third that is living in poverty and is no longer able to survive; and the Third Italy is the one that cannot go on with the salary it receives. Although in 2001 these families were able to cope fairly well until the end of the month, today the same stipend lasts only for three weeks: during the fourth week, one saves desperately" (Cillis; translation mine).

20. Low fertility and marriage rates, high survival rates, and significant levels of immigration affect the population growth in Italy. In fact, a fast-rising life expectancy and the world's lowest birthrate are combining to make Italy "the oldest country in the world." Women in Italy enjoy a relatively high social status compared to their counterparts in most developing countries. Education is as important for women as it is for men with 98 percent of males and 96 percent of females being able to read and write. Women are allowed responsibility and choice when it comes to deciding when and whether to have a family and how large the family will be. Unfavorable social conditions for having and raising children and a lack of confidence in the future seem to be resulting in smaller families later in women's lives. Most Italian women refuse to have large families because jobs and affordable housing are hard to find. See Meletti 13.

21. See "Nazioni Unite."

22. Juan Salgado-Ibarra is a program officer at the United Nations of Youth Foundation (UNOY).

23. On 10 February 2001, 600 Dayak soldiers initially attacked 300 Madurese civilians, killing 180. The death toll rose to 400 after a week. The Madurese are accused of not respecting the Dayak traditions and laws and of being more urbanized than the Dayak in general. See Oddone.

24. Littlewood, in *Sultry Climates*, affirms, "No other country like Italy was associated, for so long and repetitiously, with sexual liberty." From the Renaissance until the twentieth century, "Italy's identity was formed for the British travelers by the reputation of transgressive pleasures that started already during Roman times" (55). While in other parts of Europe, especially Britain, homosexuals were publicly hung, the Italy of the popes, priests, and bigots offered everybody great liberty, accepting tacitly sexual tourism as, in Littlewood's words, a "social escape valve for more than two centuries" (55). Charles Dickens, in *Pictures from Italy*, describes Italians as an ingenious race but corrupt, dishonest, and dissolute. Daniel Defoe, Richard Lessels, John Addington Symonds, Montesquieu, Charles de Brosses, Percy B. Shelley, and Lord Byron all created literature that envisioned an Italy of dissolute pleasures, diseases, and filth.

25. Piave is the name of the river that crosses Treviso.

26. When Gentilini walked the streets of Via Roma one day and realized that "extracomunitari" were sitting on the benches in front of the train station, he

proclaimed: "I do not tolerate that Treviso be a city of occupation," which was followed by the removal of the benches (Stella 78).

27. The Italian government, following a policy of political, economic, military, and cultural penetration of the country, granted a number of scholarships to Albanian students, recommended by the legislation of Tiranë. See Zickel and Iwaskiew 91.

28. Marmullaku 207.

29. The Sigurimi was one of the most shadowy secret police organizations in Eastern European history. It had little presence outside of the country but penetrated thoroughly Albanian society. After 1993, the Sigurimi made the transition from secret police force to Mafia faster than any organization of its kind. It is still implicated in frequent contract killings, and those who tried furiously to stomp out the fires of the "gjakmarrje" 'blood feud' are the greatest agents of its revival.

30. The Andreotti-Bufi Agreement stipulated that the Italian government would give Albania $56 million in exchange for an agreement with AGIP and major petrol companies in Albania. See Cararo.

31. Many articles from major newspapers elicit the problem: "Milan at this juncture has become a crossroads of interests for many fighting groups," a detective with the ROS explained: "These groups include also the Albanians from Kosovo who are among the most dangerous traffickers in drugs and in arms. They are determined men, violent and prepared to go to any lengths. They are capable of coming up with men and arms in a matter of hours. They have deep roots in civil society. They love luxury, fashionable clubs, and restaurants. They have an astonishing amount of ready cash at their disposal. Every night, to keep in practice, they burgle apartments and businesses, moving from one city in Lombardy to the next" (Ruscica). A report on minor crimes elicits, "More than 50 ethnic Albanians from Kosovo were arrested Tuesday on suspicion of membership in an international ring of robbers," Spanish police said. The arrested are suspected of having committed nearly 1,000 break-ins and robberies in apartments and companies in a number of Spanish regions and of laundering money from the robberies in Germany" ("Kosovo Albanian Robbers" 1). Finally, there are reports of Albanians organizing themselves in the United States: "A photograph hanging above the entrance to a Brooklyn construction company shows a young man in a white T-shirt with an AK-47 assault rifle slung across his chest and a pistol tucked into his pants. The young man, Adrian Krasniqi, 25, was a member of the Kosovo Liberation Army, a group of Albanian rebels fighting for independence in Kosovo, a Serbian province whose inhabitants are 90 percent ethnic Albanian. According to his uncle, who owns the construction company here, Krasniqi was killed last October during an attack on a Serbian police position in Kosovo. The company owner, a thirty-two-year-old Albanian American who immigrated to the United States in 1989, has been supporting the rebel group part time since 1994, before most of the world knew of its existence. But since his nephew's death, he said, he spends almost all his time organizing Albanian American support for the

guerrilla movement, which he hopes will turn into a force capable of fighting the Yugoslav Army" (Sullivan A12).

32. In a sense, the same thing was true in the United States for people of African descent. With the "one drop rule," blood content and not hue was the qualifier of "nonwhiteness." Hue only made it easier to detect the white from the nonwhite.

33. The Calabrian director had already begun his critical reflections on Italy and its generational disputes in *Il ladro di bambini* (1992), in which he exposes the realities of the prostitution of minors and denounces the inefficiency and indifference of the social services (Gianni Volpi, *Gianni Amelio* 148).

34. Amelio 3.

35. See "Viaggio anacronistico" (138–51) in Cattini.

36. Bignardi.

37. Di Francesco.

38. The English translation is mine from the Italian: "A proposito della Mediterraneità dei miei film posso dire che stranamente le mie pellicole sono capite meglio in culture diverse. Hanno avuto, infatti, molto piú successo nei paesi scandinavi piuttosto che in Spagna e in Francia. . . . Evidentemente nelle società dove certi problemi sono radicati in maniera molto forte si avverte un senso di estraneità di fronte alle pellicole che ne parlano."

39. The English translation is mine from the Italian: " La mia famiglia é emigrata per due generazioni. Mio nonno non é mai tornato dall'Argentina, mentre mio zio e mio padre ne sono tornati messi molto male fisicamente. La storia si ripete e loro sono quello che eravamo noi. Noi siamo stati i rumeni, i marocchini, gli albanesi di oggi. Non dobbiamo dimenticarcelo mai. . . . L'immigrazione é quanto di piú necessario ci sia al mondo per la nostra cultura se si vuole tentare di non estinguersi. Io coltivo l'utopia che un giorno non si emigri piú . . . e che il futuro del mondo sia una multirazzialità."

40. Italians decline menial jobs such as harvesting grapes, apples, asparagus, and oranges; working in fast-food chains; serving at beach bars and restaurants during the summer; and performing janitorial services.

41. The English translation is mine from the Italian: "'Ho visto in tivú che in Italia ci sono strade dove non si va in bici, soltanto in macchina, cento all'ora. . . .' 'Ehi amico, chi é piú meglio di squadra: Juventus o Milan?' 'Calciatore é miglior professione in Italia. Prende i soldi piú di tutti.' 'Sí, sí, giocatori. . . . A voi se vi va bene, in Italia vi fanno lavare i piatti! Già ci stanno i marocchini, i polacchi, tutti gli altri neri . . . venite . . . venite.' 'Meglio lavapiatti in Italia che affamati in Albania!'"

42. In "Seeing White," Peter Erickson suggests, "Whiteness will not go away tomorrow; what we need is a theory and a practice that will make possible living with whiteness today" (185). Henry A. Giroux, in *Fugitive Cultures*, reasons, "A critical analysis of whiteness should address its historical legacy and existing complicity with racist exclusion and oppression, but it is equally important that such an examination distinguish between whiteness as a racial practice that is antiracist and those aspects of whiteness that are racist" (310).

WORKS CITED

Altman, Neil. *The Analyst in the Inner City: Race, Class and Culture Through a Psychoanalytic Lens.* Hillsdale: Analytic, 1995.

Amelio, Gianni. *Lamerica: Film e storia del film.* Ed. Piera Detassis. Torino: Einaudi, 1994.

Andreotti-Bufi Agreement. Sept. 12, 1991. <http://www.notizie-est.com/article. php?art_id=429>.

Bignardi, Irene. "Vince il suo cinema, non il suo film." *La Repubblica* 14 Sept. 1998 <http://www.repubblica.it/online/cinema/bignardi/fine/fine.html>.

Camarca, Claudio. *Migranti.* Milano: Rizzoli, 2003.

Caputo, Livio. "Alle radici del razzismo." *Leadership Medica* Mar. 2001 <http://www. cesil.com/marzo01/italiano/3capuit.htm>.

Cararo, Sergio. "Albania in rivolta: Lira e moschetto." *Notizie Est-Balcani* July 1997 <http://www.notizie-est.com/article.php?art_id=429>.

Caritas Diocesana di Roma. *Dossier Statistico Immigrazione 2003: Italia, paese d'immigrazione.* Roma: Caritas, 2003. <http://www.caritasroma.it/ immigrazione>.

Cattini, Alberto. "Viaggio anacroinistico." *Le Storie e lo sguardo: Il cinema di Gianni Amelio.* Venezia: Marsiglio Editori, 2000. 138–51.

Cillis, Lucio. "L'Italia in crisi non spende piú: Pesano prezzi e recessione." *La Repubblica* 13 Aug. 2003 <http://www.repubblica.it/2003/g/sezioni/seconomia/ prezzi/prezzi/frenaconsumi/frenaco nsumi.html>.

Cini, Lucia. "Articolo di costume." *Strategie di Scrittura.* Roma: Bonacci, 1998.

Crowdus, Gary, and Richard Porton. "Beyond Neorealism: Preserving a Cinema of Social Conscience." *Cineaste* 21 (1995): 6–13.

Diamanti, Ilvo. "Quando la politica inventa le paure." *La Repubblica* May 19, 2002 <http://www.nextonline.it/archivio/17/12.htm>.

Dickens, Charles. *Pictures from Italy.* New York: Penguin, 1998.

Di Francesco, Tommaso. "Le due sponde dell'Adriatico." *Il Manifesto* 25 Apr. 2003 <http://www.ilmanifesto.it/25aprile/03_25Aprile/9503rs26.01.html>.

Dyer, Richard. *White.* New York: Routledge, 1997.

Erickson, Peter. "Seeing White." *Transition* 67 (Fall 1995): 166–85.

Giustiniani, Corrado. *Fratellastri d'Italia.* Bari: Laterza, 2003.

Giroux, Henry A. *Fugitive Cultures: Race, Violence, and Youth.* New York: Routledge, 1996.

hooks, bell. "Representing Whiteness in the Black Imagination." *Cultural Studies.* Ed. Lawrence Grossberg et al. London: Routledge, 1992. 338–42.

Kadaré, Ismail. *Elegy for Kosovo.* New York: Arcade: Time Warner, 2000.

Kant, Immanuel. *Geografia Fisica.* Milano: Giardini, 2004.

Kintz, Linda. "Performing Virtual Whiteness: The Psychic Fantasy of Globalization." *Comparative Literature Studies* 53 (2001): 333–53.

"Kosovo Albanian Robbers at Work." *Agence France Presse* 16 June 1998 <http://www.srpska-mreza.com/Kosovo/alb-mafia-afp-6-16-98.html>.

Il ladro di bambini. Dir. Gianni Amelio. Perf. Enrico Lo Verso, Valentina Scalici, and Giuseppe Ieracitano. Erre Produzioni, 1992.

Lamerica. Dir. Gianni Amelio. Perf. Michele Placido, Enrico Lo Verso, and Carmelo di Mazzarelli. Mario Cecchi Gori, 1998.

Littlewood, Ian. *Sultry Climates: Travel and Sex.* Cambridge: Da Capo, 2002.

Marmullaku, Ramadan. *Albania and the Albanians.* London: Hurst, 1975.

Martini, Emanuela. *Gianni Amelio: Le regole e il gioco.* Torino: Lindau, 1999.

Matteo, Sante. *Italiafrica: Bridging Continents and Cultures.* New York: Forum Italicum, 2001.

Meletti, Jenner. "Falivena, il sindaco dei bambini." *La Repubblica* 3 Nov. 2003 <http://www.comunedasa.it/gam/news_item.asp?newsid=507>.

"Le Nazioni Unite lavorano per combattere il razzismo." World Conference Against "Racism, Racial Discrimination, Xenophobia and Related Intolerance." Aug. 31–Sept. 7, 2001. <http://www.cgilscuola.it/rubriche/Varie/razz_no.htm>

"La nuova Miss Italia." Editorial. *Sorrisi e Canzoni* Oct. 2003: 8–11.

Oddone, Paolo. "Continua il massacro dei Maduresi." *War News* 26 Feb. 2001 <http://www.warnews.it/ita/borneo04.html>.

"Rapporto Annuale" ISTAT. 1998. <http://www.cestim.org/index01dati.htm>.

"Rapporto sullo stato di sicurezza in Italia." *Governo Italiano* 18 Aug. 2005 <http://www.governo.it/governoinforma/dossier/rapporto_sicurezza_2005.pdf>.

"Il razzismo in Italia." Editorial. *Unione delle Comunità ebraiche italiane.* 2003. <http://www.edscuola.com/archivio/handicap/razzismo.htm>.

Roediger, David R. *The Wages of Whiteness: Race and the Making of the American Working Class.* New York: Verso, 1991.

Ruscica, Roberto. "Albanian Mafia: This Is How It Helps the Kosovo Guerrilla Fighters." *Corriere della Sera* 15 Oct. 1998 <http://www.kosovo.com/rpc2.html>.

Salgado-Ibarra, Juan. *A Report from the United Nations World Conference against Racism, Racial Discrimination, Xenophobia, and Related Intolerance.* Durban, 2001 <http://www.unhchr.ch/htm/racism>.

Smargiassi, Michele. "I nuovi poveri con lo stipendio." *La Repubblica* 1 Apr. 2004 <http://www.repubblica.it/2004/a/sezioni/economia/redditi/poveri1.html>.

Smith, Tamsin. "Bossi Focuses Immigration Fears." BBC News. 10 May 2001 <http://news.bbc.co.uk/1/hi/world/europe/1321804.stm>.

Sozzi, Maria Assunta. "Un cuore grande per amare, forte per lottare." *Coordinamento Teologhe Italiane* 1 Jan. 2003 <http://www.teologhe.org/news01.htm>.

Stella, Gian Antonio. *L'orda: quando gli albanesi eravamo noi.* Milano: Rizzoli, 2002.

Sullivan, Stacy. "Albanian Americans Funding Rebels' Cause." *Washington Post* 26 May 1998: A12.

Vitti, Antonio. "Albanitaliamerica: Viaggio come un sordo sogno in Lamerica di Gianni Amelio." *Italica* 73 (1996): 2.

Volpi, Gianni. *Gianni Amelio*. Torino: Edizioni Scriptorium, 1995.

Wieviorka, Michel. *Il razzismo*. Trans. Maria Cristiana Carbone. Bari: Laterza, 2000.

Wollard, Elke. "Politica del corpo: Riflessioni femministe antirazziste sulla 'bianchi- tudine' come mito e terrore." Universitat Autonoma de Barcelona: *European Women's Synod*. Aug. 5–10, 2003 <http://www.synodalia.net/ita/relazioni. htm>.

Zickel, Raymond, and Walter R. Iwaskiew. *Albania: A Country Study*. Washington D.C.: Library of Congress, 1994.

Zincone, Giovanna. *Commissione per le politiche di integrazione degli immigrati*. Editorial. Roma, 13 Dec. 2000 <http://www.cestim.org/integra2/integra2_ index.htm>.

"Claiming": White Ambition, Multiracial Identity, and the New American Racial Passing

MEREDITH MCCARROLL

In *The Chronicles of Riddick*, protagonist Richard Riddick, played by multiracial actor Vin Diesel, roams his science fiction universe as a cultural anomaly. He does not belong to any of the stable ethnic communities in which individual inclusion is based upon a shared geography, physicality, and belief. His own mysterious background enables him to move through existent groups to fight the powerful Necromongers who threaten to homogenize and control the once diverse universe. In a climactic scene, one of the Necromongers asks in frustration, "Who are his people? Where does he come from?" There is no clear answer. Because of his fluid identity, Riddick eventually prevails and becomes the new lord marshal, the spiritual leader of the Necromongers. The film ends ambiguously, leaving Riddick with the potential to restore diversity to the universe or to continue the push toward homogeneity.

In the reality of the United States in the twenty-first century, as claims to multiracial identity increase and racial categories are questioned, the outcome of racial integration and hybridity is less cinematically nuanced. The multiracial is not endowed with the power to unite peacefully different races. Rather, categorical distinctions are upheld while those whose bodies are not easily read are reimagined and made to fit into one of two distinct binaries, black or white. In an American culture of unequal racial binaries, historical precedents documenting the social imbalance between these oppositions creates a desire to move out of the impotent and oppressed position into the powerful, dominant position. Historically, the desire to effect a power migration translates as a move toward whiteness. In "The Negro Artist and the Racial Mountain," Langston Hughes wrote that when he heard a Negro poet say, "I want to be a poet—not a Negro poet," he understood the poet to say, "'I want to write like a white poet,' meaning subconsciously, 'I would like to be a white poet'; meaning behind that, 'I would like to be white'" (1311). Claiming multiraciality often turns on a similar syllogistic reasoning terminating in the denial of race—most often the denial or invalidation of the darker one.

Black to white passing, especially prevalent during the early twentieth century, allowed individuals of African ancestry who could perform and appear as Anglo or European to escape from blackness in order to gain access to white spaces and privileges. Claiming multiracial identity, like black to white passing, has been read as a politically viable way to destabilize race. Maria P. P. Root, a scholar and advocate for mixed-race identity writes, "Clinging to a mixed-race identity in racialized ethnic groups, particularly if the other race is European derived, challenges the foundations on which perceived solidarity was constructed" (7). Not all see claims of multiraciality as a means to deconstruct racial hierarchy. Mary Thierry Texeira argues that "we cannot understand the movement unless it is placed in the context of white supremacy," a system in which "divisions, including racial labels and categories among people of color in the United States, have always benefited a white power structure that has often endorsed attempts to disunite nonwhites" (22). Rather than disrupting a constructed but considerable racial dichotomy of white and nonwhite, Texeira sees this multiracial identity movement developing in terms of "who is white(r) and who is not white" (33), sustaining rather than weakening racial identity. Texeira cites historical and cultural sociologist and the father of mixed-raced children Orlando Patterson as having naïve optimism about multiracial identity. Patterson states that "[racial] mixing is the best thing that could happen because . . . a middle group [makes] people feel an investment on both sides" (29). Texeira is quick to point out that Patterson fails to recognize that the "'middle races' have always identified more with the dominant group" (29). At the heart of the debate among those like Root, Texeira, and Patterson is the issue of agency and the question of sustaining an existence in the "third race" in order to challenge the racial dichotomy long in place in the United States.

Advocates of multiracial identity often envision a transgressive liminal space opening up between black and white, bridging the two while empowering the racial "other" to exist outside of racial expectations and limitations. While theories range from a liberating and fluid transnational identity that Paul Gilroy imagines in *The Black Atlantic* to an envisioned embodiment of the marginal space as a means of "recoupling" two sides of a contentious dichotomy that Gloria Anzaldúa in *"Borderlands/La Frontera"* and Donna Haraway in "The Cyborg Manifesto" reify, these idealized visions of liminality depend upon the assumption that the racialized other can achieve and maintain sufficient agency to embody and speak for a new racial identity. In this model of racial transgression, the power to interpret the sign of the body lies with the signified, the claiming or passing body. As film scholar Laura Mulvey makes clear the gaze enables the audience to make meaning by interpreting images. Similarly, reading response theorist Jonathan Culler asserts that "the reader becomes . . . a virtual site" where images are decoded and meaning is made (38). The identity of a mixed-race person becomes the object of the gaze and the text waiting to be read. Taking a page from Stuart Hall, whose historically and culturally grounded readings situate power hierarchies and textual relationships within a space and time that is specifically raced, classed, and gendered, the reading of a multiracial individual must take place within a sociopolitical climate that is built upon concrete and distinct definitions of race and tends toward monoracial readings of even the most adamantly multiracial individual. In this way, claims to multiracial identity fall short of revolutionary subversion and instead support white ambition while reinforcing a system built upon racial hierarchy.

Black Becomes White: Passing in the 1920s

In *Ethnicity and Race: Making Identities in a Changing World*, Stephen Cornell and Douglas Hartman define ethnicity as "a group of people with a shared history, culture, and symbolism—such as language, spiritual belief, geographical region, etc." They define race, on the other hand, as "a social construct, based on physical characteristics" (144). While race may well be a construct, and many theorists agree that it is, most people believe it to be a reality. The history of the United States is built on racial oppression—particularly the racial oppression of enslaved Africans, of their descendants, and of all those who bear the physical characteristics of nonwhiteness. Race, like ethnicity, carries assumptions of shared cultural experiences—particularly the experiences of privilege associated with whiteness and the prejudice whiteness heaps upon nonwhiteness. In a culture that judges others' racial reality based on a subjective reading of appearance, those judgments may often be incorrect. It is this fluid subjectivity that both supports the idea that race is a detrimental social construct and allows generalizations and judgments to hold sway. There is not, after all, any way to prove these judgments wrong when they are based on subjective perception rather than on objective fact. In the absence of "objective" genetic testing to determine "racial" heritage, presumptive skin and phenotype visual scanning suffice. Visual scanning has long allowed many exceptions to the "one-drop" rule to pass as white. Negative and limiting social strictures imposed upon the black body, combined with the desire of the oppressed to escape from the terrorism and racism of the Reconstruction period and to access power, explain the black to white passing migration that took place in the post–Civil War years.

The early twentieth century was a perilous time to be black in America. It is estimated that in the decade of the 1920s, as many as 281 people who were identified as black were lynched. During this period, the number of governmental offices held by those regarded as black was at a historic low. Although Reconstruction welcomed African Americans into positions of power, with 199 legislative representatives appointed between 1868 and 1869, their number dramatically declined by the 1920s, with only one black legislative representative appointed in 1929. Segregation was a common and legal practice throughout the nation. Whites limited occupational opportunities for those whose bodies they read as black. To be "black" in the early twentieth century was to be outside of or subservient to the dominant European-American culture. Out of this historical reality emerged two migratory political responses to circumvent racial exclusion and marginalization: the separatist migration response of Marcus Garvey, who advocated black nationalism and a return to Africa, and the integrationist migration response of subversive black to white passing.

With no physical test to assess race, many fair-complected African Americans who identified as black or whom the one-drop rule deemed nonwhite realized the potential to claim whiteness and migrate into privilege. Although statistics are inconclusive because passing is a covert activity, it has been estimated that between one hundred thousand and five hundred thousand individuals passed as white between 1900 and 1920. African-American novelist Jessie Fauset, who published *Plum Bun* (1929), a fictional account of passing, felt that clandestine transracial migrations were even more frequent and reported that twenty thousand nonwhite people were passing as white in New York City alone (Salzman 2108).

A literary trend during the 1920s and a filmic trend in the 1930s and 1940s mirrored the historical trend of passing. Nella Larsen's *Passing* (1929) follows protagonist Clare Kendry's migrations between black and white worlds that ultimately end with her ambiguous suicide or murder. Most scholars read Larsen's *Passing* as a cautionary tale mapping the pitfalls of black to white passing and negating the black self, perspectives echoed in other passing narratives of the 1920s era known as the Harlem Renaissance. Jessie Fauset's *Plum Bun* (1929), Walter White's *Flight* (1926), and George Schuyler's *Black No More* (1931) all treat racial passing as a denial of one's "true" heritage. The films of the 1930s and 1940s that narrate passing follow a similar formula. All three versions of *Imitation of Life*, the 1933 novel by Fannie Hurst, the 1934 movie directed by John M. Stahl, and the 1959 remake directed by Douglas Sirk, damn the biracial Sarah Jane for passing as white. Other passing films include Elia Kazan's *Pinky* (1949) and Alfred Werker's *Lost Boundaries* (1949).

The literary depictions of racial passing reflect a common curiosity not only in how passing works but also in what it does with respect to race and power. As an individual who has been raced in a particular way, and (mis)treated on that basis, steps outside of that racing and enters the position deemed powerful and privileged, there exists subversive potential. The concrete concept of race and the physical characteristics that categorize it lose substantive merit as one crosses the racial divide. In the revelatory moment, when the reader recognizes that the protagonist has successfully passed and simultaneously superseded categories of race, there is enormous potential for the often limiting racial category to disappear. With no means of determining black or white, black and white ostensibly cease to exist. Gender theorist Judith Butler posits that by pointing to the performativity of gender, the seemingly natural male/female dichotomy is revealed as a farce, promising liberation from narrowly defined gender roles and expectations. In *Gender Trouble*, Butler asks, "Is drag the imitation of gender, or does it dramatize the signifying gestures through which gender itself is established?" (viii). Extending Butler's speculation on gender construction to race, a black individual's performance of whiteness as a means of disrupting the white/nonwhite dichotomy is promising. In a system of oppositional definition like race and gender, inhabiting the other position offers an opportunity to disrupt the normative standards. Gayle Wald explores this potential in *Crossing the Line: Racial Passing in Twentieth-Century U.S. Literature and Culture*, writing of "the enterprise of 'crossing the line' as a strategic appropriation of race's power, emphasizing the stakes of such appropriation for racially defined subjects" (ix). Considering that everyone in the United States (and beyond) is a "racially defined subject," more overtly if the subject is not defined as white, many people have much at stake when racial passing occurs. Categorical racial judgments, as well as unearned racial privilege, are at stake if race is deemed to be fluid. Wald is interested in the ability of passing narratives "to demonstrate the failures of race to impose stable definitions of identity or to manifest itself in a reliable, permanent, and/or visible manner" (ix). This act of destabilizing alone, according to most scholars, fails to produce change. Rather than tearing apart the dichotomous system in place, passing reifies the existence of race as a stable marker of identity. Passage from one to the other strengthens the existence of both. In most passing narratives, not only are the passers punished for their transgressions, but racial difference and stability are upheld. In Fauset's *Plum Bun*, the female protagonist, Angela Murray, is unfulfilled while she passes as white. When she "comes out" as black, Fauset presents her return to her first socially constructed identity as natural and right. Murray, who is deemed black, can finally find peace as she claims her "true" racial identity. In Larsen's *Passing*, Clare Kendry refuses to admit her racial truth, and must die in order to support Larsen's moral of racial fealty. Similarly, Sarah Jane, who passes in *Imitation of Life*, is destined to live a life of regret for her refusal to admit her "true" race. In each of these cases, once an individual admits to her blackness, she is deemed thoroughly and completely black. The "one-drop" rule prevails.

Wald, for all of her hope in the subversive potential of passing, reads racial passing not as a complete failure but as an individualized effort with narrow influence outside of the personal. She explains, "Passing entails, then, not racial transcendence, but rather struggle for control over racial representation in a context of the radical unreliability of embodied appearances" (6). Ultimately, in a culture that determines race by physical characteristics, the power to interpret them lies with the gazer rather than the viewed—with the signifier rather than with the signified. Literary and media critics ranging from Stuart Hall to Jonathan Culler agree that meaning is made at the site of intersection between text and audience. A text with no audience has, according to this line of thinking, no existence. In terms of racialized bodies as texts, the reader—enveloped in a material reality built upon and influenced by monoracial categories—interprets that body-as-text based upon his or her own cultural point of reference. In passing narratives, as quickly as the gazer learns the "true" race of a passer, the novel or film wraps up tragically and, often, the career or status of a "real-life" passer dramatically changes.

These facts reveal the high stakes of racial passing and the desire to adhere to established racial categories—for a variety of reasons. The idealized concept of a colorblind United States, while theoretically appealing to some, is appalling to many. Gayle Wald investigates a colorblind approach as she shows the "potential pitfalls of such a predetermined 'blindness' to collective identities that are at once sites of self-recognition and self-identification and also regulated and enforced by racial ideology" (185). One runs into difficulty when attempting to identify as an individual who disregards the racial group to which s/he is assigned. The "imagined community," to borrow Benedict Anderson's term, which is in this case based on race, acts as an actual community that accepts, rejects, claims, or outs its members. Racial hierarchies tend to remain intact when an individual steps out of his/her prescribed racial role. As Kathleen Pfeiffer shows in her analysis of passing novels in the three decades following the *Plessy v.*

Ferguson (1896) landmark U.S. Supreme Court decision that legalized and solidified segregation, "passing for white has long been viewed as an instance of racial self-hatred or disloyalty." She argues that passing is not necessarily an act of political resistance, as Wald posits, but may in fact emerge because the passing figure "values individualism [and] . . . may be idiosyncratic, self-determining, or inclined toward improvisation" (2). Both Wald and Pfeiffer agree, however, that black to white passing "tends to reinforce the very logic of segregation by which passing is constructed" (17). Passing from black to white invites ejection from the white race if it detects "one drop" of black blood and encourages an outing from the black community—often out of a sense of injustice. After all, why should someone equally "black" get undeserved access to the white world, especially when no collective social change occurs with individual advancement? On either side of the color line, there are those that agree that passing has little result outside of the individual passer's life. It hardly challenges the status quo and certainly does not diminish race in any way. These limitations to racial passing, combined with a surge of racial pride associated with the black led civil rights movement of the mid-twentieth century, have deemed passing for white a damnable offense. In its place, claiming multiracial identity has emerged as the new passing of the twenty-first century.

Toward Whiteness: Claiming Multiracial Identity in the Twenty-first Century

While the rhetoric of colorblindness, growing out of the King era of the civil rights movement, pervades discussions of race in the United States by encouraging an ignorance of race, Cornel West and other critical race theorists have posited that race does indeed matter in America, a country in which 13 percent of today's population descended from enslaved Africans while another 1 percent descended from Indigenous Americans who were similarly disenfranchised and disempowered. Using traditional definitions of race, which physicality and presumed geographical origin circumscribe, Americans have been multiracial as long as the landmass they populated has been called

America. With European colonizers, deemed white, came the rape of and consensual relations with Indigenous and enslaved "Americans," deemed nonwhite, creating the first American multiracial generation. While multiracial Americans have long existed and identified as multiracial, as a "category" it has only begun to "count" in a more legitimate way in the past few decades as shifts in public identity and governmental classification have taken place.

From the inaugural census in 1790 until 1970, enumerators who went door to door to collect census information determined the subject's race and/or ethnicity. From the 1970 census onward, citizens have been able to identify themselves by choosing from an expanding list of possibilities (see fig. 1). On these early census forms, the conceptualization of race was limited to and limited by the census's system of categorizing. According to population scholar Tamar Jacoby, "Race was an exclusive category—if you were one thing, you were necessarily not something else, just as you were either male or female" (37). After choices for self identification increased, the next monumental change in the census came in 2000, as citizens were allowed to mark more than one race or ethnicity (see fig. 2). According to the U.S. Census Bureau, of the 281,421,906 residents of the United States on April 1, 2000, approximately 7 million (2.4 percent) marked more than one category.

The revisions to the census, which went unnoticed by many respondents, were the result of at least a decade of work by grass-roots organizers who were lobbying for a change in the racial/ethnic classification system. Multiracial organizations like AMEA (Association of Multiethnic Americans) and Project RACE (Reclassify All Children Equally) challenged the categories in place arguing that they were forced to privilege one parent's race over the other. Their plea was for "multiracial" to be included as a selection in the "race" section. A multiracial category, organizers believed, would satisfy the large number of citizens left frustrated by the lack of representation in the present classification. As the debate drew growing public attention, the National Association for the Advancement of Colored People (NAACP), the National Urban League, and the National Council of La Raza voiced concern about the proposed shift in racial classification. The burgeoning of a "nonwhite" group would place considerable strain on projects that receive Affirmative Action funding while the official count of African Americans, Spanish/Hispanics/Latinos, or American Indians or Alaska natives would decrease dramatically. Arthur Fletcher, then chair of the U.S. Commission on Civil Rights, imagined "a whole host of light-skinned Black Americans running for the door the minute they have another choice [to say], 'I am something other than Black'" (Spencer 104–5).

When the Office of Management and Budget ruled, it forwarded a compromise. Rather than adding "multiracial" as a category, the office decided to allow citizens to choose multiple categories. The multiple selection compromise was seen as a victory for some advocates of multiracial identity, while the ruling panicked other civil rights organizations. The result was a mass advertising campaign, sponsored by organizations including the NAACP and the National Asian Pacific American Legal Consortium, costing millions of dollars, to encourage individuals identifying as African Americans, Spanish/Hispanics/Latinos, and American Indians or Alaska natives to check only one box. From the racially mixed singer Lenny Kravitz's warning—"In this world, if you have one spot of Black blood, you are Black" (qtd. in Spencer 104)—to radio commercials urging African Americans to check only the black box "regardless of whether they had white or other ancestry (105), there was an urgency for African Americans to remain monoracial. Of the United States' 281,421,906 resident population, 75.1 percent (211,460,626) marked White or Caucasian and no other race, while 12.3 percent (34,658,190) marked Black or African American and no other race. Only 5 percent or 182,096 of the 34,658,190 respondents marking Black or African American also marked more than one race.

If proponents for the allowance of multiple identities in the 2000 census had hoped for clarity, they were sorely disappointed. Much confusion followed the tallying of census figures, with census workers uncertain about how to count specific citizens. As the census figures were tabulated, multiracial individuals were counted for each race or ethnicity claimed, making it impossible to compare the 2000 census with previous decades. Jacoby looks at one example from the census that shows the level of confusion resulting from the new categories:

> How many blacks are there in the United States today? If one counts only the people who check black alone, the answer is 34.7 million. But if one includes those who checked both black and

PLEASE ALSO ANSWER HOUSING QUESTIONS ON PAGE 3 ⟶

	PERSON 1	PERSON 2
Please fill one column ➤ for each person listed in Question 1a on page 1.	Last name	Last name
	First name — Middle initial	First name — Middle initial
2. How is this person related to PERSON 1? Fill ONE circle for each person. If **Other relative** of person in column 1, fill circle and print exact relationship, such as mother-in-law, grandparent, son-in-law, niece, cousin, and so on.	START in this column with the household member (or one of the members) in whose name the home is owned, being bought, or rented. If there is no such person, start in this column with any adult household member. ▪	If a RELATIVE of Person 1: ○ Husband/wife ○ Brother/sister ○ Natural-born ○ Father/mother or adopted ○ Grandchild son/daughter ○ Other relative ⌐ ○ Stepson/ stepdaughter If NOT RELATED to Person 1: ○ Roomer, boarder, ○ Unmarried or foster child partner ○ Housemate, ▪ ○ Other roommate nonrelative
3. Sex Fill ONE circle for each person.	○ Male ○ Female	○ Male ○ Female
4. Race Fill ONE circle for the race that the person considers himself/herself to be. If **Indian (Amer.)**, print the name of the enrolled or principal tribe. ⟶ If **Other Asian or Pacific Islander (API)**, print one group, for example: Hmong, Fijian, Laotian, Thai, Tongan, Pakistani, Cambodian, and so on. ⟶ If **Other race**, print race. ⟶	○ White ○ Black or Negro ○ Indian (Amer.) (Print the name of the enrolled or principal tribe.) ⌐ ○ Eskimo ○ Aleut Asian or Pacific Islander (API) ○ Chinese ○ Japanese ▪ ○ Filipino ▪ ○ Asian Indian ○ Hawaiian ○ Samoan ○ Korean ○ Guamanian ○ Vietnamese ○ Other API ⌐ ○ Other race (Print race) ⌐	○ White ○ Black or Negro ○ Indian (Amer.) (Print the name of the enrolled or principal tribe.) ⌐ ○ Eskimo ○ Aleut Asian or Pacific Islander (API) ○ Chinese ○ Japanese ○ Filipino ▪ ○ Asian Indian ○ Hawaiian ○ Samoan ○ Korean ○ Guamanian ○ Vietnamese ○ Other API ⌐ ○ Other race (Print race) ⌐
5. Age and year of birth a. Print each person's age at last birthday. Fill in the matching circle below each box. b. Print each person's year of birth and fill the matching circle below each box.	a. Age b. Year of birth 0 ○ 0 ○ 0 ○ 1 ● 8 ○ 0 ○ 0 ○ 1 ○ 1 ○ 1 ○ 9 ○ 1 ○ 1 ○ 2 ○ 2 ○ 2 ○ 2 ○ 3 ○ 3 ○ 3 ○ 3 ○ 4 ○ 4 ○ ▪ 4 ○ 4 ○ 5 ○ 5 ○ 5 ○ 5 ○ 6 ○ 6 ○ 6 ○ 6 ○ 7 ○ 7 ○ 7 ○ 7 ○ 8 ○ 8 ○ 8 ○ 8 ○ 9 ○ 9 ○ 9 ○ 9 ○	a. Age b. Year of birth 0 ○ 0 ○ 0 ○ 1 ● 8 ○ 0 ○ 0 ○ 1 ○ 1 ○ 1 ○ 9 ○ 1 ○ 1 ○ 2 ○ 2 ○ 2 ○ 2 ○ 3 ○ 3 ○ 3 ○ 3 ○ 4 ○ 4 ○ ▪ 4 ○ 4 ○ 5 ○ 5 ○ 5 ○ 5 ○ 6 ○ 6 ○ 6 ○ 6 ○ 7 ○ 7 ○ 7 ○ 7 ○ 8 ○ 8 ○ 8 ○ 8 ○ 9 ○ 9 ○ 9 ○ 9 ○
6. Marital status Fill ONE circle for each person.	○ Now married ○ Separated ○ Widowed ○ Never married ○ Divorced	○ Now married ○ Separated ○ Widowed ○ Never married ○ Divorced
7. Is this person of Spanish/Hispanic origin? Fill ONE circle for each person. If **Yes, other Spanish/Hispanic**, print one group. ⟶	○ No (not Spanish/Hispanic) ○ Yes, Mexican, Mexican-Am., Chicano ○ Yes, Puerto Rican ▪ ○ Yes, Cuban ○ Yes, other Spanish/Hispanic (Print one group, for example: Argentinean, Colombian, Dominican, Nicaraguan, Salvadoran, Spaniard, and so on.) ⌐	○ No (not Spanish/Hispanic) ○ Yes, Mexican, Mexican-Am., Chicano ○ Yes, Puerto Rican ○ Yes, Cuban ○ Yes, other Spanish/Hispanic (Print one group, for example: Argentinean, Colombian, Dominican, Nicaraguan, Salvadoran, Spaniard, and so on.) ⌐
FOR CENSUS USE ⟶	○ ○ ☐	○ ○

Figure 1. The 1990 U.S. Census Form, Page 2, Section 4 "Race," instructs respondent to "Fill ONE circle for the race that the person considers himself/herself to be."

United States
Census
2000

U.S. Department of Commerce • Bureau of the Census

This is the official form for all the people at this address. It is quick and easy, and your answers are protected by law. Complete the Census and help your community get what it needs — today and in the future!

Start Here

Please use a black or blue pen.

1. How many people were living or staying in this house, apartment, or mobile home on April 1, 2000?

[ ] Number of people

INCLUDE in this number:

- foster children, roomers, or housemates
- people staying here on April 1, 2000 who have no other permanent place to stay
- people living here most of the time while working, even if they have another place to live

DO NOT INCLUDE in this number:

- college students living away while attending college
- people in a correctional facility, nursing home, or mental hospital on April 1, 2000
- Armed Forces personnel living somewhere else
- people who live or stay at another place most of the time

2. Is this house, apartment, or mobile home — Mark ☒ ONE box.

- [ ] Owned by you or someone in this household with a mortgage or loan?
- [ ] Owned by you or someone in this household free and clear (without a mortgage or loan)?
- [ ] Rented for cash rent?
- [ ] Occupied without payment of cash rent?

3. Please answer the following questions for each person living in this house, apartment, or mobile home. Start with the name of one of the people living here who owns, is buying, or rents this house, apartment, or mobile home. If there is no such person, start with any adult living or staying here. We will refer to this person as Person 1.

What is this person's name? *Print name below.*

Last Name

[| | | | | | | | | | | | | | | | |]

First Name   MI

[| | | | | | | | | | | | | | | | |]

OMB No. 0607-0856: Approval Expires 12/31/2000

Form **D-61A**

4. What is Person 1's telephone number? *We may call this person if we don't understand an answer.*

Area Code + Number

[| |] - [| |] - [| | |]

5. What is Person 1's sex? *Mark ☒ ONE box.*

- [ ] Male [ ] Female

6. What is Person 1's age and what is Person 1's date of birth?

Age on April 1, 2000

[|]

Print numbers in boxes

Month   Day   Year of birth

[|] [|] [| | |]

→ **NOTE: Please answer BOTH Questions 7 and 8.**

7. Is Person 1 Spanish/Hispanic/Latino? *Mark ☒ the "No" box if **not** Spanish/Hispanic/Latino.*

- [ ] **No,** not Spanish/Hispanic/Latino
- [ ] Yes, Mexican, Mexican Am., Chicano
- [ ] Yes, Puerto Rican
- [ ] Yes, Cuban
- [ ] Yes, other Spanish/Hispanic/Latino — *Print group.*

[| | | | | | | | | | | | | | | | | | | | |]

8. What is Person 1's race? *Mark ☒ one or more races to indicate what this person considers himself/herself to be.*

- [ ] White
- [ ] Black, African Am., or Negro
- [ ] American Indian or Alaska Native — *Print name of enrolled or principal tribe.*

[| | | | | | | | | | | | | | | | | | | | |]

- [ ] Asian Indian [ ] Japanese [ ] Native Hawaiian
- [ ] Chinese [ ] Korean [ ] Guamanian or Chamorro
- [ ] Filipino [ ] Vietnamese [ ] Samoan
- [ ] Other Asian — *Print race.* [ ] Other Pacific Islander — *Print race.*

[| | | | | | | | | | | | | | | | | | | | |]

- [ ] Some other race — *Print race.*

[| | | | | | | | | | | | | | | | | | | | |]

→ **If more people live here, continue with Person 2.**

Figure 2. The 2000 U.S. Census Form, Page 1, Question 8, instructs respondent to "Mark one or more races."

something else, the number rises to 36.4 million. Are blacks still the country's largest minority group, or do Latinos now outnumber them? It depends on whether one includes those extra 1.7 million: yes if one does, no if one does not. (38)

The response to the new census forms was as mixed as the response to the petition to change the racial categories. A *USA Today*/CNN/ Gallup poll from March 2001 found that 64 percent of the public thought it was "good for the country" for more Americans to "think of themselves as multiracial rather than belonging to a single race" (39). Former head of the Census Bureau, Martha Farnsworth Riche, called the new census "the beginning of the end of the overwhelming role of race in our public life" (Kasindorf and El Nasser). William Frey, a University of Michigan demographer, reads the shift as a new "democratic approach to race and ethnicity."

Those engaged in the debate and hearings with the U.S. Census Bureau were less optimistic about the 2000 census. Although citizens were allowed to mark as many categories as they wished, their options were still fairly limited. There were six broad racial categories: (1) White, (2) Black, African American, or Negro, (3) American Indian and Alaska Native, (4) six Asian subcategories and one write-in "Other" box, (5) three Pacific Islander subcategories with one write-in "Other" box, and (6) Spanish/Hispanic/Latino with three subcategories and one write-in "Other" box. To provide a seventh and final option, a write-in box for "some other race" was provided (see fig. 2). Even as the various combinations of these races or ethnicities were growing exponentially, the concept of racial definition began to seem superficial when it was self-defined. As Naomi Zack, advocate for mixed-race identity, asserts in "American Mixed Race: The United States 2000 Census and Related Issues" that multiethnicity is a social construct, a fiction without biological reality. What this exercise in checking boxes proved is that all of race is a fiction:

Race, however, is a social construction on all levels. Not only are the links between so-called biological race and culture the result of history, tradition and current norms, but the existence of biological racial taxonomies is itself the result of such social factors. . . . Since human biological race is a fiction, so is mixed race. (13)

For Zack, the fiction of race was not adequately revealed with the mark all that apply compromise in the 2000 census. Zack's disappointment stems from her work for a multiracial category. Ranier Spencer, on the other hand, critiques the 2000 census for the lack of clarity it created in terms of racial categories. Spencer argues that an acknowledgment of race is the only means to acknowledge racism and statistical tracking, which relies upon racial categories, and serves to "check for indications of possible covert and institutional discrimination. . . . The point is that without the collection of racial statistics none of this kind of analysis is possible" (101–2).

For those desirous of upholding racial categories, the idea of easily choosing another category or two does not respect the legitimacy of one's primary or perceived race. For those who wanted to see an end to race as a defining category, the 2000 census shift was equally unsatisfying. Neither of these political polarities offers a subversion of the current white dominated racial hierarchy in America. Merely to preserve existent racial categories is to uphold a system that historically disenfranchises and disempowers on the basis of race. At the other extreme, to pretend that race does not matter naïvely ignores contemporary cultural characteristics and denies a history of racially determined social caste. A passive colorblind approach has failed to cause the racial revolution for which many once hoped and generally allows those in positions of power to maintain that power without any accountability. Proponents of the revised census hoped that the selection of multiple racial categories would not only more accurately represent the majority of Americans but also challenge the meaning of race as it complicates assumptions and subverts the power structure by deconstructing whiteness. Critical white studies critics like Peggy McIntosh and Richard Dyer have suggested that whiteness maintains its power because of its invisibility, which results because whiteness is unraced and thus becomes the norm. McIntosh calls for an attention to the "invisible package of unearned assets" granted by white skin (291) in order to answer Dyer's call to "make whiteness strange" by seeing it as the constructed identity that continually asserts itself as natural (4). By seeing whiteness as a race and by acknowledging the performativity of race, the elite position of white may be revealed, as in the case of black to white passing, as less powerful when claims to whiteness cease to presume exclusion of any other race.

The subversive potential of the liminal space posited by Anzaldúa and others is erased, however, when borders are patrolled by a governmental agency. The playfulness of the third race proved too uncomfortable to advocates of a revised census; rather than claiming a mutable liberatory identity, this insistence on racial categories pins down and labels all Americans, further legitimizing the stability of the constructed categories of race in America. It is said that native Alaskans have forty official words for snow—so prevalent and central to their understanding of the world; the United States now has sixty-three official races (Spencer 108).

While the statistical results of the 2000 census did alter the way that demographers think about race in the United States, their impact on the average American has been imperceptible. When the majority of Americans, especially the 97 percent of Americans who identify as monoracial, sees an individual on the street or on the television screen, most within the majority interpret that individual as a member of a designated race, and that racial interpretation may vary from person to person, from household to household. What remains to be true, even in light of a shifting focus toward multiraciality, is that an individual's self definition of him/herself often fails. Instead, the gaze empowers the viewer to read—and race—the viewed. Regardless of how emphatically the multiracial disputes monoracial reading, the viewer has the power simply to hit mute.

The "Cablinasian" Identity of Tiger Woods

When Tiger Woods entered the mainstream of American popular culture after winning the Masters Golf Tournament in 1997, the stability of race and ethnicity seemed to quake momentarily. Spectators and media identified the multiracial Woods, whose father has African, American Indian, and Chinese heritage, and whose mother has Thai, Chinese, and undisclosed European heritage as monoracially black. Many viewers took a stance on Tiger Woods's ethnicity when "white" golfer Fuzzy Zoeller made his infamous remark urging Woods not to request "fried chicken . . . or collard greens or whatever the hell they serve" for the 1998 Champions Dinner, whose menu the previous year's winner decides ("Golfer"). To the dismay of those who had claimed him exclusively as one of their own, Woods identified himself as African American and Asian American in a statement to the press:

> My parents have taught me to always be proud of my ethnic background. Please rest assured that is, and will always be, the case—past, present and future. The media has portrayed me as African American, sometimes Asian—in fact, I am both. . . . Truthfully, I feel very fortunate, and EQUALLY PROUD to be both African American and Asian! The critical and fundamental point is that ethnic background and/or composition should NOT make a difference. It does NOT make a difference to me. The bottom line is that I am American . . . and proud of it!

He later expanded his identity to Caucasian, Black, Indian, and Asian, from which he created the racially melded term "Cablinasian." Woods has maintained this multiracial identity and continually counters exclusive monoracial labels.

As someone who identifies as multiracial, it makes little—or as much—sense for Woods to identify as black as it would for him to identify as Native American. Yet despite his press statements, most of his admirers and critics deny him multiracial identity, deeming him monoracial or biracial. The African American Registry lists him as golf's "Main Man," calling him an "African and Asian American professional golfer." The motivation here, presumably, is to lay claim to a successful individual who identifies, at least in part, as African American. The African American Registry that places him in only two racial camps ignores Woods's claims of multiraciality. In other instances, as in a post on the white supremacist web site of former politician and Ku Klux Klan leader David Duke, Woods's claims of multiraciality are denied and he is made monoracially black. Given his neo-Nazi leanings, Duke must deny Woods access to whiteness, and because multiraciality is a step toward whiteness, it too must be denied. Instead, Duke ignores the complexity of Woods's identity and discusses him as a black man, which is to say, without much respect. As Duke writes to his white supremacist followers, he quells anxiety that Woods has made it into the white realm by assuring his readers that while Woods might be a golfing champion, he is still a black man living in a white world that denies him full access to power. Duke warns his audience of "racially aware Whites" that support of a "Black" athlete like Tiger Woods "affirms Black racial pride and a sense of supremacy and solidarity" ultimately "add(ing) to the myth that most Blacks are just like us."

Just as David Duke wants Tiger Woods to be black so that he is not mistaken as white, there are others invested in making Woods monoracially black to the point of calling him black in defiance of his repeated claims that he is multiracial. Woods told the *Washington Post*, "My mother is from Thailand. . . . My father is part black, Chinese and American Indian. So I am all of these. It's an injustice to all my heritages to single me out as black" (qtd. in Alsultany 153). In spite of this "injustice," many reporters waxed eloquent about the beauty and justice of Woods's 1997 Masters victory, referring to him as the first black man to win the tournament. In one of the most sentimental depictions of a golf victory, Jay Mariotti of the *Chicago Sun-Times* wrote, "On a windy Sunday in the Georgia hills that seemed to blow away sports and society evermore, the clenched fist of Tiger Woods was a vision of triumph and, let's hope, a bridge to a colorblind world" (qtd. in Futrelle). Mariotti's perspective, reflective of the general mood following Woods's victory, disregards and simplifies both Woods's multiracial identity and America's racial history. By designating Woods as black when convenient, the white media, sports community, and general populace can feel progressive and inclusive without interrogating the psychology that approves of the racial mixed over the "monoracial" yet continues to ignore his repeated claims to multiraciality.

In order to challenge racial assumptions and white privilege, multiracial individuals must continually assert their racial makeup, resisting social tendencies to view them as monoracial. Cecile Ann Lawrence, in "Racelessness," looks at the marketing and passing of multiethnic persons, revealing American society's preference for an individual whose parents come from dual or multiple racial backgrounds over the African American whose parents may be born "black." She cites cases in which "firsts" are reported as black when they are actually multiracial. The first black surgeon general, Joycelyn Elders, or the first black secretary of commerce, Ron Brown, or the first black woman to win a best actress Oscar, Halle Berry—all of these people have parents who identify with different races.

> Worse is the fact that passing off mixed-race people as "black" allows the "white" power structure to pat itself on the back for "allowing" "black" people into positions of power, when what they are really doing is letting in mixed-race people whose physical appearance is more acceptable culturally than very dark-skinned people. (Lawrence 26)

Physical and social traits that are deemed white maintain a position of privilege while the reality of multiraciality loses valence in this simplification of race.

Outing Vin Diesel

In the mid-1990s, actor Vin Diesel was having little success at finding film work. He recalls that casting agents read him as "'too Italian' for gangsta films, 'too black or Latino' for mobster things, and 'too Jewish or Asian' for commercials" (Solotaroff 110). Frustrated by these physical judgments, Diesel saved three thousand dollars and, with the guidance of a filmmaking book that his mother gave him, wrote and starred in the short film, *Multi-Facial* (1995). The film screened at the Cannes Film Festival, where Steven Spielberg saw the young actor and cast him as the Italian American Adrian Carpazo in *Saving Private Ryan* (1998). From there, Diesel went on to play Richard Riddick in the Riddick series, including *Pitch Black* (2000) and the *Chronicles of Riddick* (2004), and other "ethnically indeterminate" characters like Chris Varick in *Boiler Room* (2000) and Xander Cage in *xXx* (2002). As his résumé and his olive complexion demonstrate, Vin Diesel is the "kid who grew up checking all 12 boxes on the census form for race" (66). Although, as already pointed out, multiple selection was not an option until 2000, Diesel identifies as multiracial. Beyond that label, he is reluctant to define himself. Whereas Tiger Woods gives the ancestral equation comprising his race, Vin Diesel prefers to remain silent, repeatedly referring to himself as a chameleon when pressed by interviewers for clarity.

Diesel's fluid identity, however, has only brought more attention to the question of his race. Surfing for "Vin Diesel" on any Internet search engine quickly turns up dozens of sites devoted to the topic. Many interviews with Diesel focus on his race, as each journalist hopes to be the first to report Diesel's identification of himself. Even discussion boards on general fan sites inevitably turn to the multiracial debate swirling around Diesel. On these sites there is some allowance for Diesel's multiracial identity but an exigency for him to identify *which* of the multiple races he means by multiracial pervades the discussion. Attempts to link him to specific races reveal the instability of what constitutes race as well as the "authority" used to determine one's link to a racial group:

> I read an article that his real father is black and Vin Diesel is mixed with Dominican, Mexican and Irish. ("Multicultural")

> I heard Mariah Carey said that he was mixed black and white. ("Multicultural")

> I read an article recently in *Time* magazine that stated Mr. Diesel has a twin brother with BLONDE hair and BLUE eyes. ("Vin Diesel")

> If Vincent is his last name, then he's probably English. . . . I'd say from looking at him that he's Dominican and Italian and that's what I've always thought. ("Multicultural")

> Vin is black, I read it in a local newspaper article on him. Look at his hair and his facial features, and his voice. . . . He is also Italian, you can tell by his nose. I am black and Italian also, and many people in my fam, even me, have the same features. ("Multicultural")

> Access Hollywood showed a clip of Vin over the weekend and he had a big afro, an Adidas jog suit and he was break dancing to "Crush Groove." Now that really busted him out. ("Outing")

Based on anecdotal testimony, phenotypic outing and onomastics, discerning Diesel's race becomes fans' obsessive preoccupation. Rather than clarifying the meaning of race, these assessments anatomically dissect Diesel and depend upon rumor for validation. The need to identify Diesel and the need to identify *with* Diesel both contribute to a disregard for his desire to deny all racial affiliations. One discussant on a Diesel discussion board wrote, "I just wonder sometimes when people say that they want to be thought of as multiracial or cultural they just mean 'don't think of me as black'" ("Outing"). Adherence to race as a stable definitional category pervades discussions of race. Diesel's denial of race frustrates many viewers who identify as black. The anonymous moderator of a discussion titled "Outing Vin Diesel" on BET.com writes,

> Vin Diesel, you need to be careful. Don't worry about fighting evil spies or ferocious flying aliens. You need to keep your eyes out for.... THE BLACK COMMUNITY! You know the old saying, "it takes one to know one"? Well, you are one. One of us, that is. The Rock, Jennifer Beals, Tiger Woods—none have been able to escape! And you're next.

Although the moderator uses wry humor, the message touches on a cultural reality in which failure is associated with blackness while success is linked to whiteness. The BET moderator and others' viewing of Diesel or Woods as monoracial and black is as logical as an oppressed black American wanting to out someone passing as white in the early twentieth century. Out of fear, pride, envy, disgust, or disappointment, many who identify as black use the power of the gaze to define the multiracial as monoracial. In response to the question, "Should it bother us that Diesel doesn't play up his 'blackness'?," one contributor wrote, "I look at that like I look at Tiger Woods: he's a great champion, he makes golf more palpable, and he's part of the Family, even if he doesn't claim full membership" ("Vin Diesel"). Regardless of Woods's or Diesel's claims to multiracial identity, this viewer and others like him can disregard those claims and identify them as black—as brothers in the "Family." Diesel's coy treatment of his race potentially separates him from blackness, offering the white access and association that is more often granted to one with light skin. Ultimately, the viewer decides if Diesel's ancestry is African, Asian, or Hispanic. As one fan adamantly asserts, "He should admit his race and satisfy his fan base for we are the ones that supposedly make him the star that he is. We decide and that's what matters" ("Outing").

The New American Passing:
Claiming Multiracial Identity

Many scholars and activists maintain that multiracial identity can and will lead to a world less divided by race. Jack Foley, in "Multiculturalism and the Media," hopes that multiculturalism will offer "a way of see-ing the world *without whiteness*" because it "implies a continual effort of construction and deconstruction" (369, 370). Similarly, G. Reginald Daniel writes, "The new multiracial identity is a form of resistance to 'common sense' notions of race based on the one-drop rule" (125). Evelyn Asultany imagines a way in which insisting on a multiracial identification "poses a challenge to monoracial cultural logic and as a result might introduce the possibility of a multiethnic conceptualiza-tion into our narrow ethnic cartography" (148). Each of these writers, even in their optimism, is unconsciously acknowledging, via their talk of resistance and insistence, the powerful cultural urge to read indi-viduals as monoracial and to deny white access whenever possible. Otherwise, such assertion would not be necessary.

San San Kwan and Kenneth Speirs, editors of *Mixing it Up: Multi-racial Subjects*, explore the ways that multiracial identity has long been read:

> Historically, multiracial identity in the United States has been a mark of shame and ignominy. The need to establish and sustain firm categories of race as a way to maintain White dominance in America left no place for the multiracial. Thus the mixed blood, who threatened these categories, was either monoracialized or rep-resented as "deviant" and "pathological." (1)

There has not been a space for the multiracial in the United States, although the U.S. Census Bureau projected a 9.5 percent increase in multiracial Americans between 2000 and 2003 (U.S. Census Bureau 15). Instead, as Kwan and Speirs reveal, those who cannot be made to fit one race or another have been ostracized. Evelyn Asultany, who is Latin and Arab, finds this to be true today, noting that "identities that make sense within the cultural logic (monoracial) are rewarded with belonging, while those posited as 'illogical' (multiethnic) are denied community belonging" (143). Whether consciously or not, categorization takes place in an American climate that prides itself on being a melting pot of cultures, races, classes and experiences. Instead of melting together, there continues to be a stew, chunks of separation based on imagined communities of difference. Within this American pot there is no in-between space. Rather, an individual who might identify with multiple communities must choose, just as the early censuses forced multiracial Americans to choose. While governmental records now allow an intermediary position for those who do not easily fit one category or another, American sensibility and judgment do not allow the same flexibility. According to Asultany, there is too much at stake for most Americans:

> For some Whites, the multiethnic represents the pollution of the White race; for some African Americans the multiethnic represents an attempt to escape blackness; and for other ethnicities, such as South Asians, Latinos, or Arabs, the multiethnic can be seen as ill-equipped to perpetuate cultural traditions and therefore represents the dilution of that particular culture. (145)

The response is to monoracialize those who do not fit. These judgments are based most frequently on visual cues, and sometimes, as with Diesel above, on behavioral or cultural assumptions. What follows is the pattern that took place in the early twentieth century, in which those with light enough skin became white. In the twenty-first century, those not quite white enough to pass entirely can attempt to exist in the middle ground of multiracial—not quite black, but certainly not white, inviting fear from critics like Lisa Jones, who worries that a multiracial identity in America may be "akin to South Africa's 'colored' caste created under apartheid" (58). Not black, but still not white, those labeled as "colored" in a system of apartheid establish an ascendance toward whiteness out of blackness without subverting the system of racist oppression. Further, when a system that depends upon binaries and is uncomfortable with hybridity enables an audience to determine who is black and who is white, claims of multiraciality are subject to the judgments of viewers—viewers deeply embedded in a system of racial classification built around racial categories that only make sense in opposition to one another.

Celebrities such as Cameron Diaz, Keanu Reeves, and Benjamin Bratt are all multiracial but are read as white and have access to white privilege, while other famous and high-profile multiracials, such as Halle Berry, Paula Abdul, Mariah Carey, and Barack Obama, are continually read as black. The difference is physical. Diaz, Reeves, and Bratt are light enough to pass while Berry, Abdul, Carey, and Obama are not. Like Diesel and Woods, a greater social onus is placed on those who cannot pass entirely into whiteness to claim multiraciality as an escape from blackness. Thus the fight to identify as multiracial is also a fight for white access.

Works Cited

Alsultany, Evelyn. "Toward a Multiethnic Cartography: Multiethnic Identity, Monoracial Cultural Logic and Popular Culture." *Mixing It Up: Multiracial Subjects.* Ed. San San Kwan and Kenneth Speirs. Austin: U of Texas P, 2004. 141–57.

Anzaldúa, Gloria. "Borderlands/La Frontera." *Literary Theory: An Anthology.* Ed. Julie Rivkin and Michael Ryan. Malden: Blackwell, 1998. 887–902.

Butler, Judith. *Gender Trouble: Feminism and the Subversion of Identity.* New York: Routledge, 1990.

Cornell, Stephen, and Douglas Hartmann. *Ethnicity and Race: Making Identities in a Changing World.* Thousand Oaks: Pine Forge, 1998.

Culler, Jonathan. *The Pursuit of Signs: Semiotica, Literature, Deconstruction.* Ithaca: Cornell UP, 1981.

Daniel, G. Reginald. *More than Black?* Philadelphia: Temple UP, 2002.

Duke, David. "Tiger Woods, Race, and Professional Sports." Oct. 1997. Stormfront. org. 16 Nov. 2005 <http://www.stormfront.org/1097/sports.htm>.

Dyer, Richard. *White.* New York: Routledge, 1997.

Foley, Jack. "Multiculturalism and the Media." *MultiAmerica.* Ed. Ishmael Reed. New York: Viking, 1997. 366–70.

Gilroy, Paul. *The Black Atlantic: Modernity and Double Consciousness.* Cambridge: Harvard, 1993.

"Golfer Says Comments About Woods 'Misconstrued.'" 21 Apr. 1997. *CNN Interactive.* 16 Nov. 2005 <http://www.cnn.com/US/9704/21/fuzzy/>.

Hughes, Langston. "The Negro Artist and the Racial Mountain." *Norton Anthology of African American Literature.* 2nd ed. Ed. Henry Louis Gates and Nellie Y. McKay. New York: Norton, 2004. 1311–14.

Jacoby, Tamar. "An End to Counting by Race?" *Commentary* 111.6 (2001): 37–40.

Jones, Lisa. *Bulletproof Diva: Tales of Race, Sex, and Hair.* New York: Anchor, 1995.

Kasindorf, Martin, and Haya El Nasser. "Impact of Census' Race Date Debated." 13 Mar. 2001. *USA Today.* 1 Oct. 2005 <http://www.usatoday.com>.

Kwan, San San, and Kenneth Speirs, eds. *Mixing It Up: Multiracial Subjects.* Austin: U of Texas P, 2004.

Lawrence, Cecile Ann. "Racelessness." *American Mixed Race: The Culture of Microdiversity.* Ed. Naomi Zack. Lanham: Rowman and Littlefield, 1995. 25–37.

"The Multicultural Mysteries of Vin Diesel." 21 Aug. 2002. Online posting. 24 Apr. 2004 <http://www.sklerosystems.com/signalkorps/archives/000117.html>.

McIntosh, Peggy. "White Privilege and Male Privilege: A Personal Account of Coming to See Correspondences through Work in Women's Studies." *Critical White Studies: Looking Behind the Mirror.* Ed. Richard Delgado and Jean Stefancic. Philadelphia: Temple UP, 1997. 291–99.

"'Outing' Diesel." 2 Aug. 2002. Online posting. BET.com. 24 Apr. 2004 <http://www.bet.com/articles>.

Pfeiffer, Kathleen. *Race Passing and American Individualism.* Amherst: U of Massachusetts P, 2003.

Root, Maria P. P. "Five Mixed-Race Identities: From Relic to Revolution." *New Faces in a Changing America: Multiracial Identity in the 21st Century.* Ed. Loretta I. Winters and Herman L. DeBose. Thousand Oaks: Sage, 2003. 3–20.

Solotaroff, Paul. "Diesel Power." *Men's Journal* Mar. 2005: 62+.

Spencer, Ranier. "Census 2000: Assessments in Significance." *New Faces in a Changing America: Multiracial Identity in the 21st Century.* Ed. Loretta I. Winters and Herman L. DeBose. Thousand Oaks: Sage, 2003. 99–110.

Texeira, Mary Thierry, "The New Multiracialism: An Affirmation of or an End to Race as We Know It?" *New Faces in a Changing America: Multiracial Identity in the 21st Century.* Ed. Loretta I. Winters and Herman L. DeBose. Thousand Oaks: Sage, 2003. 21–37.

Thrupkaew, Noy. "The Multicultural Mysteries of Vin Diesel." AlterNet.org. 16 Aug. 2002 <http:/www.alternet.org/story.html>.

U.S. Census Bureau. *Statistical Abstract of the United States: 2004–2005.* <http:/www.census.gov>.

"Vin Diesel: Sellout or Smart Marketing?" 12 Aug. 2002. 3BlackChicks.com. 24 Apr. 2004 <http://www.3blackchicks.com/ubb/Forum1/HTML/000172.html>.

Wald, Gayle. *Crossing the Line: Racial Passing in Twentieth-Century U.S. Literature and Culture.* Durham: Duke UP, 2000.

Woods, Tiger. "Press Statement." 1 Oct. 2005 <http://www.geocities.com/Colosseum/2396/tigerrace.html>.

———. "American Mixed Race: The United States 2000 Census and Related Issues." *Harvard Blackletter Law Journal* 17 (2001). 27 Sept. 2005 <http://www.inter-racialvoice.com>.

Beyond the White Negro: Eminem, Danny Hoch, and Race Treason in Contemporary America

KIMBERLY CHABOT DAVIS

In the fifty years since Norman Mailer coined the term "white Negro," whites who ventriloquize African-American culture have been a frequent target for derision among left-leaning academics and cultural critics. Derision was clearly warranted in the case of Mailer's Beat generation hipsters, who idealized black masculinity as anarchic, sexually potent, antibourgeois, violent, and sociopathic—in short, "cool." Cultural critics Nelson George and Gayle Wald have deftly analyzed the romanticization and essentialism lurking behind these white fantasies of blackness, and they also unveil the imperialist desires which often turn "white Negro" cross-racial affiliations into acts of co-optation and cultural theft.[1] A long line of ethnomusicologists and music critics have criticized whites for appropriating the African-American and Caribbean styles of jazz, blues, reggae, and hip-hop; white artists who have faced such scrutiny include George Gershwin, Elvis Presley, Janis Joplin, the Police, Mick Jagger, Vanilla Ice, and the Beastie Boys.[2] Journalist Armond White, for example, lambasts the Beastie Boys' farcical rap music for evacuating hip-hop of its cultural specificity and political edge as protest music. He contends that "white appropriation [often] attempts to erase the culture it plunders" (548), a conclusion echoed by the vast majority of cultural critics writing about white identification with blackness.³ Hip-hop expert Greg Tate recently edited a collection of essays called *Everything But the Burden: What White People Are Taking from Black Culture;* the title registers an unequivocal disdain for crossover in popular culture. Bell hooks similarly describes cross-racial identification as a symbolic annihilation and incorporation, akin to "eating the other" (21–39). In the book *Racechanges,* which documents hundreds of instances of racial crossover in twentieth-century art and culture, Susan Gubar despairingly concludes that "even the most high-minded, idealistic motivations will not save white impersonators of blackness from violating, appropriating, or compromising black subjectivity in a way that will *inevitably* rebound against the ethical integrity of whites" (36; emphasis added).

While this valuable body of cultural criticism has drawn much-needed attention to the imperialist dimensions of whiteness, it also risks treating whiteness as a monolithic signifier of domination. This oft-repeated narrative of appropriation has inadvertently led to the obscuring or repression of other kinds of stories about white attraction to blackness. Relegating all white artists working with African-American cultural idioms to the same pejorative category as Mailer's white Negroes, we underestimate the potential of some instances of crossover to function as radical acts of "race treason" against white privilege, such as Noel Ignatiev and John Garvey encourage in their journal, *Race Traitor.* Vron Ware and Les Back, in their analysis of white contributions to the development of southern soul music, convincingly argue that critics must pay attention to local contexts before passing judgment on individual acts of racial crossover: "Distinctions among musicians, studio owners, producers, and songwriters are elided within the language of appropriation" (230). However, while blanket condemnations of white Negroes are problematic, so are facile celebrations of crossover as inherently subversive. As Noel Ignatiev warns in an interview, "[B]y itself crossover represents a potential for race treason, not the actuality" ("Interview" 290).

Rather than falling into essentializing generalizations about the politics of white Negroism, this essay attends to such localized distinctions by analyzing two contemporary white performers working in hip-hop media, Eminem (a.k.a. Marshall Mathers) and Danny Hoch, one an internationally famous rap star and the other little known outside of New York City and the underground hip-hop theater scene. A Jewish actor/writer of off-Broadway hip-hop "solo theater" and founder of the Hip Hop Theater Festival, Danny Hoch received acclaim for his shows *Some People* (1995) and *Jails, Hospitals, & Hip-Hop* (1998), comprised of a series of monologues in the personae of black, Latino, and white characters, each imbued with a rich individuality. Voicing a strong disidentification with white privilege and a deeply felt affiliation with the nonwhite cultures of their native urban communities in Detroit and Queens, New York, both Eminem and Hoch prompt a reconsideration of the stereotype of the white Negro as a romanticizing appropriator. Since both artists grew up in racially mixed, inner-city neighborhoods where hip-hop was the dominant cultural idiom, they cannot rightly be accused of co-opting what is in some sense their own "native" language. As historian David Roediger reminds us, the "challenges of disentangling the imaginary and the lived are great, and thinking in terms of . . . authentic/inauthentic does not help us" (*Colored White* 229). Although white rapper Eminem has been alternately vilified as a minstrel in Phat Farm sweats or celebrated as a progressive symbol of multicultural fusion, he is neither a white Negro (in Mailer's terms) nor a race traitor (in Ignatiev's). While Eminem claims that his presence in the hip-hop world is helping to erode racism, Danny Hoch's cultural work presents a far more radical political vision. Abounding in the ethical integrity that Gubar finds lacking among white Negroes, Hoch's theater and film performances offer a powerful deconstruction of white institutional racism and a model for the development of antiracist forms of white identity. His work could be read as a response to cultural critic Henry A. Giroux's call for a "rethinking [of] the subversive possibility of 'whiteness'" (91).

While little has been written about Danny Hoch, Eminem has been the subject of much debate since he burst onto the music scene in the late 1990s. Fearing that hip-hop might "slowly becom[e] bleached," a black writer in a 1999 *Village Voice* piece called Eminem a "talentless exploiter . . . who's using our form and not trying to contribute artistically to the black community" (Toure 71). Despite the initial backlash, Eminem quickly gained the respect of the black hip-hop world, partly due to the endorsement of his producer, hip-hop impresario Dr. Dre (formerly of N.W.A.). Eminem's semiautobiographical film *8 Mile*

(Curtis Hanson, 2002) further cemented his street credibility and the legitimacy of his connection to African-American musical culture. The film's plot is based upon Marshall Mathers's own poverty-stricken youth, his series of unfulfilling low-wage jobs, and his immersion in the black community near Detroit's 8 Mile Road. The title of the film literally refers to a color line, as Mathers himself notes: "[B]oth sides [of 8 Mile Road] had pretty much the same income, but when I was growing up, it was literally black on one side, and white on the other" (qtd. in Enders).[4] Mathers, however, had lived on both sides of the road during his childhood, and *8 Mile* similarly defines its protagonist, Jimmy (Rabbit), as a renegade crosser of borders struggling to fit in and survive. The film culminates in Rabbit's dramatic victory in a freestyle rap battle at a black hip-hop club, thus vindicating the act of racial crossover itself. Rabbit/Eminem clinches the victory by exposing his black opponent to be a prep school kid rather than an authentic voice of the 'hood; thus class momentarily trumps race as a sign of "realness." By emphasizing Eminem's class solidarity with African-American urban youth, the film distinguishes him from Mailer's middle-class hipsters or today's suburban white teens who fantasize about "slumming" in the ghetto. As one film reviewer writes, "white rappers have never been viable until now because white rappers have never been credible. . . . They have never been believable underdogs" (Dunlevy F1).

The film *8 Mile* provides a visual analogue to the gritty story of urban poverty already detailed in Eminem's lyrics, a story which resonates with one Latino teen from the South Bronx, who remarked in the *New York Times* that "he's rapping about . . . stuff that we go through out here. A lot of us can relate to that" (qtd. in Holloway C1). The song "If I Had," for example, speaks poignantly of the pain and rage millions of have-nots experience. "Tired of being white trash, broke, and always poor," Eminem voices the frustrations of those who work dead end jobs for a taunting boss, who eat with "plastic silverware," and who can't afford a phone or even a home ("If I Had"). Even BET vice president Stephen Hill lauds Eminem for "keepin' it real," stating that "in terms of rapping about the pain that other disenfranchised people feel, there is no one better . . . than Eminem" (qtd. in Holloway C1).

While his street credibility is undeniable, a working-class background should not simply absolve him from the charge of co-opting and romanticizing black culture. David Roediger makes a similar point in his analysis of the racism of nineteenth-century white, working class men in pursuit of "the wages of whiteness." People who have experienced poverty and class oppression are not necessarily sensitive to other forms of domination, particularly racial. Kid Rock, another self-dubbed "white trash" rapper "straight out the trailer" has been criticized for caricaturing ghetto life and slang (sample lyric from "Bawitdaba": "the Gs with the 40s and the chicks with beepers").[5] Journalist Josh Ozersky describes Kid Rock's rock-rap fusion as "completely reverential toward the 'old-school' clichés of blaxploitation" (Ozersky 62), evident in his appearance in furs at the MTV music awards and lyrics such as "I'm a pimp! / You can check my stacks! / I'm rollin' a Fleetwood / That's how I mack!" In the bombastic song "You Never Met a Motherfucker Quite Like Me," Kid Rock brags about his "pimping" of hip-hop style to white audiences: "I'll adapt to any and all situations / that's why they call me the pimp of the nation." In contrast, Eminem avoids a caricature of ghetto style often enacted by white Negroes, preferring an understated hip-hop regulation outfit of sweats, T-shirts, body tattoos, and a "do-rag." It is also important that "Eminem makes no effort to sound black" (62) in his diction, and he has even publicly refused to use the word "nigger": "It's not my place to say it. There's some things I just don't do" (qtd. in Smith). Rather than resting on his street credibility alone, Eminem is clearly conscious of the political importance of distinguishing himself from a latter-day minstrel. Avoiding outward displays of blackness common to other white pretenders, Mathers suggests that his affiliation with black culture runs deeper, a point implied by naming his MC persona with a phonetic spelling of his initials, M. M., that coincides phonetically with M&Ms, the candy manufactured with an array of colors on the outside and chocolate on the inside.

Of course, the most famous "white chocolate" performer in American music history was Elvis Presley, and it is instructive to compare Eminem to his legendary predecessor, similarly accused of co-opting black culture. Eminem explicitly invites such a comparison in his barbed-track "Without Me," mocking those who see him as just another-white Negro:

> No I'm not the first king of controversy
> I am the worst thing since Elvis Presley
> To do black music so selfishly
> And use it to get myself wealthy (Hey)
> There's a concept that works
> Twenty million other white rappers emerge.

While Eminem equates Elvis with co-optation, many cultural critics have defended the "King of Rock and Roll," arguing that he "didn't so much steal the blues as live up to them" (Lott 484).[6] Even the black nationalist rapper Chuck D of Public Enemy, who once labeled Elvis racist, later conceded that he was no thief: "Elvis had to come up through the streets of Memphis and turn out black crowds before he became famous. It wasn't like he cheated to get there. He was a bad-ass white boy. Just like Eminem" (qtd. in Blank A1).[7] Just as Elvis showed respect for the black sources of his blues style, Eminem frequently acknowledges his indebtedness to black artists and to his mentor Dr. Dre. His song "Marshall Mathers" mourns the deaths of Tupac Shakur and the Notorious B.I.G. and slams other rappers who exploit the images of these hip-hop martyrs. Chuck D praises him for having "more respect for black artists and black people and culture than a lot of black artists themselves" (qtd. in Blank A1).

Paying homage to one's African-American sources, one could argue, is not enough to repay the debt incurred. As Salim Washington argues in the pages of *Race Traitor*, to the "acknowledgement [of one's sources] must be added economic and cultural democracy" (167). More important than paying tribute to his forerunners, then, is the fact that Eminem has used his industry power to foster such democracy by promoting black protégés like 50 Cent, D12, and Royce Da 5'9. Given the context of the segregationist 1950s, Elvis could only "repay" his indebtedness to the black community indirectly, in that his sound prepared white fans to be more receptive to black-produced blues music. In contrast, Eminem chooses to repay his cultural debt more directly. His frequent collaboration with many black artists has undoubtedly boosted the sales of these MCs among white fans, as

Eminem claims in his song "White America": "every fan black that I got was probably [Dre's] in exchange for every white fan that he's got / . . . we just swapped." One multiracial Howard University student, Jozen Pedro Cummings, concurs: "[T]hink of how many new hip-hop fans know who Dr. Dre is, thanks to Eminem. He's opening doors" (qtd. in Britt B1). While critic Paul Garon believes that white blues music has been "economically crippling to black artists through loss of jobs and critical attention" (168), Eminem has actively drawn attention to black rappers and contributed to their economic success.

Although most music critics concede that Eminem is not guilty of exploiting black culture, one could still argue that he romanticizes the image of the black thug, as did Norman Mailer. While Eric Lott reasons that "nobody . . . can dismiss Presley as merely a case of racial rip-off," he nonetheless suggests that "fantasies of 'blackness' [as sexually potent] were unquestionably crucial in shaping [his] persona" (484). If, as Lott argues, "to put on the cultural forms of 'blackness' was to engage in a complex affair of manly mimicry" (479), then Eminem's attraction to black culture might simply reflect a desire to possess the hypermasculinity associated with black men. The lyrics to his song "Just Don't Give a Fuck" bear witness to Eminem's identification with a glorified image of violence and misogyny associated with famous black athletes such as O. J. Simpson and Mike Tyson. Addressing a woman referred to only as "Bitch," Eminem raps: "You getting' knocked the fuck out like Mike Tyson/ . . . I'll slit your motherfuckin' throat worse than Ron Goldman."

Clearly, a glorification of violent masculinity is a major reason for rap's popularity among white teenage boys, who are attracted to the thug posture of defiance and power. Yet how can one determine whether Eminem's fantasy of "black macho" is any more disingenuous than the macho posing of black MCs such as 50 Cent? That line of reasoning would depend on an essentialist premise that the thug persona is somehow natural to black rappers rather than learned. Eminem's assumption of the gangsta pose may simply be attributed to the streets where he grew up, an environment in which hypermasculine violence, anger, misogyny, and homophobia are strategies of survival and group acceptance.

I certainly do not mean to condone these violent fantasies of male power, but rather to suggest that race is not the central problem in Eminem's glorification of male domination, given its ubiquitous presence in American culture, both black and white. It was telling to watch how easily Eminem extricated himself from the recent controversy that erupted over the discovery of a racist track he once wrote disrespecting black women, made after Mathers was dumped by a black girlfriend in high school. On the "Yellow Brick Road" track of his CD *Encore*, he guiltily apologized to the black community while maintaining his sexist position: "I singled out a whole race and for that I apologize / I was wrong cuz no matter what color a girl is, she still a hoe." Perhaps the backlash was so shortlived, contends a *Village Voice* commentator, because his pathetic adolescent misogyny "failed to meet the level of bile that [black] rappers have been slinging toward black women for two decades" (Coates). Drawing comparisons to the misogyny of Snoop, 50 Cent, Ghostface Killah, and Slick Rick, Coates reminds us that "the house of hip-hop was built on the broken backs of black women."

If Eminem can be viewed as just another one of the b-boys rather than a white Negro who ventriloquizes a fantasized image of black culture, it is much less clear whether his own racial crossover act succeeds in deconstructing white privilege or destabilizing the color line. In an article in the *New York Times*, Neil Strauss envisions the hip-hop world as a site of multicultural fusion, a "Grey Nation" moving "beyond racial boundaries and mythologies" (1). Eminem subscribes to a similarly optimistic picture of hip-hop's power to integrate: "There's millions of white kids and black kids coming to the tour . . . having the common love—and that's hip-hop. Me and Dre are changing the world right now. I feel that we are making racism less and less and less" (*Life Story* 23). In bombastic hip-hop fashion, Eminem here claims agency for a blurring of cultural boundaries far beyond his own making, but it is still worth considering his claim. Is Eminem's music and star persona helping to erode racism or white privilege?

Eminem's angry denunciation of the white elite could be seen as participating in some aspects of *Race Traitor*'s multifaceted project aimed at the "abolition of whiteness." Eminem certainly engages in "outrageous acts of provocation" that "violate the rules of whiteness," a strategy of defection which Ignatiev and Garvey hope will lead to the end of the white race ("When Does" 36). In "The Way I Am," Eminem strongly disidentifies with whites who cannot fathom his connection to black culture. His patience is tried by white antagonists who falsely dismiss him as "some wigger who just tries to be black" and who demand to know "what 'hood [he] grew up in" ("The Way I Am"). While one might assume that African Americans would be more likely to question his credibility, Eminem imagines his chief antagonists to be "cocky Caucasians" threatened by racial transgression. Although he rarely targets black rappers for ridicule, his songs have contained many barbs directed at other white recording artists, such as Everlast, Insane Clown Posse, and Moby. Aiming to disidentify with whites whom he suspects of being middle-class pretenders, he trashes the disingenuous Insane Clown Posse for "claimin' Detroit, when y'all live twenty miles away" in the suburbs (Eminem 64).

Beyond these squabbles with other white rappers, Eminem offers a biting critique of the white establishment and the "moral majority" in his brilliant track "White America." The song rocks with fury against those who are lobbying the government to censor offensive lyrics:

> I . . . piss on the lawns of the White House . . . and
> replace it with a
> Parental Advisory sticker . . .
> To spit liquor in the faces of this democracy of
> hypocrisy
> Fuck you Ms. Cheney! Fuck you Tipper Gore!
> Fuck you with the freest of speech
> this divided states of embarrassment will allow me to
> have . . .

Eminem alternately views himself as a rebel "dumping it on white America" and a victim of governmental oppression. Once again identifying himself with black Americans, he compares censorship to a lynching: "It's like this rope / waitin' to choke, tightening around my throat, / watching me while I write this." He also rightly points out the racist hypocrisy of white elites, who were indifferent to the bad influences of gangsta rap upon *black* youth: "surely hip hop was never a problem in Harlem, only in Boston / after it bothered the fathers of daughters starting to blossom."

These antagonistic lines suggest a profound disidentification with white power, yet Eminem is also fully aware of his own complicity with the system of white privilege. He admits in the song "I'm Back" that "I'm a commodity because I'm W-H-I-T-E / cuz MTV was so friendly to me." In "White America," he offers an astute analysis of the racism fueling his own sales:

> Look at these eyes, baby blue, baby just like yourself
>
> If they were brown Shady lose, Shady sits on the shelf . . .
>
> Let's do the math—if I was black, I would've sold half
>
> . . . my skin is starting to work to my benefit now

His words imply that as long as we live in a racist country, even those who aim to be "ex-white men" will still benefit from their skin color. Eminem does not so much renounce his whiteness as own up to it ironically. In "White America," he further calls attention to himself in the act of "bleaching [his] hair with some peroxide." By going blonde, he is deliberately heightening the white star image to give the fans what they want—someone "who look[s] like them"—and perhaps to provide an ironic contrast with the "chocolate" underneath. By drawing attention to the fakeness of his platinum hair in a song about white America, Eminem also hints at the artificiality of whiteness itself, and of the whole system of race classification.

Race as a signifier of difference is something that Eminem loves to hate. Unfortunately, however, his desire to do away with racial categories often gives way to a color-blind ideology that minimizes the continued presence of power and inequality in American society. Eminem has made several public statements that echo the color-blind agenda of "polite" liberalism: "I look at myself as a white person who raps. Everyone else looks at me like I'm a white rapper. I don't understand it. Why can't we just get past the color issue and just deal with the music?" (*Life Story* 35). He also commented that "the best thing a guy ever said about me was after an open mic in Detroit. He was like, 'I don't [care] if he's green, I don't [care] if he's orange, this [kid] is dope!'" (44). Eminem's desire to "get past the color issue" is a tactic that Ruth Frankenberg has described as "power evasiveness" (14), a blindness to the realities of racism. In *Race Traitor*, Paul Garon has similarly criticized color-blind blues fans for ignoring the issue of white appropriation and arguing that "the music is all that counts" (173). Even more problematic than this naïve liberal wish that race and racism can be willed away is Eminem's deployment of the discourse of "reverse racism" common among conservative racist whites. Invoking the victim card, Eminem remarked, "I get offended when people say, 'so being a white rapper . . . and growing up white. . . . ' It's all I ever hear. I'm at a boiling point. Anybody who pulls the race card is getting it back in their face" (*Life Story* 62). Although it is undoubtedly difficult to fit in as a white man in a black cultural scene, surely there are much more devastating kinds of racism—the kinds that affect the life chances of people of color—at which Eminem ought to be taking offense. Giroux argues that the best antiracist strategy for whites would be to eschew color-blind rhetoric and instead "locate themselves within and against the discourse and practice of racism" (103). Eminem certainly locates himself within the discourse of racism, but he does not do enough to speak out *against* it, particularly in its institutional forms.

Josh Ozersky praises Eminem for steering clear of "black lifestyle issues" (62) in his lyrics, but one could interpret his omission as a liability rather than an asset. Despite his claim to be black on the inside, Eminem rarely uses his music to draw attention to the consequences of racism for African Americans, a longstanding theme of hip-hop music even in the face of recent topical shifts in the lyrics of today's most popular rappers. Culture critic Armond White defines the hip-hop ethos as a "muckraking imperative" to protest against "racial and social affronts" (543); similarly, actor/writer Danny Hoch praises hip-hop for "how it has articulated the complaints of oppressed peoples, of people of color, in a way that's unprecedented" (Croal). By these measures, Eminem's self-involved rap falls far short of the ideal, since it speaks only of social injustices that are not racialized as black.[8] Although he calls the United States a "democracy of hypocrisy" in "White America," he is protesting against the censorship of his own

free-speech rights, not the historical legacy of African-American disenfranchisement. He urges his fans to vote against President Bush
for dragging us into the Iraq War in his song "Mosh," but neglects to
address how Bush's domestic and foreign policies have disproportionately harmed the lives and livelihood of black Americans. Eminem's
newest CD, *Encore*, is at once more overtly political (in "Mosh") and
less sensitive to the racial dynamics of power, as he wastes energy
satirizing easy African-American targets such as Michael Jackson's
alleged pedophilia. Even "Mosh" offers a facile fantasy of colorblind
unity: "a sea of people some white and some black / don't matter what
color, all that matters we gathered together."

Eminem's colorblindness leads him to pay insufficient attention
to the lived reality of being black in America, of being marked as subordinate. At a 2003 Detroit Hip-Hop summit that Detroit mayor
Kwame Kilpatrick described as a convention about "social, economic,
and political consciousness," Eminem advocated for more opportunities for new rappers and declared, "hip-hop is about poverty. The
people who take the mic have the most influence. They are reflecting
the people's will" (*Life Story* 26). While hip-hop is undoubtedly about
poverty, with this reductionist definition Eminem seems to erase the
rich history of rap as a black cultural form of enunciation, of voicing racial grievances. One might ask, who are the people whose will
Eminem claims to be reflecting? Spelman professor William Cobb
has similarly criticized *8 Mile* for implying that class oppression
trumps race oppression, citing the climactic scene which portrays
Rabbit as more authentic than his middle-class black opponent. Cobb
further points out that Rabbit "has no racial reckoning of his own
to do because racism is black people's problem" in *8 Mile* (33). These
criticisms could also be applied to Eminem himself, who impatiently
hopes to "get past the color issue" but does very little to help bring
about an antiracist future. Because Eminem does not use the influence of which he speaks—his position of power as a famous white
man—to advocate for change in the racial order, he falls far short of
Ignatiev's definition of a race traitor working toward the abolition of
whiteness. While his angry disidentification with white privilege is a
move in the right direction, it is simply not enough to bring the racist
house down.

Marshall Mathers seems like a navel-gazer without political vision when compared to Danny Hoch, whose radical theater envisions hip-hop as antiracist and socialist activism. While both Hoch and Eminem disidentify with white domination and self-reflexively critique an industry that commodifies black styles and culture, Hoch aims to move beyond complaint to forge political coalitions and work actively against racism and white privilege. The affective register of Eminem's rap is that of personal pain transformed into anger, directed more often at women (both black and white) than at institutional racism. In comparison, Danny Hoch's theater and film work is full of humor, pathos, and empathy for the human casualties of racism and capitalism, and demonstrates his commitment to working against all forms of social domination.

After graduating from New York's High School of the Performing Arts, Hoch made a local name for himself in the off-Broadway circuit in the 1990s, performing solo monologues in the tradition of Eric Bogosian, Anna Deavere Smith, and John Leguizamo, yet within an explicitly hip-hop idiom and ethos of social protest. He gained a national audience by showcasing his work on HBO's Def Poetry Jam and founded the Hip Hop Theater Festival in 2000. Via the festival, Hoch helped to produce and promote the work of African-American monologue performer Sarah Jones, who recently won a 2006 special Tony Award for her show *Bridge and Tunnel*, which bears striking resemblance to Hoch's own work. In the dramatic monologues of his 1998 show *Jails, Hospitals, & Hip-Hop*, Hoch sympathetically embodies (rather than impersonates) a black rap star doing a guest spot on David Letterman, a Cuban street vendor speaking in Spanish, a light-skinned entrepreneur jailed for lacking proper permits, a disabled Puerto Rican man shot by police, a racist white prison guard undergoing psychotherapy, a white prison inmate with AIDS, and a teenage "wigger" from the rural Midwest. In his earlier show *Some People*, Hoch performed in the personae of a Puerto Rican woman, a Jewish "liberal" mother, Jamaican and Latino DJs, a white racist yuppie, and two black teens trapped by ghetto codes of male behavior. His newest play, *Taking Over* (2008), examines the gentrification of Brooklyn by middle-class whites and the resulting displacement and alienation of people of color and the poor. While Eminem's disidentification with whiteness is a posture of defiance that involves little empathy for African Americans, Danny Hoch's chameleonic performances enact a transethnic and transracial consciousness and underscore the power of empathy as a political tool. By envisioning a complex subjectivity for people of color and individuals living in poverty or in prison, Hoch's work promotes identification with people who are often devalued by the media, while offering a stinging critique of racial essentialism and the power structures that maintain white privilege.

Hoch's anti-essentialist, social constructionist perspective is evident in his shows' emphasis on cultural fusion and the fluidity of race. As he explains in the introduction to the printed text of his two shows, "Hip-Hop formed my language and my entire worldview" (Hoch, *Jails* xvi), and he sees hip-hop culture as a unifier that "crosses all lines of color, race, economics, nationality, and gender" (xii). The "wigger" (an update of the white Negro)[9] is a leitmotif of his work, but Hoch also draws attention to other acts of color crossing and cultural fusion: "rappers don themselves with Italian mafia names . . . urban youth clothe themselves with expensive sailing, skiing, camping, and hiking apparel and suburban youth copy the fashions, trying to be like the urban youth (who no doubt sail, ski, and camp in their spare time)" (xvi). A black character in *Some People* reflects on this bewildering disruption to a racially segregated universe:

> "It's already 'nuf white kids out here that's tryin' to be black . . . but what you call them white people that don't wash theyself . . . them punk-rock anarchy niggas, right? I seen a bunch of them walkin' . . . and I seen this one black son in there. . . . How a brother gonna be in that shit? . . . How a sister gonna sing opera? How a black man gonna sing backup for some Kenny G?" (Hoch, *Jails* 133)

The racial fluidity that Hoch sees in American life is also reflected in his own composite sense of cultural identity, formed from the diverse influences of his multiethnic neighborhood in Queens: "I didn't know I was a white Jewish kid. . . . I thought I was a white-Jewish-black-Latino-Russian-Georgian-Senegalese kid" (qtd. in Bravmann). He spent his youth as a graffiti-warrior breakdancing and rhyming with "this Indian kid named Prashant and this Puerto Rican kid named Jesus and this black kid named Kenny" (qtd. in Goldstein 57) and he learned fluent Spanish from his Cuban American godmother. While he acknowledges that race is ascribed, and that he has been assigned the identity of the "white Jewish kid," Hoch perceives both race and ethnicity as functions of culture and environment rather than biology. In the opening prologue to *Jails*, spoken in rhyme, Hoch notes that

> people be like shut the hell up when I talk
> Like I shouldn't be talkin' 'black' even though I'm from
> New York
> But what's that? A color, a race, or a state of mind?
> A class of people? A culture, is it a rhyme? (3)

Defending his use of African-American idioms as an expression of his own native language—New Yorkese—Hoch implies that race is a "state of mind" or a cultural affiliation rather than a state of nature. Like the *Race Traitor* editors, Hoch questions the "natural existence of 'races,'" an essentialist premise that even some antiracist activists accept (Ignatiev and Garvey 10).

Hoch's own identification with people of color has ruffled the feathers of some who aim to preserve racial boundaries and the idea of race itself. At what Hoch describes as "one of those angry panels about racial opprobrium," Harry Allen, the critic and hip-hop nationalist, confronted him, demanding him to answer the question, "Are you white?" (qtd. in Goldstein 57). Similarly, Hoch explains why a Jewish audience once booed him: "they can't stand that I'm playing complex black characters, because, like Harry Allen, they can only reference minstrelsy" (qtd. in Goldstein 57). In response to fear of crossover and fluidity, Hoch offers a skit in *Jails, Hospitals, & Hip-Hop* involving a racially ambiguous character whom he names "Bronx" to further imply that identity is a function of environment. As Bronx himself says, "I live in 163rd street, I got a certain look" (Hoch, *Jails* 11). Bronx describes how he got arrested for selling Bart Simpson and O. J. Simpson t-shirts without a license:

> So this cop . . . he had sunglasses, so when he look at me first from the car, I look darker. When he get out, he get confused. 'Cause if you put me next to the cop, I'm whiter than the cop. . . . Next thing, he throw me down in the ground, he got his nightstick in my back,

with the spit and the gum from the sidewalk is in my face and shit.
He say, 'What are you, what are you?!! Are you Puerto Rican, are
you Puerto Rican?' . . . I mean my color is white like Bill Clinton,
but that's not good enough for him, you know, in the way that I'm
speaking, or I don't even know. (11–12)

It seems as if Bronx is being arrested not for breaking the law but
for troubling the color line and threatening the policeman's sense of
the impermeability of race. A further irony is that the cop wants to
fix him as Puerto Rican, which is already an unstable racial category
given that many Latinos are of mixed race. In Bronx's monologue and
Hoch's own interviews with the press, Hoch implies that unstable
identities disturb the normal operation of a racist system dependent
upon essentialist logic.

Although Hoch embraces racial fluidity, he clearly aims to expose
the problematic essentialism underlying some acts of crossover. In
Jails, Hoch humorously anatomizes the white Negro complex in his
monologue as Flip, a white teen infatuated with gangsta rap. Imagining
himself as a famous rapper being interviewed by Jay Leno, Flip contends, "I got this rare skin disorder where I look white but I'm really
black . . . see this birthmark, Jay? Well, it's not really a birthmark,
see that's the real color of my skin, and the rest of me is a birthmark.
. . . [E]ven though I live in Montana, I still got the ghetto in my heart"
(Hoch, *Jails* 19). Flip's romanticized image of the ghetto, however, is
one "where the people just kick it every day and keep it real. And chill
in their BMWs and rap, and all the girls got on bikinis, and everybody
just . . . parties . . . and raps" (20). While Flip's myth of blackness rests
on a capitalist, MTV-fueled fantasy as opposed to Mailer's anties-
tablishment idealism, both essentialize African Americans as hypermasculine and "cool": "If I had a choice between bein' like you—Jay
Leno—or Tupac Shakur, who you think I'ma choose? . . . At least he
went out like a true thug nigga. He's cool" (21). A frequent refrain of
Flip's ghetto-speak is the phrase "keep it real," which Hoch employs
artfully to comment on the problematics of both mimicry and racial
essentialism. The last words of Flip's monologue are "keep it real, Jay"
as he dons his Hardee's cap and sets off for his dead-end job. Here
Hoch ironically draws attention to Flip's own depressing reality as

the chief motivator behind his desire to imitate the more thrilling life-style of the black gangsta rapper. Furthermore, the audience is prompted to question not only Flip's distorted sense of ghetto reality but also the pursuit of racial "realness" itself.

By emphasizing the commodification of the gangsta pose, Hoch further underscores the artificiality of a stance often associated with an essential blackness. In his show *Some People*, Hoch performed as a black teenager named Floe who shares Flip's infatuation with gangsta rap, although Floe is more concerned about proving his street credibility: "[I've] never been to Riker's Island [prison], but I almost went" (Hoch, *Jails* 94). The black and the white teens rap about a similar macho thug fantasy: "I'll shoot you point blank in the head, then fuck your sister" (*Jails* 95). But these lines are no more "authentic" for the African American Floe than they are for the white Flip. Hoch's Floe is actually a sensitive guy heartsick over being dumped by a college-bound girlfriend. The masculine bravado and stoicism of the gangsta is clearly a façade for him, since he "had like almost started like, cryin' and shit" (98) while making love to his girl. As Laurie Stone argues in the *Nation*, Hoch reveals that hip-hop masculinity can sometimes become a "gorilla suit that keeps at bay emotional expressiveness . . . and vulnerability" (34). In his performances as Floe and Flip, "keepin' it real" in ghetto terms is thus exposed to be an artificial mask, donned by both black and white boys yearning for power and acceptance. In his monologue as black rap star Emcee Enuff, Hoch further highlights how the entertainment media commodify and reify the black thug image. Rapper Emcee Enuff complains that his antiviolence and anti-drug message "wasn't sellin'" (Hoch, *Jails* 69), so in order to pay his bills, he started rapping about "runnin' up in niggas' cribs and puttin' fifty bullets in they head" (69). Of course, he notes, "those records made me more money than I ever made in my life" (70), and the sheer repetition of this narrative on the airwaves makes fans like Flip and Floe believe in its "realness." Hoch certainly does not deny the reality of violence in the ghetto, but what he does deny is the equation of such violence with a black "nature."

While Hoch is clearly invested in dispelling myths of an essential blackness, he is also engaged in a project rarely attempted in leftist circles—undermining essentialist ideas of *whiteness*. In an article he wrote for the *Nation*, Hoch questions an understanding of whiteness as monolithic by qualifying the statement "America is mostly white people" with the following aside: "whatever that means" ("Mr. Hoch" 28). I argue that Hoch bucks a trend identified by Giroux, who laments that recent scholarship in critical race studies "is troubling in its inability to capture the complexity that marks 'whiteness' as a form of identity and cultural practice" (90). For example, Giroux objects to Roediger's oversimplification of whiteness as "the terrifying attempt to build an identity based on what one isn't and on whom one can hold back" (Roediger, *Toward* 13).[10] Despite their anti-essentialist doctrine, the contributors to *Race Traitor* similarly tend to flatten out white identity and imbue it with uniform significance: "whiteness is nothing but an expression of race privilege" (Ignatiev and Garvey 289). By attending to other vectors of difference that complicate white identity—such as class, age, gender, generation, and ethnicity—Danny Hoch's theater speaks to Giroux's desire for a more complex picture of whiteness as it is lived in conjunction with other identities.

Even as Hoch's 1995 show *Some People* voices a righteous disdain for racist whites, he nonetheless aims to differentiate multiple shades of whiteness. At first glance, Hoch seems to equate the entire white race with domination, as do Ignatiev and Garvey. The epilogue to Hoch's show invokes the familiar dichotomy between "Us" and "Dem" but places Hoch firmly on the side of the othered "Dem." Thus his "some people" can be read as a retort to the white racist disdain for "those people," that is, nonwhites. Furthering this disdain for the white race, the epilogue's character, a mythical sage, raps a symbolic prophecy about the abolition of white hegemony:

> The Chickens used to live in big mansions, and the
>   other birds live in the street
>
> The Chickens used to drive BMW, and the other birds
>   walk with dem feet
>
> The Chickens used to say, Look at dem birds, dem
>   lazy bum
>
> How can they live like that really, We are so smart and
>   Dem so dumb
>
> Well today all de chickens die, and the other birds fly in
>   the sky. (147)

Hoch chooses a species metaphor to imply humorously that whites as a *race* will become extinct. This strong disidentification with whiteness as equivalent to oppression is also evident in his monologue as Bill, a white yuppie-wanna-be who spews hateful comments about Shiite Muslims, Chinese restaurateurs, AIDS victims, and Black Panthers. Typical of conservative "new racists" who feel "besieged" and bitter over "imagined racial injuries committed against whites" (Giroux 93), Bill fears being victimized by terrorist bombs and "crackhead murderers in the street" (Hoch, *Jails* 104). He also imagines he is being targeted for parking tickets because he is white and from New Jersey: "these *whatever* meter maids . . . [must be] connected to those [antiwhite] hate groups that were on *60 Minutes*" (107–8). Hoch spins out the supreme irony of "reverse racism"—that this one-man hate group believes himself to be the true victim of race hatred.

In addition to offering a scathing exposé of the new racism that conservative whites espouse, Hoch delineates another kind of white identity that hits closer to home—the hypocritical Jewish liberal, personified in a mother (Doris) arguing with her antiracist son Dave, who works for an organization "like the Peace Corps, but in New York" (124). Hoch modeled this sketch after an argument he had with his own Jewish mother (Goldstein 57). Worried that her son will be shot on the subway, Doris says, "I wish these kids didn't have to grow up with all violence and such, a mess, and my heart goes out to them. . . . [B]ut let them shoot each other and not you" (127). About "those people" who live in the South Bronx, she offers this conflicted analysis: "they're different. . . . I mean not that they're different, they're the same as us, everyone is the same, but all right, never mind, it's just different" (125). Like many white liberals, Doris has been taught that a color-blind ideology is polite and correct—"everyone is the same"— but when threatened, her deep-rooted belief in racial differences emerge.

Hoch complicates this portrait of white liberal hypocrisy by delving into the ambivalent relationship of Doris's Jewishness to her whiteness. Despite her white liberal attitudes about "those people," Doris still views herself as a persecuted minority: "How is it possible for Jews to be prejudice when everyone is prejudice all the time against the Jews? . . . David, six million . . . did you see *Schindler's List*? . . . How am I a victim in the suburbs in 1994? . . . The Jews are still victims"

(127). Rather than being proud of the history of Jewish involvement in the civil rights movement, Doris interprets that history as a wrong turn that distracted Jews on the path of assimilation into the safety of white America: "You wanna be one of the Jewish kids in Mississippi with the voter registration and they killed them?" (127). Doris's monologue offers an insightful portrait of how American Jews often view themselves as a shade of "off-white"—part of the white American "us" yet retaining their memories of victimization, their experiences of being treated as one of "them" or "those people."[11]

If *Some People* exposes variants of white racism while highlighting ethnic differences among whites, *Jails, Hospitals, & Hip-Hop* devotes more attention to working-class whites and to the possibility of an oppositional white identity, glimpsed at only briefly in *Some People* with the character of Doris's son, David. In his later and more mature show, Hoch avoids a simple denunciation of whiteness as a signifier of domination and even gives us a surprisingly sympathetic treatment of a white prison guard (Sam) reprimanded for using excessive force against an inmate. Sam directs his rage at the prisoners he calls "pollutants" (*Jails* 27) because he lacks power in his own life: he was recently denied custody of his children in a divorce court and restricted to one visit per month. Bitter about the lack of "justice in that court decision" (29) and doing time in a job he hates, Sam is more like the inmates than he would care to admit: "I did twelve years already with this [job]. I got eight more. Then I'm out" (29). While a violent white prison guard would seem to represent the white establishment, Hoch treats Sam as an object of pity, because his racist actions are a sign of desperation and frustration at his inability to access power on his own behalf. Hoch's empathetic portrait of Sam is not an apology for racism, but an elucidation of its ability to trap whites by giving them a false sense of power and agency.

To offer a contrast to Sam, who denies his similarity to others struggling against a biased justice system, Hoch gives voice to a white prison inmate with AIDS (Andy) whose own whiteness belies his solidarity with the underclass. A heroin addict who suffers without proper medical attention for his AIDS, Andy has experienced life as a perpetual servant and angrily disidentifies with white privilege: "Lemme tell ya somethin,' I SERVED! I served in Vietnam and I served in McDonalds, and I'm servin' sweepin' this fuckin' room all day. . . . And I want SERVICE! I want SERVICES because I'm DYING!" (50). Despite his rage at being disempowered, Andy does not scapegoat racial others as does Sam, but instead has built a strong kinship network with prisoners of color, including an inmate who runs Muslim services and a young black inmate angry at the recurrence of blackface minstrelsy on television. When the black youth cries in frustration at his inability to affect change while in prison, Andy helps him to channel his anger by writing protest letters to the networks: "Dear Fox, I think Martin Lawrence is fucked up" (49). With his portrait of Andy, Danny Hoch reminds his audience that class and race are intersecting vectors of identity, and that lower-class whites have the potential to become allies of people of color fighting for justice and equality.

To further complicate his representation of working-class white identities, Hoch's monologue as midwestern wigger Flip suggests that whiteness can sometimes be experienced as a liability rather than an asset. Flip struck such a chord with audiences that Hoch expanded his monologue into a feature film called *Whiteboyz*, in which he stars. In *Jails* as well as *Whiteboyz*, Flip romanticizes ghetto life as an endless party, but an experience of whiteness as not merely boring but as an economic dead-end fuels his fantasy: "I hate it sometimes . . . servin' burgers to some damn tractor-drivin' motherfuckers. . . . All they do is hang out at the mall every day . . . and then they go home and watch *Friends* and *Cops*. Yippee. . . . I don't really aspire to that in my life, man. . . . What the hell I wanna be white for?" (Hoch, *Jails* 20–21). The film version adds rich detail to Flip's experience of "white trash" poverty, as he shops for groceries with food stamps, watches his father's degradation after being laid off from a factory job, and becomes a small-time drug dealer in search of the "American dream." A central irony of the film is that Flip and his friends associate whiteness not with power and domination but with economic stagnancy and emasculation; for them, blackness and the hip-hop life represent financial empowerment, agency, and voice. As critic Paul Bravmann notes, Flip's "desire to be black, strange as it may seem, is nothing less than the desire to better himself. How's that for the old switcheroo?" Despite Flip's desire to cross over into an identification with black culture, Flip can hardly be called a race traitor, because he does not fully comprehend the national and global power of whites, and mistakes an illusion of power for the real thing. When Flip and his buddies take an ill-fated road trip to a real-life ghetto, Cabrini-Green in Chicago, they are disabused of their illusions, but not before their actions result in the police-shooting death of a black man who was trying to help them. Flip's disidentification with whiteness is even more politically anemic than Eminem's because it rests on a romanticization of blackness and a distorted understanding of the distribution of power in a racist episteme.

If part of Hoch's anti-essentialist project is to offer a multilayered portrait of diverse whitenesses, his larger goal is to attack the structures of racial inequality to which Flip is blind. The powerful prologue to *Jails, Hospitals, & Hip-Hop* reveals Hoch to be a race traitor shining a spotlight on white institutional racism. Although he takes pains at first to establish that he "ain't no cracker" (3) and aligns himself culturally with people of color, later in the prologue he shifts from the position of white Negro to one of white power broker. His goal in assuming the "I" of white privilege is to wield it in ironic self-critique:

> I can take [black] culture, soup it up, and sell it back to you / And I can sell crack to you and smack to you if you let me / I'm the president, the press, and your paycheck, you sweat me / You never even met me or can fathom my derision / You try to buck my system, son, I'll lock yo ass in prison / . . . This is my game, I can't lose / When I wanna see the score I just turn on my news. (4–5)

In addition to calling attention to white control of the major avenues of power—government, media, entertainment, and business—Hoch is particularly disdainful of whites who profit from a commodification of black culture, since he is concerned that the commercialization of hip-hop has blunted its radicalism. While whites sell goods that equate blackness with powerful revolt, Hoch argues that such commodification equals containment: "this revolution lookin' like junk, and it sunk / with all the X caps that I sold you out my trunk / You bought my revolution and you wear it on your head. . . . You got your X cap but I got you power . . . less" (6–7). It's crucial that he directs this message about white institutional control to an audience of urban youth and people of color—the "you" with which he identifies. He uses such provocation to spur audiences to take action against the "institutions that reproduce race as a social category" (Ignatiev and Garvey 3).

One of the institutions most deserving of attack is the criminal justice system, which Hoch singles out with the first word of his show's title—jails. Intimately familiar with the prison system, Hoch has devoted many hours to leading workshops for inmates about conflict resolution and racism, and he recently created a moving film version of *Jails, Hospitals, & Hip-Hop* that includes footage of the live show being performed for prisoners in a jail.[12] Several of the monologues in Hoch's show argue that people of color are not inherently criminal but are often led by structures of inequality into misguided life choices that land them in prison. His sketch as Bronx points out the bitter irony of being jailed for trying to get off welfare and pursue the American capitalist dream, just like a girl with a lemonade stand. But racism predetermined Bronx's fate, restricting his access to the American dream: "that cop see somebody that's a entrepreneur . . . and 'cause he feel threaten, that day he gonna decide that capitalism is illegal. . . . I feel like suing them lemonade motherfuckers, man . . . for false advertising" (12–13). Even more disturbing are the tales Hoch spins of police brutality. Victor, a young Puerto Rican man, walks with steel crutches and can never dance again because he was shot by overzealous cops in what the newspapers termed "an accident" (54). A gut-wrenching piece in *Some People* is told from the perspective of a grieving Latino father, Cesar, who lost his son in a similar police shooting "accident." Hoch, as the black rapper Emcee Enuff in *Jails*, attributes the criminal behavior of black youth partly to a nihilism bred from routine experiences of institutional racism, such as police brutality: "I see somebody who look just like me, getting a plunger stuck up they rectum by somebody that's supposed to protect us. Then I *wanna* go to jail. I be like, 'Joy? What's that?'" (72). Hoch suggests that for many poor urban youth, going to jail is a self-fulfilling prophecy; if the whole world views you as a criminal, then you are more likely to become one.

This negative image of people of color, Hoch contends, is perpetuated by television and film, and Hoch himself has attempted several antiracist interventions as an actor and writer in lily-white

Hollywood. In addition to the film *Whiteboyz*, which he co-wrote, he worked on the development of a series pilot for ABC about multiethnic urban teenagers. The series concept, not surprisingly, was axed by the network because they deemed it "too specific" (Hoch, "Mr. Hoch"). Hoch has been working to offer alternative nonracist media programming because of his belief in the power of images to shape attitudes. His skit as racist yuppie Bill underscores how television news fosters racial and ethnic prejudices. Bill naïvely believes that "on Dan Rather, you get the whole complete story" (*Jails* 103), and he falsely asserts, "I'm socially aware [because] I watch TV" (103). In addition to this ironic commentary on the white bias of news reporting, Hoch critiques the "one-dimensional image 'opportunities'" available for minorities on entertainment television (Hoch, "Mr. Hoch"). One of his monologues in *Jails*, told in Danny's own voice, exposes the racism he viewed on the set of *Seinfeld*, when he was offered a guest role as a "Puerto Rican pool guy who cleans up towels and jumps around like an idiot and talks with a 'funny Spanish accent'" (Hoch, "Mr. Hoch"). When he complained about the offensiveness of the stereotype, he was subjected to Jerry Seinfeld taunting, "Danny, why don't you do the next scene in blackface? . . . Oooh!" and was then summarily dismissed from the set (Hoch, *Jails* 40). Hoch surmises that "they wanted somebody that could do the real thing [accents], but still be one of them" (*Jails* 39), and they were shocked to find Hoch a race traitor, a wolf in sheep's clothing. In contrast to *Seinfeld's* form of minstrelsy, Hoch contends, his own work finds the humor as well as pathos in the lives of people of all colors without reducing them to one-dimensional racial or ethnic types.

Danny Hoch appears to subscribe to the "Abolition of Whiteness" manifesto in that he speaks out loudly against white-friendly and racist practices in a variety of institutions. But does he share the desire of Vron Ware and Les Back (and others) to "bring about an end of whiteness" itself, by attacking the "very notion of race and the obstinate resilience of racial identities" (2)?[13] Does Hoch seek to become an ex-white man? Or should he rather be positioned alongside other theorists of whiteness who argue that doing away with racial identity is neither possible nor altogether desirable? In opposition to the *Race Traitor* "new abolitionists," Giroux believes in the continued importance of racial identities as a means of asserting political agency (131). Thus he calls for a rearticulation of oppositional models of white identity, in order to "forge multiracial coalitions based on an engagement rather than a denial of whiteness" (134). In his recuperation of white identity, Giroux invokes Stuart Hall's recognition of difference while avoiding essentialism: "we all speak from a particular place, out of a particular history, out of a particular experience, a particular culture, without being contained by that position" (Hall 447). In Ruth Frankenberg's groundbreaking study of white women's racial self-images, she similarly contends that whites should acknowledge that they are fully imbricated in racial discourse by reflecting on how "racism . . . shapes our daily experiences and sense of self" (6). Like Giroux, Frankenberg advocates working toward "antiracist forms of whiteness" (7) rather than rejecting white identity altogether. The terms of the debate are whether an antiracist project can best be served by totally rejecting, acknowledging, celebrating, or rearticulating white identity. While Danny Hoch is clearly working toward the abolition of whiteness and racial essentialism, he acknowledges the necessity of owning up to his whiteness given the current racial order, as does Frankenberg. Yet he stops short of embracing a white identity as the locus of his political agency, as does Giroux.

In some moments in his shows, Hoch rejects identification as white almost too sanctimoniously. One could similarly argue that those who claim to be "ex-white men" underestimate the difficulty of erasing how one's subjectivity has been formed and continues to be shaped by social forces beyond one's control.[14] Although Hoch's antiracist principles are to be applauded, his denunciation of Jerry Seinfeld and company is a bit self-righteous in tone, as he vehemently denies that he is "one of them." In his introduction to Jails, he also writes, "It's just cooler to be the oppressed than the oppressor. Who wants to be the oppressor? Shit, not me" (xvii). Here Hoch sounds like a teenager seeking popularity and "street cred" rather than political change. He appears to be momentarily engaging in what theater professor Shannon Jackson humorously dubs "saving whiteface"—the practice of distancing oneself from racist whites with a holier-than-thou attitude. Jackson's own brilliant, risk-taking performance piece "White Noises" plumbs the contradictions of her own white liberal consciousness, showing herself "saving whiteface" while also dredging up memories of a racist inheritance, such as equating blacks with filth

when she was a child. Jackson aims to "undo oneself" (52) by showing whiteness in conflict, contradiction, and transformation, as does
Ruth Frankenberg's sociological study of white women. Jackson's soul-
baring rather than sanctimonious performance strikes me as even
more radical than other-directed denunciations of racism, because it
turns the critique on the self.

Despite moments where Hoch appears to be saving whiteface, he
does engage in meaningful self-reflection about his own complicity
with white privilege. In his introduction to *Jails*, Hoch explicitly
states that self-reflexive engagement is one of the goals of his theater,
whereas most entertainment asks audiences merely to "laugh and cry
at the characters, not at ourselves" (xii). Despite his expressed distaste
for art that is "self-centered" (qtd. in Weiner 30), Hoch does not avoid
reflecting on how his own white skin complicates his identification
with minority cultures. His prologue to *Jails* bravely employs the use
of "I," leading the audience to momentarily wonder if he himself is
engaged in "souping up" black culture and selling it back for profit.
In that same piece, Hoch calls attention to the fact that he inadvertently benefits from racism: "I'll use my skin privileges to flag you
down a taxi" (4). Like Eminem, he points out how his color has no
doubt fostered his success: "I often wonder if my skin were darker, or
if I couldn't flip my linguistics during meetings to sound 'business-
like and un-threatening' . . . if I would have had the success I've had
with these two shows. Was I a 'safe in' to the 'disenfranchised voice of
America' for the rich and middle class?" (xv). No matter how much he
might desire to be an "ex-white man," Hoch acknowledges that he will
perhaps always be drawn in by the privileges of whiteness, even against
his own political will. Unlike those who advocate a complete rejection
of whiteness, Hoch expresses a more ambivalent stance, neither dis-
avowing nor embracing his identity as white. He aims to attack white
privilege from within, by exploiting his skin privileges—such as an
ability to broker meetings with Hollywood executives—in order to
reach a "wider audience . . . and of course to make more money—money
to invest in my community and generation" (Hoch, "Mr. Hoch").[15] As
he notes in an interview: "part of me wants to say, f—k [Hollywood,]
but it's difficult. It comes back to the age-old question, do you change
the system from outside of it or from the inside? I think you can do

both. I'll run on one path and then on the other" (qtd. in Croal). The *Race Traitor* editors might consider this impure resistance a form of treason against their abolitionist goal of transcending whiteness, but Hoch might reply that he is simply "keepin' it real."

Hoch's pragmatic strategy of working simultaneously within and against whiteness is brilliantly demonstrated in his film *Whiteboyz*. The character of Flip provides a self-reflexive commentary on Hoch's own cross-racial "brotherhood trip" (Stone 34) and on his own complex attitudes toward race and "representing." Although *Village Voice* critic Richard Goldstein believes that Hoch erases and "empties his whiteness" (57) in his theater performances, I argue that the trajectory that Hoch draws for his character of FlipDogg suggests a much different goal. As part of his acquisition of a black persona in the film, Flip continually drops the hip-hop phrase "I'm here to represent," which means to stand up in solidarity with one's race or to speak out against racism. For example, Flip claims that he is "representin'" when he protests a cop's prejudiced treatment of a black teen in his town, and both boys get arrested as a result. But as Flip employs the term, "representin'" also suggests a process of standing in the place of reality, and this disjunction between the representation and the real is evident in Flip's misguided claim to *be* black. As he sits in jail, pleased at finally living out his fantasy of the ghetto life, he enrages his black schoolmate by saying "brothers gotta stick together," to which the black college-bound teenager replies, "Who the hell are you representin'?"

Flip's attitudes about race and representing are radically altered by his trip to Cabrini Green, when his own ignorance causes the death of a black man. As a result of this reality check, Flip takes off the black "mask" and begins writing rap as political protest poetry, speaking out *as a white man* against America's long history of racism. The moving lyrics to Flip's final "rap" speak volumes about Danny Hoch's own stance toward whiteness:

> I had this dream that I was on this planet
>
> But it wasn't another planet, it was like this planet
>
> And I started crying
>
> And I was embarrassed

Embarrassed that I didn't know shit

Embarrassed at my history

And I started thinking about 50,000 murders a year and two
million people in jail

And I think about Columbus Day and Columbus Circle and
Columbus, Ohio

And I started thinking about tribes, man, American tribes

Raped, murdered and moved

And I started thinking about tens of millions of Africans dying
in the sea

And Malcolm X and Jeep Cherokee and Columbus Day and
Columbus, Ohio

And I felt ashamed, man, ashamed of what I was representin.'

While Flip previously claimed to represent blackness, now he has owned up to his identity as a white man, voicing his shame at "what I was representin'"—that is, white privilege and genocidal power. Flip no longer empties his whiteness but rather poignantly acknowledges that he is imbricated in white racism against African Americans and Native Americans, which he calls "*my* history." Although earlier he had shunned white culture for being boring, uncool, and stagnant, he now disidentifies with "whiteboyz" for political rather than merely cultural reasons. In his essay "Crossover Dreams" in *Race Traitor*, Phil Rubio wonders if white Negro fascination with blackness can grow from a "cultural to [a more powerful] political" identification (151), and Danny Hoch as Flip offers us a fable of just such a transformation. Crucial to Flip's political awakening is his acceptance of his own complicity with whiteness. Abandoning his earlier attempt to become black, Flip in a sense becomes Danny Hoch, a man who has forged an antiracist yet white political identity.

Although Danny Hoch envisions an antiracist white identity, his understanding of that positionality differs slightly from that of Giroux's model of oppositional whiteness. Hoch admits that he functions in the public sphere as a white man, but he is not as concerned as Giroux about retaining a primary identification as white. For example, Giroux advocates that white youth search for oppositional antiracist models *within* white culture, while Hoch locates the sources of his political agency in black and Latino hip-hop culture rather than in his white Jewish heritage. The antiracist identity that Hoch has forged more closely resembles what Susan Gubar describes as a space of "transraciality" in which people "seek neither to become the Other . . . nor to flaunt their alienation from the other" but rather to dwell "in racial borderlands" (248). Danny Hoch's theater and film explore the possibility of a whiteness in solidarity with racial minorities and the underclass, a kind of transracial identity that is rarely explored in popular culture.

To equate Hoch's ethic of transraciality with the cultural fad of the wigger or "white Negro" is to underestimate the revolutionary power of his work as a form of race treason. As Kobena Mercer has argued, to reject all acts of racial crossover on the part of whites would be to risk reinstating the racial binary by overemphasizing racial purity as a requirement for antiracist struggle. The cultural work of Danny Hoch, and Eminem to a lesser degree, should make critics pause before dismissing all white hip-hoppers as impersonators and appropriators "aiding and abetting white rule" (Garon 175). By highlighting crossover artists who have moved beyond the paradigm of the white Negro with varying political effects, my goal is not to draw a prettier picture of whiteness but rather to show how whiteness is currently being undermined from within its gates. It strikes me as ironic that many of the cultural critics writing about whiteness and cross-racial iden-tification—David Roediger, Noel Ignatiev, Jeffrey Melnick, Michael Rogin, Susan Gubar, and Robyn Wiegman, to name a few—repre-sent white identity as an unchanging position of domination, despite the fact that these critics are themselves white and antiracist. While their own critical work attests to the radical potential of some acts of cross-racial affiliation, they universally lament that the libera-tory potential of racial crossover is almost never realized in cultural representation—least of all in popular culture.[16] Why is the only ac-ceptable critical stance one of overwhelming despair? While I do not mean to minimize the importance of these cautionary analyses of the imperialist power of whiteness, I am concerned that white critics may feel compelled to repeat the same tale as a means of "saving whiteface." This position also smacks of critical hubris, by implying that only critics and theorists, and not producers of popular culture, are capable of treason against white privilege. If scholars continue to treat whiteness as a "transhistorical essence" (Frankenberg 236) by ignoring the challenges to white hegemony and racial essentialism currently taking place in American popular culture, we risk reifying the very racial category that we set out to deconstruct and abolish in the first place.

Notes

1. See George; and Wald, *Crossing the Line*, specifically her chapter on Mezz Mezzrow.

2. See Wald "One of the Boys?" Also see George; Baraka; Alleyne; Melnick; White; Ozersky; and Garon.

3. See Roediger *Wages*. Also See Lott; Rogin; Sanchez-Eppler; Gubar; and hooks.

4. Statistics confirm Mathers's memory; one side of 8 Mile Road is 83 percent black and the other is 90 percent white (Enders).

5. When rappers Naughty by Nature warned that "if you ain't been to the ghetto, don't ever come to the ghetto, because you wouldn't understand the ghetto," Kid Rock replied, "I ain't straight outta Compton, I'm straight out the trailer" (qtd. in Strauss). The title of N.W.A's CD *Straight Outta Compton* inspired the retort.

6. For other defenses of Elvis, see Chadwick; Bertrand; and Rodman. In *Colored White*, Roediger offers an insightful analysis of Elvis's movement over time from an affiliation with blackness to a descent into "full whiteness" (220) with all its power and privilege.

7. Public Enemy had previously condemned Elvis in its song "Fight the Power": "Elvis was a hero to most / but he never meant shit to me / he's straight up racist / that sucker was simple and plain / motherfuck him and John Wayne."

8. For a view of Eminem as an "angry narcissist" (263) with "no psycho-political project" (258), see Miller.

9. For a thorough history of the term "wigger," see David Roediger's essay "Elvis, Wiggers, and Crossing over to Nonwhiteness" in his book *Colored White*.

10. To be fair to Roediger, his work is more nuanced than this sentence would imply. His 2005 book *Working Toward Whiteness* explores the process by which European immigrants moved from being an "in-between" racial group to one that was fully white. While this book questions an understanding of whiteness as unchanging over time, he is nonetheless focused on whiteness as an expression of power and privilege. I largely agree with the final chapter of his 2002 book *Colored White*, where he not only laments the failure of many wiggers to encourage antiracist politics, but also acknowledges the possibility that such cultural crossovers may inspire more politically minded coalitions.

11. For an insightful look at the complex relationship between Jewish American identity and whiteness, see Jacobson.

12. Hoch worked with the Creative Arts team, an NYU theater group that "reaches out to at-risk adolescents in prisons, detention centers and schools . . . [by doing] structured improvs about AIDS, racism, and abuse" (Stone 33).

13. In addition to Ignatiev and Garvey, and Ware and Back, see also Roediger *Toward.*

14. At least Ignatiev and Garvey admit the difficulty of abandoning one's race: "We know how devilishly difficult it is for individuals to escape whiteness . . . even those who step outside of it in one situation find it virtually impossible not to step back in later, if for no other reason than the assumptions of others" (37).

15. Hoch is not merely paying lip service to the act of "giving back" to the community. He is a founding board member of Active Element Foundation, which raises money for activist organizations such as Refuse and Resist, involved in the fight to free Mumia Abu-Jamal, a convicted cop killer.

16. For example, in *Racechanges,* Susan Gubar sees visual images of cross-racial imitation, masquerade, and identification as potentially radical in their denaturalizing function, but concludes that they so "rarely find egalitarian expression" (241). Gubar theorizes that mimetic representation "inevitably leads to the disappearance of the other's otherness" (245). Despite her confessed "utopic hopes," Robyn Wiegman reads integrationist literature and film as ultimately wedded to white authority, and concludes that "the transformatory hope of identifying with the pain and suffering of others seems ever more bound to an imperialistic cast" (200).

WORKS CITED

8 Mile. Dir. Curtis Hanson. Universal Studies, 2002.

Alleyne, Mike. "White Reggae: Cultural Dilution in the Record Industry." *Popular Music and Society* 24.1 (2000): 15–30.

Baraka, Amiri. *Blues People: Negro Music in White America.* New York: Morrow, 1963.

Bertrand, Michael T. *Race, Rock, and Elvis.* Champaign and Urbana: U of Illinois P, 2000.

Blank, Christopher. "The Artist Used Black and White; Many Still See Red." *Commercial Appeal* 18 Aug. 2002: A1.

Bravmann, Paul. "Whiteboy Deluxe: Danny Hoch's Cultural Revolution." TheStranger.com. 2 Sept. 1999 <http://www.thestranger.com/1999-09-02/theater4.html>.

Britt, Donna. "Eminem's 8 Mile Adds Distance to Rap's Reach." *Washington Post* 8 Nov. 2002: B1. LexisNexis. 8 Nov. 2002.

Chadwick, Vernon, Ed. *In Search of Elvis: Music, Race, Art, Religion.* Boulder: Westview, 1997.

Coates, Ta-Nehisi. "Caught on Tape: Eminem's Racist Rant Says Little that Hasn't Been Said by Black Rappers before Him." *Village Voice* 21 Nov. 2003 <http://www.villagevoice.com/music/0348,coates2,48918,22.html>.

Cobb, William Jelani. "White Negro, Please!" *Progressive* 67.1 (Jan. 2003): 32–33. ABI/INFORM Global. Proquest <http://proquest.umi.com/pdqweb>.

Croal, Aida Mashaka. "Danny Hoch Wants to Change the Word." Africana.com. 12 Oct. 2001 <http://www.africana.com/DailyArticles/index_20011012.html>.

Dunlevy, T'Cha. "What a Mouth He Has." *Montreal Gazette* 28 May 2002: F1.

Eminem. *Angry Blonde.* New York: Regan, 2000.

Enders, David. "Eight Mile Road: Detroit's Physical and Metaphorical Border." Associated Press, Domestic News. 5 Nov. 2001. LexisNexis.

Frankenberg, Ruth. *White Women, Race Matters: The Social Construction of Whiteness.* Minneapolis: U of Minnesota P, 1993.

Garon, Paul. "White Blues." *Race Traitor.* Ed. Noel Ignatiev and John Garvey. New York: Routledge, 1996. 167–75.

George, Nelson. *The Death of Rhythm and Blues.* New York: Random House, 1988.

Giroux, Henry A. *Channel Surfing: Race Talk, and the Destruction of Today's Youth.* New York: St. Martin's, 1997.

Goldstein, Richard. "Left Back City." *Village Voice* 14 Apr. 1998: 57.

Gubar, Susan. *Racechanges: White Skin, Black Face in American Culture.* New York: Oxford UP, 1997.

Hall, Stuart. "New Ethnicities." *Stuart Hall: Critical Dialogues in Cultural Studies.* Ed. David Morley and Kuan-Hsing Chen. New York: Routledge, 1996. 441–49.

Hoch, Danny. *Jails, Hospitals, & Hip-Hop* and *Some People.* New York: Villard, 1998.

———. "Mr. Hoch Goes to Hollywood: Why *Whiteboyz* Wasn't at a Theater Near You." *Nation* 3 Apr. 2000: 25–30. ABI/INFORM Global. Proquest <http://proquest.umi.com/pdqweb>.

Holloway, Lynette. "The Angry Appeal of Eminem Is Cutting Across Racial Lines." *New York Times* 28 Oct. 2002: C1. LexisNexis. 28 Oct. 2002.

hooks, bell. "Eating the Other." *Black Looks: Race and Representation.* Boston: South End, 1992. 21–39.

Ignatiev, Noel, and John Garvey, eds. *Race Traitor.* New York: Routledge, 1996.

———. "When Does the Unreasonable Act Make Sense?" Ignatiev and Garvey 35–37.

"Interview with Ignatiev." Ignatiev and Garvey 287–92.

Jackson, Shannon. "White Noises: On Performing White, on Writing Performance." *TDR: The Drama Review* 42.1 (1998): 49–65.

Jacobson, Matthew Frye. *Whiteness of a Different Color: European Immigrants and the Alchemy of Race.* Cambridge: Harvard UP, 1998.

Life Story: Eminem—In His Own Words. Life Story Magazine. Aug. 2003.

Lott, Eric. "White Like Me: Racial Cross-Dressing and the Construction of American Whiteness." *The Cultures of U.S. Imperialism*. Ed. Amy Kaplan and Donald Pease. Durham: Duke UP, 1993. 474–95.

Melnick, Jeffrey. *A Right to Sing the Blues: African Americans, Jews, and American Popular Song*. Cambridge: Harvard UP, 1999.

Mercer, Kobena. "Skin Head Sex Thing." *How Do I Look? Queer Film and Video*. Ed. Bad Object-Choices. Seattle: Bay, 1991.

Miller, Stephen. *Conversation: A History of a Declining Art*. New Haven: Yale UP, 2006.

Ozersky, Josh. "The White Negro Revisited." *Tikkun* 15.5 (Sept./Oct. 2000): 61–63.

Rodman, Gilbert. *Elvis after Elvis: The Posthumous Career of a Living Legend*. New York: Routledge, 1996.

Roediger, David. *Colored White: Transcending the Racial Past*. Berkeley: U of California P, 2002.

———. *Toward the Abolition of Whiteness*. London: Verso, 1994.

———. *The Wages of Whiteness: Race and the Making of the American Working Class*. London: Verso, 1991.

———. *Working Toward Whiteness: How America's Immigrants Became White*. New York: Basic, 2005.

Rogin, Michael. *Blackface, White Noise: Jewish Immigrants in the Hollywood Melting Pot*. Berkeley: U of California P, 1996.

Rubio, Phil. "Crossover Dreams: The 'Exceptional White' in Popular Culture." Ignatiev and Garvey 150–61.

Sanchez-Eppler, Karen. *Touching Liberty: Abolition, Feminism, and the Politics of the Body*. Berkeley: U of California P, 1993.

Smith, Zadie. "The Zen of Eminem." Nov. 2002. VIBE on LAUNCH. 1 Nov. 2002 <http://www.launch.yahoo.com/vibe/content.asp?id=77>.

Stone, Laurie. "Vox Populi." *Nation* 18 May 1998: 33–34. ABI/INFORM Global. Proquest <http://proquest.umi.com/pdqweb>.

Strauss, Neil. "The Hip-Hop Nation: Whose Is It? A Land of Rhythm and Beats for All." *New York Times* 22 Aug. 1999, sec. 2: 1+. ABI/INFORM Global. Proquest <http://proquest.umi.com/pdqweb>.

Tate, Greg, ed. *Everything but the Burden: What White People Are Taking from Black Culture*. New York: Broadway, 2003.

Toure. "32 Questions." *Village Voice* 30 Mar. 1999: 71. ABI/INFORM Global. Proquest <http://proquest.umi.com/pdqweb>.

Wald, Gayle. *Crossing the Line: Racial Passing in Twentieth-Century U.S. Literature and Culture*. Durham: Duke UP, 2000.

———. "One of the Boys? Whiteness, Gender, and Popular Music Studies." *Whiteness: A Critical Reader*. Ed. Mike Hill. New York: New York UP, 1997. 151–67.

Ware, Vron, and Les Back. *Out of Whiteness: Color, Politics, and Culture.* Chicago: U of Chicago P, 2002.

Washington, Salim. "Responses to Crossover Dreams." Ignatiev and Garvey 163–67.

Weiner, Wendy. "Bricks, Asphalt, and Language." *American Theatre* July–Aug. 1998: 30.

White, Armond. "The Resistance: Ten Years of Popular Culture that Shook the World." *Beyond Borders: A Cultural Reader.* Ed. Randall Bass and Joy Young. Boston: Houghton Mifflin, 2003. 538–56.

Whiteboyz. Dir. Marc Levin. 1999. Videocassette. Twentieth Century Fox Home Entertainment, 2000.

Wiegman, Robyn. *American Anatomies: Theorizing Race and Gender.* Durham: Duke UP, 1995.

Stalling Zion: Hegemony, Whiteness, and Racial Discourse in *The Matrix* Phenomenon

DOUGLAS A. CUNNINGHAM

You're white as snow, and you think like a slave.
—Philip Roth, *The Human Stain*

. . . unhappily while this class of people exists among us, we can never count with certainty on its tranquil submission.
—James Monroe, governor of Virginia, responding
to the 1800 slave rebellion of Gabriel Prosser

The great thing about being me is there's so many of me.
—Agent Smith, *The Matrix Reloaded*

In *The Matrix* (1999), cybernetic resistance leader Morpheus (Laurence Fishburne), a black man, endures Agent interrogation within the computer-generated reality called the Matrix. During his interrogation, a computer-generated white man, Agent Smith (Hugo Weaving), explains to him that the first version of the Matrix—designed to imprison the minds of humans so that their bodies could act as battery power for a world run by machines—had originally been a place in which "everyone would be happy." Unfortunately, Smith explains, humanity refused to accept the program. In other words, the captive human minds within the first Matrix could not accept the possibility of a world in which, among other things, all social and economic barriers to human happiness had been removed. In an attempt to salvage the "entire crop" of artificially produced humans lost to this "disaster," the machines reconfigured the Matrix to mirror what Agent Smith calls the "peak" of human civilization, replete with all its racial judgments and inequities. *The Matrix*, then, suggests that even within the pseudo-reality of the Matrix, racial antagonisms play a significant role in the everyday existence of human beings. That is to say, the racial antagonisms of the extradiegetic, "real" world have been purposefully recreated within the Matrix. Police swarm and violently club men of color. Marginalized peoples occupy tenement projects. Whiteness pervades assumptions about "normalcy," privilege, and power. Interestingly, *The Matrix* phenomenon foregrounds the ubiquity of whiteness in the extreme and "embodied" form of "Agents," mysterious "G-men" types who monitor and punish transgressions that threaten to expose the conceit of the Matrix. These Agents, all of them Caucasian, come to represent not simply the power structure of authority within the Matrix itself but also the power of whiteness in the extradiegetic, "real" world. Other entries in *The Matrix* trilogy and, indeed, the collective *Matrix* phenomenon—*The Matrix Reloaded* (2003), *The Matrix Revolutions* (2003), *The Animatrix* (2003), the video game "Enter the Matrix" (2003), and even *The Matrix Comics* (2003, 2005)—reinforce the first film's critical engagement with questions of racial antagonisms. On the surface, these *Matrix* products merely examine issues of race in a reductive and science-fictional way by pitting the *human* race against the "race" of machines. Ultimately, however, the conflicts on display in these films speak more to the modern racial reality in countries like the United States than to the trilogy's more simplistic universal human-machine conflict, which merely serves as a metaphor to describe real racial contentions among humans.[1]

This essay investigates the ways in which *The Matrix* trilogy and its ancillary products communicate ideas about the legacy of human racial conflict and its impact on Western, late capitalist societies. To begin, it employs Michel Foucault's theory of the Panopticon to discuss how issues of race within *The Matrix* series speak to the hegemonization of power inside the narrative and to issues of ideology outside the narrative. What arises from the phenomenon's treatment of race are subliminal scenes in the series that universalize themes of oppression and slavery by exploiting the viewer's familiarity with cinematic, literary, and televisual codes derived from past images of racial conflict residually embedded in collective memory. Of particular interest, however, are the assimilation threats portrayed in these films and the extreme whiteness they imply. The latter two *Matrix* films of the trilogy and "Enter the Matrix," in fact, present the hegemony of machine power, as maintained through the perpetuation of racial conflict among its human subjects, giving way to the greater threat of homogenized assimilation in the form of the self-replicating program, Agent Smith. Finally, since understanding the racial ambiguity of the character Neo (and of Keanu Reeves, the actor who plays him) is essential to discussions of this assimilationist threat within *The Matrix* trilogy, the essay revisits theories of both Jeffrey M. Fish and Foucault (specifically the latter's theories on governmentality) in an effort to explain how the series portrays racial ambiguity as a liberating force and, indeed, as a force that celebrates progressive theoretical ideas about individual identity. Certainly, Neo's ultimate commitment to free will and his ability to transcend traditional racial categorizations signal not only the salvation of Zion but also a new way of understanding questions of race in cinematic science fiction.

Most of the major critical publications on *The Matrix* series over the past five years have dwelled almost exclusively on its Baudrillardian and mytho-Christian/Buddhist themes.[2] Such interests are warranted, but they grow more uninspiring with each new article or volume. The unique philosophy section of the trilogy's official web page and almost all of the book-length critical studies published in early 2003 marginalized the racial aspects of the narrative. Fortunately, critical attention directed at examinations of race within the popular science fiction trilogy grew after the release of *The Matrix Reloaded*. Internet posts and bulletin boards started to exchange ideas on the subject frequently, and conference panels on the topic increased. A new anthology released in 2004, *Jacking into* The Matrix *Franchise: Cultural Reception and Interpretation*, even includes an essay, C. Richard Leonard and David J. King's "Is Neo White? Reading Race, Watching the Trilogy," critiquing whiteness. Elvis Mitchell's review of *The Matrix Reloaded* in the *New York Times* was among the very first to apply critical race theory to the series. Mitchell's review lauds the progressive racial politics at work in these films when he states, " . . . [*The Matrix Reloaded*] has one of the most excitingly subversive and radical points of view ever seen in a major motion picture: a postmodern purview that accords equal weight to philosophical ideals from people of color" (B10). The increased attention focused on the Oracle (Gloria Foster/Mary Alice), Niobe (Jada Pinkett-Smith), and several other nonwhite supporting characters, the multiracial citizens of Zion, and the casting of African-American Princeton University professor Cornel West serves all too well to drive Mitchell's point home. On the DVD box set, the Wachowski Brothers—the producers, writers, and directors of the phenomenon—devote an exclusive audio track to West's critical/philosophical commentary on the films.

Mitchell's comment is wholly appropriate; after all, within the Matrix, machines use racial conflict among humans to prevent the formation of a collective resistance to their hegemony. Is "race" in our world, however, any more of a reality than the Matrix itself? Does "race," as we have come to understand the term, even exist? Is it something— as Morpheus asks of reality in the first film—that we can see, taste, touch, or smell? Certainly Agent Smith feels he can smell the "stench" of the human race while interrogating Morpheus, but can we empirically provide proof of race, dissect it, categorize it? Eugenicists took the pseudo-science to an extreme. Can we—have we—learned from the past, or is the "color coding of American public policy and civic culture," as columnist Jim Sleeper argues, "a colossal blunder," a thorn in the side of a post–civil rights America striving to move beyond the disappointments of utopian liberalism? (2). Anthropologist Jeffrey M. Fish offers an answer:

> The fact that Americans believe that Asians, blacks, Hispanics, and whites constitute biological entities called races is a matter of *cultural* interest rather than scientific substance. It tells us something about American culture—but nothing about the human species. . . . There is no such thing [as race]. Race is a myth. And our racial classification scheme is loaded with pure fantasy. (251; emphasis added)

Fish goes on to argue that race has no basis in scientific fact, stating instead that "mutation, natural selection, and genetic drift" make up the "variance in physical appearance" among human beings (251–52). Fish's work forms a part of a larger movement within critical race theory to move beyond "traditional," biological assumptions about human difference and toward a collective understanding of race as a social construct. Bearing the tenets of this movement in mind, how is one to go about remedying issues of race through popular culture? After all, film, literature, and other critics can dismiss the biological validity of race all they want, but unless they can ensure wide acceptance of that dismissal in society, nothing changes—racism, regardless of scientific facts, remains embedded in American culture.

The Matrix phenomenon wrestles with the unchanging problem of race—but with vision and a far-reaching purpose; indeed, over the course of the series, its audience witnesses a remarkable transition in ways of looking at race and racial discourse that mirrors a similar transition within critical race theory and activism over the past fifty years. That is to say, *The Matrix* phenomenon moves from a "traditional" or "biological" view of race to one that is firmly rooted in the modern perception of race as a mere cultural construction, thereby pushing aside common categorizations in favor of individually determined identities and free will. Granted, the transition in the series is gradual; only as the credits roll after *The Matrix Revolutions* do all the pieces fall into place. The payoff is real, however, and once understood, promising as a tool for helping to open dialogues about white hegemony, race, and difference in America and, by extension, globally.

The Architecture of Divisive Power

In *Discipline and Punish* (1977), French philosopher Michel Foucault presents his theories on prison, punishment, and the disciplinary reforms of the nineteenth century and beyond. Foucault claims the control once held over the body has been replaced by a control over the soul, a "punishment that acts in depth on the heart, the thoughts, the will, the inclinations" (16). According to Foucault, discipline serves as the coercive, soul-correcting tool to ensure compliance with societal standards. The effective administration of discipline turns otherwise wrong-minded individuals into "docile bodies" that may be "subjected, used, transformed, and improved" (136). The imposition of such discipline requires, among other things, the following governances: "enclosure," a common point of collection for all individuals to be disciplined; "partitioning," the separation of individuals from each other to prevent "collective dispositions"; and the "control of activity," the delimitation of gesture, posture, and movement (141–49). What kind of structure might best serve these activities? Foucault suggests Jeremy Bentham's Panopticon. Foucault describes the structure as a cylindrical building consisting of a rotunda of cells (200). A guard or some other kind of disciplinarian stands in a watchtower in the middle of the rotunda and at any given time can see into each of the cells, which are lit by windows on the outside of a cylindrical building (200). The cells, of course, are also partitioned from each other, thereby preventing the formation of a "collective resistance" to power (200).

Because the Panopticon not only "encloses" and "partitions" but also subjects its individual bodies to constant surveillance those bodies, argues Foucault, now "docile," "self-police"; that is to say, individual docile bodies in a Panopticon take on the burden of monitoring their own activities: "Hence the major effect of the Panopticon," states Foucault, is "to induce in the inmate a state of conscious and permanent visibility that assures the automatic functioning of power" (201–2). Power maintains itself through the acquisition of knowledge and the knowledge of the inmate that s/he falls under constant surveillance and the knowledge of the guardian concerning each individual inmate—his or her case and activities (201–3). Although Foucault speaks of Bentham's Panopticon within its intended context as an architectural tool of discipline (whether for a prison, asylum, schoolhouse, hospital, or factory), he seems to hint that the Panopticon, removed from its corporeal stricture, represents power on a much larger, more abstract scale. Rather than viewing the Panopticon as a mere building, we can use its tenets of enclosure, partitioning, and activity control to describe marginalization tactics of dominant, hegemonic ideologies.

Unlike the inmates of a Panopticon, however, most inmates of the Matrix do not know of their imprisonment. On the contrary, knowledge of mental imprisonment within the Matrix can lead to freedom of both mind and body. Rather than relying on the self-policing concept so central to Foucault and Bentham's design, the Matrix employs its massive, computer-generated reality to create the docile bodies necessary to fuel—quite literally—the machine society. Even without the effect of self-policing created by the awareness of constant surveillance, however, the Panopticon still serves as a useful model for analyzing the Matrix. For example, like the Panopticon, the Matrix encloses its inmates mentally and physically in order to exert discipline. Also, despite their blissful ignorance, the inmates of the Matrix, after all, are, persistently watched and monitored to ensure compliance and mental docility. Finally, like a Panopticon, the Matrix replicates the partitions and divisions, in this case, those social partitions and divisions inherent to a late twentieth-century capitalist society, in an effort to prevent collective resistance.

The Matrix follows a Panopticonic model to secure and perpetuate power. The racial divisions replicated within the Matrix serve figuratively as partitions, occupying the collective conscious of the inmates and thereby suppressing the impulse for revolution. But how does the narrative of the first film in *The Matrix* trilogy confirm these arguments? In what ways does the film address issues of race? And how do these issues contribute directly or indirectly to themes of power?

"Residual" Racial Identity (Part I)

From a biological point of view, race remains a constant both within and outside the Matrix. If, for example, one is born black within the real world, that same person within the Matrix will also be black. The film provides a partial explanation for this constant when Morpheus explains the concept of "residual self-image" to Neo in the first film's Matrix orientation sequence. Here, Morpheus states that residual self-image is "the mental projection of your digital self" within a given virtual reality. All Matrix humans, then, must possess a degree of self-awareness and identity unique to their bodies in the "real" world. Otherwise, how could a Matrix human construct an accurate residual self-image?[3] Of course, such a concept raises the following question: Is this sense of self-*inherent* to the Matrix humans (i.e., have they developed the identity codes necessary for the construction of their residual self-images on their own), or have the machines programmed them with essential building blocks of identity information as part of the "growing" process? Lacan might argue that these Matrix children submit to both processes. They independently form identities to facilitate entry into the symbolic order, but they can only do so in the realm of the imaginary through "gestalt," that is, external identifications that create an illusion of wholeness. In this case, those external identifications take the form of images provided to them by the Matrix (Lacan 2). What other images *could* they have? Just as in the "real" world, knowledge of racial identity and/or difference originates from a source external to the subject. And since the Matrix provides all stimuli external to Matrix humans, the machines ultimately carry the burden of introducing the concept of racial difference.

But why? Why should the machines care about initiating racial identities within Matrix humans and then further cultivating and exploiting those identities after formation? Quite simply, the machines recognize racial difference and conflict as divisive and "othering." As Foucault's model of the Panopticon demonstrates, raising partitions—figurative or literal—between inmates prevents rebellious unity and revolution. By perpetuating racial conflict, the Matrix distracts its humans from asking the bigger questions that might some day lead to freedom. As a result, the machines hegemonize their own power.

For example, consider the two "realities" represented in the first film. The reality in the Matrix follows very closely the model of a Western, late capitalist society. Whites hold positions of power in the corporate sector and in law enforcement (a close viewing reveals that only whites serve as representative of the law within the series). Nonwhites even seem absent from the prosperous streets of the Matrix metropolis. Of the very few persons of color who appear within the Matrix in the first film, at least three—an elderly Aboriginal man, the Oracle, and the Oracle's assistant—live in a ghettoized high rise project with graffiti on the walls. The original film does not address the state of other nonwhites further, but given their lack of representation in the workplace and on the streets of the city, one might assume that they have been boxed into segregated or ghettoized communities and prevented from entering the upper and middle classes.

The second reality—the reality outside the Matrix—is that of Morpheus and the crew of his hovercraft, the *Nebuchadnezzar*. In their "real" human world, to which our exposure at this point is limited, the Panopticonic effects of the Matrix have far less power, in part because the machines have no means by which to monitor continually or effectively either the roving hovercraft or the inhabitants of Zion. More important, however, Panopticonic power fails in the "real" world primarily because the conditions necessary to perpetuate human existence cannot allow racial differences to obstruct the rebellious unity of the humans waging war against the machines, although, as the later films reveal, the inhabitants of Zion do insist on recognizing certain kinds of difference. On the *Nebuchadnezzar*, with the obvious exception of the traitorous Cypher (Joe Pantoliano), all humans work toward two common goals—finding "the One" and preserving Zion. The "real" human world confounds the Panopticonic power of the machines. Indeed, machine-specific efforts at splintering human unity only seem successful within the Matrix. For example, Agent Smith virtually "wines and dines" Cypher at a posh restaurant inside the Matrix in order to convince him to betray Morpheus and the crew of the *Nebuchadnezzar* outside the Matrix. Given that race normally plays such a central role in mass, interhuman contention, the accepted racial heterogeneity among humans in the "real" world of the film frustrates machine hegemony. After all, based solely on phenotypes, skin color, and hue, those ever-present markers of "traditional" racial discourse, the crew of the *Nebuchadnezzar* represents a kind of racial diversity and human cooperation not seen within the Matrix—four whites (Switch, Cypher, Mouse, and Trinity), two blacks (Dozer and Morpheus), one Pacific Islander (Apoc), and two characters of ambiguous ancestral categories (Tank and Neo).

The Codes

The frustration and exposure of the perpetuation of racial conflict also serves an important purpose outside the diegesis. Several scenes within the first film, most of which feature Morpheus, draw upon cinematic, literary, and televisual codes of African-American enslavement and oppression. These codes, in turn, serve to universalize those same horrific experiences for racially diverse audiences. In other words, while a typical spectator may not experientially understand what being an unwary human slave in a world dominated by machines is like, he or she *can* sympathize with the enslaved position through exposure to subliminal images of racial oppression. Subliminally, vicarious universalization of oppressive experience ultimately helps the spectator to identify his/her own place within—and even collusion with—the Panopticonic forces at work in the real world outside the film. Exposing the Panopticon and the ways in which it partitions human social consciousness mark the first step toward undoing what Foucault calls the "technologies of domination" (Gabrielson).

A prime example of subliminal coding of racial oppression appears during a long pair of sequences in the middle of *The Matrix*. Having tested his protégé's mettle in a number of combat training programs, Morpheus decides to take Neo into the Matrix to see the Oracle. As they return to the abandoned building that serves as their dial-up transport site back to the real world, three agents and a host of law enforcement officers ambush Morpheus's entourage. The pursued group attempts to escape by descending a cavity between the building's walls, only to be discovered by the Agents. To ensure Neo's escape, Morpheus bursts through the wall of a bathroom and tackles the only person in the room, Agent Smith.

> "The great Morpheus," Smith monotonically proclaims.
> "We meet at last." Morpheus, attempting unsuccessfully to choke Smith, asks, "And you are?"
> "Smith. Agent Smith."
> "You all look the same to me," Morpheus retorts
> sarcastically.

Morpheus's sarcasm acknowledges a common racially derogatory comment that whites use to allege that members of other races are indistinguishable from one another. Cleverly, however, Morpheus appropriates the original intent of the phrase and inverts it, thereby insulting the whiteness inherent to the world of the Matrix while simultaneously offering a sort of extradiegetic "wink" that mocks the idiocy of such a statement in the real world of the spectator.

Of course, despite the double entendre, Morpheus actually speaks the truth: all the Matrix Agents *do* look the same in their black suits, black ties, and rectangular dark glasses, a point which becomes even more significant in *The Matrix Reloaded* and *The Matrix Revolutions*. As extreme representatives of authority, their intimidating presence signals a brand of whiteness within the Matrix that appears all the more stark and unforgiving when contrasted with the warm, human, and black presence of Morpheus. In fact, Morpheus—in his role as mentor, prophet, militant, and zealot—combines diametrically opposed African-American resistance leaders Martin Luther King Jr. and Malcolm X. His ability to call these historical figures forth from the subliminal to the liminal level demonstrates the extent to which the film encourages its audience to identify real-world racial protest and resistance with the overall human struggle depicted in the narrative. The first film's tendency to encourage associations with codes of racial conflict becomes even more disturbing in the moments following the telling and slightly humorous exchange between Morpheus and Smith. A battle ensues between the two, and while the combat-skilled Morpheus makes a valiant effort, he proves no match for Smith whose moves derive from a "superior" program. Morpheus receives a terrible bludgeoning until he lies prostrate on the bathroom floor. At this point, we see a hitherto unseen view of the bathroom doorway. Smith has not, in fact, been alone during his battle with Morpheus; an entire cadre of policemen donned with full assault gear has patiently and wordlessly watched the fight from outside the doorway. Smith moves to the doorway and speaks to the gathered policemen. "Take him," Smith says dismissively. The film cuts to an overhead point-of-view shot as a swarm of riot police batter the helpless body of Morpheus with clubs.

The fight scene and its aftermath trouble the audience on many levels because the audience sympathizes and identifies with Morpheus. But its sympathy derives from other sources—most specifically, the codes inherent to the historical representation of racial conflict. The abuse suffered by Morpheus recalls the controversial 1991 George Holliday video of white Los Angeles Police Department members using excessive force to subdue offending motorist and African American Rodney King.

As in the Holliday video, the scene in *The Matrix* involves a black man who, despite continuous physical punishment, continues to resist authority with unexpected resilience. In 1991, many of the officers involved in the beating maintained that King's stamina came as the result of a PCP high; *The Matrix*, of course, provides its own explanation for Morpheus's stubborn resistance. Also, as in the Holliday video, the beating of Morpheus continues even though the immediate danger to authority has passed. These details become even more relevant given the countless screenings of the King video in 1991 and later. Repeated viewings of those images created within the American collective subconscious racialized codes for the representation of racial conflict. In America and abroad audiences saw the powerful echoes of the Los Angeles police officers' beating of King displayed in American cinema soon after the incident in *Natural Born Killers* (1994), which uses footage from the Holliday video, and in *Strange Days* (1994), yet another film dealing with the societal effects of racism and simulated realities. In the latter film, Mace (Angela Bassett), an African-American woman, attempts to flee two renegade members of the LAPD during a New Year's Eve celebration on the crowded streets of downtown Los Angeles. Finding no escape, she turns to face her attackers. Using martial arts, she fights, defeats, and handcuffs the two policemen. Before she can explain her motives, riot policemen assault her with their clubs. These actions, in turn, incite a riot among the thousands of citizens on the streets, and the city teeters on the brink of a race war. Like the beating of Morpheus in *The Matrix*, the police battery scene from *Strange Days* seeks to capitalize psychically on its audience's familiarity with the Rodney King beating.

As Stan Chambers, the KTLA television reporter who covered the King story, and others have pointed out, the first thirteen seconds of the King beating were edited out of the original airing of the video, and the events leading up to the beating were not captured. Chambers describes the editing decisions made with regards to the tape as follows:

> The first ten seconds or so were out of focus as George Holliday started shooting his new camera. There were images there, but you could not tell what was happening, once he was in focus, the images were clear and the action mesmerizing. We decided to pick it up there. The officers swarmed around Rodney King. We let the tape play until the beatings stopped. The tape was so brutally powerful, we just used Holliday's voice as he described what he saw. That is the way it went on the air that night. Of course, the tape could not show what had gone on before. The camera wasn't rolling during the high-speed police pursuit down the San Fernando Freeway. The large number of officers at the scene were there because they were part of the pursuit and follow up. The camera did not show that Rodney King threw off four officers who tried to subdue him after the freeway chase. The camera did not show Sgt. Tracy Koon use a taser gun twice in an effort to subdue Rodney King. Nothing that preceded the beatings on the tape had been recorded except the out-of-focus footage taken by George Holliday before the clear pictures appeared in his view finder. The fact that the officers thought

he was on PCP, a drug that seems to give super powerful strength to someone under its influence was, of course, not seen on the video tape. King, a huge powerful man, fought all of the officers until he was finally subdued.

Arguments about the contextualization of the taped footage helped to acquit the LAPD officers charged with King's brutalization. Those acquittals, in turn, sparked the worst race riot seen in the United States since Watts in 1968 (Chambers). *The Matrix* and *Strange Days*, however, remove ambiguity by providing the contextual information necessary to generate audience sympathy for, and identification with, the victims of the beatings. As stated previously, the ultimate purpose of these codes is to draw upon the audience's familiarity with representations of racial violence and oppression. Its familiarity, in turn, facilitates suture; that is to say, the audience becomes more easily woven into the emotional and psychological power of the narrative history of slavery and oppression as a result of recognizing codes from previous cinematic or, in this case, televisual experiences. Similar codes are at work in the lengthy interrogation scene between Smith and Morpheus; they act as reifying elements here, although they take both visual and rhetorical forms. In the follow-up scene to his beating, Morpheus sits handcuffed and drugged in a large room in a Matrix government skyscraper. Agent Smith sits smugly before the drugged Morpheus, issuing a soliloquy that seems uncharacteristic for a sentient, law-enforcing computer program:

"I'd like to share a revelation that I've had during my time here. It came to me as I tried to classify your species, and I realized that you're not actually mammals. Every mammal on this planet instinctively develops a natural equilibrium with its surrounding environment, but you humans do not. You move to an area and you multiply and multiply until all the natural resources are consumed. The only way for you to survive is to spread to another area. There is another organism on this planet that follows the same pattern. Do you know what it is? A virus. Human beings are a disease, a cancer of this planet. You are a plague. We are the cure."

Smith's comments reverberate with Nazi rhetoric regarding the non-humanity of Jews, not to mention the myriad pseudo-scientific methods of eugenics developed by Nazi doctors to measure, classify, and sort humans according to race. Smith reaches the conclusion that human beings are a "virus," yet another term that echoes Nazi rhetoric categorizing Jews. Here that rhetoric has been adopted to condemn humanity as a whole; however, the codes help to reify racially for the audience that condemnation. The spectator can see and hear the technologies of domination in action; in fact, the specific words Smith uses evoke the cold precision of scientific classification and objectification. His rhetoric, coupled with the familiar image of a black man in chains—Morpheus's hands are shackled—brings the racial undercurrent of the filmic text to the surface, adding tension and pathos to a narrative sequence that might otherwise seem simply formulaic and gratuitous.

Ultimately, the codes at work in *The Matrix*—the historical representations of racial conflict—help audiences sympathize with states of oppression for the sake of more than just the narrative. Indeed, the film seeks to enlighten the spectator's understanding of his or her own Panopticonic world where racial divisions among peoples and nations continue to divide human resistance to corporate and despotic power.

The Codes Reloaded

Just as subliminal images resembling past representations of racial conflict help to universalize feelings of oppression and enslavement for racially diverse audiences in *The Matrix*, effective examples of the suturing codes arise again in *The Matrix Comics*, several episodes of *The Animatrix*, *The Matrix Reloaded*, and *The Matrix Revolutions*. For example, "Bits and Pieces of Information," the first story in the first volume of *The Matrix Comics*, and "The Second Renaissance, Part I," an episode from *The Animatrix*, co-opt significant historical moments from African-American literature, slave history, the Million Man March, the Vietnam War, the Tiananmen Square massacre, and ethnic cleansing in Rwanda and Bosnia in order to fill in essential elements of *The Matrix's* origin narrative—elements that lay the groundwork for interpreting the coded representations of racial conflict that follow in the trilogy. "Bits and Pieces of Information" and "The Second Renaissance, Part I" both tell a portion of the story of B1-66ER, the first robot servant to murder its master. B1-66ER's very name references "Bigger Thomas"—the troubled and persecuted African-American protagonist of Richard Wright's seminal novel, *Native Son* (1940). But B1-66ER's crime alludes more specifically to the 1831 slave rebellion that Nat Turner led in Virginia, an uprising that began with the killing of Turner's slave master and eventually resulted in the deaths of some sixty whites (Foner 152). Almost two hundred blacks, most of whom did not even participate in the uprising, were butchered in the white retribution that followed (153). Although B1-66ER does not lead an insurrection following the master's murder, "The Second Renaissance, Part I" makes clear that the slave machines monitor very closely the discourse surrounding B1-66ER's crime. Construction-worker robots even watch the proceedings on TV during their "lunch" hours.

Later, as "Bits and Pieces of Information" depicts closing statements at B1-66ER's trial, the lawyer for the defense cites the 1857 Supreme Court case of *Dred Scott v. John F. Sandford*. With this allusion, the historical moment morphs from African-American slave insurrections to African-American pleas for status as "legal" human beings. Using the courts, Scott, a slave, argued that he should be freed because he and his master, for a time, had lived in states and territories where the practice of slavery had been deemed illegal (Franklin and Moss 178). Chief Justice Roger B. Taney, speaking on behalf of the majority opinion, declared Scott's claim invalid, thereby remanding Scott to slavery (178). Conversely, in "Bits and Pieces of Information," B1-66ER's legal counsel, Clarence Drummund, ridicules the decision in the Scott case. Nodding to the unfortunate court decision, Drummund addresses the jury:

> "Chief Justice Taney believed, truly believed, the black race to be an inferior species to the white race. In fact, it was widely believed at the time that the black man was not even a human being, that he was a kind of animal, a two-legged brute incapable of the same thoughts and feelings of the white man. I know most of you feel

the same way about B1-66ER as Taney felt about Dred Scott. . . .
Over a century ago, Taney made a great mistake. . . . I will admit
to you that I am afraid, afraid of what will happen to this world if
we continue to repeat our mistakes." (15–16)

Despite Drummund's pleas, however, the jury finds B1-66ER guilty
of murder. The decision is ironic considering that a guilty verdict
acknowledges the robot's "humanity." In response to the verdict,
robots and liberal "robot rights" activists riot after a peaceful demonstration, the "Million Machine March" in Washington, D.C., erupts
into violence (Wachowski 16). This allusion to the 1995 peaceful
African-American demonstration, the Million Man March, is obvious. Although *The Animatrix* perverts the outcome, the "racial" conflict in "The Second Renaissance, Part I" has transgressed far beyond
peaceful resolution.

The trend of coded historical representations of racial conflict continues in more stunning imagery from the "The Second Renaissance,
Part I." For example, an image of a robot's execution following the
Million Machine March lends a different racial bent to its recreation
of Eddie Adams's 1968 photo depicting a suspected Vietcong captain being summarily executed on a Saigon street. Adams snapped
his shutter just as the South Vietnam national police chief fired his
gun at the captive's head. Similarly, images depicting the dumping
of hundreds of "murdered" robots into mass graves, by "The Second
Renaissance, Part I" director Mihiro Maedra's own admission, seek
to invoke memories of televised images of ethnic and racial cleansing in Rwanda and Bosnia, as well as the Jewish Holocaust. Even the
episode's preliminary images of machine subservience come loaded
with historical racial baggage, as in scenes where slave robots march
to and from their labors in a drudgery reminiscent of the marching
of exploited underground workers in the beginning of Fritz Lang's
Metropolis (1927). To echo the Fascist appropriation of Socialist imagery that took place during the last days of Germany's Weimar Republic,
these same robot workers later appear in an image directly reminiscent of Nazi propaganda films on the order of Leni Riefenstahl's
Triumph des Willes (1935). Each of these covert images helps to weave
effectively diverse audiences into the narrative's backstory, encouraging them to grapple with familiar and disturbing images ingrained

within the popular psyche which, in turn, helps them to process the racial significance of the overt events on the screen in opposition to a collision with whiteness.

And yet, despite codified imagery, the machines do not stand as the worst harbingers of doom in these films. They oppress, inveigle, and control, but they do not do so at the expense of human individuality and identity; indeed, as posited earlier, the machines *want* to magnify differences—particularly racial differences—among Matrix humans in order to sublimate collective resistance. The true threat in the trilogy is assimilation: the radical and complete elimination of human difference. If, as concluded earlier, the Matrix embodies its enforcers of authority within extreme whiteness, the new Smith, formerly an "agent of the system" and now "unplugged" and operating independently, represents white authority gone fanatical; his autonomous rise depends almost exclusively upon the homogenization, or if necessary, the elimination, of difference. Smith achieves homogenization by penetrating others with his palm, initiating a copying process that remakes the victim into an exact replication of himself. Each new Smith possesses this replicating impulse and capability, resulting in a viral infection that spreads quickly throughout the Matrix. *The Matrix Reloaded* codes this idea of white homogenization marvelously by deliberately linking the new Smith with a horde of cawing crows reminiscent of those seen in Alfred Hitchcock's film, *The Birds* (1963). The birds in that film represent a type of operating behavior and mass psychology characteristic of the way in which the assimilated Smiths behave. As even the shocked ornithologist in the Hitchcock film's bayside diner witnesses, birds of different feathers can and will, in fact, flock together (read: assimilate) to overwhelm a common humanity—just like the assimilated Smiths.

After a short meeting with the Oracle, Neo confronts the unplugged Smith and ninety-nine viral Smith clones in an over-the-top courtyard fight sequence. Prior to the actual fight, Neo, although still unsure of his own capabilities, finds he can resist Smith's penetrating assimilationist threat, a topic addressed in-depth below. Important to the discussion at hand, however, is the fact that Neo has, through a process that his own literal "leap" into Smith at the end of the first film triggers, enabled Smith to replicate himself endlessly. In his treatise on whiteness, Richard Dyer argues that to be white is, essentially, to lack, to be empty, or to be dead (211–12). Neo himself hints at these perceptions of whiteness immediately following his escape from the fight with the hundred Smiths. Referring to Smith's penetrating attempt to assimilate Neo, Morpheus questions Smith's activities. Neo can only reply, "I don't know what he was doing. But I know what it felt like. . . . It felt like dying." Here, assimilation, or more specifically, the emptiness of its whiteness, is, as Dyer suggests, equated to death. Emptiness, he argues, derives from an absence of cultural roots or identity. Citing critics such as Tom DiPiero, Dyer maintains that "the representation of both whiteness and masculinity [are] not so much identities as 'hysterical responses to a perceived lack of identity' . . . [and that certain films] 'endorse the position that white men are justified in asking others to determine their identity'" (212). Whiteness, in fact, implies not only literal emptiness and death, posits Dyer, but also the "sense of the dead-end, the death, of whiteness is also suggested in relation to [sexual] reproduction" (218). Dyer also paraphrases Barbara Creed's concept of the "monstrous-feminine" when he states, "It is a specifically white, aghast perception of the unstoppable breeding of non-whites, that deep-seated suspicion that non-whites are better at sex and reproduction than are whites, that, indeed, to be truly white and reproductively efficient are mutually incompatible, and that as a result, whites are going to be engulfed and swamped by non-white multitudes" (216). Smith's new power, his new reproductive capability, has come as the result of his emptiness being filled by Neo, an "other" possessing an empowering racial ambiguity. In Dyer's theory, when the film's personification of extremist whiteness connects with otherness, the end result is a sense of identity, a purpose that was previously lacking. With Smith, this newfound sense of purpose brings with it a desire to strip others of individual identity and purpose: "We are here because of you, Mr. Anderson," Smith says, his clones surrounding Neo in the courtyard. "We're here to take from you what you tried to take from us: PURPOSE." Neo's "leap" into Smith has facilitated and affirmed white reproductive capability on a massive scale, temporarily filling Smith's emptiness as the embodiment of white authority with meaning and purpose. That purpose is the mass assimilation of everything into Smith's whiteness.

How fitting their encounter and the massive fight that follows take place in a courtyard of the projects. While this space, like the Oracle's home, seems to act as a site of minority resistance—what bell hooks calls "homeplace"—it transforms here into a site of racial conflict, contention, and invasion (41–49). This sense of white violation is echoed in a spooky scene from *The Matrix Revolutions* in which the Smiths calmly invade the apartment of the Oracle (now Mary Alice) and palm-penetrate her arm, infusing one of the trilogy's most powerful symbols of nonwhite resistance with assimilated—and assimilating—whiteness. Initially, this white invasion is even more troubling given the fact that the Oracle's *personal* selection of "homeplace" extends beyond her physical surroundings to the deliberate choices of *physiological* surroundings, or human shells, that she—as an ancient and "intuitive" computer program—chooses to inhabit. *The Matrix Revolutions*, for example, reveals that the Oracle has lost her original human "shell" as punishment for disclosing to Neo the location of the Keymaker (Randall Duk Kim), an exiled computer program who, like the Oracle, has taken bodily form in the Matrix. The Oracle finds a new shell, however, choosing once again to inhabit the body of a black woman. Granted, this plot twist was, at least in part, driven by real-life events: Gloria Foster—the first actress to play the Oracle—died of diabetes after filming her only scene in *The Matrix Reloaded*. Yet the casting of Mary Alice to play the Oracle in "Enter the Matrix" and *The Matrix Revolutions* works within the racial politics of the series because it reinforces the fact that the Oracle elects to inhabit the shell of a black woman by *choice*. The Oracle's strategy, in fact, recalls Edward Soja's concept of a "Thirdspace of political choice," that personally and deliberately selected spot of "decenteredness" from which one can effectively launch revolutionary efforts (97). Significantly, the Oracle's own choice, her selection of the decentered position as the site from which to exercise her free will, foreshadows Neo's actions during his confrontation with the Architect (Helmut Bakaitis) in *The Matrix Reloaded* and during his climactic battle with Smith in *The Matrix Revolutions*. Thus, while Smith's white, assimilationist penetration/invasion of the Oracle's Thirdspace initially disrupts, ultimately it contributes to Smith's defeat, destroying him, quite literally, from the inside out—again.

"Residual" Racial Identity (Part II):
Why Penetration Matters

In "Penetrating Keanu: New Holes but the Same Old Shit" (2003), Cynthia Freeland dwells extensively on the many penetrations Neo receives in the first film. Freeland fails, however, to explore cogently the potential significances of these penetrations, why they are important, or how they form an essential link between sexuality and race. To be fair, Freeland wrote her article before the release of the remaining films in the trilogy, but even examinations of penetrations present in the first film help illuminate the racial politics at work. Most notable among these is the fact that to be free born in Zion is to exist in an unviolated state, while conversely, the *substantiated* (that's Zion talk meaning "liberated from the Matrix") "pod-borns" carry the scars of machine penetration with them, constant reminders—to themselves as well as to their free-born colleagues—that they hail from an unholy union with the enemy "other." (Such scars are, in fact, reminiscent of the concentration camp numbers tattooed onto Jews and other prisoners during the Holocaust—yet another example of the suturing codes at work.) And yet these "scars" also prove useful, even emancipatory, offering substantiated Matrix humans opportunities and unique abilities not available to their free-born cousins. The films do not dwell on animosities between "pod-borns" and "free-borns," but hints of supremacism and even a strange form of racism between the two types of humans occasionally slip into the narrative, as exemplified by Tank's pride in being a "100-percent pure, old-fashioned, homegrown human, born free, right here, in the real world. A genuine child of Zion." In *The Matrix Revolutions*, too, the free-born leader of Zion's APU Corps, Captain Mifune (Nathaniel Lees), voices his dismay that Kid (Clayton Watson), whose self-substantiation we witness in the "Kid's Story" episode of *The Animatrix*, presumes to serve in "his" Corps. Neither grouping seems to have much regard for "Coppertops"—a racializing epithet that Switch (Belinda McClory) uses to label nonliberated Matrix humans in the first film; the liberated Matrix humans kill them without conscience, reasoning as Morpheus does when he points out that "most of these people are not ready to be unplugged" and hence must be considered unwitting collaborators with the machines. We know, of course, that the machines can "grow" human members of every conceivable race in their massive fields. How else do we explain Zion's healthy racial mix of "pod-borns" who are able to jack in to the Matrix? In the *Animatrix* episode titled "World Record," a black man awakens in his pod. Ironically, although "traditionalists" might argue that his racial origin is still recognizable by his facial phenotype, his skin color appears almost a deep pink in the red glow of the pods—a commentary, perhaps, on the irrelevance of phenotypes and skin color among the slave humans serving as "Coppertops."

The machines, then, do more than assign racial identity to their Matrix subjects, as I indicated earlier; they also deliberately *produce* a diverse racial populace within the *real* world. Why, exactly, the machines do this is unclear—particularly if they are capable of creating a racial identity for a subject regardless of that subject's actual racial origin. Perhaps the machines see the divisive potential for racial diversity in the "real world" as it is within the Matrix. Admittedly, the oblivious, pod-bound humans are far from forming any kind of collective resistance to machine power.

The point here is that as far as the machines are concerned racial origin and racial identity are one and the same. At no point within the Matrix do we see a Matrix human—substantiated or Coppertop— "performing" race or "passing" for any other aspect of human variability that is different from his or her natural state in the real world. Unlike the real world, then, Matrix humans cannot reach for additional privilege by "passing" as Coleman Silk attempts to do in Philip Roth's novel *The Human Stain* (2000). Liberated Matrix humans, however—like those from the crews of the various Zion hovercrafts who regularly plug in to the Matrix—do achieve a Matrix form of "passing" in that they effectively masquerade as Coppertops. They move in and out of the arenas of corporate and hegemonic power, and, indeed, in and out of the Matrix itself, apparently recognized only by Agents and other "in the know" computer programs; the Oracle, the Merovingian, and so on. Here, passing as a Coppertop is likened to any other form of passing—whether based on skin color, cultural habits, or both—and like those who pass, the liberated Matrix humans strategically employ their pass-ability in order to manipulate corrupt and oppressive systems for their own benefits.

While racial concerns within Zion may seem inconsequential or even eradicated altogether, the truth is these concerns merely take different forms—forms based not necessarily on skin color, hue, or phenotype but on a criterion that nevertheless resembles the "one-drop" or "hypo-descent" theory. This theory posits that any genetic coupling with the "other" automatically classifies the progeny as a member of the "other" grouping. The progeny of the other are usually considered a people of inferior status, tainted by their mixed blood and shamed by the taboo-breaking sins of their forbears (Fish 255). In this respect, the trilogy nods again to the Holocaust as well as to its science fiction and horror film predecessors—most notably to *Blade* (1998), in which "pure blood" status among a hidden but powerful society of affluent vampires implies some greater degree of power, authority, privilege, and authenticity. Played by African-American actor Wesley Snipes, the film's title character is also called the "Daywalker," the prophesied half-human half-vampire enemy of a secret vampire society, a warrior endowed with all the powers of his different forbears yet none of their weaknesses. Blade's status as a "genetic freak," a fact often referenced within the film, marginalizes him from each of his societies of origin, and the entire premise of his racial isolation and difference is indexed by the decision of Blade's original comic-book creators, Marv Wolfman and Gene Colon, to depict him as black. Interestingly, in *The Matrix* trilogy, just as in *Blade*, the power to effect true revolutionary change rests with a character of "mixed blood"—a substantiated Matrix human of ambiguous raciality whose diverse genetic ties grant him power far beyond the inhabitants of either of his societies of origin.

The Anomaly

Is Neo, in fact, a character of mixed blood? Although traditionally coded as white within his films, the actor behind Neo—Keanu Reeves—hails from a rich racial heritage—part Polynesian, part Caucasian. But does the extradiegetic racial heritage of Reeves "matter" when discussing his role as Neo? Certainly few things in the trilogy overtly mark him as anything other than white, particularly given his Anglo-Nordic Matrix name (Thomas Anderson) and the fact that his hacked-goods customer, Choi, even comments that Mr. Anderson/

Neo looks "whiter than usual" near the beginning of the original film. And yet, the series does seem to rely heavily on the physical hints of "otherness" (what Mitchell labels "pan-Asian exoticism") personified by Keanu Reeves in order to set Neo apart as somehow separate from his Matrix and Zion colleagues. It employs the same aura of difference that empowered this *Bill and Ted's Excellent Adventure* alum to portray an ascetic Buddhist in ancient India in the Bernardo Bertolucci film *Little Buddha* (Mitchell B10). His dark eyes and dark hair contrast sharply with his pale skin and high cheekbones, as if to suggest that he, in fact, is the human amalgam of two (or more) collided worlds. Also, as Carol Siegel has suggested, Mr. Anderson/Neo's affinity for technology (he is an expert computer hacker) and his loose associations with the "Goth" scene (evidenced by the aforementioned visit from Choi and his Goth-like, "white rabbit" friends) tie Mr. Anderson/Neo to certain stereotypes of angst-ridden, Asian American youth culture. Mr. Anderson/Neo's reification of such Asian American stereotypes alludes to the film's anime and manga source material and lends even more weight to his status as an invisible, ambiguous, and unknowable "other" in a world populated by representatives of white authority. In other words, he represents difference on both the diegetic and extradiegetic levels. As Neo, Reeves represents a type of "neo"-multiculturalism that stands as a threat to the stark whiteness of authority and normalcy within the Matrix, and his place with the crew of the *Nebuchadnezzar* sends a clear message that the future of humanity will not fall into easy categories of black or white.

Neo's ability to defy racial classification plays a crucial role in helping to fell partitions between the figurative "cells" that divide humanity and prevent collective resistance. Tania Gabrielson effectively paraphrases Foucault when she describes governmentality as "a form of activity designed to shape, affect, or change the conduct of a person or persons." More specifically, we are concerned here with governmentality's

> ... technologies of domination ... that classify, objectify, and normalize us as persons who will lead useful, docile, and practical lives. ... Thereby, power/knowledge involves a particular kind of truth which is located within the deep regimes of discourse and practice. The path to freedom requires us to detach ourselves from

the regimes of truth associated with the human sciences, because these have become manipulative, if not dominating and enslaving. (Gabrielson)

Neo finds this "path to freedom" because he is able to achieve, both racially and spiritually, the detachment to which Gabrielson alludes. When acting within the Matrix, he stands apart from its categories and proscriptions to define his own sense of self and identity. He ceases to act as a subject of the system, rejects its technologies of domination, and becomes instead a subject of his own construction. Hence Neo persistently rejects Smith's calling him by his Matrix name, "Mr. Anderson," in much the same way that many African Americans have chosen to shed the last names of their slave masters in favor of self-selected, individual names. The ambiguity of Neo's racial identity, therefore, serves as at least part of his liberating potential as "the One"; he upsets the perpetuation of racial conflict because he represents the potential for independent self-definition and for collective human resistance to machine power. It is this same ability to rise above racial categorization that enables Neo to resist the assimilationist threat of Agent Smith in *The Matrix Reloaded* and ultimately to conquer it in *The Matrix Revolutions*. In short, Neo represents choice.

The Problem—and Solution—Is Choice

What viewers know of Neo's origins they learn during his confrontation with the Architect—the creator of the Matrix—in *The Matrix Reloaded*. Dressed in a silver-gray three-piece suit resembling that of the nineteenth-century American rail barons who were symbols of an imperializing and genocidal white manifest destiny, the Architect explains that Neo's life is "the sum of the remainder of an unbalanced equation inherent to the programming of the Matrix"; the unbalanced equation is caused by the 1 percent of all potential Matrix humans (Coppertops) who at a "near unconscious level" refuse the Matrix program, thereby creating what the Architect calls the "systemic anomaly" or Neo. Restated, Neo is, quite literally, the personification of free will and choice brought about as a result of the 1 percent sum of all those humans in this integration of the Matrix who chose to reject the program. Neo learns from the Architect that five other "integral anomalies" have iterated before Neo, making him the sixth "One" to emerge. The Architect implies that the emergence of each "integral anomaly" ultimately brings about the complete destruction of Zion. The fact that Neo is the sixth anomaly recalls what scientists today call the Sixth Extinction, a massive self-imposed genocide of humanity resulting from an overconsumption of natural resources—a human practice Agent Smith alludes to in the first film. The Sixth Extinction, which evolutionists claim is already underway, has been preceded by five other mass extinctions that have occurred on Earth over the course of millions of years—including that of the dinosaurs.

Eventually, the Architect offers Neo a choice—he can save some minuscule vestige of Zion and all those connected to the Matrix, as his five predecessors have done, or he can try to save Trinity (Carrie-Anne Moss), the woman he loves. The choice is, the Architect admits, based on the One's programmed "attachment to the rest of [his] species"—in other words, on the One's connection to his race, the race of humanity. The Architect, in fact, expects Neo to act on this race-centric precedent, just as the five "systemic anomalies" did before him. Neo resists easy classification, however, and because he personifies free will and choice, Neo finds he is capable of making decisions independent of racial ties or bonds. He makes a choice based on individuality and an emotional connection, and this choice, a celebration of individual free will but delusional at the time, ultimately empowers Neo to face the unplugged Smith at the climax of *The Matrix Revolutions*. In that last battle, Neo, acting once again of his own free will and choice, submits to the assimilating penetration of Smith, knowing full well that his individual choice and identity, regardless of attempts to categorize racially and proscribe, homogenize, or erase, will ultimately win out over Smith's homogenizing whiteness. His self-actualization as "the One," his purpose, is complete.

This climax and its aftermath resolve *The Matrix* phenomenon's mediation of the conflicting discourses surrounding racial identity politics, for just as Neo has defied the technologies of domination that would categorize, classify, and label him, so too has the series itself challenged traditional, biological conceptions of personal identity.

Indeed, *The Matrix* phenomenon goes to great lengths to expose racial inequalities and sufferings by presenting its audience with many thought-provoking questions about the building blocks of racial formation and the way that we come to interpret those identity formations through coded representations of racial conflict. In this way, the series adheres to very traditional, biologically based ways of looking at race. But not satisfied with its own achievements, *The Matrix* series actually offers us a way forward—a set of parameters gleaned from the progressive developments within critical race theory since the 1950s that deny categorizing proscriptions and celebrate individuality.

However, the challenge of putting theory into practice remains. While *The Matrix* phenomenon should be applauded for its progressive ideologies, the general public's disappointment with the series suggests that its message may have initially fallen upon many deaf ears. As Kalpana Seshadri-Crooks states, "Unlike other forms of socially constructed difference . . . 'race,' like sex, appears as something that one inherently is from birth. Thus, despite historicist arguments about its social construction . . . there is a powerful *semblance* of necessity built into race that makes it ultimately intractable to constructionist claims" (20). As the critical evaluation of *The Matrix* phenomenon continues to grow, however, so too will its reflective impact on Western, twentieth-century, late capitalist society. The Internet launch of the multiplayer role-playing game, *The Matrix Online*, contribute to future discourses about race in the Matrix universe, particularly because the game allows players to customize racially their onscreen characters. Thoughtfully communicating ideas and feelings about race, as these films and products do, expose stereotypes and lies, while fostering good will and understanding. And if an effective entry into the discourse comes packaged as a multi-million-dollar science fiction film series, then all the better. Like *2001: A Space Odyssey*, *Blade Runner*, and the *Alien* series, *The Matrix* phenomenon has a cinematic future as a cultural masterpiece that inspires people to take a revisionist look at human existence. Indeed, that future has long since begun. If the series has a cultural impact equal or even greater to its predecessors, the efforts will have been worth the trouble. The potential for inspiring progressive thoughts—particularly thoughts about race and identity in America—is what makes *The Matrix* phenomenon truly revolutionary.

NOTES

The James Monroe epigraph is quoted in Foner.

1. One of the great ironies of life is the fact that, in order to discuss race with any degree of frankness, intelligence, or specificity, one must sometimes (as bell hooks is fond of saying) "use the master's tools." I here acknowledge my own use of traditional and biological categorizations and classifications of race for a good portion of this essay, but I stress that I use these tools in an effort to reach a higher goal: the demonstration of the ways in which *The Matrix* phenomenon encourages us to leave such proscriptions behind. I ask the reader's indulgence of this contradiction so that I might attain that higher goal.

2. See, for example, Seay and Garret. Also see Brannigan; Fontana; and Ford 159–84.

3. Throughout this essay, I use several names to identify the various states of humans within the Matrix. "Matrix human," for example, a general term, refers to humans who, consciously or not, are "jacked in" to the Matrix. I break this category down further by differentiating between "Coppertops" (the Matrix humans serving unwittingly as batteries) and "liberated" or "substantiated Matrix humans" (those Matrix humans who have been freed from the Matrix and now dwell in Zion). As I point out later in the essay, the residents of Zion also draw a distinction between "pod-borns" (those humans living in Zion who once served as mere "Coppertops" after having been conceived by the Matrix and raised in a pod) and "free-borns" (those humans born by natural processes). This process of assigning categories and names, in its own right, is consistent with the very practices the series itself seeks to undermine. For the purpose of my discussion of these issues, however, the terms prove useful.

WORKS CITED

Blade. Dir. Stephen Norrington. Perf. Wesley Snipes, Kris Kristofferson, and Stephen Dorff. New Line Cinema, 1998.

Brannigan, Michael. "There Is No Spoon: A Buddhist Mirror." The Matrix *and Philosophy: Welcome to the Desert of the Real*. Ed. William Irwin. Peru: Carus, 2002. 101–10.

Chambers, Stan. *Stan Chambers Home Page*. 5 June 1997. Civitu.com. 12 Jan. 2003 <http://www.citivu.com/ktla/sc-ch1b.html>.

Dyer, Richard. *White*. New York: Routledge, 1997.

Fish, Jeffrey M. "Mixed Blood." *Conformity and Conflict: Readings in Cultural Anthropology*. Boston: Allyn and Bacon, 2000.

Foner, Philip S. *History of Black Americans*. London: Greenwood, 1983.

Fontana, Paul. "Finding God in *The Matrix*." *Taking the Red Pill: Science, Philosophy and Religion in* The Matrix. Ed. Glenn Yeffeth. Dallas: BenBella, 2003. 159–84.

Ford, James L. "Buddhism, Mythology, and *The Matrix*." *Taking the Red Pill: Science, Philosophy and Religion in* The Matrix. Ed. Glenn Yeffeth. Dallas: BenBella, 2003. 125–44.

Foucault, Michel. *Discipline and Punish*. Trans. Alan Sheridan. New York: Vintage, 1995.

Franklin, John Hope, and Alfred A. Moss Jr. *From Slavery to Freedom: A History of Negro Americans*. 6th ed. New York: Knopf, 1988.

Freeland, Cynthia. "New Penetrations but the Same Old Shit." *The Matrix and Philosophy*. Ed. William Irwin. Chicago: Open Court, 2003.

Gabrielson, Tania, et al. "Postmodern Thinkers: Michel Foucault." *Education in the Postmodern* 12 Oct. 2003 <http://www.edb.utexas.edu/faculty/scheurich/proj6/pags/thinkers.htm>.

hooks, bell. *Yearning: Race, Gender, and Cultural Politics*. Boston: South End, 1990.

King, C. Richard, and David J. Leonard. "Is Neo White? Reading Race, Watching the Trilogy." *Jacking into the Matrix Franchise: Cultural Reception and Interpretation*. Ed. Matthew Kappel and William G. Doty. New York: Continuum, 2004.

Lacan, Jaques. "The Mirror Stage as Formative of the Function of the I as Revealed in Psychoanalytic Experience." *Ecrits: A Selection*. Trans. Alan Sheridan. New York: Norton, 1977.

Maedra, Mihiro, dir. "The Second Renaissance, Part I." *The Animatrix*. DVD (commentary). Warner Bros. Home Video, 2003.

The Matrix. Dir. Andy and Larry Wachowski. Perf. Keanu Reeves, Laurence Fishburne, Carrie-Anne Moss, and Hugo Weaving. Warner Bros., 1999.

The Matrix Reloaded. Dir. Andy and Larry Wachowski. Perf. Keanu Reeves, Laurence Fishburne, Carrie-Anne Moss, and Hugo Weaving. Warner Bros., 2003.

The Matrix Revolutions. Dir. Andy and Larry Wachowski. Perf. Keanu Reeves, Laurence Fishburne, Carrie-Anne Moss, and Hugo Weaving. Warner Bros., 2003.

Mitchell, Elvis. "An Idealized World and a Troubled Hero." Rev. of *The Matrix Reloaded*, dir. Andy and Larry Wachowski. *New York Times* 14 May 2003, late ed.: B1+.

Roth, Philip. *The Human Stain*. Boston: Houghton Mifflin, 2000.

Seay, Chris, and Greg Garret. *The Gospel Reloaded: Exploring Spirituality and Faith in* The Matrix. Colorado Springs: Piñon, 2003.

Seshadri-Crooks, Kalpana. *Desiring Whiteness: A Lacanian Analysis of Race.* London: Routledge, 2000.

Siegel, Carol. Conversation with author. 14 Jan. 2003.

Sleeper, Jim. *Liberal Racism.* New York: Putnam, 1997.

Soja, Edward. *Thirdspace: Journeys to Los Angeles and Other Real-and-Imagined Places.* Malden: Blackwell, 1996.

Strange Days. Dir. Kathryn Bigelow. Perf. Ralph Fiennes, Angela Bassett, Tom Sizemore, and Juliette Lewis. 20th Century–Fox, 1994.

Wachowski, Larry, and Andy Wachowski. "Bits and Pieces of Information." The Matrix *Comics.* Ed. Spencer Lamm. New York: Burlyman Entertainment, 2003.

Contributors

DOUGLAS A. CUNNINGHAM is a doctoral student in film studies at the University of California, Berkeley. His primary research interests are the study of race and gender in cinema, particularly representations of whiteness and masculinity. He has published articles in the *Moving Image* (U of Minnesota P), *War, Literature, and the Arts* (U.S. Air Force Academy), *Critical Survey* (Berghahn Journals), and *Screens* (Oxford UP). His dissertation centers on the history of the U.S. Army Air Forces' first Motion Picture Unit during World War II and constructions of masculinity in its training films. He was born and grew up in Salt Lake City.

KIMBERLY CHABOT DAVIS received a Ph.D. in English from the University of Virginia. She is presently assistant professor of twentieth-century U.S. literature and film at Bridgewater State College in Massachusetts. She is the author of *Postmodern Texts and Emotional Audiences* (Purdue UP, 2007) and has published essays on race in contemporary American culture in the *International Journal of Cultural Studies, LIT, South Atlantic Review, Modern Fiction Studies,* and *Twentieth Century Literature.* Her essay in this collection is drawn from a book manuscript in progress, "Beyond the White Negro: Cross-Racial Empathy, White Audiences, and Contemporary African-American Culture." Dr. Davis was born in Fall River, Massachusetts.

RENÉE D'ELIA-ZUNINO, a lecturer of Italian at the University of Tennessee, Knoxville, graduated with an M.A. in comparative literature, achieving the License of Doctor in Modern and Foreign Languages and Literatures from the University of Genova. Her first article on whiteness, "Passing for Black or Passing for White: Authenticating Middle-Class American Whiteness Through Blackness," appeared in *Reconstructing Societies in the Aftermath of War: Memory, Identity, and Reconciliation* (Bordighera, 2004). A native of the province of Genova, Italy, she moved to the United States in 1998.

DAWN DUKE completed a Ph.D. in Latin American literature at the University of Pittsburgh and is presently assistant professor of Spanish and Portuguese at the University of Tennessee, Knoxville. She previously taught at the University of Guyana. Specializing in issues of race, gender, and writing in Hispanic, Caribbean, and Brazilian literatures, she is the author of

Literary Passion, Ideological Commitment: Towards a Legacy of Afro-Cuban and Afro-Brazilian Women Writers (Bucknell, 2008). A native of Georgetown, Guyana, Dr. Duke has also lived and studied in Brazil.

BALTASAR FRA-MOLINERO completed a Ph.D. at Indiana University and is now associate professor of Spanish at Bates College in Lewiston, Maine. His research focuses on the representation of blacks and racial difference in Spain, Latin American, and Equatorial Guinea. Among his publications are *La imagen del Negro en el teatro del Siglo de Oro* (Siglo XXI, 1995) and "Juan Latino and Racial Difference," included in the volume *Black Africans in Renaissance Europe* (Cambridge UP, 2005). He is a native of Ponferrada in northern Spain.

PETER HÖYNG earned a Ph.D. from the University of Wisconsin, Madison, and is presently associate professor of German in the German Studies Department at Emory University. His areas of research are German drama and theater of the late eighteenth and twentieth centuries and German-Jewish culture from the mid-eighteenth century to the present. His publications include *The Stars, Censorship and Fatherland: History and Theater in the Late 18th Century* (Böhlau, 2003) and *Embodied Projections of History: George Tabori's Theater Work* (Francke, 1997), an edited collection of essays on the Jewish playwright. He has also published essays on Beethoven's intellectual life in Vienna. A native of Germany, Höyng has taught study abroad courses in Berlin and Vienna, emphasizing the German-Jewish cultural and literary influences on both cities.

LA VINIA DELOIS JENNINGS earned a Ph.D. at the University of North Carolina at Chapel Hill specializing in twentieth-century American literature and is presently Lindsay Young Professor of English at the University of Tennessee, Knoxville. Her books include *Toni Morrison and the Idea of Africa* (Cambridge UP, 2008) and *Alice Childress* (Macmillan, 1995), a critical introduction to the novelist and playwright. Born in Virginia, she has traveled extensively throughout North America, South America, the Caribbean, Europe, and Africa.

AMY KAMINSKY earned a Ph.D. in Spanish at Pennsylvania State University and is presently professor of women's studies and global studies at the University of Minnesota, where she is also a member of the graduate faculty in Spanish and Portuguese. Among her numerous scholarly essays, the award-winning "Gender Race Raza" (*Feminist Studies*, 1994) is her most outstanding. Her books include *Reading the Body Politic: Feminist Criticism and*

Latin American Women Writers (U of Minnesota P, 1993), *Water Lilies: An Anthology of Spanish Women Writers from the Fifteenth through the Nineteenth Century* (U of Minnesota P, 1996), *After Exile: Writing the Latin American Diaspora* (U of Minnesota P, 1999), and *Argentina: Stories for a Nation* (U of Minnesota P, 2008). Born in New York City, she has lived in Spain and Sweden and traveled in the Americas, India, and other parts of Europe.

SUZANNE LEONARD completed a Ph.D. at the University of Wisconsin, Milwaukee, and is currently assistant professor of English at Simmons College in Boston. In addition to studying unfaithful wives in contemporary American fiction and film, her research interests include twentieth- and twenty-first-century women's literature, film studies, and feminist theory. Her published work has appeared in *Women's Studies Quarterly*, *MELUS*, and in various anthologies, including *Interrogating Postfeminism: Gender and Politics of Popular Culture* (Duke UP, 2007) and *Feminism, Domesticity, and Popular Culture* (Routledge, 2008). She was born in Hartford, Connecticut.

MEREDITH MCCARROLL earned a Ph.D. from the English Department at the University of Tennessee, Knoxville, and wrote her dissertation on the topic of literary and cinematic whiteness. Her dissertation draws from cultural, literary, and critical race studies in order to interrogate moments of racial transgression, particularly those that attempt to disrupt white normativity as reflected in American film and literature of the twentieth century. She rereads written and visual texts ranging from Richard Wright's *Native Son* (1940) to Spike Lee's *Bamboozled* (2000), recognizing the mutability of white dominance that remains stable as long as the racial hierarchy remains dichotomous. Dr. McCarroll grew up outside of Asheville, North Carolina.

EMILY SATTERWHITE earned a Ph.D. from the Institute of Liberal Arts at Emory University and is presently assistant professor in the Department of Interdisciplinary Studies at Virginia Tech. She specializes in critical regionalism, Appalachian studies, and American studies. Her articles have appeared in *American Literature*, *Appalachian Journal*, and *Journal of American Folklore*. "Bestselling Appalachia: Readers and the Geographic Imagination of Race, Place, and Nation, 1873–2003," her current book project, examines fan mail in order to assess readers' investments in the idea of Appalachia. Born in Greenville, South Carolina, she grew up in Louisville, Kentucky.

Index

8 Mile (2002), 223–24, 232
50 Cent, 226, 227, 228

Abdul, Paula, 219
Adams, Eddie, xxvi, 270
Africa, 13, 21, 22, 122, 153
Africa Vive (Africa Lives), 8, 25n18
African Americans, 35–36; devices (marking, mythification, omission) used in American cinema to define, 154–55, 156, 159, 160; as a reminder of slavery in America and Europe, 154. *See also* racial passing
Africanness, xv
Africans, 2; loss of identity and collective consciousness because of slavery, 174
Afroargentinos (2005), 25n21
Albania, xxiv, 180–82, 183, 191n27, 191n30; criminal elements of, 191–92n31; racing of Albanians as inferior, 182; Sigurimi Albanian secret police, 181, 191n29. *See also Lamerica* (1998)
Albania: A Country Study (Zickel and Iwaskiew), 181
Allen, Harry, 235
Almodóvar, Pedro, xxiii, 164–65
Altman, Neil, *Analyst in the Inner City*, 176
Amelio, Gianni, xxiv, 173, 182; criticism of, 185; on estrangement, 185–86
American Anthropological Association, statement on racial grouping, xiv
"American Mixed Race: The United States 2000 Census and Related Issues" (Zack), 209–10
"Americanness," 93
Analyst in the Inner City (Altman), 176
Anderson, Benedict, 203
Andreotti, Giulio, 181
Andreotti-Bufi Agreement (1991), 181, 191n30

Andrews, George Reid, 10, 11
Anglos, xvii
Animatrix, The, xxvi, 256, 274; codes that perpetuate racial conflict in, 270–71; "The Second Renaissance, Part I" episode of, 268, 269, 270; story of B1-66ER in, 269; "World Record" episode of, 275
anti-Semitism, 14, 39–40, 57n30; in Austria, xx–xxii, 29–30, 30–34, 40, 52; in Italy, 188n9
Anzaldúa, Gloria, 211; *Borderlands/La Frontera*, 199
Aponte-Ramos, Dolores, 15
Appalachia, xxi–xxii; as a bastion of racially "pure" white Americans, 93–94; Celtic, Scottish, and Scots-Irish ancestry of Appalachians, 97, 98, 110; class and social disparity in, 95–96; distinctiveness of mountain people in, 94–95; ethnic revivalism in, 97–98; ethnicized vision of, 109–11; fiction concerning, 103, 109–11, 96, 112–13n9, 114–15n23; Gothic depictions of, 96; as "home" and the "real America," 97; mountain residents of as "barbarians," 95; perception of as dangerous, 98–99; post-1990 novels concerning, 96–97; revival of interest in Appalachian heritage (white ethnic revivalism), 97–98, 110; as victimized, 110
Apuntes sobre poesía popular y poesía negra en las Antillas (Franco), 76
Aranda, Vicente, 151–52
Argentina, xix–xx, 23–24n3, 26n25; abolition of slavery in, 11, 14; Argentine elites' rejection of the other, 20–21; Blackness in, 4, 8, 11, 14–15; color line in, 6–8, 10–14; Conquest of the Desert campaign in, 11, 17; conscription of

Argentina (cont.)
black slaves in, 11; cultural codes of
Whiteness in, 7; dispute concerning
"authentic" Argentina, 11–12; dissem-
ination of family portraits from to
Central America, 2–3; Federalists
and Unitarians in, 11–12; immigration
policy of, 10; lack of black Argentine
literary voices, 7–8; marginalization of
indigenous peoples in, 12–13, 19, 25n22;
mestizo identity of, 24–25n14; pavilion of at the 1900 Paris international
exposition, 20; racial anxiety in, 21;
racial system of, 4; racial taxonomy in,
2; racism in, 12, 24–25n14; relationship
between Argentina and Africa, 22;
removal of Blacks from census reports
in, 10; slavery in, 8; use of Black troops
to kill indigenous peoples in, 10–11;
visible markers of Whiteness in, 7; as
a White country, 22–23; Whiteness in,
1–2, 4, 6, 7–8
Argentina (Bona), 22–23
Argentina: Stories for a Nation
(Kaminsky), 26n25
Argentina White, 1–2, 14; Europe and
the making of, 19–23
Arias, Aurora, 83
Armendáriz, Montxo, xxiii, 154, 155
Aryans, xvi
Asians, xvii, 2
Association of Multiethnic Americans
(AMEA), 205
Asultany, Evelyn, 217, 218
At Home in Mitford (Karon), 96
Australia, 179
Austria, 58n34; anti-Semitism in, 30–34;
ethnic groups within, 30–31; First
Republic of, 29; post–World War I,
30; racism in, 29–30, 46. *See also* anti-
Semitism, in Austria; Vienna
Austria-Hungary dual monarchy, 30, 33;
ethnicities within, 30–31
Austrian-Hungarian Empire, 30, 40, 44

Bacher, Eduard, 55n9
Back, Les, 222, 244
"Bad Faith and Antiblack Racism"
(Gordon), 119
Badawi (Sheik Badawi), xv
Balaguer, Joaquín, 64
Balderson, Daniel, 25n22
Batista, Celsa Albert, 89n11; on
Dominicans as a mulatto race, 83;
Mujer y esclavitud en Santo Domingo,
83
Beastie Boys, 221
Benedikt, Moriz, 55n9
Benegas, Noni, 25n16
Bentham, Jeremy, 260
Bernal, Martin, xvi; *Black Athena:
The Afroasiatic Roots of Classical
Civilization,* xvi
Berry, Halle, 219
Bettauer, Hugo, xx, 29–30, 34; attempts
to redefine whiteness, 53–54; *Blaue
Mal, Das* (*The Blue Stain*), xx, xxi,
29–30, 34, 46–54; conversion of to
Christianity, 39, 53; desire and failure
of to become an "invisible" Jew, 38–41;
expulsion of from Berlin, 39; frankness
of concerning sexuality, 40, 41; murder
of, 39, 40, 56n24, 57n30; in New York,
39, 56n20; popularization of Freud
by, 40; publishing career of, 39–40,
56n22; racism of, xx, 29, 30, 47; reifying
of white values in his novels, 53; *Die
Stadt ohne Juden: Ein Roman von
Übermorgen* (*The City without Jews: A
Novel of Our Time*), xx, xxi, 29–30, 34,
41–46, 56–57n26, 57n30;support of for
gay rights and legalized abortion, 40;
whiteness as visible and invisible force
in his novels, 52–53
*Bettauers Wochenschrift: Probleme des
Lebens* (*Bettauer's Weekly: Problems of
Life*), 39–40, 56n22
"Beyond Neorealism: Preserving
a Cinema of Social Conscience"
(Crowdus and Porton), 184

Bhabha, Homi, 73

¡Bienvenido, Mr. Marshall! (1952), 150

Big Stone Gap (Trigiani), 96

biological race, and national identification, 13

Birds, The (1963), 271

Black Athena: The Afroasiatic Roots of Classical Civilization (Bernal), xvi

Black Atlantic, The (Gilroy), 199

black culture, white appropriation of, 221–22

Black No More (Schuyler), 201

blackface minstrelsy, 235, 241, 244

blackness, xiv–xv, xxi, xxiv, 4, 10, 64–66, 82, 84, 216; acceptance of, 49–50, 53; and black femaleness, 67; connection of to subhumanness, xiv; decentering of, xxv; denial/erasure of by postcolonized and postenslaved peoples, xv–xvi, xx; escaping from, 218, 219; fantasies of, 221, 227; hidden blackness, 120; romanticization of, 242; white blackness, 119, 131; white identification with, 222, 225

Blade (1998), 276; "Daywalker" in, 276

Blaue Mal, Das (The Blue Stain [Bettauer]), xx, xxi, 29–30, 34, 46–54; acceptance of Carletto by blacks in, 49–50; as a Bildungsroman, 46–47; Carletto as the "other," 50; "Carletto" section of, 46, 47–48; "The Colored Gentleman" section of, 45; "Georgia" section of, 46, 47; Karola Sampson in, 47, 51; New York City as a mythical space in, 48; projection of racism outside of Europe in, 50–51; racial categorization of Carletto in, 49, 50; racism of Wilcox in, 50–51; reduction (whitewashing) of Carletto's "blackness" in, 51–52; Rudolf Zeller in, 47, 51; theme of accepting blackness in, 46, 49–50

Bollaín, Incíar, xxiii, 154, 159

Bona, Dominique, 22; Argentina, 22–23

Boorman, John, 96

Borderlands/La Frontera (Anzaldúa), 199

Borghezio, Mario, 179

Bosnia, racial cleansing in, xxvi, 270

Bossi, Umberto, 176, 189n12

Brainin, Neumark, 56n20, 57n30, 58n33

Bratt, Benjamin, 219

Bravmann, Paul, 241–42

Brazil, 10, 62, 77

Breslauer, Hans Karl, 43

Bridge and Tunnel (S. Jones), 233

Brontë, Charlotte, 129

Brown, Jonathan, 10, 11

Budapest, 32

Buenos Aires, 8, 21; reasons for decline in the black population of, 8, 10, 25n19

Bultman, Britney, 97; Redneck Heaven, 97

Buñuel, Luis, 164

Bush, Barbara, 73

Butler, Judith, Gender Trouble, 202

Bwana (Lord [1996]), 154; colonial role reversal in the naming of Bwana in, 157; as an exercise in white guilt, 156; gendered discourse of whiteness in, 158; internalized sexual frustration in, 159; intimidation of the family patriarch by skinheads in, 157; language as a factor of characterization in, 156–57; loss of patriarchal privilege in, 158; role of the Bubi language in, 157; skinheads in, 157, 158, 159; whiteness as violent religion in, 159

Camarca, Claudio, 179; Migranti, 181

capitalism, 95; industrial capitalism, 100

Carey, Mariah, 219

Carmen (Gautier and Mérimée), 149

Carmen (1983), 151, 166n4

Carmen (2003), 151–52; Basque origin and devout Catholicism of Don José in, 152; Carmen as a "witch" in, 152; flamenco music in, 152; possession of whiteness by Don José in, 152

Cartas de Alou, Las (Alou's Letters [1990]), 154, 167n11; Alou as one of the three Magi, 156; narration of the variety of immigrant experiences in, Cartas de

Alou (cont.)
155–56; racist policies of the state in, 155; sympathy with the black African protagonist of, 155

Casa por la Identidad de la Mujer Afro (Center for Afro-Women's Identity), 89n11

casta paintings (family portraits), 2–4, 24n7, 24n10; depiction of children in, 24n11; depiction of flora in, 3; depiction of the "gente blanca" in, 5; gendering of, 5–6; origins of, 3; Peruvian, 3, 5; racial significance of the captions accompanying, 4–5; stability of gender in, 5

casta racial system, 2, 3, 23n5; whiteness within, 4. *See also* family portraits (casta paintings)

Ceballos, Diego, 25n16

Centro Cultural Eduardo León Jiménez (León Museum), 78–79

Cervantes, Miguel de, 164; *Don Quijote*, 161

Chambers, Stan, 266

Chávez, Fermín, 15

Chile, 25n15

Christendom, xxiii, 163

Christianity, xxvii, 62, 147, 148, 163, 172, 186; Christian hegemony, 188n7; hierarchy of spiritual qualities within, 35; Pentecostal Christianity among Gypsies, 151; and whiteness, 172, 187n1

Chronicles of Riddick, The (2004), 197

Chuck D, 226

cinema: "marking" of blacks in, 154–55; "mythification" of blacks in, 154, 156; "omission" of blacks in, 154, 159

Clay's Quilt (House), 94, 96, 103, 106–9; ethnic variations on whiteness in, 108–9; images of whiteness in, 106–8; nostalgic representation of Appalachia in, 106; threats to whiteness in, 108; visual whiteness of the characters in, 108

Clinton, William Jefferson, xi–xii

Cobb, William, 232

Cold Mountain (Frazier), 94, 96, 103–6; Appalachian justice/egalitarianism contrasted to northern imperialism in, 104; common Appalachian tropes in, 103–4; commercial success of, 103; contrast of white characters to Indians in, 105; distinctions marking mountain characters' whiteness in, 105–6; ethnic difference of white characters in, 103; portrayal of Charleston's citizens relationship to "outsiders," 105; portrayal of Cold Mountain's citizens as racially innocent, 104–4; purported cause of the Civil War in, 104

Colombia, 62

Colon, Gene, 276

colonialism, xix, 13, 55n8, 62, 121, 141n8, 142n16, 174; gender roles under, 141n5; organizational system of, 141n3; parallels with patriarchy, 140n2; and the reproduction of whiteness, 139–40

Conquest of the Desert, 11, 17

Cornell, Stephen, *Ethnicity and Race: Making Identities in a Changing World*, 199–200

Cosmic Race, The (Vasconcelos), 24–25n14

Creed, Barbara, 272

Creoles, 4

Crisis, 49, 58n38

Crossing the Line: Racial Passing in Twentieth-Century U.S. Literature and Culture (Wald), 202

Crowdus, Gray, 184

Cuba, 77

Culler, Jonathan, 203

cultural assimilation, "whitewashing" effects of, xxvi

cultural identity, 112

Cunningham, Douglas A., xxv

Curiel, Ochy, 89n11

"Cyborg Manifesto, The" (Haraway), 199

Dalí, Salvador, 164

Daniel, G. Reginald, 217

Davis, Kimberly Chabot, xxv
"defensive xenophobia," 178–79
Délia-Zunino, Renée, xxiv
Deliverance (1972), 96
Derby, Lauren, 64, 65
Diaz, Cameron, 219
Díaz, Fermín del Pino, 3
Dickey, James, 96
Diesel, Vin, xxv, 197, 218, 219; casting of
    to play "ethnically indeterminate" char-
    acters, 214; films of, 214; multiracial
    identity of, 214–16
DiPiero, Tom, 272
*Dirt and Desire: Southern Women's
    Writing, 1930–1990* (Yaeger), 107
Discipline and Punish (Foucault), 259–60
Dominican Republic, xv–xvi, 61, 62;
    abhorrence of the term "black" in, 65;
    anti-Haitianism in, 65–66, 80, 86–87;
    contact of with North American cul-
    ture, 79–80; "Dominican identity," 70;
    Dominican whiteness, 63, 70, 77–82;
    Dominicans as a miscegenated race,
    66, 67; fabrication of a white social
    identity in, 63; Haitian occupation
    of (1822–44), 64–65, 77, 86; lack of
    black activism in, 77; mass marketing
    of female ceramic dolls to tourists,
    88; Negrophobia in, 70; persecution
    of Haitians in, 86; poetic movements
    in, 64, 89n3; preference for "white"
    or "indio" racial designations in, 63,
    77, 79, 80, 81, 83; racial identity in,
    63, 66, 77, 80–81, 83, 84; racism in, 61;
    rejection of Negritude as a paradigm
    for its national existence, 62, 80–81;
    "white" Dominicans, xvi; women of
    Haitian descent in, 87–88. *See also*
    whiteness, Dominican
"dominicanidad," 70
Dominicanness, 82, 86
Don Quijote (Cervantes), 161
Dr. Dre, 223, 226, 227
Dred Scott v. John F. Sandford (1857), xxvi,
    269

Du Bois, W. E. B., 49; on "double-
    consciousness," 150; on the "problem of
    the color-line," xii, 6
Duke, David, 212–13
Duke, Dawn, xxi
Dyer, Richard, xii, xxii, 52, 55n11, 148,
    188nn3–4; on the projection of
    sexuality to dark races, 37; on racial
    concepts of the body, xiii; on seeing
    "whiteness," 34–35; on white women's
    threat to the colonial mission, 120–21;
    on whiteness and Christianity, 172,
    187n1; on whiteness as emptiness, 272;
    on whiteness as invisible, 210

East Africa, xv
Eastern Europe, ethnic revivalism in, 97
Economic Recovery Program (ERP
    [Marshall Plan]), 150, 166n2
Ecuador, 153
Egypt, xvi
El Ejido (Spain), attack on immigrants
    in, 161
Eminem (a.k.a. Marshall Mathers), xxv,
    222–32, 233, 242, 246, 249; black pro-
    tégés of, 226; on censorship, 229–30,
    231–32; collaboration of with black
    artists, 226–27; colorblind ideology of,
    230–32; compared to Elvis Presley,
    225–26; complicity with white privilege,
    230; denunciation of whiteness and the
    white elite, 228–29; street credibility
    of, 224, 225
Enlightenment, the, 3
Enriquillo (Galván), 63
Enter the Matrix (video game), xxvi, 256,
    257, 273
*Er und Sie: Wochenschrift für Lebenskultur
    und Erotik (He and She: A Weekly for
    Life-Style and Eroticism)*, 39–40, 56n22
"español," as a racial category, 4
ethnicity, 112n3, 205, 206, 029, 211; defini-
    tion of, 199–200; ethnicity-based con-
    structs of race, 97; ethnicity-based
    racial distinctions, 86

Ethnicity and Race: Making Identities in a Changing World (Cornell and Hartman), 199–200

ethnics (Southern and Eastern European), xvii, 2, 14

eugenics/eugenicists, xii, 136, 142n17, 258, 268

Eurocentrism, 66

Europe, 14, 26n30; and the making of Argentine white, 19–23; Northern Europeans, xi, xii; post–World War I, xx, 29–30, 32, 34, 38, 150; projection of its racial anxieties onto Argentina, 21; white anxiety in European literary texts, 21–22. *See also* Eastern Europe, ethnic revivalism in

Everything But the Burden: What White People Are Taking from Black Culture (Tate), 222

expansionism (U.S.), xvii

extradiegetic markers, 154, 167n10

family portraits. *See* casta paintings (family portraits)

Fauset, Jessie, *Plum Bun*, 201, 202

Ferrusola, Marta, 153

Fish, Jeffrey, 257; on race as a myth, 258–59

flamenco, 150, 152

Fletcher, Arthur, 206

Flight (W. White), 201

Flores de otro mundo (*Flowers from Another World* [1999]), 154, 159–61; beating of Black Cuban Milady in, 160; economic subjugation of Patricia in, 160–61; gendering of immigration as female in, 159–60; omitted narrative of, 159; Patricia in, 159–60; theory of omission in, 159; as a "veridic documentary" of women immigrants in Spain, 159; white territorialization of Almería and Castile in, 159

Foley, Jack, 217

Fortes, Jorge, 25n16

Foucault, Michel, 256, 262, 277; *Discipline and Punish*, 259–60; on the "technologies of domination," 264; theories of governmentality, 257

Fox, John Jr., 94, 98, 113nn16–17, 114n20; as a correspondent for *Harper's Weekly* during the Spanish-American War, 102; linkage of Cuba with Appalachia, 102; *The Little Shepherd of Kingdom Come*, 104; opinion of mountaineers, 99–100; *Trail of the Lonesome Pine*, 94, 99–102; relocation to Big Stone Gap, 99; white imperialist worldview of, 114n21

Fra-Molinero, Baltasar, xxiii

Franco, Francisco, xxiii, 148; exploitation of Gypsy Spain for tourism purposes, 149–50

Franco, Tomás Hernández, xxii, 61, 66, 75, 87–88; allegiance of to Trujillo, 64, 89n5; *Apuntes sobre poesía popular y poesía negra en las Antillas*, 76; persecution of homosexuals by, 167n17

Frankenberg, Ruth, 231, 245, 246

Franz Joseph I, 30, 31

Frazier, Charles, 94; *Cold Mountain*, 94, 103–6

Freeland, Cynthia, 274

Freud, Sigmund, 39; popularization of, 40

Frost, William Goodell, 93, 95, 99, 112n

fundamentalism, 163

Gabrielson, Tania, 277–78

Galicia, 32, 44, 54n2

Galván, Manuel de Jesús, *Enriquillo*, 63

Gardner, Ava, 158

Garon, Paul, 227, 231

Garvey, John, 222, 238, 251n14

Garvey, Marcus, 201

Gates, Henry Louis, Jr., xv

Gates, William H., Sr., 112n6

Gaucho Martín Fierro, El (*The Gaucho Martín Fierro* [Hernández]), xx, 15; Cruz in, 18, 19; as a discourse of othering, 18; Fierro's designation of his brother as "Moreno" (dark), 18; Fierro's insulting of a black woman in, 15–16; Fierro's killing of a black man in, 16–18; foundational myth of the gaucho in, 19; rejection of "civilized" society in, 18; representation of Indians in, 18–19

gauchos, 11, 12, 14–15, 17, 18, 19, 26n26, 26n28

Gautier, Théophile, *Carmen*, 149

gay marriage, 163–64

gender, xiv, 12, 24n12, 66, 112n3, 124, 149, 162; gender identification, 119; gender roles, 164, 202; gender roles under colonialism, 141n5; gender studies, 55n11; performativity of, 202; and racial ideology, 5. *See also* casta paintings (family portraits), gendering of

Gender Trouble (Butler), 202

genetics, human, xii, xiii, xvii

genocide, xx, 279

Gentilini, Giancarlo, 179–80, 190–91n26

George, Nelson, 221

German-Austria, 31, 33

Germany, 13; culture of, 33; racism in, 55n11. *See also* Nazis/Nazism

Gershwin, George, 221

Gesunde Juden—Kranke Schwarze (Hödl), 55n15

Gilded Age, 95, 112n6. *See also* neo-Gilded Age

Gilman, Sander L., 35, 37, 38, 73; on Eastern and Western Jews, 54n5

Gilroy, Paul, 80; *The Black Atlantic*, 199

Giroux, Henry A., 223, 231, 238; model of oppositional whiteness, 248–49; on the "new abolitionists," 245

Giustiniani, Corrado, 177

Gobineau, Arthur de, xii; *The Inequality of the Human Races*, xii, xiii

God, xiv

Goldstein, Richard, 247

Gordon, Lewis, 119

"governmentality," 257, 277–78

Goytisolo, Juan, 153, 161, 167n13

Grant, Madison, xii, xxviin2

Grass Is Singing, The (Lessing), xxii, 121, 122–29, 139, 141n9; assertion of white masculinity in, 125; Charlie Slatter's "law" in, 126; conflicting roles of Mary in, 124; criticism of, 128–29; destabilization of white privilege in, 128; Dick in, 122, 123; Gothic elements in, 141n4; idealized notions of femininity and masculinity in, 126; as indictment of colonial racism in Africa, 122; maintenance of white racial superiority by women in, 123–24; Mary's mental and physical breakdown in, 122–23, 127; Mary's sexual obsession with Moses in, 126–27; mistreatment of black laborers by Mary in, 124; Moses in, 124; murder of Mary in, 127–28; racial identity of Mary in, 124, 131; sexual paranoia of Mary in, 125; shifting self-designation of Turner in, 124; whiteness as a category in, 122, 123

Great Chain of Being, xiv, xv

Greece, xvi

"group-based" difference, 93, 112n1

Gubar, Susan, 222, 223; *Racechanges*, 251n16; on transraciality, 249

Gutiérrez, Chus, 161

Gypsies, xxiii, 31; Andalusian Gypsies, 151; appropriation of Gypsy culture in post-Franco Spain, 150; exploitation of for the Spanish tourism industry, 149–50; exploration of Gypsy culture by French writers, 166n1; films of, 166nn3–4; "Gitano" Gypsy as an insult, 151; growth of Pentecostal Christianity among, 151; identity of, 149, 150

Habsburg Monarchy, 30; dissolution of, 31

Haiti: occupation of the Dominican Republic by Haiti (1822–44), 64–65, 77, 86; status of Haitians in the Dominican Republic, 65

Haitian Revolution (1791–1804), 77

Haitianness, xxi, 76–77, 82; demonization of by Dominicans, 65, 70, 76–77, 86

Hall, Stuart, 199, 203, 245

Hanley, Lynee, 127

Haraway, Donna, "The Cyborg Manifesto," 199

Harlem Renaissance, 201

Harris, Cheryl, 6

Harris, Trudier, 141n7

Hartman, Douglas, *Ethnicity and Race: Making Identities in a Changing World*, 199–200

Heat and Dust (Jhabvala), xxii, 121, 133–39, 140; biological reproduction as serving the goals of patriarchy in, 137–38; colonial context of the "white wife" in, 133–34; consequences of Olivia's choice to abort her child in, 138; Douglas's dismissive treatment of Olivia in, 135; ideology of whiteness and the organization of marital behavior in, 139; Major Minnies's assertions of masculine concern for India in, 138; Olivia's desire for children as a recommitment to whiteness in, 136–37; Olivia's fatigue/boredom with the imperial atmosphere surrounding her in, 134–35; paradoxical position of white women in, 138–39; question of Olivia's child's paternity/race in, 137–38; relationship of Olivia and the Nawab in, 135–36; romantic fictions comprising the marriage of Olivia and Douglas in, 134

"Hermandad del Espíritu Santo de los Congos de Villa Mella, La" ("Brotherhood of the Holy Spirit, the Congos of Villa Mella"), 78

Hernández, José, xx, 15; *El Gaucho Martín Fierro* (*The Gaucho Martín Fierro*), xx, 15–19

Herzl, Theodore, 33, 34, 39, 54–55n7; *Der Judenstaat* (*The Jewish State*), 33, 34; move of to Zionism, 38, 55nn8–10; "Neue Nasen" ("New Noses"), 36–37, 56n17

hip-hop: commercialization of, 242–43; hip-hop culture as a unifying force, 234; hip-hop masculinity, 237; as socialist activism, 233; themes and ethos of, 231, 232

Hip Hop Theater Festival, 223, 233

Hispanic-Caribbean negrismo movement, 69

Hispanidad, 2, 65, 70; ideology of, 79

Hispaniola, 61

Hitchcock, Alfred, 271

Hitler, Adolf, xi, 43

Hoch, Danny, xxv, 222–23, 233–49, 251n12; and the abolition of whiteness, 244–45; anti-essentialist perspective of, 234, 236–37, 242, 245; casting of in *Seinfeld* episode, 244; complicity with white privilege, 246–47; criticism of, 245; cultural identity of, 234–36; and the ethic of transraciality, 249; exposure of white racism in his monologues, 240–42; founding of the Active Element Foundation, 251n15; in Hollywood, 244; *Jails, Hospitals, & Hip-Hop*, 233, 235–36, 240, 241–43, 246; opinion of ethnicity as culture-based, xxv, 235; opinion of liberal Jewish hypocrisy, 239–40; opinion of whiteness, 237–39; *Some People*, 233, 234, 237, 238–39, 240, 243; *Taking Over*, 233; *Whiteboyz*, 241–42, 244; work of with prisoners, 243

Hödl, Klaus, 35–36, 37; *Gesunde Juden— Kranke Schwarze*, 55n15

Holliday, George, 265, 266

Holocaust. See Shoah

hooks, bell, 173, 188n5, 222, 281n1; on "homeplace," 273

House, Silas, 94; *Clay's Quilt*, 94, 96, 103

Hoxka, Enver, 183

Höyng, Peter, xx–xxi

Hughes, Langston, 198; "The Negro Artist and the Racial Mountain," 198

Human Stain, The (Roth), 255, 275

humanity, 158, 171, 255, 267, 277; common humanity, xi, xvii, xxvi, 271; "standards" of, 34

Hurst, Fannie, *Imitation of Life*, 6, 201, 203

"hypo-descent" theory, 276

iconography, Medieval, 35

"If I Had" (Eminem), 224

Ignatiev, Noel, 222, 232, 249, 251n14

"imagined community," 203

Imitation of Life (Hurst), 6, 201, 203

Imitation of Life (1934), 201

Imitation of Life (1953), 201

immigration, 103, 113n10, 149;
anxiety concerning, xxii, 95, 103;
European, 1, 10, 11–12; gendering
of, 159; geographical distribution of
immigrants in Spain, 153, 166n6; in
Italy, 176–77, 182, 185, 190n20; Jewish,
32; Latin American and African, 149;
Spanish immigration issues addressed
in film, 153–54

imperialism, 55n8, 173, 186; British, xvii;
European, xix. *See also* United States,
imperialism of

India, xix; feminization of, 142n16

Indianness, 65

"Indigenous Movement" ("movimiento
indigenista"), 65

industrialization, 98–99

Inequality of the Human Races, The
(Gobineau), xii, xiii

Ingram, Penelope, 62

International Exhibition (1900 [Paris]),
xx, 20, 26n30

*Interracialism: Black-White Intermarriage
in American History, Literature and
Law* (Sollors), 120

Irish, the, xvii; Scots-Irish ancestry in
Appalachia, 97, 98, 110

Irving, Washington, *Tales of the
Alhambra*, 149

Italy, xxiv, 188n8; Albanian refugee
issue in, 180–82, 191n27; "binary
consciousness" of Italians, 173;
changing attitude toward race in,
175; constructions of whiteness
in, 186–87; correlation of racism
to immigration in, 176–77; as a
country of disenfranchised societies,
176, 190n19; emigration from, 176;
fascism in, 174–175, 188n9; foreign
population of, 188n6; the foreigner
("extra-comunitario") as scapegoat
in, 177; identification of with sexual
liberty, 190n24; immigration to, 173,
174, 177, 179; intolerance of foreigners
in, 179–80; Italians as "non visibly
Negroes," 179; multicultural society of,

177, 189n17; "new racism" and identity
crisis in, 177–82; Northern League
party of, 179, 189n12; "otherness" in the
Italian imagination, 177; paradoxes
within, 174–77; possible extinction
of nonimmigrant Italians, 177–78,
190n20; racism in, 174–75, 189n17;
unification of as a nation, 175–76

"Italian-ness," 173

Iwaskiew, Walter, 181

Jacobson, Matthew Frye, *Whiteness of a
Different Color*, 63

Jacoby, Tamar, 205

Jackson, Shannon, 245; "White Noises,"
245–46

Jagger, Mick, 221

Jails, Hospitals, & Hip-Hop (Hoch), 233,
235–36, 240, 241–43, 246

Jamaica, xix

Jews, xvii, 2, 31, 151, 189n17, 239–40;
association of with Blackness, 35;
conceptions of the Jewish nose
in caricatures and anti-Semitic
discourse, 36–37; Eastern European
Jews (Ostjuden), 14, 32, 35–36, 37,
44; Galician, 44–45; gentrifying of,
32; the "invisible Jew," 38; negative
stereotyping of the Eastern European
Jewish body, 36–37; Orthodox, xx–xxi,
37, 38; perception of as "dark" and
"feminine," 35–36; pogroms of, 51;
Western, 37; as "white negroes," 35.
See also Vienna

Jhabvala, Ruth Prawer, *Heat and Dust*,
xxii, 121, 133–39, 140

Jiménez, Blas R., 78, 81

Johnson, Anthony, xxvii–xxviiin3

Jones, Lisa, 218

Jones, Sarah, 233

Joplin, Janis, 221

Judenstaat, Der (*The Jewish State*
[Herzl]), 33, 34

Kadaré, Ismail, 185

Kaminsky, Amy, xix–xx; *Argentina:
Stories for a Nation*, 26n25

Kant, Immanuel, 171
Karon, Jan, *At Home in Mitford*, 96
Katzew, Ilona, 7, 24n6
Kazan, Elia, 6, 201
Kennedy, Brent, 113–14n18
Kenya, xv
Kid Rock, 225
King, David J., 257
King, Jeanette, 126
King, Rodney, xxvi, 96, 265–66
Kingsolver, Barbara, *Prodigal Summer*, 96
Kintz, Linda, 172
Kolchin, Peter, 63
Kraus, Karl, 56n21
Kravitz, Lenny, 206
Kwan, San San, 217

Labanyi, Jo, 161
Lacan, Jacques, 261
Lamadrid, María Eugenia, 8
Lamerica (1998), xxiv, 173, 182, 183–87;
    Albanians' view of Italy in, 183; Gino's
    loss of identity in, 184; message of social
    displacement in, 183; plot of, 183–84;
    racism of Fiore in, 184; transformation
    of Fiore in, 184–85
L' America, 183
Lamu, xv, xvi
Lander, Eric, xii
Lang, Fritz, xxvi, 270
Larsen, Nella, *Passing*, 201, 202–3
Latin America, 153; colonial period in, 2;
    political exiles of, 165; racial categories
    in, 7, 24–25n14
Latins, xvii
Lawrence, Cecile Ann, 213
Leonard, C. Richard, 257
Leonard, Suzanne, xxii–xxiii
Lessing, Doris, xxii; *The Grass Is Singing*,
    121, 122–29, 139
Lewis, Marvin, 8
Limerick, Patricia, 115n31
Listín Diario, 78
Little Buddha (1993), 277
Little Shepherd of Kingdom Come, The
    (Fox), 104

Llamazares, Julio, 159
local–color literary movement, 94,
    114–15n23
Lorca, Federico García, 149, 165
Los Angeles Police Department, 265–66;
    acquittal of officers involved in the
    Rodney King beating, 267
Lost Boundaries (1949), 201
Lott, Eric, 227
Lueger, Karl, 54–55n7, 57n28, 57n30
Lugones, Leopoldo, 26n26
lynching, 200

Maeder, Mihiro, 270
Mahler, Gustav, 56n21
Mailer, Norman, xxv, 221, 223, 224, 227,
    236
Manion, Eileen, 14n5
Mariotti, Jay, 213
Marshall, George Catlett, 166n2
Martini, Emanuela, 185
masculinity, 102, 141n5, 272; black, 221;
    darkness as a sign of, 237; heterosexist,
    165; hip-hop, 237; idealized, 126;
    idolization of, 36; violent, 227–28
Matos, Lucretia Pérez, 159
Matrix, The (1999), xxv–xxvi, 255–59, 280,
    281n1; Agent Smith in, 255–56, 258,
    263, 264, 279; Agent Smith's soliloquy
    on humans as a "virus," in, 267–68;
    assimilation threats portrayed in, 257,
    271; beating of Morpheus in, 265–66;
    codes that perpetuate racial conflict in,
    256–57, 263–71; "Coppertops" in, 274,
    281n3; "Coppertops" and racial passing
    in, 275; critical response to, 257–58, 280;
    cultural impact of, 280–81; foreground-
    ing of whiteness in, 256; historical
    figures (Malcolm X and Martin Luther
    King, Jr.) in, 264–65; Morpheus in,
    255, 258, 261, 262–63, 264; Neo in,
    257, 261, 264, 278; the Oracle in, 258,
    262, 264; a Panopticon as a model
    for analyzing *The Matrix*, 260–61,
    262–63; penetrations of Neo in, 274;
    "pod-borns" and "free-borns" in, 274,

275; racial identity in, 275, 278, 279;
racial makeup of Neo in, 276–77;
"residual" racial identity in, 261–63,
274–76; sympathy of the audience for
Morpheus, 265; two realities represented in, 262–63; view of race presented in, 259; whiteness as inherent
to the world of the Matrix in, 264
Matrix, The (comic books), xxvi, 256;
"Bits and Pieces of Information" story
in, 268, 269; Clarence Drummond's
ridicule of the *Dred Scott* decision in,
269–70; Million Machine March in,
270; story of Bi-66ER in, 269
Matrix Online, The, 280
Matrix Reloaded, The (2003), 256,
257, 264, 268, 273, 278; birds as
representative of mass psychology in,
271; confrontation of Neo and Agent
Smith in, 271–73; confrontation
of Neo and the Architect in, 278;
"systemic anomaly" of Neo in, 278–79
Matrix Revolutions, The (2003), 256,
259, 264, 268, 274, 278; assimilation
of whiteness in, 273; final battle of
Neo and Agent Smith in, 279–80;
Keymaker in, 273; Neo's choice
between saving Zion or Trinity in,
279; the Oracle in, 273
Matteo, Sante, 174
McCarroll, Meredith, xxiv–xxv
McIntosh, Peggy, 210
McWhitney, Grady, 97–98; *Cracker
Culture,* 98
Meisel, Seth, 10, 11
melanin, xiii–xiv, xv
Melnick, Jeffrey, 249
Melungeons, 100, 113–14n18
Mendez, Denny, 175
Mercer, Kobena, 249
Mérimée, Prosper, *Carmen,* 149, 151
"mestizaje" (racial mixing), 7, 24–25n14
mestizo, 19, 21, 80; Argentina as a mestizo
country, 22, 23, 24–25n14; mestizo
culture, 23
Metropolis, xxvi, 270

Mexico, 7
Migranti (Camarca), 181
Million Man March, xxvi, 268, 270
*Mirrors of the Heart: Race and Identity
(Bolivia, Haiti, the Dominican Republic)*
(1993), 79, 80, 81–82
miscegenation, xxii–xxiii, 62, 64, 119,
74, 76, 119, 127; and Caribbean racial
identity, 69; regulations outlawing, 120
misogyny, 227–28
Mitchell, Elvis, 257–58, 277
modernism, xxiii, 40, 25n56
Mogambo (1953), 158
Molina, Rafael L. Trujillo, 64, 65, 77;
execution of Haitian soldiers by, 65,
86; "hispanidad" ideology of, 65, 67;
transformation of race relations under,
65–66
Monroe, James, 255
Morocco, 153
Morrison, Toni: on white writers, 141n10;
on whiteness, 107
Mota, Mercedes, 83
Movimiento de Mujeres Dominico-
Haitianas (Movement for Dominican-
Haitian Women [MUDHA]), xxii,
61, 84–88, 89n11, 90n15; creation of, 85;
mission statement of, 85–86; work of
among bateyes, 85
Muhammad, xv
Mujer y esclavitud en Santo Domingo
(Batista), 83
mulatto, 5, 24n9; Dominicans as, 65, 81,
83; "requinterona de mulato," 24n9
mulattoness, 65, 70
multiculturalism, xiv, 217; "colors of
Benetton" multiculturalism, 111; in Italy,
177, 189n17; multiculturalism "lite," 103
multiracial identity, xxv, 197–99, 205–6,
209–11; challenge of to white privilege,
213–14, 217; claiming multiraciality,
198, 217–19; as a mark of shame, 217;
ostracizing of multiracial persons,
217–18
Muñoz, Julián Fernández, 64
Murfree, Mary Noailles, 98, 101

Museo del Hombre Dominicano, 78
Muslims, 163, 189n17
Mussolini, Benito, 188n9

Najmi, Samina, 121–22
National Asian Pacific American Legal Consortium, 206
National Association for the Advancement of Colored People (NAACP), 49, 205, 206
nationalism, xxi, 98, 112–13n9; American, xxii; Basque, 153; black, 201; as a component of Fascism, 188n9; selective, 110
Native Son (Wright), xxvi, 269
nativism, 103
Natural Born Killers (1994), 266
Nazis/Nazism, xvii, 34, 42, 43
Negrismo literary movement, 76
Negritude, 76; regional consciousness of, 69; rejection of, 62
"Negro Artist and the Racial Mountain, The" (Hughes), 198
neo-Gilded Age, 95, 96, 112n6; folk-life festivals of, 97
Neue Freie Presse, Die (The New Free Press), 33, 54n6, 55n8, 56n17
"Neue Nasen" ("New Noses" [Herzl]), 36–37, 56n17
New York HipHop Theater Festival, xxv
Newman, Judie, 142n16
nonwhiteness, xiii, xvi, xviii, xix, xxviin3, 39, 150, 161, 192n32; and racial oppression, 200
Nordics, xvii
Northern European peoples, perceived racial superiority of, xi–xii, 2

Obama, Barack, 219
"one-drop" rule, 7, 200, 201, 203, 217, 276
Orientalism, 135. *See also* "Spanish Orientalism" (Tofiño-Quesada)
Other, the/othering: Appalachian whiteness/otherness, 94–95, 108; "eating the other," 222; otherness,

177, 180; "otherness" in the Italian imagination, 177; sexual control of the other, 73. *See also* Argentina, Argentine elites' rejection of the other; *Gaucho Martín Fierro, El (The Gaucho Martín Fierro* [Hernández]), as a discourse of othering; *Poniente (West* [2002]), the other as "Moor" and "Black" in
Ozersky, Josh, 225, 231

Pagan Spain (Wright), 149
Página Abierta (Open Page), 78
Palestine, 55n8
Panopticon, 255; as a model for analyzing the Matrix, 260–61
Paris, 21
Passing (Larsen), 201, 202–203
patriarchal systems, need of for white women, 120
patriarchy, 136, 138, 141n8; parallels with colonialism, 140n2
Patterson, Orlando, 198–99
Paturuzú, 13, 25–26n23
Pérez Martín, 25n17
"Performing Virtual Whiteness" (Kintz), 172
Peru, Viceroyalty of, 3
Pfeiffer, Kathleen, 203–4
Phoenicia, xvi
Pierre, Sonia, 61, 85, 86
Pinky (1949), 6, 201
Plessy v. Ferguson (1896), 203–4
Plum Bun (Fauset), 201, 202
Poniente (West [2002]), 154, 161–63; feminism and progressive politics in, 162; feminization of whiteness in, 162; Lucía in, 162–63; murder of Curro in, 163; omitted narrative in, 161; the other as "Moor" and "Black" in, 162; title of the film as translation of the Arabic "Maghreb," 161; white Christian iconography in, 163
Portalatín, Aída Cartagena, 89n11
Porton, Richard, 184
Portugal, slave trade of, 147–48

Presley, Elvis, 221, 225–26, 250n7
Prodigal Summer (Kingsolver), 96
Project RACE (Reclassify All Children Equally), 205
Proposition 187 (California), 96, 113n10
Public Enemy, 226, 250n7
Pujol, Jordi, 153
Punch, John, xxvii–xxviiin3

Quinterno, Dante, 25–26n23

race, 112n3, 202; biological, 13; and census forms, xxiv, 205–6, 209–10; classifications of, 7, 24n13; as a detrimental social construct, 200; and ethnicity, 199–200; importance of in the United States, 204–5; instability of, 3–4; myth of, 258–59; as a signifier of difference, 230; skin color as a demarcation of, xiii; as a sociopolitical construct, xiv, 84–85, 209, 280; as a state of mind, 235; visual reading of race on the body, xvi
Race Traitor, 222, 226, 231, 238, 247; project of for the "abolition of whiteness," 228, 244–45
"race treason," 222
Racechanges (Gubar), 251n16
"raceless" identity, 172
racial binaries, 7, 197–98
racial categories. *See* multiracial identity
racial "heritage," 200
racial identity, xxvi, 80, 198, 199, 202, 244, 262; Caribbean, 69; Dominican, 63, 66, 77, 84; Spanish, xxiii, 148. See also *Matrix, The* (1999), racial identity in
racial passing, xv, xxiv–xxv, 198–99; in the 1920s, 199–204; literary depictions of, 201–4; multiracial identity in the twenty-first century, 204–6, 209–11; narratives of, 6–7, 24n12; and racial hierarchies, 203–4
racial superiority. *See* white supremacy/superiority
racial vocabularies, 112n3
racism, 24–25n14; 55n11, 172, 174, 210, 225, 245–46, 259; colonial, 122; as "defensive xenophobia," 178–79; discourse of, 23n1; during reconstruction, 200; during the shooting of *Seinfeld*, 200; and immigration, 176–77; institutional, 223, 242, 243; of the Nazis, 34; nineteenth-century, 225; "reverse racism," 231, 239; scientific, 3. *See also* Argentina, racism in; Italy, "new racism" and identity crisis in
rap music, misogyny and the glorification of violent masculinity in, 227–28
Redneck Heaven (Bultman), 97–98
"redneck" manifestos, 97–98
Reeves, Keanu, 219, 257, 276–77
regional fiction, and changes in the publishing industry, 114–15n23
Reigen (*Rondel* [Schnitzler]), 40
Rhodesia, xix
Rhys, Jean, *Wide Sargasso Sea*, xxii, 121, 129–33, 139–40
Riche, Martha Farnsworth, 209
Riefenstahl, Leni, 270
Rivadavia, Bernardino de, 7, 25n16
Roberts, Sheila, 127
Rodríguez, Juan M., 78; criticism of the León Museum, 79
Roediger, David R., 181, 223, 238, 249, 250–51n10; analysis of nineteenth-century racism, 225
Rogin, Michael, 249
Roman Catholicism, 151, 163, 164
Rondón, Pura Emeterio, 89n11
Roosevelt, Theodore, 100; preoccupation of with the "strenuous life," 101–2, 114n20
Root, Marcia P. P., 198, 199
Roth, Philip, *The Human Stain*, 255, 275
Rothstock, Otto, 40, 56n23
Rotker, Susana, 10, 11
Roussel, Raymond, 22
Rozenblit, Marsha, 31, 32
Rubio, Phil, 248
Ruchansky, Emilio, 25n19
Rue Cas-Nègres, La (*Sugar Cane Alley* [1983]), 85
Rwanda, racial cleansing in, xxvi, 270

Said, Edward, 135

Salgado-Ibarra, Juan, opinion of racism as "defensive xenophobia," 178–79

San Martín, José de, 11

Sarmiento, Domingo Faustino, 14

Satan, xiv

Satterwhite, Emily, xxi–xxii

Saura, Carlos, 151, 166n4

Savigliano, Marta, 11

Scandinavians, xvii

Schnitzler, Arthur, 40, 44, 57n30; *Reigen* (*Rondel*), 40

Schönberg, Arthur, 56n21

Schönerer, Georg, 54–55n7

Schuyler, George, *Black No More*, 201

secularism, 163

seduction theory, xix

Seinfeld, Jerry, 244, 245

Seipel, Ignaz, 57

Seshadri-Crooks, Kalpana, 280

sexuality, 41, 72–73, 120–21; control of by church or state, 163; fear of projected onto Jews, 40; myth of the sexually potent black male, 141n7; projection of onto dark races, 37; sexual control of the Other, 73

Shelton, Anthony Alan, 20

Shoah, 34, 58n34, 270, 276

Shumway, Nicolas, 15

Siegel, Carol, 277

"Signos de Identidad" ("Signs of Identity") exhibit, 79

Sirk, Douglas, 201

Sixth Extinction, 279

slavery, xv; Atlantic slave trade, 147–48; displacement of white male impropriety onto the female slave, 73; effects of on African identity, 174; expansion of in the Caribbean, 66; memory of, 154

Sleeper, Jim, 258

Snead, James, on the racial representation of African Americans in film, 154–55, 156, 159, 160

Snipes, Wesley, 276

Soja, Edward, 273

Sollors, Werner, 120; *Interracialism: Black-White Intermarriage in American History, Literature and Law*, 120

Some People (Hoch), 233, 234, 237, 238–39, 240, 243

Soriano, Florinda ("Mamá Tingó"), 83

South, the, post-bellum, 114n21

Spain, xxiii–xxiv, 3, 178; Basque region of, 153; Christianity of, 147; conquest of the Americas, 147; gender roles in, 164; geographical distribution of immigrants in, 153, 166n6; Hispanicizing of its colonies, 2; incorporation into the European Union, xxiii, 148; Jewish minority in, 147; legalization of gay marriage in, 163; loss of empire by, 148; as a "mingled nation," 147; "movida" cultural move as providing "Europeanness" to, 164; Muslim/Christian division in (twelfth century), 153; non-white immigration to, 153; sexual politics in, 149; slave trade of, 147–48

Spain, whiteness in, xxiii–xxiv, 147, 161, 164; and the concept of "limpieza de sangre" ("purity of blood"), 148; connection of with Christianity, 163; escalation of, 148; and Gypsy Spaniards, 150; "payo" (non-Gypsy Spaniard) essentialist view of Gypsies, 150–51; "payos" (non-Gypsy Spaniards), 150; social paradigms defining, 148–49; Spaniards' vision of themselves as white, 147–48

Spanish America, racial category of the "español" in, 4

Spanish American War (1898), 102, 148

"Spanish Orientalism" (Tofiño-Quesada), 149

Speirs, Kenneth, 217

Spenser, Edmund, 147

Srikanth, Rajini, 121–22

Stadt ohne Juden, Die: Ein Roman von Übermorgen (*The City without Jews: A Novel of Our Time* [Bettauer]), xx, xxi, 29–30, 34, 41–46, 56–57n26; absence

of Eastern Jews in, 44; adaptation of to the stage, 57nn31–32; anticipation of Hitler's racial politics in, 43; commercial success of, 43, 57n30; criticism of, 43–44; Karl Schwertfeger character in, 41–42, 57n30; lack of Orthodox Jewish characters in, 44, 45–46; Leo Strakosch character in, 45, 51–52; movie adaptation of, 43, 57n31; as a roman à clef, 57n30; stereotypes of Jews in, 44; subtext of, 45–46; temporal structure of, 41
Stahl, John M., 201
Stella, Gian Battista, 179
Stoddard, Lothrop, xii, xxviin2
Stone, Laurie, 237
Strange Days (1994), 266, 267
Sullivan, Shannon, xix
Sweden, 13

Taíno Indians, xvi, xxi, 63, 78
Taking Over (Hoch), 233
Tales of the Alhambra (Irving), 149
Taney, Roger B., 269
tango, the, xx, 11, 25n21
Tanzania, xv
Tarantos, Los (1960), 166n2
Tate, Greg, *Everything But the Burden: What White People Are Taking from Black Culture*, 222
Taylor, Gary, 67
"technologies of domination," 264, 268, 277–78, 279
Teutons, xvii
Texeira, Mary Thierry, 198, 199
Tiananmen Square, xxvi
Tietze, Hans, 43–44
Todo sobre mi madre (*All About My Mother* [1999]), 164–65; AIDS theme in, 165; Christian nature of, 165; democratic spirit of, 165; multicultural urban background (Barri Gotti) of, 165; whiteness as "raceing" of the self as Gypsy in, 165
Tofiño-Quesada, Ignacio, "Spanish Orientalism," 149

Trail of the Lonesome Pine, The (Fox), 94, 99; appeal of to advocates of the "strenuous life," 101–2; civilization/savagery conflict in, 101; eye and hair color of white characters in, 100–101; John Hale character in, 99, 100; June Tolliver character in, 99, 101; planning of, 114n21; racial makeup of mountaineer characters in, 99–100; Ruff Tolliver character in, 101; Sam Budd character in, 100, 101; transformation of John and June in, 99, 100
Trigiani, Adriana, 96; *Big Stone Gap*, 96
Triumph des Willes (1935), 270
Trujillo. *See* Molina, Rafael L. Trujillo
Turner, Nat, 269
tyrosinase, xiii
tyrosnase inhibitor, xiii

UNESCO (United Nations Educational, Scientific, and Cultural Organization), 78
"Unitarios" (Unitarians), 11
United States, xv, 6, 7, 50, 51, 174, 179; as a "colorblind" nation, 203; expansionism of, xvii; imperialism of, 102–3, 104, 111; as a multiracial nation, 204–5; racial classification in, 24n13, 197–98, 205–6, 209–11; scholarship in, 55n11; segregation in, 182, 192n32; as victimized, 110, 115n31; white studies in, 186
United States Census, and multiracial definition, xxiv, 205–206, 209–11, 217
Uruguay, 10, 25n15
Uribe, Imanol, xxiii, 154, 156

Vanilla Ice, 221
Vasconcelos, José, 13–14, 26n24; *Cosmic Race, The*, 24–25n14; idea of the "cosmic race," 13, 26n24
Vega, Bernard, 64
Venezuela, 62
Ventura, Miriam, 83
victimization, 110, 115n31

Vienna: acculturation and assimilation of Jews in, 32–33, 37–38; anti-Semitism in, xx–xxii, 29–30, 40, 52, 54–55n7; conflicting identities of Jews in, 32, 33; identity crisis of Jews in Vienna, 31; importance of Jews to, 58n33; Jewish neighborhoods in (Ringstrasse Boulevard and Leopoldstadt), 38, 44, 56n18; Jewish population of, 32; "white" Vienna, 44

Viñas, David, 25n22

"Voudun Sala" exhibit, 78

Wald, Gayle, 203, 204, 221; *Crossing the Line: Racial Passing in Twentieth-Century U.S. Literature and Culture*, 202

Washington, Salim, 226

Ware, Vron, 222, 244

Welt von Gestern, Die (The World of Yesterday [Zweig]), 33–34, 54n6

Werker, Alfred, 201

West, Cornel, 204, 258

White, Armond, 221, 231

White, Walter, *Flight*, 201

"White America" (Eminem), 229, 230, 231

"white negro," the, xxv, 221, 223, 225, 236, 242, 249; condemnation of, 222; Jews as, 35

"White Noises" (Jackson), 245–46

white persons, 171, 172, 188n2; ambition of, 199; privileged and underprivileged, 173

White Porteños, 8

white privilege, 128, 213–14, 223, 228, 232, 233, 234, 250

White Screens, Black Images (Snead), 154–55

white studies, 186–87

white supremacy/superiority, xi–xii, 165, 171, 173

"white trash," 225

Whiteboyz (1999), 241–242, 244; Flip and "representin" whiteness in, 247–48

whiteness, xvii, xviii, xxii, xxiii, xxiv, 55n11, 62, 66–67, 107, 192n42, 217, 223; abolition of, 228–29, 232, 238–39, 244–45; Appalachian whiteness/otherness, 94–95, 108; ascent of, xiv; biological, xii; as the color of danger in southern women's fiction, 107; as a communication phenomenon, 181; conception of as corporeal, 35; Dominican, 63, 70, 77–82; essentialist ideas of, 237–38; and European perfection, 75; as an expression of white privilege, 238; gendered construction of, 67; genealogical, xii; and the German term "Rassismus," 55n11; generic, 96; global communication concerning, xix; ideologies of, xii–xiii; internal hierarchies within white ethnic groups, xvi–xviii, xxvi; as invisible, 210; myth of, 171–72; and national identity, 14n6; oppositional, 248–49; paradoxical nature of, 172; possessive geographies of, xix; preoccupation with by post-colonized peoples, xv; as a race, 210; representation of, xviii, xix; resecuring of, xxvi–xxvii; reproduction of, 139–40; seeing whiteness, 34–35; stability of, xx; and unconscious archetypes, 181; undermining of, 249–50; variegated, 63

Whiteness of a Different Color (Jacobson), 63

"Whiteness Studies" (Kolchin), 63

Wide Sargasso Sea (Rhys), xxii, 121, 129–33, 139–40, 141n8; alignment of Antoinette with the dark land of the Caribbean in, 130, 142n12; Antoinette's "confession" in, 133; Antoinette's relationship with Sandi in, 132; blackening ("othering as dark") of Antoinette by Rochester in, 129, 130, 132, 133, 142n13; mixed racial status of Antoinette in, 130; renaming of Antoinette as "Bertha" in, 132; as a rewriting of *Jane Eyre*, 129; Rochester's affair with Amelie in, 132–33; Rochester's justification for his hatred of Antoinette in, 132; Rochester's view of his marriage to Antoinette in, 129–30; "savage" desires of Rochester for Antoinette in, 131; sexual and racial identity of Antoinette in, 131–32, 133

Wiegman, Robyn, 249, 251n16

Wieviorka, Michel, 176–77

"wigger," 229, 233, 234, 249. 250–51n10

Williams, Claudette, 69

Williams, Tennessee, 165

Wills, Christopher, on the effects of melanin in skin, xiii–xiv

Wilson, Darlene, 100

Wister, Owen, 101–2

Wistrich, Robert, 31–32

Wolfman, Marv, 276

women: black female identity, 76; derogatory terms for nonwhite females, 83–84; relegation of black women to the status of sexual animal, 73; women's writing (Afro-Dominican) and feminist-based activity, 82–84. See also women/wives, white

women/wives, white: and colonial ideology, 121–22; command over biological reproduction, 120; gendered role of in sustaining colonial whiteness, 121; as racially privileged and sexually marginalized, 122; and the reproduction of whiteness, 120; sexual identity of, 121; sexual vulnerability of as threat to the colonial mission, 120–21; threat of a hidden "blackness" in, 119–20

Woods, Tiger, xxv; "Cablinasian" identity of, 211–14, 216, 219

World War I, 53

World War II, xi, 166n2, 180, 188n8

Wright, Richard: Native Son, xxvi, 269; Pagan Spain, 149

xenophobia, xxiv. See also "defensive xenophobia"

Yaeger, Patricia, 107, 108

"Yélida" (Franco), xxi, 61, 62, 80, 87–88; celebration of mulattoness in, 70; destruction of Erick's Aryanism in, 67–68, 70, 71–72; imagery of Christ's resurrection in, 72; negrista poetic aesthetic of, 71; othering of the black female figure in, 70–71; portrayal of white innocence in, 70; power of contrasting binaries in, 68; privileging of whiteness in, 72; privileging of Yélida's European ancestry in, 67; prominence of in Dominican literature, 66; resurrection imagery in, 72; role of Erick's Nordic ancestry in, 67, 69; role of Voudun in, 68, 69, 70, 71; sexual and religious power of Suquí in, 71, 72–73; Suquí as the Other in, 67; vilification of Suquí in, 71–72; Voudun divinities in (Legba, Ogun, loa, Wangol, Badagris, Agoue, Ayida-Queddo), 69, 75–76; Yélida as a symbol of Dominican hybrid racial identity, 67, 68, 69, 74; Yélida's mulattoness as symbol of the Dominican Republic's racial conflict, 74–77

Yiddish, 31, 36

Zack, Naomi, 209–10

Zanzibar, xv

Zickel, Raymond, 181

Zweig, Stefan, Die Welt von Gestern (The World of Yesterday), 33–34, 54n6

At Home and Abroad was designed and typeset on a Macintosh OS 10 system using CS3 InDesign software. The body text is set in 10/13 Adobe Jenson Pro and display type is set in Calligraphic 421 BT. This book was designed and typeset by Barbara Karwhite and manufactured by Thomson-Shore, Inc.